OTAKU AND THE STRUGGLE FOR IMAGINATION IN JAPAN

秋葉原
ゲーム
メイド喫茶
ムービー
テレビ

OTAKU AND THE STRUGGLE FOR IMAGINATION IN JAPAN

Patrick W. Galbraith

DUKE UNIVERSITY PRESS *Durham and London* 2019

Printed in the United States of America on
acid-free paper ∞
Designed by Matthew Tauch
Typeset in Arno Pro by Westchester Book Group

Library of Congress Cataloging-in-Publication Data
Names: Galbraith, Patrick W., author.
Title: Otaku and the struggle for imagination in Japan /
Patrick W. Galbraith.
Description: Durham : Duke University Press, 2019. | Includes
bibliographical references and index.
Identifiers: LCCN 2019008724 (print) | LCCN 2019016967 (ebook)
ISBN 9781478007012 (ebook)
ISBN 9781478005094 (hardcover : alk. paper)
ISBN 9781478006299 (pbk. : alk. paper)
Subjects: LCSH: Mass media and culture—Japan. | Fans (Persons)—
Japan. | Popular culture—Japan. | Animated films—
Japan—History and criticism. | Japan—Social life and
customs—21st century.
Classification: LCC P94.65.J3 (ebook) | LCC P94.65.J3 G353 2019
(print) | DDC 306/.10952—dc23
LC record available at https://lccn.loc.gov/2019008724

IMAGINATION is the key to empathy, and if we're not able to imagine peoples' lives, then our empathy diminishes. Translation is a bridge that serves to enlarge imagination, to connect to the world. We're impoverished without it. **PHILIP BOEHM, 2017**

CONTENTS

DEDICATION/ ACKNOWLEDGMENTS

To my big brothers, Russ and Joe, who taught me that, no matter our circumstances, we can always seek ways to alter our consciousness and see and be in the world differently. They were rough times, but for opening my eyes to anime and Japan, I owe you my life. And my mother, Denise, for the unending support and imparting a love of reading and the written word. To my friend Chris, who approached an awkward, angry young man, fresh off the boat and itching for a fight, and just kept on smiling. For that, and teaching me to smile again, I owe you more than you know. To my mentors inside and outside the academy, David H. Slater, Anne Allison, and Yoshimi Shun'ya, who took me under their wing and encouraged me to think in new ways—as consciousness altering as anything that happened up north, but decidedly less dark and more disciplined. To Keiko, the only person I watch anime with regularly. You saw me at my worst and stayed. I am better for having met you, and knowing that we will watch anime again keeps me going. While this project occupied me for many, many years, and often pulled us apart, know that I love you. And to those I came to know in Akihabara, for sharing your lives and stories, for showing me other worlds. Thank you. All of you, each and every one, I love.

INTRODUCTION "OTAKU" AND THE STRUGGLE FOR IMAGINATION IN JAPAN

The sun is rising to illuminate the hazy sky over suburbia in Japan. A Japanese man in his twenties begins to stir in bed, prompted by a voice. "It's morning! Wake up!" The words are spoken in Japanese, gently, melodically. The man rustles under the sheets, alone in a spacious but minimally decorated apartment. "Hey, wake up!" The voice is insistent. Without opening his eyes, the man sits up and turns to a device next to the bed. A designer alarm clock, perhaps, that produced the voice that woke him and he now means to shut off. As the man pries his eyelids apart, however, he sees the face of a girl, not a clock. The tiny face of a girl standing approximately twenty centimeters tall and seeming to bounce with energy. With a breathy giggle, she tilts her head to the side and says, "Good morning." The man leans toward the device, which looks to be a container for the girl, who is visible as a full-body hologram inside a central, clear cylinder. He taps a button on the base of the device—not to turn it off but instead to respond to the girl. A microphone icon appears on the clear surface, letting the man know that she can hear him. "Good morning," he says, sleepily. As he gazes out the window, the girl tells him that it might rain later and he should take an umbrella. After putting on a suit for work, the man slips a folding umbrella into his satchel and heads for the door. "Hurry, or you'll be late." She is right, but he nevertheless turns around, bends down to the device, and says, "I'm going now." The girl smiles, waves, and replies, "See you later."

This is an advertisement for Gatebox, which its developer, Vinclu, describes as a "virtual home robot."[1] Vinclu appeals to those who might buy the device not by demonstrating its functions as an alarm clock, weather report, and scheduling tool but by foregrounding a relationship. Steps to activate and use the device are shown but fall away as the focus shifts to interactions between the man and girl. These are routine interactions not in the sense of mechanical repetition but rather the rhythm of living together. The routine exchange of set phrases—"I'm going now," or *ittekimasu,* said by someone going out and coming back, and the reply, "See you later," *itterasshai*—is part of a relationship. At a time when more and more people are living alone in Japan, a country facing declining dating, marriage, and birth rates to the extent that the entire population is shrinking (for an overview, see Allison 2013), these routines can mean a great deal. Vinclu's Gatebox advertisement seems to suggest that this is true even when interactions and relations are with a "virtual home robot," or rather the virtual girl inside of it.

As the advertisement continues, the man, now on a bus commuting into the city, receives a text message telling him to have fun at work. It is from her, the girl in the Gatebox at home. During lunch, the man sits by himself but receives another text: "Come home early." "It's only noon," he replies, and she responds, and he smiles. Stuck working late, again alone, the man looks at his phone and the previous exchange. Pausing momentarily, he punches in, "I'm heading home now." Her response is immediate—"Yaaay!"—and elicits a smile. As the man runs out into the rain, armed with folding umbrella, the Gatebox girl turns on the lights at home. They continue texting as he approaches. Coming through the door, he rushes over to the Gatebox—no, to her—and leans in close. "Welcome home," she says. The Japanese here, *okaerinasai,* is another set phrase, this one so charged with the affect of the relationship that one set of English subtitles translates it, "Missed you, darling!" They sit together and watch television, sipping beverages. Finally back in bed, this time lying awake, the man says, "You know, someone waiting at home . . . is great. I thought so on the way back." From the street outside, he had seen his brightened window. "Good night," he says. "Good night," she responds. As the advertisement concludes its narrative day, the dark room is bathed in a soft glow from the Gatebox, and the girl seems to be watching over the man.

FIGURE I.1 Gatebox: "Missed you, darling!"

When it was released online in December 2016, Vinclu's Gatebox advertisement found a ready, if not always receptive, audience. In anglophone news, it was slotted into a genre of stories about "Weird Japan," or the Japanese as socially dysfunctional and sexually deviant others. Collectively, the reports told a story: "The Creepy Virtual Assistant that Embodies Japan's Biggest Problems," specifically how alienated young men are turning to a company selling a "holographic 'girlfriend'" (Liberatore 2016), "pseudo-girlfriend" (Morris 2016), or "anime girlfriend" (Szondy 2016). Even as putting "girlfriend" into scare quotes implies a question about how the Gatebox girl could be anything of the sort, so does modifying it as "anime girlfriend," which draws attention to her as a Japanese cartoon character, or one with a distinct look shared with the characters of manga (comics) and anime (animation). Few seemed interested in seriously entertaining such a question, however. After all, it was patently obvious to critics that what the Gatebox offers is not a real relationship by any stretch of the imagination.

On the contrary, almost diametrically opposed to its critics, Vinclu presents interactions and relations with a manga/anime character as a significant other, both fictional and real. According to her official bio page, the Gatebox girl is twenty-year-old Azuma Hikari.[2] She likes donuts and watching anime. From her distinctive appearance to the prominence of anime on her list of hobbies, it is apparent that Azuma is meant to appeal to manga/anime fans. If such fans interact with characters from manga/anime franchises in various media and material forms in Japan today (Allison 2006;

Steinberg 2012; Condry 2013), then Vinclu has developed a device that allows for new forms of interaction and relation with a character as part of everyday life. They imagine that the Gatebox makes possible "Living with Your Favorite Character," as the official English-language slogan puts it.[3] The English-language website confirms this vision: "Gatebox is a project that grants the dream of closing the distance between you and characters. The reason why we develop[ed] Gatebox is not because we are just pursuing entertainment or convenience. We want the characters [to] be naturally [present] in our daily lives and [to] spend relaxing time with us. 'I want to live with my favorite character.' We dreamed of such [a] world and we started this project." Vinclu's description of the technology behind Gatebox begins, "Everything is in here for living together." With Gatebox, the character, who recognizes movements, faces, and voices and responds to them, "comes to life." Although Gatebox is designed to be "an interface between two people," the website explains that the "interface [is] centered around communication with the character." The point thus seems to be interacting with a character as a person, or someone alive and real in a relationship. While currently in the spotlight, Azuma Hikari is only the first step toward "living together with the character of your choice"; one day fans may draw from their favorite manga/anime franchises.

Note that the emphasis is on bringing manga/anime characters into our world and spending time with them, which is about adding new dimensions to life, not necessarily shutting off others. The climax of Vinclu's Gatebox advertisement comes when the man refers to Azuma Hikari—waiting at home, there in the room with him—as "someone" (*dareka*). Soon after the man says this aloud, the camera shifts to show the room from above and the Gatebox at an angle, which sets up a contrast. From above, Azuma appears as not only a cartoon character but also a flat image, her full-body hologram an illusion next to the human body in bed. And this comes precisely as the distance between the man and Gatebox girl has closed in his recognition of her as someone and their relationship as real. The revealing view from above is not meant to undermine the moment but rather to underscore it as something other than misrecognition of a character as human. Visually, the view from above reminds us that Azuma is a character, a flat image, *and at the same time someone*. Put another way, Vinclu shows Azuma as a significant other, even as she is also a character, a form of existence that is separate and distinct from human. The point here is emerging forms of interaction and relation with characters as such.

This book is an anthropological study of people living with and loving characters in contemporary Japan. Such people are often called "otaku," which requires some unpacking. As defined in the Japanese dictionary, "otaku" are "people who are interested in a particular genre or object, are extraordinarily knowledgeable about it, but are lacking in social common sense" (Kam 2013b, 152). This seems straightforward enough, but one wonders why certain people and their interactions and relations with certain objects are consistently deemed to be lacking in "social common sense," and indeed what that common sense entails. Conducting fieldwork in the 2000s in the Akihabara area of Tokyo, which had come to be associated with "otaku," I encountered men who, like the protagonist of the Gatebox advertisement, were engaged in intimate interactions and relations with manga/anime characters, specifically *bishōjo*, or cute girl characters. Rather than lacking common sense, however, they seemed to be going against it in public performances of their affection for these characters. During archival research, I found that this same issue was the primary impetus for originally constructing "otaku" as a label in Japan in 1983. Over time, I came to understand "otaku" as connected to the imagined excesses and perversions of manga/anime fans. From another perspective, however, "otaku" point to imagining and creating alternative social worlds with characters.[4] This all speaks to the contestation of "common sense," not consensus. In this way, the book positions "otaku" in an ongoing struggle for imagination in contemporary Japan.

"Otaku," Margins, Imagination

In the literature on manga and anime in North America, examples abound of referring to manga/anime fans in general, if not also viewers/readers, as "otaku." There are a variety of reasons to avoid doing this (Galbraith and Lamarre 2010; Kam 2013a, 2013b; Galbraith, Kam, and Kamm 2015), but suffice it to say here that "otaku" means very little out of context. While discussions of "otaku" often assume understanding, we must scrutinize the term to get at its significance in time and place. This book thinks with "otaku" as it was articulated in Japan in the early 1980s, which speaks back to the 1970s and forward to the 1990s and 2000s. This approach allows us to consider what it was about *specific* manga/anime characters and fans in Japan at *specific* times that required a label for *specific* imagined excesses and perversions. For all that has changed, analysis reveals remarkable resonances and resilient strands of discourse. Even as manga and anime have spread around the world, and "otaku" have in some ways been normalized as manga/anime fans, the imagined excesses and perversions remain and are revived in specific ways (Kelts 2006, 69, 162–64). While the manga/anime fan might be treated as normal, the "otaku" might not be, and while the "otaku" might be normal, the "weird otaku" in Akihabara or Japan might not. Some interactions and relations with some manga/anime characters might be treated as normal, but others might not. It is important to recognize normalization as a process that is also a struggle with the "abnormal."

In this book, I have decided to keep "otaku" in scare quotes and draw attention to it as a label, which is to be interrogated in context rather than taken for granted at large. More concretely, I present "otaku" as a label that is applied in response to the imagined excesses and perversions of "male" fans of manga and anime, namely an attraction to and affection for cute girl characters. The point is not to exclude other objects or subjects but to think "otaku" in terms of the label that emerged in Japan in the early 1980s. Rather than participate in what theorist Thomas Lamarre describes as discourse about "otaku" meant to "define a historical moment, promote a set of objects, or establish an identity" (Lamarre 2006, 365), the book explores how and why the label has been constructed and applied in contemporary Japan. If, as Lamarre suggests, much of the academic discourse about "otaku" leaves the lines and hierarchies of gender, sexuality, and nation undisturbed (368, 387), then we should not overlook the fact that the imagined excesses and perversions to which the label responds tend to trouble a "straight," "male," "Japanese" position. It is only by being specific that one begins to see politics in sociohistorical context, which opens into questions about the struggle for imagination.

Crucial to these questions are interactions and relations with manga/anime characters as fictional and real others, which can challenge common sense. Why, for example, was the reaction to the Gatebox advertisement and its imagined life with a character so negative? When sharing this advertisement with friends and colleagues in North America, I was surprised that many shook their heads and muttered, "How sad." When pressed, they expanded on how lonely the man must be. This is sad, and turning to a pseudo relationship for solace sadder still. Life with a human partner, a real relationship, would be better, more rewarding and fulfilling. This commonsense position speaks to hegemony, which produces norms and persuades people of their rightness (Hall 1987). To these friends and colleagues, the life portrayed in the Gatebox advertisement registered as abnormal, somehow wrong. What fascinates me about this interpretation is that it completely ignores the narrative of the Gatebox advertisement, which is explicitly about how the man is not alone, but rather living with a character; there is no indication that he is anything but happy with that character, and the score builds to a crescendo in his recognition of her as someone; the Gatebox advertisement is a celebration of the possibilities of living life otherwise. This did not make sense to friends and colleagues in North America, but it did make sense to manga/anime fans in Japan. Undergirding this are different understandings of interactions and relations with characters, different ways of evaluating them, different ways of seeing and being in the world.

When discussing the Gatebox advertisement, friends and colleagues in North America found equally nonsensical the terms "two-dimensional" (*nijigen*) and "three-dimensional" (*sanjigen*), which have circulated widely among manga/anime fans in Japan for decades. In practice, they mean the manga/anime world or "dimension" and the human world or "dimension," rather than literally two-dimensional and three-dimensional. For example, a manga/anime character in the form of a figurine is still said to be two-dimensional. This is not a distinction between fictional and real, because a two-dimensional character is both fictional and real, but real in a different way than a three-dimensional human. Using the terms "two-dimensional" and "three-dimensional," manga/anime fans talk about their interactions and relations with characters as separate and distinct from humans. One might critique this as "binary thinking," but I am fundamentally skeptical of the assumption that we already know more and better than those we engage with.[5] If, as anthropologist Gabriella Coleman argues, researchers can expect that interactions with media and technology will lead some to "indigenously conceive of the relationship between the screen and the physical space where bodies meet" (Coleman 2013, 49), then researchers can also expect that interactions with manga and anime contribute to a similar phenomenon. In the spirit of anthropology, researchers might try to learn to see the world and be in it differently.

Things make a good deal more sense if one keeps track of "dimensions." For example, in the Gatebox advertisement, the Japanese catch copy reads, "Crossing Dimensions, Coming to You" (*Jigen wo koete, ai ni kuru*). In her official English-language bio, Azuma Hikari is introduced as a "dimension traveler," who will "fly over dimensions to see you." Included is a short comic showing her as a flat character image before entering another dimension, the one where humans live. This explains the revealing view from above in the advertisement and that shot's very intentional juxtaposition of Azuma inside the Gatebox and the man beside it, with the device allowing for intimate interactions and relations between them and their dimensions. We thus realize that, for Vinclu, the innovation is enabling interactions and relations between the two- and three-dimensional: "Enjoy this unprecedented jump between dimensions that will result in a new, shared lifestyle." The imaginary is one of characters and humans, the two- and three-dimensional, coexisting in the same world, living together. In contrast, not keeping track of dimensions can lead to misunderstanding, as, for example, when critics look at "maid cafés" in Akihabara and see no more than women serving men, while regulars instead draw attention to their interactions and relations with characters. Salient terms such as "2.5-dimensional" (*nitengo jigen*) slip past observers unless they follow that two-dimensional is the manga/anime world and three-dimensional is the human world, and the maid café is somewhere in between. Such "in-between spaces," theorist Jack Halberstam reminds, can "save us from being snared by the hooks of hegemony" (Halberstam 2011, 2), but we first need to learn to recognize them.

On the subject of hegemony, let us return to the Gatebox advertisement and situate its protagonist in the imaginary of Japan. Commentators in the anglophone news describe the Gatebox man as not only an "otaku" but also a "salaryman" (Gallagher 2016). Setting aside for now that these are labels, the Gatebox man appears to be a white-collar worker at a large corporation—that is, a "salaryman"—as well as someone involved in intimate interactions and relations with a manga/anime character—an "otaku." For much of the second half of the twentieth century, however, the salaryman was a figure of success in stark contrast to the "otaku." Defined by his institutional belonging, the salaryman was a middle-class, masculine hero whose efforts were imagined to support his company, family, and nation (Roberson and Suzuki 2003, 1). This is an example of "hegemonic masculinity," which need not be the most common or comfortable form but is still the common sense of what a man ought to be and is judged against (Connell 2000, 10–11). As opposed to the salaryman, the "otaku" was seen as an institutional outsider, individualistic and self-absorbed, unstable and undisciplined, engaged in consumptive rather than productive activity, and so on. Simply put, if success in many capitalist societies is tied to achieving "reproductive maturity" (Halberstam 2011, 2), then the "otaku" was seen as a failure, unproductively immature. Nevertheless, with the recession that rocked Japan in the 1990s and subsequent destabilization of institutions

FIGURE I.2 Vinclu CEO Takechi Minori and Azuma posing together. The two-dimensional character shows what appears to be a wedding ring, which suggests an intimate relationship.

(Allison 2006, 74–75), some dramatically proclaim that the salaryman has lost to alternatives such as "otaku," which "have won" (Frühstück and Walthall 2011, 12). Perhaps, then, the Gatebox man is that winner, the successful man, the "otaku" that replaced the salaryman.

This, however, overlooks critical aspects of hegemony in contemporary Japan. To be blunt, the "otaku" does not stand for a new hegemonic masculinity. Few in Japan see "otaku" in ways corresponding to the salaryman ideal. Far from it, in fact: Even a cursory glance at the sociological literature shows "otaku" to be historically suspect (Kinsella 1998), which has led to lingering suspicions of dysfunction and deviance that come out in both longitudinal survey data (Kikuchi 2015) and relatively recent qualitative interviews with even younger Japanese (Kam 2013a, 2013b). That the majority of respondents do not have positive impressions, even in the 2000s, should not go unnoticed. From the commonsense position, the Gatebox man is still a failure, employed and earning enough to afford a device that retails for around US$2,500, but not achieving reproductive maturity. The Gatebox advertisement effectively sabotages its protagonist's salaryman status by portraying him alone during lunch, without his work cohort, texting Azuma Hikari. The impact of the scene is amplified by seating a man and woman chatting directly behind the Gatebox man, who has his back to them. He is alone again in the office working late, thinking of Azuma, without any sign of his coworkers. Not only is the Gatebox man's heart not in the corporate institution, but his significant other waiting at home is a manga/anime character, and interactions and relations with her cannot produce human children. Rather than framing this as "sad," however, Vinclu triumphantly declares the arrival of a new, shared lifestyle "between dimensions." This imaginary is not of the salaryman but of the "otaku" living life otherwise. If, as anthropologist Ian Condry suggests, affection for manga/anime characters contributes to "the emergence of alternative social worlds" (Condry 2013, 203), then researchers need to account for what makes these social worlds alternative and why that distinction matters.

Hints to such an approach can be found in work on "otaku" outside of Japan. Writing on anime fandom in North America from the mid-1980s to the late 1990s, science and technology scholar Lawrence Eng describes "otaku" as "reluctant insiders" (Eng 2006, 24, 34). Reluctant insiders, Eng explains, feel somehow alienated by their inclusion and seek alternatives through unanticipated consumption and appropriation. This is often consumption and appropriation of media and material that are not intended for the reluctant insider, who crosses boundaries to get them (158–59). In the case of Eng's anime fans, the consumption and appropriation was of Japanese cartoons, which meant crossing national boundaries and escaping an alienating inclusion in "the United States." Others add that these reluctant insiders, alienated by their inclusion in "American masculinity," crossed gender/genre boundaries in seeking alternative imaginings of relationships and romance in Japanese cartoons (Newitz 1995, 4–7).[6] For Eng, "otaku" are those that "consciously make choices to self-marginalize" (Eng 2012, 102), or become marginal as a way out of the main body.[7] To rephrase, they choose to move toward the margin and become other than what inclusion in the main body allows and demands. Much of this also strikes a chord in Japan, where "otaku" began crossing gender/genre lines in consumption and appropriation of *shōjo* (for girls) manga and shōjo (girl) characters in manga and anime in the 1970s, and in imagining interactions and relations with bishōjo (cute girl) characters in the 1980s. One way to understand this is by viewing "otaku" as reluctant insiders of the hegemony of masculinity seeking alternatives.

In Japan, not only did "otaku" consume and appropriate across gender/genre lines, but they also produced new spaces to gather and share shōjo manga and fan works such as the Comic Market, new character forms such as the bishōjo, new niche and specialty magazines to share these characters as objects of desire and affection, a new language to discuss this affection, new online and offline sites to share affection, and new ways of interacting with and relating to characters. This is not just about emerging alternative social worlds but also about the movement of actively imagining and creating them. Again, thinking outside Japan can provide clarity. In North America, theorist bell hooks shines a light on movement that takes one "out of one's place," which requires "pushing against oppressive boundaries set by race, sex, and class domination" (hooks 2000, 203). This can be understood as movement toward the margin, or, in the language of reluctant insiders, choosing to self-marginalize. Distinct from marginality that is structurally imposed, hooks advocates cultivating marginality as openness. Choosing such marginality offers "the possibility of [a] radical perspective from which to see and create, to imagine alternatives, new worlds" (207). For hooks, these alternatives, these imagined and created worlds, are a form of "counter-hegemonic discourse," which goes beyond just words to ways of seeing and being. In its radical openness, the margin is also an invitation to, as hooks puts it, "Enter that space" (208). One not only imagines and creates alternative worlds, not only lives them, but also draws others in.

We can take this further by considering manga and anime, or comics and animation, as media of imagination. In *Understanding Comics*, theorist Scott McCloud argues that comics are radically open in ways that encourage artists and viewers/readers to get involved in shared worlds of imagination—to enter that space, as it were. Three points are germane: iconic characters, gutters, and shared imagination. On the first point, McCloud makes a distinction between "lines to *see*" and "lines to *be*" (McCloud 1994, 43), with the former being more realistic or natural looking, and the latter more iconic or cartoony. If lines to see are objects in a world, then lines to be draw subjects into a world. This informs McCloud's discussion of the effect of iconic characters: "When you look at a photo or realistic drawing of a face you see it as the face of another. But when you enter the world of the cartoon you see yourself. . . . The cartoon is a vacuum into which our identity and awareness are pulled, an empty shell that we inhabit, which enables us to travel to another realm. We don't just observe the cartoon—we *become* it" (36). By McCloud's reckoning, iconic characters are open to diverse identifications, or identification across boundaries as one is pulled out of place and into other spaces and forms. In manga, characters tend to be more iconic than realistic (44).

On the second point, gutters, McCloud states that comics make the viewer/reader "a willing and conscious collaborator" (65) in moving images. Comics are a series of still drawings arranged in panels on the page,

FIGURE I.3 McCloud explains the gutter.

and there is space between deliberately juxtaposed images, which is called the gutter. The viewer/reader looks at the images and fills in the blank between them, and in the process moves the still drawings. To demonstrate this, McCloud presents a pair of panels (figure I.3): the first with two men, one raising an axe and shouting "Now you die!" to a terrified response, and the second a city skyline in which the night air is pierced by "Eeyaaa!" Moving between the images, the viewer/reader fills in the blank—the axe man swings and the other man screams before his demise. In this way, McCloud elucidates, comics excel at compelling viewers/readers to "use their imaginations" (69).

This transitions to the third and concluding point, which McCloud makes through a theory of media: "Media convert thoughts into forms that can traverse the physical world and be re-converted by one or more senses back into thoughts" (195). In the case of comics, this means converting thoughts into drawings, or a series of deliberately juxtaposed images, for the viewer/reader to access visually. Put somewhat differently, the artist and viewer/reader share thoughts through images, or share imagination. The images are open, yes, but also concrete and immediate. Furthermore, for McCloud, comics stand out in that basically all one needs is a pencil and paper, and the artist is intimately involved in forming the thoughts into images from mind to hand to page (197, 204–5). The images are flexible, there are few limitations on what can be drawn, and the viewer/reader is brought close to what the artist imagines by filling in blanks in and between images.

Given that they often do not feature the "realism" of much of mainstream media, McCloud counts comics among "minority forms," which offer other ways of seeing the world (McCloud 2000, 19). One could also call comics a marginal form, or a medium of imagination, which highlights how artists imagine and create alternative worlds, opening spaces for the viewer/reader to move out of place. In the literature on Japanese comics, a well-documented example of this is a subgenre of shōjo manga focusing on romance and sex between male characters, which in Japan is produced and consumed primarily by heterosexual girls and women but also appeals to a wide range of others (for an overview, see Galbraith 2015a). Thus while manga critic and editor Sagawa Toshihiko provocatively suggests that the "male" characters might better be described as "young women wearing cartoon-character costumes" (quoted in Schodt 1996, 123), it is not only women who are wearing these costumes to move out of place. Indeed, researchers of this subgenre of shōjo manga and its fans have applied McCloud's understanding of iconic characters to propose that the open image invites broad, fluid, and shifting identifications (Isola 2010, 86). In short, in such comics, one can become other by being drawn into character images across lines.[8] Not coincidentally, Sagawa Toshihiko himself was among the early generation of male fans of shōjo manga featuring "male" character romance and sex in the 1970s (Schodt 1996, 120). Like other reluctant insiders seeking alternatives and crossing gender/genre lines, Sagawa opened a shared space of imagination and creation in the form of *June* magazine, which became a flagship of "boys love manga."

Not only do comics offer other ways of seeing the world, they also offer other worlds and ways of being in the world. Again turning to an example from shōjo manga, artist Hagio Moto is renowned for producing stories about male-male romance in the 1970s, but more generally pushed the boundaries of gender and sexuality in works of speculative fiction that imagined ways out of the hegemonic family and related roles and responsibilities (Suzuki 2011, 59–60).[9] To Hagio's mind, this family was an illusion that many took to be "reality," which she wanted to challenge. Imagining and creating other worlds, Hagio estranges "our naturalized view of the world" and encourages us to question "dominant social norms" (60, 70). Significantly, this sort of shōjo manga spoke to men such as Sagawa Toshihiko as well as critic Yonezawa Yoshihiro, who was involved in founding the Comic Market and providing a shared space of imagination and creation for early "otaku" in the 1970s. For his part, Yonezawa recognizes that comics can be especially effective for unsettling norms because "manga constitutes a realm of imagination, a power to give illusions concrete form" (Yonezawa 2004, 44–45). The imagined and created worlds of comics can be inhabited and shared as alternatives to the illusions of commonsense, hegemonic "reality." If, as scholar of religion Joseph P. Laycock argues, "hegemony can be resisted only if we can imagine new possibilities" (Laycock 2015, 215), then it is perhaps not so surprising that regulators in Japan have had their sights set on manga since the institutional instability of the 1990s.

With a history of substantial connection and crossover between manga and anime in Japan (Steinberg 2012), there are practical reasons to consider the two together, but there are also theoretical reasons. Like comics, much of animation departs from "reality." If film captures movement in the world and turns it into a series of still images, then animation takes a series of still images and turns them into an illusion of movement in imagined and created worlds (Bukatman 2012, 47).[10] This movement is not always or necessarily continuous or "natural." Moreover, while animation on the whole tends to focus on fiction as opposed to preformed entities in front of cameras, the vast majority of characters in Japanese animation are intentionally crafted in a manga/anime style that is "unrealistic." So distinctive is it that critic and editor Ōtsuka Eiji postulates the existence of "manga/anime realism," which points to the reality of manga/anime worlds rather than an approximation of the natural world (Ōtsuka 2003, 24).

Despite linkage and overlap, manga and anime are best grasped as separate but complementary media of imagination. Drawing from manga, anime present images that move and transform onscreen in ways that still ones on the page cannot. The most eloquent assessment of this characteristic of animation comes from Sergei Eisenstein, a Russian filmmaker and theorist intrigued by Walt Disney's early work: "What's strange is that it attracts! And you can't help but arrive at the conclusion that a single, common prerequisite of attractiveness shows through in all these examples: a rejection of once-and-forever allotted form, freedom from ossification, the ability to dynamically assume any form. An ability that I'd call 'plasmaticness,' for here we have a being represented in drawing, a being of a definite form, a being which has attained a definite appearance, and which behaves like the primal protoplasm, not yet possessing a 'stable' form, but capable of assuming any form" (Eisenstein 1986, 21). In that it leaves room for the imagination and stimulates it, imagines and creates worlds of fluid and shifting form, and draws viewers in, animation joins comics as a medium that is marginal.[11] Small wonder, then, that theorists such as Halberstam look to animation for alternatives to commonsense, hegemonic "reality" and the world as it is known and inhabited "naturally" (Halberstam 2011, 17, 89).[12]

Although Halberstam at times seems dismissive of "two-dimensional cartoons," there is certainly potential in interactions and relations between the two- and three-dimensional, not least of which is "otaku" movement in response to characters. In his work on the topic, Lamarre refers to such movement as a "collective force of desire" (Lamarre 2006, 359). This desire is quite visible in Japan, where manga and anime are robust media drawing large and diverse audiences with attractive characters (Schodt 1996, 19; Steinberg 2012, 41–45; Condry 2013, 86), but Lamarre would no doubt agree that there is nothing about it that is uniquely "Japanese." Indeed, in North America, theorist W. J. T. Mitchell develops the concept of "drawing desire," which gets at the dual meaning of drawing as inscribing lines and attracting (Mitchell 2005, 59). I find Mitchell helpful for addressing desire among those living with and loving characters in not only contemporary Japan, but beyond. Of particular interest is "desire generating images and images generating desire" (58), which resonates with the discussion of "otaku" (Lamarre 2006, 382–83). In Akihabara, I found that such desire could transform a neighborhood, interactions and relations between dimensions, and even worlds.

Acknowledging those actively imagining and creating alternative social worlds, discourse that hastily normalizes and nationalizes "otaku" strikes me as every bit as problematic as discourse about socially dysfunctional and sexually deviant others. The risk is collapsing together the margin and main body, which smooths over, on the one hand, the contestations of those choosing the margin, and, on the other, efforts to close in-between spaces and discipline and domesticate what is reincorporated into the main body—simply put, missing the process of normalization and attendant conflict and compromise. Queer theory, carefully conceived, can provide analytic guidance. In her work on male-male romance and sex in manga, psychological researcher Anna Madill writes, "Queer theory . . . draws attention [to], and celebrates, slippage between dichotomously conceived categorization and in so doing challenges a hegemonic worldview that disavows that which is betwixt and between. Where categories are placed in opposition, one is usually associated with greater hegemonic value and the second Othered. Hence, queer theory is also a critique of dominant status and power hierarchies" (Madill 2015, 280). Dwelling on and with what is in-between and out-of-place can challenge hegemonic worldviews. In this way, it is possible to disrupt dominant status and power hierarchies, whereas uncritically accepting the normalization and nationalization of "otaku" can serve to reinforce them. As I learned in Akihabara, where I became enmeshed in struggles over imagination and in shared spaces of imagination, "otaku" movement continues to be unsettled and unsettling, even when seemingly aligned with the powers that be.

Toward an Anthropology of Imagination

This book is based on long-term engagement with Akihabara and the people, characters, and ideas that I encountered and became entangled with there. I initially arrived in Akihabara in 2004, and soon was visiting several times a week, then daily, to hang out for hours at a stretch. Intensive fieldwork took place between 2006 and 2008, and regular commuting to the area continued until 2011. (Afterward, I phased into a project on adult computer games, also situated in Akihabara.) During that time, I was most immediately involved in Akihabara and the happenings in that corner of Tokyo, which led to many of my most enduring relationships with people that I learned with over the course of months and years. From the streets of Akihabara, I followed people into maid cafés, back out, and elsewhere. While conducting this fieldwork in the 2000s, I was made aware of histories that I needed to know to keep up. First it was *moe*, or an affective response to fictional characters, which I was told had much to do with the transformation of Akihabara into an "otaku" haven and the emergence of maid cafés there in the 1990s. Some said that moe dated back further to artists such as Takahashi Rumiko, Miyazaki Hayao, and Tezuka Osamu, whose manga/anime works I was instructed to read and view for reference and discussion, drawing me deeper into shared worlds of imagination.

From the moment that I set foot in Akihabara, "otaku" was a word that I could not ignore, but it profoundly puzzled me, because that word seemed as though pulled between competing definitions in the 2000s. "Otaku" were at once creepy and cool, and I was adrift in some chaotic flux. I eventually turned to historical research, which took me back to the 1990s, then the 1980s, where I discovered that the imagined excesses and perversions of interactions and relations with characters was key to labeling some manga/anime fans "otaku." Much of this seemed familiar from the street in Akihabara, and I began to notice that those negatively labeled "otaku" were almost always "male" manga/anime fans attracted to "female" manga/anime characters, specifically bishōjo, or cute girl characters. The longer I spent digging around the archives, the more I saw these characters as vital to the imagination of "otaku." Exploring their origins in the 1970s led to new insights about "otaku," margins, and seeking alternatives in manga and anime.

The order of my learning in the field is reversed in the order of chapters in this book, which starts with manga and anime in the 1970s and works its way up to Akihabara in the 2000s and beyond. Chapter 1 traces the origins of bishōjo. Although now seen as characteristic of manga and anime overall, bishōjo emerged from the movement of men and women imagining and creating alternatives as they crossed gender/genre lines in the 1970s. Again dealing with origins, chapter 2 turns to discourse about "otaku" and draws attention to the formation of it as a label in response to the imagined excesses and perversions of "male" fans of cute girl characters in Japan in the 1980s, as well as mutations of the label amid mounting concern about the impact of manga and anime on psychosexual development and society in the 1990s. Identifying a number of "reality problems," the chapter sketches the terrain of "otaku" and the struggle for imagination in contemporary Japan. Chapter 3 explores discourse about moe. Born from fans discussing cute girl characters online, this neologism allowed "otaku" to share movement. With a rising tide of bishōjo in games such as *Tokimeki Memorial* (Tokimeki memoriaru, 1994–) and anime such as *Neon Genesis Evangelion* (Shinseiki Evangerion, 1995–), and a tsunami of fans moved by them, moe came to be understood as a social, economic, and political phenomenon in Japan from the 1990s into the 2000s.

Pivoting from the archive of published accounts and personal interviews to the field, chapter 4 zooms in on the Akihabara area of Tokyo, which was a central hub for bishōjo games that blew up as an "otaku" hotspot with the manga/anime explosion from the late 1990s into the 2000s. Even as the number of men sharing moe responses to cute girl characters in the area attracted national and international attention, Akihabara was also becoming a symbolic site of "Cool Japan" culture and a tourist destination, which thrust "otaku" there into the spotlight. Core to the chapter is a simultaneous promotion and policing of "otaku" performances, which throws into relief the tension between normalized and nationalized "otaku" and "weird otaku." The focus then shifts in chapter 5 to interactions and relations between two-dimensional characters and three-dimensional humans in maid cafés in Akihabara in the 2000s. From the streets to these establishments, in spaces between dimensions and bodies, fictional and real, we can observe alternative ways of interacting with and relating to others in worlds of shared imagination. The conclusion examines a series of exhibitions of cute girl character art held in Akihabara in the 2010s, which brought bishōjo game makers and government ministries into an uneasy alliance. The exhibitions allow us to consider not only the contested imaginary of "otaku" domestically and internationally, but also the role that academic writing on "Japanese" media and popular culture plays in the ongoing struggle for imagination.

Although the result of reordering my learning in the field is a roughly chronological sequence in the chapters, this book is not intended to be an authoritative or general history of "otaku." My movement backward in time was specifically driven by engagement with Akihabara and the people, characters, and ideas that I encountered and became entangled with there. From participant observation on the streets and in maid cafés, I arranged personal interviews with manga/anime creators, fans, and critics that had lived through earlier decades, and I scoured the wealth of published interviews, dialogues, and firsthand accounts. This is, of course, only a partial view, which reflects where I was positioned and who I was talking with, pointed toward, and learning from. Taking a cue from the word *sōzō*, a homonym in Japanese that can mean "imagination" or "creation," I realize that in imagining "otaku" and bishōjo in relation to one another I am also creating them.[13] For me, the process is a collaborative one. In the field, I checked my "constructive attempts" (Malinowski 2014, 13) with others, who affected my thinking and writing. This book is another constructive attempt, but produced at a distance from my initial collaborators. In presenting it to readers, I anticipate different checks in different fields, which will contribute to open-ended discussion.

In this book, I try to draw readers in by imitating the media of imagination that I shared with "otaku" in the field. Drawing from participant observation, personal interviews, and archival research, I construct and frame images in text, which I imagine like panels in a comic.[14] The images are drawn in a particular way from a particular point of view and position. They are put into a sequence with space between them, which I hope will encourage readers to use their imagination. If this is at times unsettling, then that is also one of the aims of this book, which pushes back on common sense about "otaku" and predictable readings of psychological, sexual, and social dysfunction and deviance. Like theorist Eve Sedgwick, I fear that readings of this sort often only serve to confirm what critics already "know," which closes down the possibility for encounters with the unknown and where the outcome is not known in advance. To borrow Sedgwick's words, I worry that the prevalence of these readings "may have made it less rather than more possible to unpack the local, contingent relations" (Sedgwick 2003, 124). So I stick with those relations, which speaks to an ethics of learning with others, or a methodological commitment to be open to encounters and entanglements that can surprise, unsettle, and affect ways of thinking and seeing, if not also being, in the world.[15]

Against the backdrop of countries across the globe regulating some manga and anime under the assumption that they are pornography appealing to perverts, pedophiles, and predators (McLelland 2013), it is more urgent than ever to unpack local, contingent relations that may challenge what critics already "know." To return to the Gatebox advertisement and responses to it, many seem certain that Azuma Hikari is "a little girl" (Siciliano 2016) and that "Japan has a sex problem" (Gilbert 2017). Is this really all that we can imagine? Inspired by fieldworkers finding that interactions and relations with characters are increasingly part of everyday life around the world (Allison 2006; Ito 2008; Condry 2013), we must do better. In her monograph on mushrooms, anthropologist Anna Tsing offers what I take to be an invitation: "We might look around to notice this strange new world, and we might stretch our imaginations to grasp its contours" (Tsing 2015, 3). In the process, we might also imagine other possibilities in the world, other possible worlds. We might even try to live in shared worlds of imagination—to create them, together. This, too, is part of the struggle.

ONE SEEKING AN ALTERNATIVE

"Male" Shōjo Fans since the 1970s

As groundwork for the discussion of "otaku" and the struggle for imagination in Japan, this chapter focuses on male engagement with shōjo (for girls) manga and shōjo (girl) characters in manga and anime from the 1970s to the early 1980s. It is well known that shōjo manga underwent a renaissance in the 1970s (Thorn 2001; Suzuki 2011; Shamoon 2012), when female artists such as Hagio Moto, Takemiya Keiko, and Ōshima Yumiko began to experiment with speculative fiction, poetics, the grammar of comics, depictions of psychological conflict, and sexuality. What is less known is that men were also attracted to works by these and other shōjo artists in the 1970s. The existence, let alone motivation, of male shōjo fans seems sketchy at best. When mention is made of them, their attraction to shōjo is often understood as a crude desire to "deflower" (Mackie 2010, 200).[1] Discussion of male shōjo fans typically comes with critique of *lolicon*, or the "Lolita complex," which conjures mental images of creepy older men lusting after little girls. So certain are some critics that they know the meaning of lolicon that they comfortably gloss it as part of the "normalization of a wide range of pedophilic and misogynistic ideas" and "men's sexual abuse and objectification of girls" (Norma 2015, 85). To stop circulation and harm, one is told to consider refusing to translate related material, and perhaps even burning it (86). As "lolicon" has become a keyword in global criticism of manga, anime, and games from Japan, activists and academics alike seem confident in passing judgment. Indeed, when I presented on lolicon at an international conference in the summer of 2017, and made the rather modest proposal that researchers explore what it means to manga/anime fans in Japan, a member of the audience asked incredulously, "What more do we need to know?"[2]

If one can avoid thinking about lolicon in the familiar terms of Vladimir Nabokov's *Lolita* (1955) and Russell Trainer's *The Lolita Complex* (1966), and instead attempt to understand the word as it was used among manga/anime fans from the 1970s to the early 1980s, an often-obscure phenomenon begins to come into focus.[3] Consider that Akagi Akira, a manga editor and critic, connects what came to be known as lolicon not to sexual desire for little girls but rather attraction to "cuteness" (*kawai-rashisa*) and "girlness" (*shōjo-sei*) in manga and anime (Akagi 1993, 230–31).[4] Further, as articulated by Nagayama Kaoru, a manga editor and critic, the spirit of lolicon was not "I like girls" but rather "I like cute things" (Nagayama 2014, 83). As Nagayama sees it, "the cute movement" (*kawaii undō*) came out of growing up with weekly manga magazines and television anime, which gave rise to desire for manga/anime-style cute characters. Akagi, Nagayama, and other Japanese critics argue that lolicon refers to a desire for "manga-like" (*manga-ppoi*) or "anime-like" (*anime-ppoi*) characters, for "cuteness" (*kawai-rashisa*), "roundness" (*maru-kkosa*), and the "two-dimensional" (*nijigen*) as opposed to "real." The orientation of the cute movement, of lolicon, was not toward the girl per se, but rather the shōjo, or girl character, and the bishōjo, or cute girl character, specifically.

This chapter adds to the story of the cute movement the dynamic of men consuming and producing shōjo manga and characters, which is a phenomenon of crossing gender/genre lines. If, as manga editor and critic Fujita Hisashi suggests, "'cute' = shōjo manga-like" (Fujita 1989, 127), then it is clear from the proliferation of cute in manga and anime that the boundaries between shōjo and genres for men are increasingly blurred. In fact, the bishōjo character emerged out of responses to and appropriations of shōjo manga and characters, and evolved in collaborations between male and female artists across gender/genre lines. Diverse participation in the cute movement, and the shifting gender identities and sexualities of those involved, not only disrupts overly simplistic discourse about lolicon and men desiring to deflower girls but also raises the possibility of men seeking an alternative to hegemonic forms of masculinity and media and finding it in shōjo manga and characters (Ueno 1989, 131–32). More broadly, this movement and responses to it throw into relief, on the one hand, the imagined excesses and perversions associated with "male" shōjo fans, and, on the other, the struggle to imagine and create alternative social worlds. At this conjuncture appeared the figure of the "otaku," which is discussed in chapter 2, building on the understanding developed here.

Seeking an Alternative

Despite massive social and economic changes that have led to more opportunities for women and transforming relations between the sexes, Itō Kimio, a pioneer of men's studies, notes that expectations for men remain stubbornly rigid in Japan (Itō Kimio 2005, 149–51). To a certain extent, Itō's concerns stem from his own struggles with masculinity, which date back to at least the early 1970s. At the time, Itō was a student at Kyoto University involved in the movement against the political arrangement that made Japan an accomplice to the United States and its wars in East Asia. Itō found himself uncomfortable with not only his adult male role models—the salaryman, professor, and bureaucrat, for example—but also with the machismo of others in the movement, who wore military-inspired garb and engaged in sometimes violent standoffs with authorities on the street. It was a kind of masculinity familiar from popular media, as well, which was increasingly alienating for the young man (Galbraith 2014, 26).

Seeking an alternative, Itō began to read shōjo manga. In his essay "When a 'Male' Reads Shōjo Manga," Itō recalls those days: "I began to seriously read shōjo manga at the beginning of the 1970s, right in the middle of the aftermath of the explosion of counterculture and in the continuing wave of political youth rebellion. . . . In that period, I was reading the manga magazine *Shōjo Margaret* every week as well as the supplementary edition of *Shōjo Friend* and the magazines *Nakayoshi*, *Ribon*, and I bought every monthly I could lay my hands on, my favorite being the supplementary edition of *Seventeen*" (Itō Kimio 2010, 171–72). Looking back, Itō connects his intense attraction to shōjo manga and growing discomfort with masculinity: "In the last phase of the countercultural wave, when I was feeling a kind of alienation from the so-called male culture, shōjo manga offered me the opportunity to reconsider masculinity and to critically review the present situation of gender. . . . My encounter with shōjo manga has been of great importance to me. I suppose it has brought about one of the starting points for my research into masculinity" (175–76). In shōjo manga, specifically stories about male-male romance and relationships, a subgenre called "boys love" pioneered by Hagio Moto and Takemiya Keiko, Itō gained access to what he describes as a "minority" view:

> Having always been put into the margins, the minority is forced to face itself. To be excluded from the mainstream generates various feelings of alienation and discrimination. The majority though does not become aware of its own majority-ness, unless something extraordinary happens. . . . In a certain sense it is through the circuit of shōjo manga that I have been able to reflect upon male-dominated society from a male point of view. Above all, it was of great importance to me that the development of shōjo manga at the beginning of the 1970s started with boys' love stories, because the marginal male/homosexual perspective (as opposed to the heterosexual majority of society) turned my eyes to the indifference of the social majority hidden in gender and sexuality. (Itō Kimio 2010, 176)

In moving to the margins with and through shōjo manga, Itō gained a minority view, or, to rephrase somewhat, he moved away from the majority or mainstream to see things that he had not as a "heterosexual male." He was thus able not only to critique hegemonic masculinity but also to think differently as a man. With and through shōjo manga, Itō came to problematize his own position. It is for this reason that Itō puts "male" into scare quotes when he refers to himself as a reader of shōjo manga.

What Itō describes in his engagement with shōjo manga is remarkably similar to what others present as a survival strategy of queer youth. In her essay "Queer and Now," theorist Eve Sedgwick notes that many queer youth share the memory of attaching to cultural objects that did not match up with the dominant codes available to them. "We needed for there to be sites where the meanings didn't line up tidily with each other," Sedgwick explains, "and we learned to invest in those sites with fascination and love" (Sedgwick 1993, 3). Sedgwick is astute in appreciating that these objects, which "became a prime resource for survival" (3), can be drawn from popular media and material culture. While this seems to speak to Itō's experience, he notably did not identify as gay but rather as a queer person attracted to shōjo manga, which did not match up with the dominant codes of masculinity available to him. This is even more striking given Itō's attraction to boys love manga, which features romance and relationships between "male" characters that typically do not identify as gay (Akatsuka 2010, 167). With and through such shōjo manga, Itō gained access to an "open mesh of possibilities, gaps, overlaps, dissonances and resonances, lapses and excesses of meaning when the constituent elements of anyone's gender, of anyone's sexuality aren't made (or *can't be* made) to signify monolithically" (Sedgwick 1993, 8). Hence the questioning of Itō's position as a "male" reader of shōjo manga, which opens into other possibilities.

While Itō remembers being essentially alone, there were in fact many others like him. In a self-published book, sociologist Yoshimoto Taimatsu reports interviewing men who read boys love (BL) manga and *yaoi,* or fanzines focusing on boys love, in the 1970s. Among other things, the men said, "BL was salvation for me. And I think that it would be the same for a lot of men in contemporary Japan"; "BL/yaoi was a tool that my generation... could use to liberate ourselves from the pretense that we were tough guys"; "I was really saved by [the magazine] *June* and by yaoi, which offered me a new perspective on accepting [myself] being a passive man"; "I started getting the idea that men can enjoy specific texts, like yaoi, that were originally made by and for women, in order to live with less stress and psychological pressure" (translated in Nagaike 2015, 193–94). Much of this resonates with Itō, which suggests a larger phenomenon of men seeking an alternative. In Japan in the 1970s, new forms of shōjo manga offering alternative views of gender and sexuality became part of the survival strategy of queer youth that felt alienated by hegemonic masculinity and related institutions (Suzuki 2011, 59–61).

This was not limited to boys love manga, either. Later in the decade, Itō reports witnessing other men reading shōjo manga by Mutsu A-ko (Galbraith 2014, 27–28), who has not received the same critical praise as revolutionaries such as Hagio and Takemiya, but rather produced "girly" (*otome-chikku*) stories about romance and everyday life. As with Itō and boys love manga, one can see among Mutsu fans a move to the margin away from the masculine, mainstream, or majority. For Itō, in both cases, the interest in shōjo "started from a small sense of discomfort towards the contemporaneous male-dominated society" (Itō Kimio 2010, 177). In a personal interview, Itō expanded on this to argue that the turn toward shōjo manga was part of a larger one toward girls' culture and cuteness in Japan (Galbraith 2014, 28–29). Shōjo fans, Itō elucidates, "managed to preserve their own space by enjoying the commodified world through their own point of view, or by manipulating the commodified objects of consumption and adopting them to their own needs" (Itō Kimio 2010, 174). On the one hand, attracted to shōjo manga and characters, men began to consume across gender/genre lines. On the other hand, they began producing their own shōjo manga and characters, or rather bishōjo manga and characters, in dialogue and collaboration with female artists. Space was opened for men to share responses to (bi)shōjo manga and characters. Alternative social worlds were imagined and created. This is the story of "male" shōjo fans seeking an alternative in Japan.

The Comic Market

In the early 1970s, Harada Teruo (aka Shimotsuki Takanaka) was a student at Wakō University in the suburbs of Tokyo. He was born in 1951, the same year as Itō Kimio, and, like Itō, was a reader of shōjo manga. This is not entirely surprising, given the impact of Hagio, Takemiya, and Ōshima. "In the early 1970s when these female artists were working," Harada recalls, "even male fans got caught up in the boom, and each artist had fan clubs across the country" (Shimotsuki 2008, 12). Critics recall that, at the time, anyone who was a manga fan read shōjo manga (Nagayama 2014, 56, 233–34).[5] For his part, however, Harada was unaware of this larger phenomenon when he first encountered Hagio's work in COM magazine in 1971. He writes evocatively of the moment when "a university student on the verge of adulthood, who knew nothing of the 'shōjo mind' (*shōjo no shinsei*), was ensnared by it" (Shimotsuki 2008, 45). Following this exposure, Harada—again, like Itō—became fanatical in his pursuit of what seemed to him a singular interest. He bought *Bessatsu Shōjo Comic* and other magazines in which Hagio published, and sought out her work at new and used bookstores. In this way, reading *Bessatsu Shōjo Comic*, Harada stumbled onto Hagio's "November Gymnasium" (11 gatsu no gimunajiumu, 1971), a groundbreaking work in the shōjo manga subgenre of boys love. Overwhelmed with emotion, Harada was completely hooked, absorbed in shōjo manga and drawn into its world (Shimotsuki 2008, 46).

It was not until the following year, in July 1972, that Harada discovered he was not alone. He relays the happenings of a fateful night at the First Japan Manga Festival, which he spent in the company of fellow fans:

> A bunch of manga fans were in the same room talking and the topic turned to Hagio Moto's works. As soon as it did, men began to reveal that they, too, were Hagio fans. I did the same, and things got very lively. One man showed me a massive collection of Hagio works that he had cut out of magazines. I was truly surprised to meet fans who were passionate

to that degree. It was the first time that I met Matsuda Shin'tarō, who I learned was a Hagio fan just like me, and I ended up promising him that we would make our own fan club. (Shimotsuki 2008, 62)

That fan club, Moto no Tomo, connected Harada with not only Matsuda but also others across the country. Among them was Y-jō, representative of the Postwar Shōjo Manga History Research Group, and Yonezawa Yoshihiro, who came from Kumamoto to Tokyo to enroll in Meiji University. In 1973, Harada published his first fanzine, which was dedicated to Hagio and brought him into contact with even more fans. Against the backdrop of Hagio's *The Poe Family* (Poe no ichizoku, 1972–76) earning her a larger following of female fans, at the Second Japan Manga Festival in August 1973, Harada remembers spending the night at a hotel where he and others held a "meeting for men only to discuss shōjo manga" (Shimotsuki 2008, 68). In November 1973, Harada and his friends published another fanzine devoted to shōjo manga.

Gaining momentum and drawing others in, Harada's passionate pursuit of shōjo manga yielded spectacular results. In 1973, inspired by techniques of "still animation," Harada began to float the idea of producing an animated version of Hagio's "November Gymnasium."[6] To complete this "fan letter in visual form" (Shimotsuki 2008, 92), Harada enlisted the help of the Wakō University manga club, and tapped into the network of his fan club and publications. Composed of four hundred drawings and running forty-five minutes, the finished animation was screened in Shibuya, Tokyo, in 1974. In no time, universities and high schools were requesting screenings, and Harada was happy to oblige (Shimotsuki 2008, 20, 97). Interest in shōjo manga was building, as can be deduced from not only the screenings but also the Shōjo Manga Festival held in Yokohama in 1974. The following year, in April 1975, Harada joined Yonezawa Yoshihiro, Aniwa Jun, and others to form Labyrinth (Meikyū), a group that produced a legendary series of fanzines focusing on manga criticism, with heavy emphasis on shōjo manga.[7] Yonezawa, for example, used materials collected by contacts such as Y-jō to write articles on shōjo manga history, which would later become the book *Postwar Shōjo Manga History* (Sengo shōjo manga shi, 1980). Others turned a critical lens on themes such as light and darkness in Hagio's works, and Harada contributed a parody of *The Poe Family*.

Among the most important occurrences in 1975 was the founding of the Comic Market, with Harada acting as representative (something like president) and other members of Labyrinth playing crucial roles. Today, the Comic Market is the world's largest gathering for self-published manga artists and their fans, but in December 1975 it was a relatively small affair that drew around seven hundred people. Significantly, but perhaps not surprisingly given the steering of Harada and other members of Labyrinth, the Comic Market was biased toward shōjo manga and its fans. The only manga magazine in which the organizers advertised the Comic Market was *Bessatsu Shōjo Comic,* which published work by Hagio and was a favorite of Harada (Shimotsuki 2008, 11). About 90 percent of attendees at the Comic Market in December 1975 were young women (18). In a survey of favorite manga artists, attendees chose Hagio as number one, followed by Takemiya Keiko, Tezuka Osamu, and Ōshima Yumiko (12). No wonder, then, that attendees cried out in joy when Harada's *November Gymnasium* was screened, and lined up to buy a special issue of Labyrinth's fanzine dedicated to Hagio. By Harada's own estimation, the first Comic Market was almost a "Hagio Moto fan festival" (13). Among the young women dominating the event were Harada and other "male" shōjo fans, who organized the Comic Market to socialize and share their interests. If the event was part of the broader "shōjo manga movement" (*shōjo manga mūbumento*), to borrow Harada's turn of phrase (Shimotsuki 2008, 16; also Yonezawa 1989; Tamagawa 2012), then this movement included "male" shōjo fans.

When the second Comic Market was held in 1976, the event was still attended primarily by young women drawn to groups focusing on shōjo manga, for example, Hagio fan clubs (Shimotsuki 2008, 157). The title of Labyrinth's fanzine for the event was *To Hagio Moto with Love.* There was also a special exhibition of works by Okada Fumiko, a female artist whose unique style had been featured in COM magazine. As late as 1979, the last year that Harada served as representative of the Comic Market, Labyrinth's fanzine was still dedicated to shōjo manga (178–79). It was, after all, their genre, what moved them, brought and held them together. If, as Itō Kimio suggests, the manipulation of commodities allows for the production of "space" (Itō Kimio 2010, 174), then Harada and his friends manipulated shōjo manga—producing fanzines, criticism, parodies, a visual fan letter—and produced a shared space, a space for sharing, in the Comic Market (Fujita 1989, 130; Yonezawa 1989, 88; Kinsella 2000, 136). This space would go on to support "manipulating the commodified objects of consumption and adopting them to [. . . meet fan] needs" (Itō Kimio 2010, 174). One clear example of this dynamic is women poaching male characters from manga/anime franchises to cast in boys love fanzines, which was observed at the Comic Market in the 1970s, as it has been in other parts of the world

(Jenkins 1988, 87). Another example is the appropriation and use of shōjo manga and characters to explore and express sexual alternatives.

The Lolicon Boom

Writing of 1979, the last year of his tenure as representative of the Comic Market, Harada Teruo notes the rise of lolicon, or "manga works that take shōjo as sexual objects" (Shimotsuki 2008, 178). While this may sound like a shocking and unexpected development, Yonezawa Yoshihiro, who would take over as representative of the Comic Market, submits that some shōjo fans were already aware of lolicon and were discussing it earlier in the decade.[8] There is evidence to support Yonezawa's claim. Consider, for example, that the first appearance of the words "Lolita complex" (*rorīta konpurekkusu*), which would be combined into the Japanese portmanteau "lolicon," in manga was in a shōjo magazine. In the June 1974 issue of *Bessatsu Margaret,* in a work titled *Stumbling Upon a Cabbage Patch* (Kyabetsu batake de tsumazuite), which draws heavily on *Alice in Wonderland,* a male character describes Lewis Carroll as a man with a Lolita complex, or someone with the "strange character of liking only small children." One suspects that the young girls that *Bessatsu Margaret* ostensibly targeted were not interested in seeing a male character gush about another man's infatuation with little girls like Alice, which makes the inclusion of this reference all the more interesting. With the knowledge that men were reading manga magazines such as *Bessatsu Margaret* in the 1970s (for example, Itō Kimio 2010, 171–72), it appears that Wada Shinji, the author of the work and a "male" shōjo artist, was sharing an inside joke with "male" shōjo fans.

In discussing the rise of lolicon at the Comic Market in 1979, Harada mentions *Cybele* (Shibēru, 1979–81), a series of fanzines as legendary as Labyrinth's own. In the pages of *Cybele,* one finds parodies and commentaries celebrating shōjo produced by men. In the first issue, one work in particular stands out, which is a parody of *Little Red Hiding Hood* focusing on a cute, cartoony girl character and her sexual encounters with various animals in the woods. Although drawing under a pen name, the man behind this work is unmistakably Azuma Hideo, one of the most influential manga artists of the 1970s. Born in 1950, one year after Hagio Moto and before Harada Teruo and Itō Kimio, Azuma was "among the earliest male artists responding to shōjo manga" (Sasakibara 2003, 120). By Azuma's own estimation, his work shares with shōjo manga a "lack of reality" (*riaritī no nasa*)

FIGURE 1.1 Wada explains the Lolita complex in shōjo manga.

FIGURE 1.2 Azuma's first contribution to *Cybele.*

(Azuma and Yamada 2011, 30). Clearly Azuma did not want to draw in the "realistic" style of *gekiga,* or the countercultural comics that were popular among adolescent boys and young men from the 1960s into the 1970s. Despite being the dominant form of "adult comics" in Japan at the time, gekiga's influence is notably absent from Azuma's work. Instead of sharp angles, dark hatching, and gritty lines, there is roundness, light shading, and clean line work (figure 1.3). As he recalls, Azuma's style comes from combining the squat and round character bodies of Tezuka Osamu's manga with the round and emotive faces of shōjo manga, which formed something that he

FIGURE 1.3
Azuma's bishōjo experiments.

found thoroughly erotic (30–31). Responding to manga for children and girls—to "God of Manga" Tezuka's foundational cartoony style and shōjo, as opposed to gekiga, which was intended for mature audiences—Azuma developed a style across gender/genre lines (Fujita 1989, 127). The result was the bishōjo, or cute girl character, and a form of eroticism based on manga-like, cartoony, or cute characters.

In producing bishōjo manga and pursuing "cute eroticism" (*kawaii ero*), Azuma was seeking an alternative to the mainstream, masculine imaginary and its particular iteration of "reality." Like Hagio, Azuma tends to reimagine male-female relations in order to get out of normative gender roles, reproductive maturity, and dominant ideals of the family (Sasakibara 2003, 120; Suzuki 2011, 59–60).[9] In works from the 1970s leading up to *Cybele,* Azuma mixed elements of sci-fi, fairytales, and the absurd with bishōjo characters and cute eroticism. In *The Two of Us and Five People* (Futari to gonin, 1972–76), for example, the protagonist cannot tell which of the members of a family is the girl that he is attracted to and wants to have sex with, because they all—men and women, young and old—look exactly alike. When the perpetually frustrated protagonist final does "get the girl," he cannot consummate the relationship and instead runs away. In *The Two of Us and Five People,* men exist in a world of infinitely deferred climax and dispersed cute eroticism. Seeming to parody men whenever he draws them, Azuma would just as soon not draw them at all, and expresses a desire to "erase himself" (Azuma and Yamada 2011, 35–36) from the work, which leaves a world of cute eroticism without male intervention (see also Tsuchimoto 1989, 110). Things are taken further in Azuma's contribution to the first issue of *Cybele,* which does include sex scenes, but in them the human male is replaced by silly little animals that seem only to tickle the girl with their tiny members (figure 1.2); the story ends with a wolf trying to sexually assault the girl and snapping his giant erection in half. Gone is the "heroic male inserter" (Akagi 1993, 231–32), who was a staple of power fantasy in the pornographic gekiga that was undergoing a boom in the late 1970s—precisely when Azuma contributed his parody to *Cybele.* Figured as silly little animals and a panting wolf with a broken penis, the would-be inserter is pathetic. One very well might be aroused by these drawings, but also laughs at that arousal. In sum, Azuma, drawing across gender/genre lines—appropriating, parodying, and sexualizing works and styles for children and girls, which were intended neither for men nor to be sexual—produced an alternative to the mainstream, masculine imaginary.

Many of the contributors to *Cybele* wanted to be shōjo manga artists, but Azuma, who published in a shōjo magazine in 1979 and was recognized by influential critics as a shōjo artist, had something else in mind with the fanzine.[10] For him, it was about parodying Tezuka and shōjo manga and characters and exposing an eroticism that had been "taboo" and "unspeakable."[11] Doing so, he hoped, would open a space to share this hidden eroticism with others. "I wanted friends," Azuma explains. "I thought that there absolutely must be others that like this sort of thing somewhere" (Azuma and Yamamoto 2011, 141). The contributors to *Cybele*—who were coming out as lolicon, or people with a Lolita complex, while gathering in cafés and sharing drawings of cute girl characters (Morikawa 2011a, 184)—produced a fanzine to share their interests at the Comic Market, which was itself a space founded by "male" shōjo fans in order to socialize and share interests. Faced with the overwhelming presence of girls and women at the Comic Market, and the dominance of fanzines by and for girls and women focusing on sexual and romantic relationships between male characters, Azuma and his friends were opening space for boys and men. In fact, even as Azuma was responding to shōjo manga in his bishōjo manga, lolicon fanzines were responding to yaoi fanzines by and for girls and women (Sasakibara 2003, 118–19; Yoshimoto 2009, 81–83; Takatsuki 2010, 105–11; Morikawa 2011a, 181–82; Azuma and Yamada 2011, 32). If imagined and created relations with, between, and through male characters provided girls and women with space to more flexibly play with gender and sexuality (Fujimoto 2015, 79), Azuma and his friends raised the possibility of something similar for boys and men. Indeed, Harada Teruo, the first representative of the Comic Market and a fan of boys love, saw in lolicon fanzines such as *Cybele* a complementary phenomenon, namely "a pure apparatus for the pursuit of pleasure that can only exist as manga" (Shimotsuki 2008, 179).[12]

The work that Azuma and his friends were producing was a departure from the norm, and it inspired criticism from gekiga artists and fans (Takekuma 2003, 107), but that did not stop boys and men from lining up at the Comic Market to buy print copies of *Cybele* in 1979.[13] While Azuma had at least in part sexualized Tezuka and shōjo manga and characters as a form of parody, the popularity of his work spoke to a growing number of boys and men that found cute and cartoony characters to be sexually attractive (more on this in chapters 2 and 3). Indeed, also in 1979, the young heroine of *Lupin III: The Castle of Cagliostro* (Rupan sansei: Kariosutoro no shiro, 1979), the first animated film directed by Miyazaki Hayao, inspired her own smash-hit series of fanzines (Takatsuki 2010, 102). Drawn to *Cybele, Clarisse Magazine*, and other related material, male attendance at the Comic Market skyrocketed—and even briefly eclipsed women as the statistical majority (Aida 2005, 157). *Cybele* and *Clarisse Magazine* laid the groundwork for parodying shōjo manga and characters and elaborating cute eroticism, and ushered in what came to be known as the "lolicon boom" (*rorikon būmu*) from 1980 to 1984.

Contemporaneously, shōjo manga continued to attract male readers in the late 1970s and early 1980s. In a personal interview, manga and anime critic Sasakibara Gō recalled reading introductions to shōjo manga (of the sort that Labyrinth had been publishing in its fanzines) in sci-fi and anime specialty magazines from around 1977 or 1978.[14] These brought him to works published by Hakusensha, and magazines such as *Hana to Yume, LaLa,* and *Shōjo Comic.* In our interview, Sasakibara highlighted the emergence of a new kind of "male" shōjo fan at the time:

> There were basically two ways to get into shōjo manga. With artists such as Hagio Moto and Ōshima Yumiko, people were saying, "Shōjo manga is better than stuff for boys," so you could get into it as a manga fan. You might praise a work for being technically superior, or as an excellent form of manga expression, or maybe as just good science fiction. Separate from this critical praise, others were attracted to shōjo manga because it was shōjo manga, which they liked. So they got into it not from a critical perspective, but rather as something that moved them, or touched them in a deeply personal way. For people like this, it wasn't just about science fiction, but also love comedies. There were many artists popular as creators of love comedies. To speak personally, I was into Hikawa Kyōko. From the time that I was a senior in high school to my first year of college, my favorite manga artist was Hikawa Kyōko. She produced extremely cute love comedies.

As Sasakibara remembers it, men like him sought in shōjo manga "a medium to enjoy moe," or an affective response to fictional characters (more on this concept in chapter 3). Even as Sasakibara and men like him were crossing gender/genre lines in their attraction to shōjo manga and characters, Takahashi Rumiko, a female artist with a sense not unlike Azuma Hideo, was producing bishōjo manga and love comedy for male readers. Takahashi's *Urusei Yatsura* (Those Obnoxious Aliens, 1978–87), which stars a cute girl character beloved by fans, is often said to be "the origin of moe" (Galbraith 2009b, 46–48, 74–77; Galbraith 2014, 175–76; see chapter 3). Having started her career selling self-published work, the anime adaptation of Takahashi's *Urusei Yatsura* caused another spike in male fanzine production and attendance at the Comic Market (Comic Market Committee 2014, 28). All of this, too, fed into the lolicon boom.[15]

In stark contrast to the beginning of the 1970s, "male" shōjo fans were a recognized force by the end of the decade, when figures such as Ōtsuka Eiji started to rise. A manga writer, critic, and editor, Ōtsuka describes himself as growing up with girls, or as "their male classmate, the boy sitting next to them during their shōjo years" (Ōtsuka 1991, 31). If the older Itō Kimio recalls reading *Ribon* (Itō Kimio 2010, 171–72), a shōjo manga magazine intended for girls between the ages of nine and thirteen, and seeing men reading Mutsu A-ko's work, which was made popular by *Ribon* (Galbraith 2014, 27–28), then Ōtsuka speaks as one of those men. In the late 1970s, following the shōjo manga renaissance, *Ribon* improved in quality to such an extent that university-aged women were reading it. Artists such as Mutsu, famous for her "girly" style, moved to the fore in producing promotional giveaways for *Ribon*. It was at this time that Ōtsuka became an avid reader, along with other men, who offered the magazine their "strange support" (*kimyō na shiji*) (Ōtsuka 1991, 221). A fan of Mutsu and Tabuchi Yumiko, Ōtsuka went as far as to send letters to them and brag about receiving a response. Just as university students gained attention at the end of the 1960s for reading *Shōnen Magazine*, which did much to mainstream gekiga, Ōtsuka and others, inheritors of the quiet revolution of "male" shōjo fans, gained attention at the end of the 1970s for reading *Ribon*. The Japanese media made much of the phenomenon of male university students reading shōjo manga generally and *Ribon* specifically, which of course reached the editors of the magazine. For example, in the August 1978 issue, there appears an advertisement for next month's promotional giveaway, which is a bag emblazoned with a design by Mutsu A-ko. The catch copy reads, "Whether it be elementary school kids or University of Tokyo students, this high fashion sense bag is sure to be the perfect fit" (Ōtsuka 1991, 221). The catch copy is responding to reports of students from the University of Tokyo forming a shōjo manga club. Although Ōtsuka was not affiliated with the University of Tokyo at the time, he does count himself among the larger population of "troubled students" that were flocking to shōjo manga at the end of the 1970s. As he began to work in industry niches in the early 1980s, Ōtsuka cultivated "shōjo manga for boys" (Nagayama 2014, 235) and played a key role in the lolicon boom.

In substantial ways, the lolicon boom is tied to "male" shōjo fans since the 1970s, who established the space of the Comic Market, where Azuma Hideo and others released fanzines featuring shōjo as objects of desire and affection. This continued with increasing interest in shōjo characters in manga and anime, as well as interest in girly or cutesy shōjo manga for younger readers. Furthermore, as Fujita Hisashi explains, the style that came to prominence during the lolicon boom is the result of both men and women crossing gender/genre lines to produce (bi)shōjo manga: "What is called the lolicon style is something with a strong influence from shōjo manga. During lean years when they were not selling well, more than a few female manga artists passed through this genre. It is only relatively recently that female manga artists have become active in comic magazines targeting male readers, but the exception to this rule is lolicon, where many female manga artists started out. This is because this genre in particular sought shōjo manga images" (Fujita 1989, 129). At the same time, male manga artists who had learned to draw for shōjo magazines were transitioning into producing work for men. For example, Yuzuki Hikaru, the male manga artist behind *Give It All* (Minna agechau, 1982–87), an erotic comedy serialized in a young adult magazine called *Young Jump,* got his start publishing in *Ribon* (Fujita 1989, 129). While the anime adaptation of *Give It All* was derided as "Japanese pornography" when imported to the United States (Right Stuf 1998), the original manga and its heroine are characterized by an unmistakable shōjo aesthetic. Crudely speaking, Yuzuki simply combined cute and eroticism, shōjo and sex, much as Azuma Hideo had done in the 1970s, but what was once reserved for niche magazines and fanzines was possible in even mainstream manga magazines during the lolicon boom.[16]

Perhaps Uchiyama Aki provides an even better example of the connection between lolicon and shōjo manga. A popular artist in the early 1980s, Uchiyama is often heralded as "the King of Lolicon," because his work became so emblematic of the lolicon boom. In a personal interview, Uchiyama explained how he ended up in such a position:

> I started drawing when I was a university student. I was in the manga club, and was producing fanzines. I was a fan of Azuma Hideo, who really influenced my work. . . . There was a guy in the manga club who was drawing shōjo manga. He said, "I'm going to submit something, so why don't you submit, too?" I wasn't particularly interested in shōjo manga, but I wanted my work to be published, and shōjo manga magazines accept a lot of reader submissions. So I drew shōjo manga and submitted it to *Ribon,* which is a pretty famous shōjo manga magazine. They rejected my submission. I had put a lot of work into it and didn't want the manuscript to go to waste. I started to think of places where I could resubmit. At the time, publishing companies could make money selling a variety of niche magazines. Of course, sex sells, and that was what most niche magazines were dealing in. So I added some pages of nudity and resubmitted my manuscript to a niche magazine [*Gekkan Out*], which accepted it. I submitted similar manuscripts to other magazines, all of which were accepted. Then publishers started coming to me with requests.[17]

It is hard not to see how Uchiyama fits in the history of "male" shōjo fans: a young man inspired by Azuma Hideo and producing fanzines is approached at university by a man interested in shōjo manga and submits work to *Ribon*, a shōjo magazine with a strong male readership; when rejected, the young man adds sex to his shōjo manga and sends it to a niche magazine, where he finds a passionate fan base that supports his professional rise; the expanding influence of these fans and visibility of media targeting them contributes to what would be called the lolicon boom. Highly sought after in the early 1980s, Uchiyama published not only in *Lemon People* (Remon pīpuru), established in 1982 as the first specialty magazine dedicated to "lolicon comics" (*rorikon komikku*), but also in mainstream manga magazines. For example, Uchiyama's *Andro Trio* (Andoro torio, 1982) appeared in *Shōnen Champion* alongside Tezuka Osamu's *Prime Rose* (Puraimu rōzu, 1982–83), which speaks to the increasing demand for, and influence of, lolicon material at the time. To put it another way, Tezuka, called the God of Manga, was publishing in the same magazine as Uchiyama, called the King of Lolicon. The distance between mainstream and niche was collapsing. Indeed, not only did Uchiyama publish in *Shōnen Champion*, but he also published a parody of his own work in *Lemon People*.

In the early 1980s, the lolicon boom was making waves, but manga/anime producers were not always aware of it, even as the cute girl characters appearing in their work became objects of desire and affection. A striking example of this is *Magical Princess Minky Momo* (Mahō no purinsesu Minkī Momo, 1982–83), which targets little girls with a transforming heroine and her animal sidekicks, but was also among the first television anime of its kind to have a fan club composed of adult men. In a personal interview, producer Satō Toshihiko recalled his surprise at encountering "male" shōjo fans attracted to *Magical Princess Minky Momo* and its eponymous heroine:

> The anime started in spring 1982 and these guys started showing up after about six months. It was completely unexpected, but this guy came to our studio asking for permission to make something for his fan club. I was shocked! He told me that he was the head of this fan club, which was made up of members between eighteen and thirty years of age. He told me that he was attracted to the character Minky Momo. He thought that she was cute. It is still hard for me to understand. Minky Momo is cute, yes, and she is someone that everyone likes. I expected this response from five-year-old girls and their mothers, who might be watching the anime with them, but not adult men.[18]

Curious, Satō attended a fan club meeting, where he came face to face with apparently normal university students and salarymen talking about the main character Minky Momo in a way that profoundly upset him:

> They said Minky Momo is cute. They said they wanted a little sister like her, or a girlfriend like her, or something. They said this stuff, but the character is a child. The things they imagined were beyond anything that we expected. We were simply making animation for three-to-five-year-old children, which was interesting enough that mothers could also enjoy it. And then we learned about this fan club and the guys there told me that Minky Momo is sexy. We never thought that way. We still don't think that way.[19]

To a certain extent, Satō's confusion and disbelief are understandable in context, given that *Magical Princess Minky Momo* was among the first anime of its kind to have a fan club with a membership like this one. Many were disgusted by these "male" fans of Minky Momo, including Satō, who dismissed them and their attraction to the cute girl character as frankly "gross" (*kimochi warui*). (More on this in chapter 2.)

Be that as it may, it is worth underscoring that there was nothing straightforward about the desire and affection. These fans wanted Minky Momo to be a little sister but also a girlfriend; they found her cute but also sexy; she was something to them, but what that was is not immediately apparent; responding to the character, their imaginations were running wild, beyond anything that the original creators had anticipated. Subsequent character designers came to expect this desire and affection, which they grasped in nuanced ways. In a personal interview, Itō Noizi, known for designing cute girl characters such as Suzumiya Haruhi, explained the appeal of magical girls for men: "Magical girls originally appeared in television anime targeting young girls, so they are cute young girls. A cute young girl gets magical powers, and the young girls watching dream of being like her. If you stop and think about it, men just want to be part of that world. They think that it would be splendid if such girls existed and they could be close to them. Men desire a world where magical girls exist."[20] In the world of *Magical Princess Minky Momo*, the story is all about lost people finding their dreams with the help of the transforming heroine and her animal sidekicks. There are no villains to defeat; it is a peaceful, happy, colorful world where anything seems possible. Possible, that is, as long as Minky Momo is around. The character anchors a world of dreams, transformation, and possibility, drawing viewers in and holding them there. If "male" shōjo fans were seeking an alternative in "the bright colors of girls' culture" (Itō Kimio in Galbraith 2014, 29), then it makes some sense that characters that stand for this alternative became objects of desire and affection, even if desire and affection are complex and contradictory, perhaps unsettling.

When another magical girl anime, *Creamy Mami, the Magic Angel* (Mahō no tenshi Kurīmī Mami, 1983–84), drew an adult male audience the year after *Magical Princess Minky Momo*, producer Nunokawa Yūji was not as critical of the development. In a personal interview, Nunokawa reflected on the phenomenon:

> From about the middle of the series we became aware of the male fans. I was surprised to find that when we did events for *Creamy Mami*, the audience was predominately male. Before that, magical girl events didn't really draw male fans. They might have been there, but they weren't really visible. Male fans of magical girls increased after *Creamy Mami*. . . . I think that people still long for protagonists that show their kindness rather than strength. Of course our company, Pierrot, makes the *Naruto* and *Bleach* anime based on the manga for boys about epic adventures, but I personally can no longer believe in male heroes. Maybe fighting isn't the way to resolve conflict. But if a male character said that, it would seem weak and pitiful, because we judge them based on some notion of what it means to be a man. The solution is to have female characters resolve the conflict in a way that is impossible for men. In the 1980s, [manga/anime producer] Miyazaki Hayao shifted from boy to girl protagonists. I think that he did this because it allowed for a different approach to the world. It's the same for those who prefer magical girls to male heroes. Regardless of what era people live in, they desire change, and that is ultimately what the magical girl is all about.[21]

In this dense and rich statement, three points stand out: first, seeking an alternative to the masculine imaginary and finding new ways of seeing and being in the world; second, the increasing visibility of men responding to cute girl characters and coming together in public; and third, transformation, which features prominently in *Magical Princess Minky Momo*, *Cream Mami, the Magic Angel*, and magical girl anime generally. Using magic, the girl transforms, which, according to Nunokawa, appeals to a "desire to change" (*henshin ganbō*). While Nunokawa primarily associates this desire with children, it also appears in adults and others seeking an alternative. Mirroring the plasmaticness of animation (Eisenstein 1986, 21), a medium of transformation from one image to the next, the magical girl has the ability to dynamically assume other forms. She is connected to other worlds and alien forces. In her movement, the magical girl crosses and blurs borders, opening a space of imagination into reality that can potentially change it.[22]

The lolicon boom, however, encompassed more than sweet dreams. There was also the sex that Satō and others condemn so strongly. Indeed, manga, anime, fanzines, and games of the time could be disconcertingly sexual and violent, even as they proliferated and diversified. This was especially apparent in the adult, or pornographic, market. Companies such as Enix produced games with titles like *Lolita Syndrome* (Rorīta shindorōmu, 1983), in which winning is rewarded with cute girl characters stripping and losing is punished with them being butchered in gory fashion. When Wonder Kids produced the first pornographic anime series in Japan, they gave it the title *Lolita Anime* (Rorīta anime, 1984–85). Trying to cash in on the phenomenon, Nikkatsu responded by producing its own pornographic anime series, also called *Lolita Anime* (Rorīta anime, 1984–85).[23] By this time, Uchiyama Aki was producing 160 pages of manga a month, and had become such an established brand that Nikkatsu paid to simply use his name to promote their series.[24] Despite high-profile features about it in publications such as *Gekkan Out*, *Animec*, and *Animage*, the lolicon boom is one of the lesser-known chapters in the history of manga and anime in Japan. What "lolicon" meant then is often buried under the baggage of what "Lolita complex" means to critics now. To explore lolicon in context, and return it to the larger narrative of "male" shōjo fans since the 1970s, we now turn to open the pages of *Manga Burikko*. Crucially, during the lolicon boom, this magazine became a platform for "male" shōjo fans imagining and creating alternative social worlds, as well as critics responding to imagined excesses and perversions.

Inside *Manga Burikko*

Manga Burikko was first published in November 1982, which is to say in the thick of the lolicon boom. Indeed, it is often remembered as a lolicon magazine (e.g., Kinsella 1998, 311), which was established to compete with the already successful *Lemon People*. What, however, is meant by the description of *Manga Burikko* as a lolicon magazine? In the beginning, it looked more like an adult gekiga magazine carrying gag strips and pornographic comics. The cover image of the first issue was drawn by Minami Shinbō, best known for illustrated essays (figure 1.4); in the front pages were photographs of

FIGURE 1.4
Manga Burikko, November 1982.

nude women; works inside included four-panel strips by Takahashi Haruo and adult gekiga (read: realistically drawn, pornographic comics) by the likes of Ishi'i Takashi, Hachū Rui, and Tomita Shigeru. In other words, initially, *Manga Burikko* appeared to be an adult gekiga magazine that bore few similarities to *Lemon People*.

It was only later, in 1983, that *Manga Burikko* transformed into what might be called a lolicon magazine, and this clear change provides a unique opportunity to consider what exactly constituted a lolicon magazine at the time. As *Manga Burikko* struggled with sales, editorial control shifted from a senior man to Ōtsuka Eiji and Ogata Katsuhiro. Soon enough, Ōtsuka was for all intents and purposes the chief editor (Yamanaka 2009, 23–25). Recall that Ōtsuka was a "male" shōjo fan, who as a university student had been reading *Ribon* and praising the "girly" manga of Mutsu A-ko and

Tabuchi Yumiko. The transformation of *Manga Burikko,* which earned its reputation as a lolicon magazine, occurred primarily as a result of Ōtsuka's increased editorial control. The direction that Ōtsuka pushed *Manga Burikko,* which is to say the nature of its transformation, was toward "shōjo manga for boys" (Nagayama 2014, 235).[25] In the May 1983 issue, a new cute or shōjo manga aesthetic was apparent in the cover art drawn by Taniguchi Kei, and the subtitle of the magazine was "Bishōjo Comic Magazine for Dreaming Boys" (figure 1.5). This does seem to suggest shōjo manga for boys—as an adjective, "dreaming" (*yumemiru*) conjures images of the starry-eyed girls drawn in, and drawn to, shōjo manga—or what was at times called bishōjo manga. While sales had been lagging for months, the May 1983 issue of *Manga Burikko* sold out (Ōtsuka 2004, 26–27, 47–49) because it successfully tapped into the energy of the ongoing lolicon boom.

Much of the following issue in June 1983, again featuring cover art by Taniguchi Kei, was devoted to celebrating the work of Uchiyama Aki, which firmly aligned *Manga Burikko* with lolicon. Significantly, there was also a contribution by Okazaki Kyōko, a female artist that would go on to earn critical acclaim for her shōjo manga. Indeed, in addition to Okazaki, coming months saw contributions from female artists such as Shirakura Yumi and Sakurazawa Erica that reflected Ōtsuka's interest in shōjo manga and intention to promote shōjo artists in the magazine. In general, for the rest of the year, *Manga Burikko*'s cover art was drawn by Taniguchi Kei and moved increasingly toward a cute or shōjo aesthetic until November and December 1983, when the cover art was drawn by Apo in a style obviously inspired by shōjo manga (figure 1.6). The subtitle of the magazine also changed to "Two-Dimensional Idol Comic Magazine for Boys" (October 1983) and, finally, "Totally Bishōjo Manga" (November 1983). As these subtitles suggest, gravure photography, nude or otherwise, disappeared from the pages of *Manga Burikko* in favor of drawings of manga/anime-style cute girl characters. In just eight months in 1983, then, there was a double move away from "reality," first from more "realistic" drawings in the gekiga style, and second from photographs of "real women." The dramatic transformation further included a move away from explicit depictions of sex. In *Manga Burikko,* as it transformed into a flagship of the genre, lolicon appears as a departure from photographs and hard sex in the realistic style of gekiga and a move toward soft, light, and cute eroticism in the unrealistic style of shōjo manga.[26] (Recall the "lack of reality" in Azuma Hideo's bishōjo manga and lolicon fanzines, which he sees as shared with shōjo manga, and was part of his conscious move away from the reality of gekiga and photographs. In fact,

FIGURE 1.5
Manga Burikko, May 1983.

Azuma also pioneered presenting bishōjo characters as "two-dimensional idols" by, for example, releasing *Myā-chan's Erotic Photo Album* [Myā-chan kan'nō shashin shū, 1981], a book of drawings of the heroine of his manga *Scrap School* [Sukurappu gakuen, 1981–83] as a pinup girl. A transformation similar to that of *Manga Burikko* also occurred in *Lemon People*.[27])

The transformation of *Manga Burikko* under Ōtsuka Eiji casts into relief key features of lolicon specifically and of "male" shōjo fans more generally. First, and most obviously, the bishōjo or cute girl characters in *Manga Burikko* were clearly differentiated from the "real thing," "reality," and "realism." The magazine moved away from not only adult gekiga, but also gravure photography. At the risk of redundancy, let us repeat that lolicon here appears to be about cute girl characters—manga/anime characters—rather than flesh-and-blood girls and women (Ueno 1989, 134; Akagi 1993,

FIGURE 1.6
Manga Burikko, November 1983.

230–31; Shigematsu 1999, 129–32; Nagayama 2014, 129–30; Galbraith 2015b, 24–30). This redundancy is built into the title of *Manga Burikko*, which translates as "Comic Fake Girl/Child," and is reinforced by subtitles such as "Two-Dimensional Idol Comic Magazine." The orientation is toward fiction as such. Second, depictions of explicit sex decreased in *Manga Burikko* as it became a lolicon magazine. Third, the bishōjo characters in *Manga Burikko* were not fetish objects drawn solely by and for men, but rather were the culmination of movement across gender/genre lines—of men consuming and then producing shōjo manga, women drawing for men, and the emergence of a space of fluid and hybrid expression. It is not a coincidence that Ōtsuka, in his historical breakdown of manga, places *Manga Burikko* in the lineage of *Ribon*, or that he situates female artists such as Okazaki in both the shōjo manga renaissance and the lolicon boom, which he sees as connected (Ōtsuka 1991, 236). The shōjo manga movement, which included "male" shōjo fans and crossing gender/genre lines, affected the lolicon boom.

The influence of shōjo manga is apparent in *Manga Burikko* beyond the cute aesthetic and focus on cute girl characters. Consider, for example, "cat ears" (*nekomimi*), which critics often associate with the fetishism of male fans of manga and anime (Azuma [2001] 2009, 42–47), if not also their dehumanization of girls and women (Sharp 2011, 64–65). Sure enough, cat ears appear frequently in *Manga Burikko*, but they were first seen in the shōjo manga of female artist Ōshima Yumiko in the 1970s (Nagayama 2014, 61–62). The pages of *Manga Burikko* are brimming with such references. For example, in *Manga Burikko*, Nakata Aki, a female artist, drew parodies of works by Ōshima, Hagio Moto, and Takemiya Keiko. As chief editor, Ōtsuka solicited work from Nakata with the assumption that *Manga Burikko* readers knew these shōjo manga artists and would get the jokes.[28] Given that only 15 percent of *Manga Burikko* readers responding to surveys identified as female—a number that, while low, undermines the stereotype of lolicon as something exclusive to men—Ōtsuka assumed that the remaining 85 percent—"male" or otherwise—were also shōjo fans.[29] These were the manga fans that Ōtsuka was targeting in *Manga Burikko*, and he did so by publishing work by a female artist parodying shōjo manga of the 1970s. While Nakata indulged in sexual parody, and turned boy characters into bishōjo, her work is, stylistically, shōjo manga. To put it another way, Nakata and women like her were producing "shōjo manga for boys," which is precisely what Ōtsuka wanted.

That said, rigid distinctions between "female" or "male" artists drawing in "female" or "male" styles for "female" or "male" readers quickly come undone in *Manga Burikko*. Alongside women drawing for the magazine appeared artists whose names sound like those of women—Hiromori Shinobu and Sawaki Akane—but who might also be men. Other artists used gender-neutral, cute names such as Maneki Neko and Apo. The more that one investigates these artists, the less clear their gender/sex becomes. Apo, for example, is a pen name used by Kagami Akira, who is male, but also drew as Yamada Eiko, a female. If we follow his/her story, Apo is the younger brother of Kagami but draws in a style influenced by shōjo manga (Nagayama 2014, 234–35). Recall that it was Apo who drew shōjo manga cover art for *Manga Burikko*'s November and December 1983 issues. While we may know that the imaginary character of Apo is "male" (Kagami's younger brother), it is significantly more difficult to grasp the gender/sex of someone such as Hiromori Shinobu, who does not make that information public and also publishes under the names Miyasu Nonki and, appropriately enough, Lolicon Maker. The gender/sex of the imaginary characters attached to those pen names is, like Hiromori's own, uncertain.

Even when gender/sex can be determined, the imaginary identifications of artists in specific works are murky at best. Consider, for example, Hayasaka Miki, who turns out to be a "male" artist. In his contribution to the August 1983 issue of *Manga Burikko,* Hayasaka uses four color pages and four black-and-white pages to introduce a cute girl character named Takanezawa Moe. The drawings are presented as photographs, some even as film straight from a camera. In a panel on the third page, Moe's older sister is introduced as a female manga artist in charge of shooting Moe for this section in *Manga Burikko.* The drawings on the page are thus revealed to be the "photographs" that the older sister took of Moe, who is posing as an "idol." The older sister calls Moe cute, but the gaze, while voyeuristic, is presented as feminine and familial. In drawing what the older sister saw through the camera's viewfinder, Hayasaka is not just drawing a cute girl in a cute style inspired by shōjo manga; he is also visualizing Moe from the position of a cute girl character—that is, Hayasaka as female manga artist and older sister.

This cross-gender/sex identification is striking but not entirely unexpected. We have already seen that Itō Kimio, Harada Teruo, and Ōtsuka Eiji, in various ways and to varying degrees, present themselves as identifying with shōjo. In his own way, each was a "reluctant insider" choosing to "self-marginalize" (Eng 2012, 102), or seeking an alternative and becoming marginal by crossing gender/genre lines. If adult gekiga represents a masculine or majority view of gender/sex, then the bishōjo manga produced by Hayasaka and others in *Manga Burikko* represents a feminine or minority view. This is nothing as naïve as saying that Hayasaka was, really, a girl—any more than it is saying that Itō Kimio, as revealed in his engagements with boys love manga, was, really, gay—but rather that bishōjo manga allowed for an opening into a mesh of possibilities, gaps, overlaps, dissonances, and resonances where gender/sex no longer signifies monolithically (Sedgwick 1993, 8). This is what it means to say that Hayasaka was a "male" shōjo artist, just as Itō was a "male" shōjo reader. Gender/sex begins to blur in the shared space of shōjo.[30] We miss much by reducing interactions and relations with, between, and through shōjo to "straightforward male-looking-at-female pornography" (Nagaike 2003, 100).[31]

In fact, even the most explicit of drawn pornography that sexualizes shōjo and imagines sex with them is not as straightforward as it is often made out to be. Many scholars of manga and sexuality problematize "male" engagement with shōjo characters. As is the case with boys love manga, the majority of these approaches propose that the cartoon character is "open" and invites broad and diverse reader identifications, or, more specifically, that men imaginatively become shōjo and share their movements (Tsuchimoto 1989, 109–10; Akagi 1993, 232; Kinsella 2000, 122).[32] Nagayama Kaoru exemplifies this when he refers to the shōjo as a "virtual body" for producers and consumers of manga (Nagayama 2003, 52). For his part, Ōtsuka Eiji talks about characters as both a "container of 'self'" and an "escape" (Ōtsuka 2015, xxv), which highlights the complex and contradictory relations between them and producers and consumers of manga. If *Manga Burikko* can be described as "a pornographic manga magazine" (Ōtsuka 2013, 251), as Ōtsuka himself does, then we must acknowledge that there is nothing straightforward about pornographic manga, lolicon or otherwise. Crossing gender/genre lines, men consume and produce shōjo media and appropriate the shōjo form—just as girls and women do with media for boys and men and the *shōnen* form—to express sexuality with, between, and through characters.

Conclusion

From the Comic Market to *Manga Burikko,* this chapter has shown that "male" shōjo fans have been a significant presence in the history of manga and anime in Japan since the 1970s. Indeed, this history is thoroughly entangled with that of "otaku," which is used today as a general term for manga/anime fans but is in fact wrapped up with very specific concerns about lolicon and the imagined excesses and perversions of "male" shōjo fans. In referring to desire and affection for manga/anime-style, cute girl characters, lolicon was more than a minor phenomenon by the early 1980s. During the lolicon boom, Uchiyama Aki published alongside Tezuka Osamu in a mainstream manga magazine, even as Azuma Hideo's *Cybele* fanzines were published alongside fanzines devoted to the heroine of Miyazaki Hayao's *Lupin III: The Castle of Cagliostro*. It is all too easy to side with critics that are disgusted by lolicon, and hard to reserve judgment and try to understand "male" engagement with shōjo manga and characters, but that is precisely what is necessary as we move forward. Continuing the discussion of "male" shōjo fans, the next chapter turns to "otaku" and responses to interactions and relations with cute girl characters. Not coincidentally, it was in the pages of *Manga Burikko* that certain fans of manga and anime came to be labeled as "otaku," specifically those attracted to manga/anime-style, cute girl characters.

TWO "OTAKU" RESEARCH AND REALITY PROBLEMS

In 2001, when cultural critic Azuma Hiroki began his influential book on postmodernism with the sentence "I suppose that everyone has heard of 'otaku'" (Azuma [2001] 2009, 3), he was acknowledging decades of discourse in Japan. When his book was translated into English in 2009, the title was changed to *Otaku*, a decision that speaks to decades of global interest in this aspect of Japan. Since appearing untranslated on the cover of the premiere issue of *Wired* magazine in 1993, being introduced in William Gibson's novel *Idoru* in 1996, and making its way into the Oxford English Dictionary in 2007, "otaku" is a word that, like "sushi" and "geisha," is now part of the English language (Schodt 2009, 6). Be it in the Japanese-speaking world in 2001 or the anglophone world in 2009, Azuma is right to assume that people have heard of "otaku," but that does not correspond to everyone knowing what the word means. And what does it mean for those who think that they know? The assumption of knowledge about "otaku" tends to close down discussion of what is known, and how, and to reinforce received stereotypes. This is particularly problematic with regard to "otaku" because media has played such an important role—arguably the most important role—in the spread and establishment of knowledge (Galbraith and Lamarre 2010, 362). To put it plainly, discussions of "otaku" are often responding to and building on media representations and discourse. In this respect, Azuma is wise to put "otaku" into scare quotes, which draws attention to the word and elicits doubt.

If "otaku" have become a "taken-for-granted feature of the global cultural landscape" (Ito 2012, xxvii), then much, perhaps too much, is taken for granted. On the one hand, there is a normalizing of "otaku" as manga/anime fans. With the mainstreaming of fannish media and activities and spread of manga and anime around the world, it seems that "there is a little bit of otaku in all of us" (Condry 2013, 203). On the other hand, there is a normalizing of discourse about "otaku" as abnormal others. So while all of us might be a little "otaku," it is still possible for researchers to write that, because "otaku" "cannot love real women, they consequently fail to marry, and their sexual desires (assuming they have a heterosexual orientation) cannot be fulfilled or realized in biological terms" (Yiu and Chan 2013, 862).[1] Such pathologizing discourse about manga/anime fans might elicit a chuckle were it not part of a pattern of "repetitive academic attention" (Kinsella 2014, 18) that allows experts and authorities to "know" certain things about "otaku." And this quickly becomes deathly serious, as when looking at cute girl characters in manga/anime and masturbating, which is taken to be characteristic of "otaku," is compared to the "self-gratification of pedophilia" (Yiu and Chan 2013, 862). This comes packaged with the ominous threat of "fatal consequences" (862). Somewhere—in Japan, over there, somewhere—there is an abnormal other to the normalized self and/as "otaku." As a taken-for-granted object of discourse, "otaku" are at the same time normal and abnormal, trivial and dangerous, us and them. In all of this, the significance of the word in the context of its emergence and use is lost.

This chapter examines "otaku" as a label for manga/anime fans perceived as somehow problematic in Japan since the 1980s. Stated somewhat differently, even as manga/anime fans imagined and created alternative social worlds, critics responded to the imagined excesses and perversions of these fans by labeling them "otaku." The chapter begins with the column "'Otaku' Research" (*"Otaku" no kenkyū*), which was published in *Manga Burikko* in 1983. Written primarily by Nakamori Akio, but also including a contribution by Eji Sonta, the column has been memorialized as the beginning of media discourse about "otaku." While many note that its overall tone was negative (Kinsella 1998, 311; Ito 2012, xxi; Toivonen and Imoto 2013, 69), not much space is devoted to the specific concerns raised in "'Otaku' Research," which would be debated for decades after its publication. Rather than the sci-fi fans most often identified as ancestors of "otaku" (Morikawa 2004, 22–27; Murakami 2005, 122; Azuma [2001] 2009, 6), Nakamori and Eji Sonta wrote about men attracted to cute girl characters. These writers considered such men socially and sexually immature; for them, "otaku" had problems accepting and living in reality. From this, "otaku" came to be associated with a "reality problem" (*genjitsu mondai*). Despite harsh words from Nakamori and Eji Sonta, some manga/anime fans nevertheless claimed an orientation of desire toward fiction and an identity as "otaku" in the 1980s. In 1989, however, with the arrest of a serial killer and child molester labeled an "otaku," the reality problem transformed into concern about manga/anime fans attracted to cute girl characters being unable to distinguish between fiction and reality. In media discourse, in addition to being perverts, "otaku" were now also potentially pedophiles and predators. These strands of the reality problem, or rather these reality problems, are implied in much of what is said about "otaku" today. Grasping them is key to understanding the struggle for imagination in Japan and beyond.

An Orientation toward Fiction

The word "otaku," which means "your home" and is used in some locales and settings as a second-person pronoun, came to be associated with the imagined excesses and perversions of fans in Japan in the early 1980s. Words such as "fan" (e.g., *fanjin*, "fanzine") and "maniac" (e.g., *manga mania*, "manga maniac") were already in circulation, and "otaku" was meant to highlight something different, strange, weird, problematic, bad, wrong, and/or abnormal about certain fans and maniacs. To understand the emergence of "otaku" as a label, it is necessary to consider the historical moment. In the late 1970s and early 1980s, a significant number of Japanese men were reading shōjo (for girls) manga, watching anime featuring shōjo (girl) characters, and experimenting in niche magazines and fanzines with bishōjo (cute girl) characters and what would come to be called cute eroticism. All of this was wrapped up in lolicon, which in this specific conjuncture meant not attraction to young girls per se, but rather attraction to shōjo manga and characters, cuteness, and, ultimately, an orientation of desire toward fiction. From this, concerns about "otaku" can be contextualized in three ways: one, cuteness; two, (bi)shōjo manga and characters; and three, an orientation of desire toward manga/anime, fiction, and "the two-dimensional" (*nijigen*). All three are related, and each requires unpacking.

In manga and anime in Japan, cuteness is tied to a particular aesthetic that is often opposed to "realism." In Japanese comics, bold and gritty lines, sharp angles, and dark hatching are associated with realism, most notably gekiga, or dramatic pictures, which were all the rage with young men and activist types from the 1960s into the 1970s. As comics scholar Shiokawa Kanako notes, "This style is a direct antithesis of the *manga* (whimsical picture) style, from which many 'cute' icons of today have emerged" (Shiokawa 1999, 97). "Cute" is about soft and clean lines, round shapes, and light shading, a style often seen in manga and anime for children and girls, but popular with a much broader demographic in contemporary Japan. As editor and critic Nagayama Kaoru sees it, men and women that grew up with manga and anime became attracted to the cute style and to cute characters, which they embraced as adults in the 1970s. This cute movement, as Nagayama calls it, was guided by a simple principle: "I like cute things" (Nagayama 2014, 83). This liking of cute things, specifically manga/anime-style characters, was perceived as a rejection of reality and an orientation toward fiction. It was, editor and critic Sasakibara Gō argues, no less than a "change in values" (*kachi tenkan*) (Sasakibara 2004, 37), which some found troubling. The dominant form of adult comics at the time, gekiga was praised not only for its realism but also for being socially engaged, mature, and masculine. The cute movement, which was intertwined with the movement of those seeking an alternative, is thus for critics associated with problems with reality, society, adulthood, and masculinity. All of this, as we shall see, comes out in *Manga Burikko* and "'Otaku' Research."

Equally important are ties to shōjo manga and characters as men consumed and produced across gender/genre lines, which resulted in bishōjo manga and characters. Part of the shōjo manga movement (Shimotsuki 2008, 16), the movement of "male" shōjo fans is foundational to concerns about "otaku." According to editor and critic Fujita Hisashi, "male" shōjo fans "sought friends that shared their interests and became the early 'otaku'" (Fujita 1989, 130). More concretely, the founders of the Comic Market, the largest gathering of manga/anime fans in Japan, were "male" shōjo fans seeking others like them. The man credited with adapting shōjo characters into bishōjo, or cute girl characters, sexualizing shōjo characters in fanzines, and amplifying male attendance at the Comic Market is Azuma Hideo, who was influenced by shōjo manga (Azuma and Yamada 2011, 18–19, 27, 30–32; Azuma and Yamamoto 2011, 148–49; Sasakibara 2003, 120). Even as Azuma sought friends and published *Cybele* at the Comic Market, which played a role in triggering the lolicon boom, design theorist

Morikawa Ka'ichirō dubs him "an ancestor of otaku culture" (Morikawa 2011a, 179). Of this moment in history, sociologist Sharon Kinsella further writes, "New genres of girls' manga written by and for boys sprouted from the fertile bed of the amateur manga medium. Some colleges and universities began to boast not only manga clubs (*manga kenkyūkai*), but also girls' manga clubs for men. This manga and those men became the focus of the otaku panic" (Kinsella 2000, 112). Resonating with Kinsella, feminist thinker Kotani Mari argues that part of the "otaku panic" was a gender panic in response to men moving toward girls and girls' culture (Kotani 2003, 118–21).[2] Indeed, it was not just Azuma and "boys" producing girls' manga and fanzines, but also a wide range of men, women, and artists identifying as neither, and their numbers were increasing. In the same year that Azuma's *Cybele* rocked the Comic Market, fans of Miyazaki Hayao's *Lupin III: The Castle of Cagliostro* (Rupan sansei: Kariosutoro no shiro, 1979) began creating their own fanzines devoted to its heroine. By 1982, there were dedicated magazines such as *Lemon People* (Remon pīpuru, 1982–98) catering to fans of manga/anime-style, cute girl characters, and adult men had started fan clubs for series such as *Magical Princess Minky Momo* (Mahō no purinsesu Minkī Momo, 1982–83). Founded in 1982 as a niche magazine featuring gekiga-style drawings and gravure photography, the transformation of *Manga Burikko* into a lolicon magazine featuring cute girl characters occurred in 1983.

The transformation of *Manga Burikko* is significant because it was here, in the pages of this magazine, in 1983, that "otaku" became a label for manga/anime fans attracted to cute girl characters. In Japan, where manga is ubiquitous enough to be compared to "air" (Gravett 2004, 17), manga/anime characters are an intimate part of everyday life. Characters proliferate across media and material forms; they ground franchises as "a technology of attraction and diffusion" and "expand outward through the media and social environment" (Steinberg 2012, 44–45). This is also to say that characters anchor media worlds, and subjects exist in these worlds in affective relations with characters. Growing up with these characters, it is not uncommon to develop deep attachments to them. Even as adult manga/anime fans emerged in the 1970s and early 1980s, fan clubs and niche magazines reproduced and circulated images of characters as shared objects of desire and affection. When fans wanted more from characters than producers would provide, they created fanzines and organized events to buy and sell them. Fan activities affected manga/anime production, and characters subsequently became more and more attractive. Sharing manga/anime characters as objects of desire and affection, an orientation toward them emerged (Saitō [2000] 2011, 30–31, 87–89). Invoking the vernacular distinction between the world of manga/anime as two-dimensional as opposed to the three-dimensional one of humans, and highlighting what is understood to be a problematic orientation, since the 1980s, some manga/anime fans have been said to suffer from a "two-dimensional complex" (*nijigen konpurekkusu*), "two-dimensional fetishism" (*nijikon fechi*), or "two-dimensional syndrome" (*nijikon shōkōgun*) (Tsuchimoto 1989, 102; Schodt 1996, 48; Yamanaka 2010, 17). Others refer to this as a "cute girl syndrome" (*bishōjo shōkōgun*), "Lolita complex" (*rorīta konpurekkusu*), or simply "sickness" (*byōki*). Strikingly, in niche magazines and at events, in fan clubs and fanzines, manga/anime lovers claimed their complex, syndrome, or sickness as an orientation. By the early 1980s, during the lolicon boom, men with such an orientation had gained enough visibility to become a consumer demographic and target of criticism.

Such was the case with *Manga Burikko* in 1983, which began to focus on bishōjo characters as "two-dimensional idols" (*nijigen aidoru*) for readers that identified themselves in letters to the editor as having a "two-dimensional complex" (figure 2.1). Some even requested that photographs be removed from the magazine, defying conventional editorial logic at the time that sex sells and that every publication should feature at least a few scantily clad models. In *Manga Burikko,* however, these photographs stood out to readers, who reacted against them. For example, in the October 1983 issue of *Manga Burikko,* a section titled "School Uniforms Are Correct! Sailor Suit Illustration Collection," which presents cute girl characters posed as pinups, is followed by a section of steamy photographs of Kawai Kazumi. The end of the first section on the right-hand page faces the beginning of the next on the left-hand page, creating a side-by-side contrast, which is stark (figure 2.2). Significantly, the photographs were reportedly the least popular aspect of the issue, while the illustrations were by some of the most popular contributors.[3] Writing on intermedia reflexivity, comics scholar Matthew Jones explains that juxtaposed images can make readers aware of differences, for example, placing line drawings beside a photograph, where "the hand-drawn icons are . . . revealed as constructions when viewed in relation to the photograph" (Jones 2005b, 284). This is precisely what happened in *Manga Burikko,* but readers then actively chose the revealed constructions. Not confused about the distinction between fiction and reality, manga/anime fans were aware that they were viewing fiction, which they desired as such. Given that the subtitle of the October 1983 issue of *Manga Burikko* was

"Two-Dimensional Idol Comic Magazine for Boys" (figure 2.3), the orientation of its readers is perhaps not so surprising, but recognizing that they did not want or need "the real thing" was a major turning point. As photographs disappeared from its pages in the following months, *Manga Burikko* shifted from a mixed two- and three-dimensional idol magazine to a strictly two-dimensional one. For some observers, this spoke to the excesses and perversions of manga/anime fans in Japan in the early 1980s.

"Otaku" Research and Failed Men

Published at a time when Ōtsuka Eiji was becoming increasingly influential, but actually commissioned and managed by another editor (Nakamori 1989, 94), Nakamori Akio's "'Otaku' Research" debuted in *Manga Burikko* in June 1983. This was just as the magazine was transitioning to shōjo manga for boys, cute eroticism, and bishōjo characters as idols. Writing content often explicitly linked with *Tokyo Adults Club* (Tōkyō otona kurabu, 1982–), a separate, smaller subculture magazine, Nakamori was not fannishly familiar with manga (Nakamori 1989, 94), let alone with *Manga Burikko*. Rather than playing along, Nakamori decided to position himself as the voice of reason against the wild extremes of fandom. In the initial installment of his column, Nakamori begins with his first visit to the Comic Market, which he estimates drew over ten thousand people in the summer of 1982. Although women originally dominated the event, *Cybele, Clarisse Magazine,* and the lolicon boom had inspired more men to participate, and a scandalized Nakamori describes those that he encountered. To his eyes, these men and women are all "manga maniacs"; their shared excitement for fictional characters, reflected in their fanzines and behavior, reveals them to be lonely losers that are freaking out in the presence of other manga maniacs. In this initial installment of his column, titled "The City Is Full of 'Otaku'" (*Machi niwa "otaku" ga ippai*), Nakamori zooms out from the Comic Market to lambaste a wide range of people—fans lined up outside of theaters waiting to see animated films, trainspotters, idol chasers, sci-fi enthusiasts that collect and cherish pulp fiction, and more—all of whom he lumps together and labels "otaku." A good deal of time is spent analyzing their poor fashion sense and physical appearance, which is simply to say that these weird men and women look uncool.

While the installment reads like a laundry list of critiques of fans in general, Nakamori reserves a special disdain for manga maniacs, and

女の子にも買い易い表紙が好きです 東京都にゃんこ♡

あなたは大阪商人ですか。

◎ミニスカートのかわゆい(?)私が本屋で「ブリッコ」を買ったら変な目で見られて損したケド、谷口先生がいっぱい載ってたから得した。プレゼントはBね。女の子の下着ならうちにいくらでもある。私は4人姉妹の長女だもん。 兵庫県 谷口K

いくらでもあるんなら一つ余分なのを送って下さい。待ってます。

◎損したか得したかなどというのは愚問です。読みたいと思って買うんだから、損をしたという答はないはず。自信をもって出版して下さい。 匿名希望

聞いてみただけなんです。怒らないで下さい。

◎今月号はまだわからないけど、先月号は損した。机の上に本を置きっぱなしにしといたら、弟が見てしまった。兄としての人格をかえせ！ 俺のプライドは四百円じゃ足りないぜ！

ブリッコ程度で壊れるプライドだったらチリ紙交換に出してトイレットペーパーに換えてもらった方がまだ役に立ちます。

◎「ブリッコ」が落ち込む谷口敬に安保だって、暗いラブコメだって何だって描かせる場になって欲しい。「ロリコンマンガ誌」なんてのが売れている今だからこそ、そんな事も出来るのじゃないか。3年前「ダメ」と言われたものも今なら出来るのじゃないか。好評でなくともある程度大丈夫なんじゃないか。 東大阪市 さきとうる

感情的には賛同しますが、何だってというわけにはいかないのです。我々は「ガロ」ではない、商業誌なのですから

◎漫画家のインタビューが良かった。来月号もやってほしい。藤原カムイの漫画は新鮮だが6月号の方が良かった。これからもこんな新鮮な漫画を載せて欲しい。全体的にもっと女の子を可愛いく(特に顔)描いてほしい。せめて江口寿史くらいの女の子の顔を描いてほしい。内容がよほどよくない限り女の子の顔が可愛いくない漫画はカスです。逆に女の子の顔が可愛いければ大抵のことを僕は許す。 吹田市 洛城琴

正しい態度だと思います。しかし本誌に江口寿史を求めるのは酷というものです。

◎某社の「ヤングキッス」にのっていた大原氏の作品を見て感激し次号に買いに行ったらもうつぶれていた。それ以来失望していましたが、ブリッコの表紙に大原氏の名を見つけすかさず買ってしまいました。これからもずっと載せて。 山形県 八幡均

大原さんには次号で16頁の書き下し作品をお願いする予定です。その他に、一～二号後になりますが中島史雄さんの書き下し作品がいただけそうです。それに合わせて中島さんの特集をやろうかという話もありますがどーでしょーか。

◎よくいわれることですが、情事のたやすさからは決してエロチシズムは出てこないと思うのですよ。脱がないエロ、精神のエロスを追究してみてほしい。 静岡県 落合康彦

む・む・むずかしい……

美少女マンガ家第3世代ですかあ？ とーぜん 緋田久美さんもその中に入りますよね。
う〜む、でもねえ、確かにトリマから出てる彼女の漫画なんてモロ・ロリコンだけど普段描いてる漫画の本質はもっとやさしさがうちだされてて特にロリコンじゃないんですよね。
彼女自身はどう思ってるか知らないけど、彼女にエロを求めるのはやめて欲しいものです…。
東京都 高橋桂

◎ぼくは2次元コンプレックスです。従って巻頭の写真あたりには特に何も感じません。という訳で、その①の写真を全部やめて漫画のみにしてもらいたい。実はこの本割と気に入ったんで、定期購読を大学の生協でしようと思ったんですが、あの手の写真が載ってるとさすがにやりずらい。なくなったらします。それまでは責任を持って、定期で買うとは言いきれない。 北海道 川口俊彦

会社上層部よりの絶対命令で、写真ページがなくなることはありません。だから残念だけど気の向いた時に買って下さい。

◎ガキのSEXなんて見たくない。女の子はそんなもんじゃないんだよ。だからサ、もうサ「いつか見た夢」みたいな写真のページを増やして健全なロリコン雑誌にしちゃいませう。 From Smi

そーゆー考え方があってもいいと思います。

◎プレゼント全員もらえるんでしょ？ え、ちがうんですか？ 名古屋市 座光寺徹

書き忘れちゃったんですが抽選で5名なのですゴメンナサイ。

アンケート&プレゼント

なんかオジンくさくっていやなんだけど、最初に注意。ハガキの宛先は、個人宛には〜様、団体や〇〇係宛には〜御中と書くのが常識です。今回の全80通以上のハガキの中で御中を使ってあるのは、ほんのわずかだった。知っていて常識を破る分にはかまわないけど、知らないで手紙を出すのは、はっきり言って恥です。見苦しいです。

さてまいどおなじみアンケート。今月は全部で74通も答えてくれた。来月は何通かな。

①今月号を買って損したか得したか、その理由も一緒に書く。
②今月号のなかで面白かったものを3つあげてその理由も書く。
③今月号のなかでつまらなかったものを3つあげて理由も書く。
④漫画ブリッコのここが好き、ここが嫌い、こうして欲しいなどがあったら書く。
⑤登場して欲しい作家、やって欲しい特集などがあったら書く。

アンケートを送ってくれたキミには抽選で各5名様にアッと驚くタメゴロー

Aウソ!!少女のヌード組写真
Bこれは欲しい 有名マンガ家家ハガキセット

プレゼントはABどちらが希望か明記して、職業・年令を書き、匿名希望の場合はその旨書いて、次の住所まで

〒160新宿区高田馬場4-28-12 漫画ブリッコ8月号係宛

締切りは7月1日まで。

さあ！明日のブリッコをキミの手で!!

五藤加純センセーのを毎月読みたいよ〜〜〜 埼玉県 西尾孝

可愛 かずみ アンコール!! kazumi
撮影■青柳有信

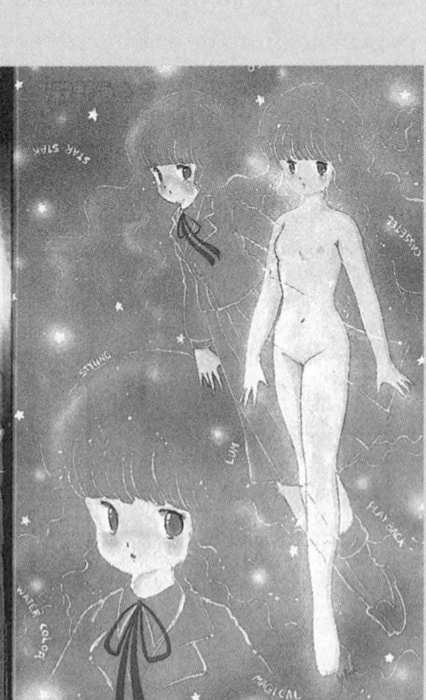

FIGURE 2.1 (above) *Manga Burikko* reader letter claiming a "two-dimensional complex," August 1983.

FIGURE 2.2 (left) The two- and three-dimensional juxtaposed in *Manga Burikko*, October 1983.

FIGURE 2.3 (opposite) *Manga Burikko* cover claiming that inside its pages are "two-dimensional idols," October 1983.

漫画ブリッコ
定価 400円
昭和57年9月7日(第3種郵便物認可)
雑誌第6386号 昭和58年10月1日
発行(毎月1回1日発行)第2巻第12号
愛の2大ゲスト
大原彩生
五藤加純
男の子のための
2次元アイドル
コミック誌
表紙イラスト/谷口敬
ブリッコ♥オールスターズ
藤原カムイ
中田雅喜
計奈恵
沢木あかね
洋森しのぶ
白倉由美
あぽ(匿名希望)
愛の特集
まるまるセーラー服まんが大全集
発表!第1回ブリッコ新人まんが賞/猫耳イラストコンテスト
MONTHLY
10
BURICCO

some among them in particular, which comes through in passages such as the following: "There are those dressing up as anime characters, those in the creepy style you see in Azuma Hideo's manga, those simpering and pushing girls to buy their lolicon manga, those running around for no reason. . . . Man, my head was about to explode." The people that Nakamori reacts to here and labels "otaku" are clearly part of the controversial fandom of men producing fanzines featuring cute girl characters and cute eroticism, as can be deduced from the references to Azuma Hideo and lolicon. The city may be full of "otaku," but these men at the Comic Market are some of the most viscerally repugnant. Indeed, in the next installment of the column, Nakamori reveals that "otaku" is a term that fans use to refer to one another at the Comic Market and similar events, where they intimately share interests but do not necessarily know names, which he found "gross" (*kimoi*) and adopted as a label for them (also Nakamori 1989, 94). That is, he starts at the Comic Market during the lolicon boom and extrapolates out from there a core disgust at imagined excesses and perversions.

In the second installment of "'Otaku' Research," published in *Manga Burikko* in July 1983, Nakamori clarifies the primary target of his criticism. Rather than devoting an entire installment of the column to trainspotters, idol chasers, sci-fi enthusiasts, or any other conceivable fan grouping, Nakamori focuses on lolicon and men oriented toward cute girl characters. The title sets the tone in the form of a question: "Do 'Otaku' Love Like Normal People?" (*"Otaku" mo hitonami ni koi wo suru?*) For his part, Nakamori comes to the conclusion that no, "otaku" do not love like normal people, because they are attracted to manga/anime characters, which makes them abnormal. In a key passage, he explains: "'Otaku' definitively lack masculine ability. So they're content with carrying around pin-ups of anime characters like Minky Momo [from *Magical Princess Minky Momo*] and Nanako [from *Nanako SOS*, a manga by Azuma Hideo that was adapted into an anime in 1983]. Maybe I'll call it a two-dimensional complex. They can't even talk to real women. In less extreme cases, they gravitate toward idol singers that don't really appeal as women, or they become warped and get into lolicon. These guys will never accept nude photographs of mature women." Considered against the first installment of the column, it is obvious that Nakamori has refined and narrowed his critical assessment of "otaku." Note that female fans of manga and anime, who were included in the first installment of Nakamori's column, have completely dropped out of the discussion. In this second installment, the problem is a lack of women, and men that are not real men and are attracted and attached to fictional girls.

A dedicated (three-dimensional) idol fan himself, what seems to bother Nakamori is the possibility that "otaku" are not interested in real women.[4] He establishes a hierarchy of objects of desire and affection: real women (*onna*), nude photographs of mature women (*seijuku shita onna no nūdo shashin*), idol singers that do not really appeal as women (*josei-teki sonzai wo anmashi apīru shinai aidoru kashu*), and, finally, anime characters (*anime kyara*) such as Minky Momo and Nanako. At the top of the hierarchy, desire is normal and healthy, while at the bottom it is abnormal and sick; only those that are warped get into lolicon (*rorikon shitari suru*). Lest we forget, the lolicon that Nakamori discusses here is not about adult men lusting after young girls per se, but rather men desiring the cute girl characters of manga and anime. This is confirmed by what Nakamori calls the abnormality, a two-dimensional complex, which is a turn of phrase that was likely already in circulation. *Manga Burikko* essentially catered to people associated with it. Readers of the magazine rejecting photographs of provocatively posed women and claiming to have a two-dimensional complex were most certainly "otaku" as defined by Nakamori, who perceived in them a disturbing lack of desire for real women. These "otaku" instead prefer, in some warped way, fictional girls, cute girl characters, manga/anime girls.

Not only is Nakamori distressed by a lack of real women and desire for them, but also real men in relation to them. To him, that is, "otaku" do not register as men. Nakamori argues that these manga/anime fans "definitively lack masculine ability" (*kettei-teki ni dansei-teki nōryoku ga ketsujo shi*), or, put differently, "otaku" turn to cute girl characters because they are not real men. This turn away from the real thing makes "otaku" sexually suspect for Nakamori: "And, maybe because of the lack of masculine ability, but these guys are strangely faggy, you know? These are adult men in their twenties, who, when they get their hands on a poster or something with their favorite anime character on it, get so overwhelmed with happiness that they jump up in the air with their legs bent behind them. . . . It just makes me sick. Really, there's no way that guys like this could ever get with a woman." From simply lacking masculine ability, "otaku," referring to men with a two-dimensional complex or lolicon, are now portrayed as "strangely faggy" (*myō ni okama-ppoi*). The word translated as "fag" is *okama*, which in Japan at the time was a pejorative for effeminate men or those that cross-dress and act like women. Nakamori's associative thinking is that "otaku" are not only unable to "get with" women, but also that they are women, failed men, fags. The issue thus shifts from a lack of real women in the lives of "otaku" to "otaku" men as women. In comparing the uncontrolled excitement and bodily response of "otaku" looking at posters of anime characters to men cross-dressing as women, Nakamori suggests that both are abnormal. "Otaku," like okama, are for Nakamori frankly "gross" (*kimochi warui*). These are adult men, Nakamori reminds the reader, and they ought to behave in line with their age and gender/sex.

The third installment of the column, published in *Manga Burikko* in August 1983, continues to expose the queer existence of "otaku" through episodes from Nakamori's ongoing "research." In this installment, Nakamori reports visiting a hangout for manga/anime fans in Shinjuku, Tokyo, called Free Space. In contrast to his visit to the Comic Market the previous year, Nakamori this time brings his young girlfriend along so that he can point out "otaku" to her and document her reactions.[5] In one memorable scene, Nakamori and his girlfriend pass the café area, where they spot a group of seven or eight men at a table with anime magazines and posters spread out between them. The men talk excitedly about the material, and respond boisterously to jokes that make no sense to Nakamori. In exaggerated terms, Nakamori relays his girlfriend's reactions, which include an involuntary shriek, goose bumps, and shaking. Calling them "otaku among otaku" (*otaku no naka no otaku*), Nakamori is equally unsettled by these creatures, whose laughter no longer even sounds human—regardless of gender/sex—but rather like "slugs" (*namekuji*) or "leeches" (*hiru*).[6] What some might see as friends talking about shared interests in manga/anime instead appears to Nakamori to be a "hellish festival" (*jigoku no shukusai*), and he cannot suppress a shudder of his own.

In some ways, Nakamori's bald bias, which has only become more brutal from the first to the third installment of his column, is comical. It could almost be read as a parody of an outsider's view of manga/anime fans. The stylistic flair of the writing, which makes Nakamori sound like a consummate comedian, supports such a reading. The consistency and persistence of the joke, however, indicates something more serious. Plainly stated, the joke is on "otaku" in contrast to Nakamori and normal men. If taken seriously, in Nakamori's writing, the "otaku" is abnormal and needs to be researched by the normal man, and if taken as a joke, the "otaku" is the funny man, whose antics beg the comedic intervention of the straight man. The result is basically the same, namely othering, which intensifies as the column proceeds. Indeed, in this third installment, Nakamori introduces his girlfriend, a further removed outsider whose utter horror lends credibility to his condemnation of "otaku" as failed men unable to get with real women. Worse, they might be "fags" unwilling to do so. While these "men" huddle around images of anime characters, Nakamori is on a date, which seems to drive home the social and sexual immaturity of "otaku." Standing with his girlfriend looking down at the seated "men," Nakamori is positioned as different from, and above, them. The punch line is that "otaku" are different from normal, straight men, which is the position of Nakamori as he tells the "joke."

Due to chief editor Ōtsuka Eiji's discomfort with his content as offensive and discriminatory (Nakamori 1989, 94–95; Yamanaka 2009, 25–28), *Manga Burikko* cut ties with Nakamori, but a fourth and final installment of the "'Otaku' Research" column nevertheless did appear in the December 1983 issue. Written by Eji Sonta, identified as a member of Nakamori's circle at *Tokyo Adults Club*, "Otaku Research: General Remarks" (*Otaku no kenkyū: Sōron*) served as a conclusion to the column. Even if earlier installments were intended to be humorous, Nakamori himself evaluates this last installment as thoroughly "serious" (*majime*) (Nakamori 1989, 94). As such, it brings Nakamori's column to an end with an earnest consideration of the issues that he raised. The tone is indeed different, calm and measured, but the problematic is the same; the author makes lolicon central and builds an argument about the social and sexual immaturity of "otaku" around it.

By Eji Sonta's estimation, "otaku" are men that are unwilling or unable to grow up and face reality; that is, "otaku" are unwilling or unable to take on the roles and responsibilities of adults that make them full members of society in Japan. While acknowledging the widespread appeal of youth in opposition to adult society at the time (Kinsella 1995, 250–52; also Kinsella 1998), Eji Sonta insists that "otaku" take things further: "The essence of manga maniacs and anime fans . . . insisting on 'lolicon' is the feeling of not wanting to mature and wanting instead to maintain a state of moratorium. . . . Usually, as we stretch ourselves and act grown up, we get closer and closer to real adulthood, but 'otaku' absolutely refuse to vector themselves toward general psychological maturity." Rhetorically, Eji Sonta sets up a contrast between what is "normal" (*futsū no ba'ai*) and the "case of otaku" (*otaku no ba'ai*), who refuse to grow up and face reality. What makes "otaku" abnormal is insisting on lolicon, which is to say holding on to cute girl characters. For Eji Sonta, manga/anime fans, or rather the "otaku" among them associated with lolicon and the two-dimensional complex, have allowed attraction and attachment to fictional characters to disrupt a normal social and sexual life. As a wake-up call, Eji Sonta writes, "A famous lolicon manga artist once said, 'Even otaku boys have plenty of chances to be friendly with girls in reality, so rather than being broody and closed off you should be proactive.' That's exactly right." Here Eji Sonta enlists the testimony of a lolicon manga artist, who stresses that "otaku boys" (*otaku shōnen-tachi*) have opportunities "in reality." The message is clear: manga/anime fandom generally, and lolicon specifically, should not foreclose interactions and relations with the opposite sex. Interactions and relations with characters, even those designed as girls and women, are not a substitute. Somewhat more emphatically, the cute girl character should not displace the real woman as the object of desire and affection. This is the message for "otaku boys," who can still become real men if they face reality and grow up.[7]

In this concluding installment of the column, the message is at last explicitly directed at *Manga Burikko* readers, who are assumed to be "otaku boys" oriented toward cute girl characters: "As a real problem, take a good look at your reflection in the mirror. There you are with a smirk on your face as you look at this lolicon magazine. After all, it's weird. Not to mention that you are seriously jerking off to this stuff, which I just can't think of as anything to celebrate." Here Eji Sonta builds on Nakamori's earlier critique of manga maniacs and lolicon, which was also implicitly about *Manga Burikko* readers. Indeed, while it is most often translated as "'Otaku' Research," another plausible English title for Nakamori's "*'Otaku' no kenkyū*" is "(My) Research of 'You.'" Punning on the double meaning of "otaku" as a second-person pronoun and the label that he was defining, Nakamori ended his first installment of the column by asking *Manga Burikko* readers, "Incidentally, are you an 'otaku?'" (*Tokoro de, otaku, "otaku"?*) Eji Sonta appears to have come to the conclusion that yes, they are "otaku," and need to be called out as such.

This is no less than an intervention. In his direct critique of readers, Eji Sonta makes clear that sexual attraction to cute girl characters, localized in the act of masturbating to a lolicon magazine such as *Manga Burikko*, is "weird" (*bukimi na mon*). The word translated here as "weird" (*bukimi*) can also mean "creepy," "uncanny," or "ghastly." The word before it, translated as "after all" (*yappari*), gives what follows the connotation of something that was already known and has been confirmed. After all, Eji Sonta tells readers, desire and affection for cute girl characters, which was beginning to be discussed among manga/anime fans as an orientation, is abnormal and nothing to celebrate. It is time to face reality, grow up, and get a life, which apparently means get a girlfriend—a real one.[8] Those that fail to do so—or worse, that refuse, "otaku" that insist on cute girl characters or prefer them in some warped way—have a real problem, which makes them a real problem.

The "Real(ity) Problem(s)" of "Otaku"

In the eyes of Eji Sonta, "otaku" are not only abnormal but also a "real problem," which requires some unpacking. To begin, it is important to keep in mind that the discussion of "otaku" here is entangled with the term "lolicon," which had a very specific meaning. Among manga/anime fans in the early 1980s, as editor and critic Akagi Akira points out, "lolicon" was used in reference to "an existence that seeks two-dimensional images (manga, anime) rather than realistic things" (Akagi 1993, 230). In addition to two-dimensional images, Akagi continues, lolicon was associated with desire and affection for "cuteness" (*kawai-rashisa*) and "girl-ness" (*shōjo-sei*). While it may seem idiosyncratic, in fact Akagi's understanding of lolicon resonates with Azuma Hideo's professed love of "roundness" (*maru-kkoi no ga suki*), which he connects to manga, cuteness, and something "girly" (*shōjo-pposa*).[9] Azuma's bishōjo are characterized by their cuteness and "lack of reality" (Azuma and Yamada 2011, 30), and the success of his commercial work and fanzines, not to mention the subsequent lolicon boom, heralded burgeoning support for the manga/anime aesthetic as opposed to realism. As Azuma had before them imagined and created something other than the reality of photographs and adult gekiga, the readers of *Manga Burikko* rejected photographs, as well as more realistic drawings, because they preferred manga/anime-style, cute girl characters. These are the "otaku" that Nakamori and Eji Sonta identify as a real problem. Translated more literally, the phrase that appears in Eji Sonta's writing is "reality problem" (*genjitsu mondai*). The implication is that "otaku," or men of the sort that masturbate to images of cute girl characters in *Manga Burikko*, have a problem with reality, which makes them a real problem.

For Nakamori, Eji Sonta, and other early critics of "otaku," lolicon seemed to be an orientation toward cute girl characters that reflected and reinforced sexual and social immaturity, if not dysfunction. Drawing on Akagi, feminist psychoanalyst Setsu Shigematsu elegantly summarizes the reality problem of "otaku": For Nakamori and Eji Sonta, "lolicon" meant an orientation toward fictional girls or "two-dimensional images of cuteness," which "replace a lack of desire for the 'real thing'—a lack of desire that young men are 'naturally' supposed to possess for real young women" (Shigematsu 1999, 131–32). Men with such an unnatural lack of desire for the real thing, and an unnatural abundance of desire for fictional girls, fail as "men," which led to their being labeled "otaku." Shigematsu astutely describes lolicon as a "fetishism for cuteness," which speaks to the critique of "otaku" as men oriented toward manga/anime characters known for their cuteness, specifically bishōjo. Even more than fetishism, however, desire and affection for cute girl characters—an orientation toward the fictional, unreal, or two-dimensional—was at times portrayed as sickness. In Nakamori and Eji Sonta's "'Otaku' Research," such sickness is an obstacle to achieving reproductive maturity, which is to say becoming a man by forming a relationship with a woman, having sex, and starting and supporting a family. The perceived reality problem of "otaku" is thus also a refusal to face reality and grow up, which means taking on roles and responsibilities that make one an adult member of society in Japan. In insisting on fictional alternatives, the "otaku" becomes a failed man, adult, and member of society.

More mortifying still for the critics, as they began to communicate through niche media, at events, and in their own publications, manga/anime fans increasingly came out and shared an orientation as "otaku" (Yamanaka 2009, 29–31; also Yamanaka 2010). In the process, manga/anime fans reclaimed concepts such as two-dimensional complex, lolicon, and even sickness in ways that were not pathologizing and could be a source of pride. For example, in *Gekkan Out,* Azuma Hideo is praised as "the man that spread lolicon and sickness in the world" (*yo ni rorikon to byōki wo hirometa hito*).[10] For some, an orientation toward fiction seemed like a form of resistance to commonsense norms. One can see a brisk summation of this opinion in *The Book of Otaku* (Otaku no hon, 1989), in which the editors claim, "we have determined that the characteristic preference of 'otaku' called lolicon is actually a manifestation of the desire of 'not wanting to become men.' By acquiring the 'platform' of shared fantasy called the fictional bishōjo, it was no longer necessary for boys to force themselves to date flesh-and-blood women [and become men]" (Bessatsu Takarajima Henshūbu 1989, 3). "Otaku" are again presented as queer men, or men that are not "men," but, if for Nakamori and Eji Sonta this was something to critique, then it is here celebrated as part of sexual politics. If, as queer theorist Jack Halberstam argues, success in contemporary, heteronormative, capitalist society is often equated with achieving reproductive maturity, then there are those that struggle against "growing up." In their perceived failure, such people imagine and create "other goals for life, for love, for art, and for being" (Halberstam 2011, 88). Many of Halberstam's examples are drawn from the queer lives of cartoon characters and interactions and relations between them, but *The Book of Otaku* provocatively contends that a large number of people are also imagining and creating queer ways of life with cartoon characters.

In line with manga/anime fans in Japan in the 1980s, the editors of *The Book of Otaku* make a distinction between bishōjo and women, which they emphasize by modifying them as "fictional" (*kakū no*) and "flesh-and-blood" (*namami no*), respectively. The point is that they are distinct, and "otaku" are consciously oriented toward the former and not the latter. "Fictional" here is not opposed to "real," because manga/anime characters are fictional, but also real in their own way. The distinction is between two-dimensional and three-dimensional, or manga/anime characters and human beings. As legal scholar Aleardo Zanghellini puts it, "deliberately rejecting three-dimensionality . . . signifies a break from reality" (Zanghellini 2009, 173), or rather a turn toward another reality. This is what Ōtsuka proposes in his conceptualization of "manga/anime realism" (Ōtsuka 2003, 24), or a reality distinct to manga and anime, but what fans more casually call "the two-dimensional." For the uninitiated, the distinction between "two-dimensional" and "three-dimensional" leads to statements that can be cognitively challenging. As a case in point, in a dialogue published in *The Book of Otaku*, feminist thinker Ueno Chizuko argues that "the Lolita complex is completely different from pedophilia" (Ueno 1989, 134). Depending on the reader's background, this might sound obvious or absurd. While "lolicon" is often almost synonymous with "pedophilia" for critics today (Norma 2015, 85–86; also Adelstein and Kubo 2014), Ueno, like many observers of manga/anime fans in Japan in the 1980s, understood it to be an orientation toward fictional bishōjo (the two-dimensional) and thus distinct from sexual desire for flesh-and-blood women (the three-dimensional), regardless of age.

Indeed, the editors of *The Book of Otaku* and its contributors tend to avoid the language of pedophilia and paraphilia altogether, and instead speak in terms of orientation and queer movement. In "otaku," Ueno, for example, sees "male" shōjo fans seeking an alternative: "The word 'cute' is key. The boys that draw such cute pictures want to be part of the 'cute' world of shōjo. They find it to be too much to be a man. To go a little further, aren't they thinking, 'I don't want to become a man'?" (Ueno 1989, 131–32). Drawing and drawn to cute girl characters, "otaku" seem to Ueno to be refusing to become adult men. This is precisely the reality problem highlighted by Nakamori and Eji Sonta, but the dialogue with Ueno instead raises the possibility of a "sex revolution" (*sekkusu reboryūshon*) (also Hinton 2014, 60–61). When she is asked whether or not orientation toward fiction is normal, or whether or not "otaku" are abnormal, Ueno suggests that the line of questioning really ought to be why people are forced to be "normal" and what exactly that means (Ueno 1989, 136). In seeking alternatives, she implies, "otaku" are also imagining and creating alternative social worlds. To rephrase somewhat, their interactions and relations with fictional and real others are part of new, emergent social realities.

By the estimation of the editors of *The Book of Otaku*, alternative values and lifestyles are easier to develop and maintain when one is not alone (Bessatsu Takarajima Henshūbu 1989, 3), which is why an orientation toward fiction appeared in Japan from the late 1970s into the 1980s. Through events and their own media, which promoted manga/anime characters as objects of desire and affection, fans imagined and created alternative social worlds. The Comic Market, fanzines, and niche publications such as *Manga Burikko* were all platforms and spaces for imaginative, creative, and social activity (Bessatsu Takarajima Henshūbu 1989, 3; Morikawa 2011a, 186). In his contribution to *The Book of Otaku*, Yonezawa Yoshihiro, a "male" shōjo fan and representative of the Comic Market, writes, "If anything is scary, it might be that such spaces exist" (Yonezawa 1989, 88). Scary, that is, because this is where alternatives emerge that can threaten common sense and norms. This, then, is one face of the reality problem and attendant politics. It begins with recognition of "otaku" as what psychiatrist Saitō Tamaki calls "people that can take fiction itself as a sexual object" (quoted in Morikawa 2003, 94; also Saitō [2000] 2011), which snaps into focus new ways of seeing and being with manga/anime characters.[11]

This is not, however, the only face of the reality problem, which has mutated over the decades. Along with the publication of *The Book of Otaku*, the year 1989 also saw the arrest of Miyazaki Tsutomu, a twenty-six-year-old printer's assistant from the suburbs of Tokyo, who was apprehended after attempting to insert a zoom lens into the vagina of a grade-schooler in a public park. The subsequent investigation revealed Miyazaki to be the man that had over the past year murdered, mutilated, and molested four girls between the ages of four and seven. The details of his ghoulish crimes include keeping one of the corpses in his room, posing it for photographs, having sex with it over the course of days, and eventually dismembering it and drinking its blood. These heinous acts shocked Japan, which is known for its statistically low rate of violent and sexual crime, especially involving children (Schodt 1996, 50–53; Diamond and Uchiyama 1999, 11; Ishikawa, Sasagawa, and Essau 2012, 308). For a year, the specter of Miyazaki had terrorized the nation, for example, in news reports of his mailing pieces of a victim to her family. In the media frenzy following his arrest, commentators discussed everything that they perceived to be wrong with youth, society, and Japan (Kinsella 2000, 129).

Among the many reasons advanced for Miyazaki's crimes, one that seemed convincing was confusion about the distinction between fiction and reality. The primary evidence: photographs of Miyazaki's room, which was filled with 5,763 videotapes, including a series of horror/slasher/gore films upon which he based some of his crimes, as well as recordings of those crimes (figure 2.4). The mountains of media surrounding the isolated man literally shut out the sun, and figuratively seem to shut out the outside world and reality. Responding to Miyazaki, cultural theorist Yoshimi Shun'ya argues, "For him, the sense of reality, or the reality of killing, was already virtual" (quoted in Galbraith 2012, 226). There are at least three ways to interpret this statement: one, Miyazaki had seen so much sex, violence, and crime in virtual worlds that it no longer seemed real to him; two, he had rehearsed his crimes virtually before acting them out in reality; and three, even after committing his crimes, they appeared virtual to him. Related are three points about media effects: one, media had reduced Miyazaki's resistance to committing violent sexual crimes; two, the line between media and reality became blurred for him; and three, he committed crimes based on media and returned them to media through recording and placing them in his videotape collection.[12] While media and material consumption is normal in contemporary Japan, the sheer volume of Miyazaki's collection was enough to convince many of excess and perversion, and the confusion of fiction and reality made him a folk devil for a society struggling to negotiate boundaries. As anthropologist Ian Condry relates, "a public debate was initiated about the dangers of youth who live in worlds conveyed by media as a substitute for reality" (Condry 2006, 125). The distinction between normal and abnormal was formalized by calling Miyazaki an "otaku." In this way, certain fans, already perceived as abnormal and labeled "otaku" in the 1980s, came to be associated with a serial killer that was also a pedophile, cannibal, and necrophiliac.

Despite the fact that horror/slasher/gore films in Miyazaki's collection were used as models for some of his crimes, it was not exclusively or even necessarily these films that were mobilized to explain his dangerous break

FIGURE 2.4
Miyazaki's room and the connection to media effects.

from reality, but rather manga. Photographs of Miyazaki's room show adult manga in the foreground next to his bed, which suggest that the piles of boxes behind must contain more manga and that the videotapes must be anime. Based on the accounts of some journalists that were in the room, however, it seems that Miyazaki owned only a few adult manga, which were actually moved and placed together for the photographs, hence stimulating discussion of their link to his crimes (Nagaoka 2010, 151–52). This discussion gained traction because Miyazaki had participated in the Comic Market, where fanzines featuring cute girl characters engaged in explicit and sometimes violent sex did not escape notice. As "lolicon" became a keyword, the message of the photographs shifted to Miyazaki being an "otaku" attracted to fictional girls that acted out his perverse desires in reality.[13] The story was thus not only that Miyazaki had blurred the line between fiction and reality, as would seem to be the case when he watched ultrarealistic violence in horror/slasher/gore films and then enacted violence to record and add to his collection, but also, and more importantly, that his attraction to manga and anime had warped his sense of reality and sexuality. With Miyazaki as their representative, "otaku" were now understood to be men harboring "dangerous sexual proclivities and fetishes," "who might be mentally ill and perhaps even a threat to society" (Schodt 1996, 46).[14] They were "a reserve army of criminals" (*hanzaisha yobigun*), primed by manga and anime and waiting to be called up as the next Miyazaki. As Ōtsuka Eiji and Nakamori Akio debated whether or not Miyazaki was an "otaku," and creative types such as Miyazaki Hayao and Murakami Ryū discussed the need for manga/anime fans to get out of their "closed rooms," a perceived connection between manga/anime images, the pedophile predator, and "otaku" was established in the popular imaginary.[15] For many, this prolonged media debate was their first introduction to "otaku," which gave the word and fans tied to it unmistakably negative connotations.

The fallout of Miyazaki fundamentally changed the image of "otaku," but it is crucial to note that the reality problem associated with him differs in significant ways from the one discussed in *Manga Burikko* and elsewhere earlier in the decade. In fact, confusing and conflating the cute girl character with flesh and blood—as Miyazaki is said to have done—has little at all to do with what was originally thought to be abnormal about "otaku," which was manga/anime fans making a conscious distinction between fiction and reality and orienting themselves toward the former, taken by critics to be a rejection of the latter. The reality problem of 1983 concerns manga/anime fans holding on to fictional girls and unwilling or unable to "face reality," "grow up," and "get a life." They were understood to be failed men, socially and sexually immature, perverts. In the wake of the arrest of Miyazaki in 1989, the reality problem shifted to concerns about manga and anime warping minds and turning men into pedophiles and potential predators. The reality problem thus splits into two reality problems, which are intertwined in contemporary discourse about "otaku." For many, "otaku" are socially and sexually immature manga/anime fans, or perverts, who are attracted to cute girl characters (Kam 2013b, 159–61, 163–65; Kikuchi 2015, 154–55). For many others, "otaku" are manga/anime fans whose attraction to cute girl characters reveals them to be pedophiles and potential predators (Cather 2012, 237–47; Galbraith 2015c, 213–15). Strikingly, following Miyazaki, the reality problem of "otaku" traveled from *Manga Burikko* through the Japanese media to the world.

Imagined Sex and Crime in Japan

In North America, manga/anime fans organize conventions such as Otacon, the "Convention of Otaku Generation"; publish magazines such as *Otaku USA*; and purchase books such as *Otacool*, which expresses the cool of "otaku" in photographs of the stylish rooms of manga/anime fans from around the world.[16] Even so, stereotypes of "otaku" have been repeated enough to have become common sense. Consider how, for example, a reporter for BBC *News Magazine* explains the problem of a declining birth rate in Japan: "One reason for the lack of babies is the emergence of a new breed of Japanese men, the otaku, who love manga, anime and computers—and sometimes show little interest in sex" (Rani 2013). Although coming from outside of Japan decades later, the words might have been written by Nakamori Akio or Eji Sonta in 1983, as could a *Guardian* story about how "young Japanese aren't having sex," which includes descriptions of men interacting with cute girl characters (Haworth 2013). This sort of journalism is part of a cottage industry dedicated to reporting on "weird" and "wacky" Japan, which dovetails with long-standing discourse about "Japan" as the deviant sexual other to "the West." In such writing, the Japanese are having too much sex, or the wrong kinds of sex, or no sex at all. The "otaku" has become a stock figure here, and appears in not only journalistic writing but also academic articles (recall Yiu and Chan 2013). To talk of "otaku" this way is often to talk of "Japanese perversion," even as "otaku" are normalized outside of Japan as something contrastively different.

More troubling is how the "otaku" becomes a figure of "Japanese pedophilia and predatory sexuality." Consider, for example, how international outlets reported the 2014 decision by the Japanese government to ban the possession of child pornography but not to follow nations such as Canada, Australia, and the United Kingdom by including comics, cartoons, and computer/console games featuring underage characters engaged in explicit sex (for a review of relevant laws, see McLelland 2013). While legal action against imaginary sex crimes raises serious issues that are being fiercely debated in Japan (McLelland 2011), news networks such as CNN instead opted to show manga/anime images, interview activists connecting them with the sexual abuse of children, and conclude that "cartoons might be fueling the darkest desires of criminals" (Ripley, Whiteman, and Henry, 2014). This is coming from outside Japan decades later, but the suggestion that manga/anime fans might be pedophiles and predators is essentially the same discourse that swept Japan after the arrest of Miyazaki Tsutomu in 1989. Then, as now, sta-

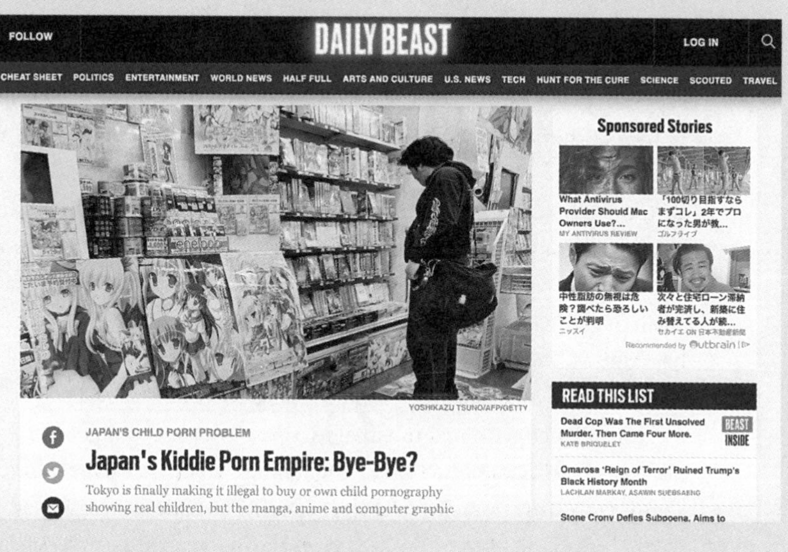

FIGURE 2.5 *The Daily Beast*: "Japan's Child Porn Problem."

tistics and substantial linkages are less significant than the possibility. Importantly, Japan itself is now imagined to be a nation of "otaku" and sex criminals. So it is that *The Daily Beast* shows a photograph of a Japanese man browsing shelves of adult computer games featuring cute girl characters and captions it "Japan's Child Porn Problem" (Adelstein and Kubo 2014) (figure 2.5). Note three things here: one, manga/anime images are described as child pornography; two, a Japanese man attracted to manga/anime-style, cute girl characters is implied to be a pedophile and potential predator; and three, all of this is made Japan's problem, which is safely located over there with them and not here with us. Even as Japan is again positioned as an abnormal other, it threatens to warp normal people with manga and anime, which are spreading like a virus around the world (Hinton 2014, 56). "Lolicon" is again a keyword, going from "otaku" and Miyazaki to Japan and beyond.

Increasingly, such critique filters back into Japan and affects evaluations of manga, anime, and "otaku." Responding to reports that paint Japan as "the Empire of Child Pornography" (Adelstein and Kubo 2014), *TV Takkuru*, a popular television show hosted by iconoclastic filmmaker Beat Takeshi, staged a debate about whether or not the nation should do more to rein in imaginary sex, violence, and crime (TV Takkuru 2014). The question, more specifically, was, "Is it necessary to regulate violent lolicon anime?" The objects under discussion ranged from adult manga and anime depicting explicit sex with underage characters—which could not be shown on television, and thus details were left to the imagination—to suggestive and sexualized images of cute girls. A panel of guests, including both a criminal psychologist and an elected politician affiliated with the ruling Liberal Democratic Party, watched as a prerecorded video roll of cartoon characters flashed before their eyes. One is in grade school; she is shown as a nude silhouette when transforming into a magical girl; and here she is in the bathtub with her friend. How about this? The protagonist is again in grade school, but she is in love with her teacher; here she is pulling her panties down. What connects these examples, the panel is told, is that the protagonists are bishōjo, which casts a wide net indeed.

Not satisfied with just the images, three men are brought out and introduced as "bishōjo anime otaku" (figures 2.6–2.10). The panel launches into a group interrogation. Do they have a Lolita complex? Are they attracted to normal women? One of them, a twenty-one-year-old university student, confesses to committing crimes in his imagination. Leaving the studio, a camera crew follows another set of bishōjo fans onto the street and into stores where they shop for manga/anime media and merchandise. The men—a twenty-two-year-old university student and two company employees, twenty-one and twenty-four years old—look normal enough, but are said to have no experience with the opposite sex and to love bishōjo. One tells the camera crew that he is married, but then holds up an image of a cartoon character. This is his "wife" (*yome*)—a character that is ten years old. Another says that he wants nothing more than a character as his wife, but doubts linger. Over images of streets and stores overflowing with cute girl characters in various media and material forms, a voice-over tells the panel and viewers at home that the number of bishōjo fans is increasing in Japan. "What do you think of this reality?" Back in the studio, the psychologist, who is said to have examined over ten thousand criminals, argues that stricter regulation is necessary, because imaginary crimes "will escalate." The politician agrees, drawing attention to a case in Kumamoto Prefecture in which a three-year-old girl was murdered by "a lover of cartoons depicting child rape."

Note the knotted strands of discourse about the reality problems of "otaku." On the one hand, the bishōjo fans on *TV Takkuru* are presented as perverts that are oriented toward and involved in intimate relations with cute girl characters; they are abnormal, weird, and socially and sexually immature; although funny rather than frightening, one hopes that they can also be attracted to "normal women" like "normal men." On the other hand, bishōjo fans appear dangerously close to pedophiles and might even be predators; one commits crimes in his imagination, while another

FIGURE 2.6
"Bishōjo anime otaku" questioned on *TV Takkuru*, September 2014.

FIGURE 2.7
Do they have an interest in Lolita?

FIGURE 2.8
Are they attracted to "normal women?"

FIGURE 2.9
No experience with the opposite sex.

FIGURE 2.10
Imaginary crimes "will escalate."

is attracted to cute girl characters that are children; viewers are told by an expert that imaginary sex crimes will escalate and spill over into reality; the case in Kumamoto immediately brings to mind Miyazaki Tsutomu. In the interwoven strands of discourse, "otaku" take cute girl characters as objects of desire and affection, which speaks to an orientation toward fiction that emerged among manga/anime fans in the late 1970s and early 1980s. However, "otaku" are also potentially harboring harmful desires that they might act on, which raises concerns about a reserve army of criminals that spread in the Japanese media in the late 1980s and early 1990s. In either case, "otaku" and their desires are abnormal. They might have a problem with reality, or might be a problem in reality, but there is a problem nonetheless. Hence the question: "What do you think of this reality?" Whatever the case may be, something is not right. Confronted by "otaku" and their reality problems, something must be done, which could be a step toward getting things back to normal in Japan.

Conclusion

In some ways, the story of "otaku" is an old one. In his foundational work, media scholar Henry Jenkins points out that fans are often depicted as feminine or asexual due to the stereotype that excessive consumption forecloses other types of social experience (Jenkins 1992, 10). Treated as "crazies" or "misfits" for being too interested in the wrong things (11), fans are told to "get a life," by which critics imply that the lives that fans already have are unacceptable. In Japan in 1983, the discussion of "otaku" clarified that what was unacceptable was manga/anime fans oriented toward fictional girls as opposed to the real thing, which was taken to be a rejection of reality, manhood, and adulthood. This discourse evolved in 1989, when "otaku" were reimagined as antisocial, lost in media worlds, and a threat to children. Today, interwoven concerns about reality problems inform much of what is said about "otaku": on the one hand, a rejection of reality or escape from it, or "otaku" as manga/anime fans oriented toward fiction, the unreal, or the two-dimensional; on the other, potential confusion and conflation of fiction and reality, which makes interactions and relations with cute girl characters suspect and dangerous.

Even as "otaku" are in some ways normalized in Japan and around the world, the labeling process and issues that instigated it persist in discourse about abnormal manga/anime fans, or manga/anime fans as perverts, pedophiles, and predators. "'Otaku' Research" in 1983 and the "otaku" panic in 1989 reveal deep-seated anxieties about deviation from proper social and sexual development in media consumer society. In this sense, "otaku" are akin to the prewar Japanese *moga*, or "modern girl," in that both are simultaneously media creations and lived identities that crystallize concerns about consumption, media effects, gender and sexuality, and acceptable socialization in times of change (Ortabasi 2008, 279–80). From another perspective, "otaku" are an example of what anthropologist Paul Amar calls "hypervisible subjects," or "fetishized figures that preoccupy public discourse and representations" (Amar 2011, 40). In his work on the Middle East, Amar shows how such hypervisible subjects are men taken as problems to be solved. Much of this resonates with "otaku" (Kinsella 2000, 132; Azuma, Saitō, and Kotani 2003, 180; Cather 2012, 231), but there are key differences.

Not merely a discursive construct, "otaku" is a label used in response to the movement of manga/anime fans, most often those moved by interactions and relations with characters.[17] Beyond the label, then, is movement, which is shared. Since the 1980s, manga/anime fans have come to recognize themselves and others as "otaku." They speak to and as "otaku," in the terms available, and in ways that make sense to manga/anime fans. As in the example of *The Book of Otaku*, the terms used can be the same, but their meanings are quite different. The terms are productive, shifting, drawing attention to other ways of seeing and being in the world. To turn the page on "otaku" research, scholars might try to learn how terms are used and made significant by manga/anime fans in everyday life and practice. This means getting past concerns about reality problems to observe how new realities are imagined and created, shared and lived. It means imagining and creating, sharing and living those realities with others. This is the approach of this book, which follows the movement of manga/anime fans in response to cute girl characters and one another. The next chapter focuses on "moe," which became a keyword among manga/anime fans in Japan from the 1990s into the 2000s. As we shall see, moe is movement that contributes to the emergence of alternative social worlds.

THREE MOE

An Affective Response to Fictional Characters

"Are you familiar with Japanese 'moe' relationships, where socially dysfunctional men develop deep emotional attachments to body pillows with women painted on them?" asks James Franco, guest starring on *30 Rock*, a primetime television series in the United States.[1] Elsewhere in the episode, the actor appears holding a pillow with a manga/anime-style girl crudely drawn on it (figure 3.1). Franco calls her Kimiko. His costars look distraught, but the audience is cracking up. The laughter comes from a growing awareness of Japanese popular culture, including manga, anime, and fans of such media. Just as manga and anime are understood to be distinct forms of comics and cartoons, manga/anime fans are in a category of their own: "otaku." Succinctly described by Franco as socially dysfunctional men, "otaku" seem entirely too attracted and attached to fictional characters, or manga/anime girls as opposed to real women. Depicting "otaku" this way is nothing new, and Franco's portrayal resonated with a then recent *New York Times Magazine* article on moe relationships, body pillows, and "love in two-dimensions," all reportedly part of a Japanese social "phenomenon" (Katayama 2009a) (figure 3.2). Given the prevalence of such stories, many watching *30 Rock* no doubt shook their heads and said, "Yes, James Franco, we know about moe!"

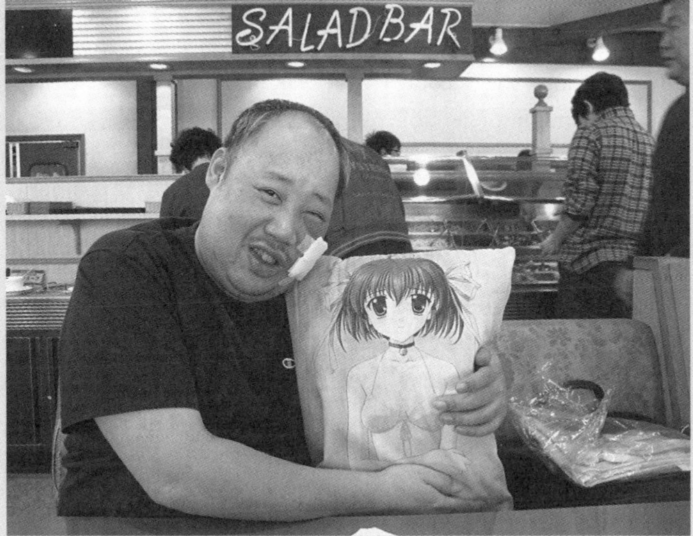

FIGURE 3.1 (above)
Franco explains moe.

FIGURE 3.2 (right)
New York Times Magazine: "Love in 2-D."

While many in the anglophone world have heard the word "moe," however, they might struggle if pressed to define it. On *30 Rock,* the audience sees a man and his body pillow, but what does it mean to call this relationship a "moe relationship?" For the joke to work, it matters less that everyone understands moe than that the Japanese modifier indicates the relationship to be "Japanese." The audience recognizes that this is weird, and it is funny to watch Franco act weird, or the American act out a Japanese moe relationship, which is incongruous.[2] Indeed, in the United States, Japan stereotypically occupies a position of contrastive difference. When American gunboats forced Japan to open its borders in the mid-nineteenth century, ending over two hundred years of isolationism, visitors were quick to denounce the Japanese as vulgar (Allison 2000, 163).[3] Even as perceived differences repulsed some, they enthralled others, and writing on "things Japanese" flourished. By the time anthropologist Ruth Benedict published *The Chrysanthemum and the Sword* in the mid-twentieth century, she took for granted that, "No one is unaware of the deep-rooted cultural differences between the United States and Japan," with the latter generally taken to be "phenomenally strange" (Benedict [1946] 2006, 1–2, 10). Numerous sections of that seminal study are devoted to sex and sexuality, which both reflects and contributes to the long history of imagining Japan as an exotic and erotic "other."[4] Even as the nations became close allies and trade partners after the Second World War, in the United States, Japan remains distant and impenetrable for many. Alongside the increased flow of Japanese media and popular culture into the United States since the 1990s (Jenkins 2006b, 154; also Allison 2006), reporting on the imagined excesses and perversions of Japan has become standard.

Much of this brings to mind Orientalism, or a system of producing knowledge about "the Orient" that is also filtering "the Orient into Western consciousness" (Said 1978, 6). In this system, "the Orient" is other to "the West," "different" to the "normal" (40). The critique of Orientalism exposes the relations of power involved in producing knowledge about others. As part of a discipline that emphasizes encountering and writing about others, anthropologists risk sliding into Orientalism by "making statements" about, and "authorizing views" of, those that are "different" (3). I was reminded of this during an interview with Ōtsuka Eiji, who edited *Manga Burikko* during its dramatic transformation in 1983. In his office in the western suburbs of Tokyo on a rainy night in October 2009, I asked Ōtsuka about *Manga Burikko* specifically and an orientation toward fiction generally. He used the word "moe," and I was keen to hear his interpretation of it, but my follow-up question offended Ōtsuka, who snapped, "There is an expression in Japanese, *macchi pompu*, which means to set a fire and pretend you are a firefighter to get credit for putting it out. Moe is like that. There is no fire besides the one that we ourselves started and poured oil on. It is simply the Orientalism of Europeans and Americans thinking that Japan possesses something special."[5] Bristling at an inferred attempt to make moe into something about "Japan," Ōtsuka dismissed it as an addition to distorted discourse about "samurai geisha Fujiyama." But he was not content only to confront an American about Orientalism. After all, someone had started the fire, which then drew the attention of those who thought that they saw something of Japan revealed by its light. The culprits, Ōtsuka seemed to be saying, are Japanese, and he warned me not to be lured to flames that were set and stoked by people with agendas. The words flowing from him as if a dam had been breached, Ōtsuka railed against academics and their theories, government officials and their campaigns, and everyone else fueling the overheated discussion of moe in Japan.

Thoroughly chastised by the end of the interview, I said my thanks and turned for the door, only to be stopped by Ōtsuka. Standing behind a desk covered with papers and artifacts, Ōtsuka had picked up, seemingly on a whim, a framed, full-color drawing, which he showed me. Published in *Manga Burikko* in August 1983, it was an original illustration of Takanezawa Moe, a cute girl character or bishōjo (figure 3.3). An example of the "two-dimensional idols" appearing in the magazine at the time and appealing to manga/anime fans, Moe looks out at the viewer, almost as if in direct address. As I gazed at the character, my eyes meeting hers, Ōtsuka interjected, "This might be the origin of moe." Smiling at my apparent confusion, he then sent me out into the black and wet dark. Walking back to the train station, it occurred to me that Ōtsuka might have been teaching me a lesson about evaluating claims, regardless of who is making them. In his writings, Ōtsuka explains the success of *Manga Burikko* in terms of an emerging orientation of desire toward fiction in Japan in the 1980s (Ōtsuka 2004, 16–58), and explicitly positions the magazine as an origin of moe (Ōtsuka 2013, 251; 2015, xix). He did it again as I left that night, even as he told me that moe is just a false alarm and so much smoke. What we presume to know might be a bunch of bunk, but that does not mean that there is nothing to know, if we are willing to listen carefully and learn from our interactions and relations with others.

Based primarily on personal interviews and published accounts, this chapter focuses on moe as a keyword among manga/anime fans and critics in Japan in the 1990s and 2000s. The goal is to explore the meaning of

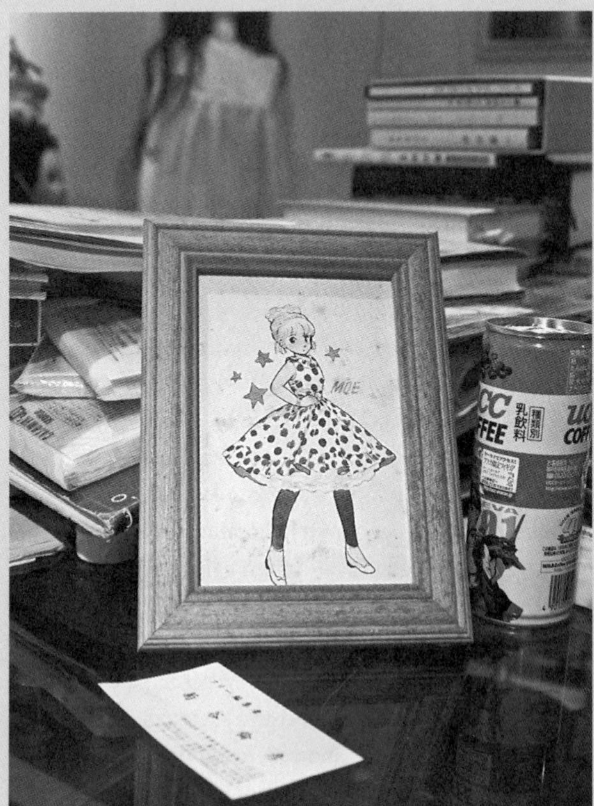

FIGURE 3.3 Framed drawing of Takanezawa Moe on the desk of Ōtsuka. The image appeared in *Manga Burikko*, August 1983. Photo by Fritz Schumann.

moe, in the sense not necessarily of its definition but rather its significance. In our interview, for example, Ōtsuka elaborated that moe is "something you feel when looking at a character." This does much to clarify the "moe relationship" in *30 Rock*: It is not about "body pillows with women painted on them," as James Franco suggests, but rather the character, Kimiko; the pillow provides her with a material form. "Something you feel," however, is still vague. As I have come to grasp it, moe is an affective response to fictional characters. Precisely stated, affect is a modification or variation produced in a body by interaction with another body (Spinoza 2005, 70), but in practice it is often close to a body moved by another body.[6] While the capacity of human bodies on screen to affect has been discussed (Hardt 1999, 96; also Williams 1989), moe highlights this capacity of fictional characters. The fictional character is a body, which can affect the human body interacting with it. So while Ōtsuka was perhaps being facetious when announcing that Takanezawa Moe is the origin of moe, the character design reflects consciousness of her affective relations with the viewer, which speaks to a pivotal moment in the late 1970s and early 1980s.[7] And while Ōtsuka is right to challenge fetishization of Japaneseness by underscoring relations with characters and their affect in other places and times, in Japan in the 1990s and 2000s, manga/anime fans and critics were thinking on this topic in increasingly sophisticated ways. This chapter presents three perspectives on moe, which trace it back to manga/anime creators such as Tezuka Osamu and Miyazaki Hayao and franchises such as *Urusei Yatsura* (Those Obnoxious Aliens, 1978–87) and *Neon Genesis Evangelion* (Shin seiki Evangerion, 1995–96). Rather than an authoritative history, these perspectives are examples of the stories that manga/anime fans and critics tell about moe. In these stories, moe is connected to shared worlds of imagination and new ways of seeing and being with fictional and real others, which can be transformative.

Some General Orienting Remarks

Before the perspectives, some general orienting remarks. "Moe" is the noun form of *moeru,* a Japanese verb meaning "to burst into bud" or "to sprout." Written Japanese employs modified Chinese characters, including "moe," which is composed of the symbol for "grass" over another for "bright, cheerful" (Condry 2013, 190–91). There is a youthful vitality to moe that is on display in its use in Japanese poetry from as early as the eighth century (Macias and Machiyama 2004, 50). It can also be a given name, which in manga and anime tends to be reserved for young girls, for example, Takanezawa Moe. In the 1990s, manga/anime fans gathering online were sharing their excitement for characters such as Takatsu Moe from *Sun Smash!* (Taiyō ni sumasshu, 1993) and Moe from *Dinosaur Planet* (Kyōryū wakusei, 1993–94). Incidentally, the verb *moeru,* "to burst into bud," is homonymous with *moeru,* "to burn." The two are distinguished through context in conversation, and Chinese characters in writing, but computer-mediated communication requires an extra step of converting typed input into corresponding Chinese characters (Nishimura 2012, 39–40). Due to errors in this process, fans writing about burning with passion for manga/anime characters—"I am hot for Moe!"—often instead wrote that they were bursting into bud (Morikawa 2003, 30–32). This led to a productive blurring of meaning in "moe," which was adopted as slang among manga/anime fans as the decade progressed. By the mid-2000s, moe was in wide use among fans—male, female, and other—of manga/anime characters—male, female, and other—in Japan and beyond.

As slang among manga/anime fans, "moe" refers to an affective response to fictional characters.[8] There are three things to note here: first, moe is a response, something that occurs, not a state; second, moe occurs in interactions and relations with images, objects, and so on, but is not located in that to which one responds; and third, the response is to fictional characters. This last qualification is crucial, because "moe" is a term that emerged out of manga/anime fan interactions and relations with fictional characters and indicates an affective response to them. Interactions and relations with fictional characters are not unique to Japan—in *Time* magazine's special issue on "the 100 most influential people who never lived," contributors lovingly describe characters (Time 2013); some are even more direct, for example, comics scholar Will Brooker, who confesses, "I love that man: I love Batman" (Brooker 2000, 8)—but manga/anime fans in Japan crossed a critical threshold in developing specific and shared language to discuss their affection. Further, given the vibrant media and material culture of manga and anime in Japan, there is more of a tendency to treat fictional characters not as "people who never lived," but rather as distinct existences that are part of everyday life (Condry 2013, 71, 190).

In contemporary Japan, characters said to trigger moe most often come from manga, anime, and games and novels featuring manga/anime-style characters. As designs have become more and more refined and intended to trigger an affective response, manga/anime fans have come to speak about "moe characters" (*moe kyara*). Be they specific entities or general types, these characters can be broken down into constituent parts, or moe elements, that spread like memes (Azuma [2001] 2009, 42–53; also Nagayama 2014). Manga/anime characters appear not only across media but also in various material forms—figurines, dolls, body pillows—and these, too, can trigger moe. Voices can be called moe when attached to characters. Plants, animals, inanimate objects, machines, buildings, countries, and more can be morphed into moe characters (for examples, see Galbraith 2015a). The response to a human can be moe when that human is approached as a fictional character, which is made separate and distinct; costumes, poses, and so on can contribute. At the heart of this culture are interactions and relations with manga/anime characters. Encountered in various media and material forms, manga/anime fans come to interact with characters as others that are both fictional and real. Nevertheless, the realness of characters does not make them the same as humans. While anthropologist Anne Allison is certainly right that fictional characters are part of everyday life in Japan today (Allison 2006, 180–91), and anthropologist Ian Condry is certainly also right that characters are real to the extent that relationships with them are real (Condry 2013, 71, 200–201), they are real and part of everyday life *as fictional characters*. Tracing this back to manga/anime creators and franchises, the following three perspectives attempt to explain how this came to be.

Perspective One: Tezuka Osamu and the Eroticism of Movement

No single figure has influenced postwar manga and anime as much as Tezuka Osamu. After the Second World War, his manga was read by hundreds of thousands, then millions, of children, and inspired others to become manga artists. In 1963, he kick-started television anime by adapting his popular manga *Astro Boy* (Tetsuwan Atomu, 1952–68) into the format of a weekly serial broadcast, built up lucrative ties with sponsors and merchandisers, and pushed for licensing outside of Japan. Imitators and rivals rose in his wake; where there had been a weak industry overwhelmed by imported American cartoons came a strong industry exporting its own content. Upon his death in 1989, newspapers opined that Japan has such a robust culture of manga and anime, which appeal to men and women of all ages, because Japan had Tezuka Osamu (Schodt 2007, vii–viii). Certainly Tezuka, who was exposed to foreign films and cartoons, literature, and theater from a young age, raised the level of manga by introducing long-form, complex, challenging stories. Of Tezuka in his early years as a creator, comics scholar Natsume Fusanosuke writes, "Even though this young man of eighteen says he's drawing it all for children, he is in fact drawing what he wants. He's drawing exactly what he wants to see drawn, what he longs for" (quoted in Miyamoto 2011, 85). What Tezuka wanted to see drawn was something as interesting as the best of film, literature, and theater, which, arguably because of his impact on subsequent artists and readers, many Japanese have come to expect of manga (Schodt 1983, 16), as well as the anime into which it feeds. At the same time, however, Tezuka maintained a "cute," "cartoony," or "child-like" aesthetic in his characters, who were placed in mature scenarios where violence and sex, suffering and death, were all possible (for a general introduction, see Randall 2005).

Identified as the source of practically everything manga/anime related, to such an extent that this lionization draws criticism (Itō Gō 2005), Tezuka has in recent years been reimagined as one of the founding fathers of moe. An example of this is *Osamu Moet Moso* (Osamu moetto mosso), an exhibition that I visited at the Tokyo Anime Center in Akihabara on September 18, 2010. In promotional material, the exhibition claimed its mission was "to extract and embody Akiba-like elements contained in Tezuka Osamu's works."[9] An abbreviation of Akihabara, "Akiba" is not the generator of any particular manga/anime style, but, since the 1990s, the Tokyo neighborhood has come to be deeply associated with fans of cute girl characters and affective responses to them (more on this below). For *Osamu Moet Moso*, extracting "Akiba-like elements" meant extracting moe elements from Tezuka's characters and aligning them with manga and anime popular in Akihabara.[10] Among those contributing illustrations of Tezuka's characters were Itō Noizi, Kei, and Yoshizaki Mine, all known for their cute girl characters.[11] Resonating with contemporary and local tastes—and despite the involvement of Tezuka Productions, a company entrusted with preserving the creator's legacy—many of the characters on display in the Tokyo Anime Center appeared as erotic as they did cute.

A rendition of Astro Boy caught my eye. The lines were softer than Tezuka's, the colors pastel, but what drew my attention was the eroticization of the little robot with a big heart. As originally designed, Astro Boy wears black briefs, a green belt, and red boots, but here the belt does not fully go around his waist, which reveals a belly button; the briefs have seams and look more like underwear; and the boots have been elongated to resemble "knee socks," which emphasize fleshy thighs (figure 3.4). This is unmistakably the work of the artist Pop, who rocketed to stardom with his illustrations for *Moetan* (2003). Even a cursory examination of signage in Akihabara demonstrates wide support for Pop, but global audiences concerned about manga and anime shading into child pornography criticize combining cuteness and eroticism as he does. Nonetheless, one of his illustrations was in the Tokyo Anime Center, a tourism hub and showcase for Japanese media and popular culture, in the form of Tezuka's most iconic and beloved character. And *Osamu Moet Moso* did not stop there. It traveled on to Marui One in Shinjuku, Printemps in Ginza, the Osamu Tezuka Manga Museum in Takarazuka, and so on (figure 3.5). Along the way, it connected unlikely sites and audiences. Reproductions of Pop's Astro Boy were sold at both high art galleries and the Comic Market. Even as the exhibition moved

FIGURE 3.4
Tezuka meets Pop in Akihabara.

beyond Akihabara, manga/anime fans were encouraged to see elements of their favorite characters in classic Tezuka. This exposure to an Astro Boy made strange—or, rather, strangely familiar—disrupted assumptions about Tezuka and opened up new possibilities. At *Osamu Moet Moso*, one could comment, "Astro Boy is practically the original moe!"[12]

Like many in Japan and around the world, *Osamu Moet Moso* provided me with a new set of lenses through which to view "the God of Manga." Gazing at Pop's illustration, I could not help but recall an interview in which Tezuka said that Astro Boy was initially intended to be a "beautiful female android," and descriptions of the character as "attractive and androgynous" (Schodt 2007, viii, 51).[13] From here I was led to another association, this time a dialogue between opinion leaders Yonezawa Yoshihiro and Azuma Hideo, which I came across in archival research. Published in *Gekkan Out*

FIGURE 3.5 *Osamu Moet Moso* on the road.

in March 1982, which is to say at the height of the lolicon boom, the dialogue features an exchange about eroticism in manga and anime. Bringing up the "Astro Boy is erotic theory" (*Atomu iroppoi setsu*), which apparently had currency in fandom at the time, Yonezawa argues, "In manga, something like eroticism has been an attraction from the beginning."[14] In agreement, Azuma responds that he vividly remembers the "sexy poses" (*iroppoi pōzu*) that Tezuka put his characters in. By his own estimation, Azuma took the already existing eroticism of Tezuka and, combining it with shōjo manga, developed his contributions to bishōjo manga from the 1970s into the 1980s (Azuma and Yamada 2011, 30–31). The explicit eroticism of "cute characters of the Tezuka lineage" (*Tezuka keitō no kawairashii kyara*) (Takekuma 2003, 107) rallied fans and riled up critics, who seem to concur that this was a decisive turning point.

Since receiving the Tezuka Osamu Cultural Prize for his *Disappearance Diary* (Shissō nikki, 2005), Azuma has been at the center of a major revival in Japan, including critical commentaries, reprints of his manga, and retrospective exhibitions. Already interesting is the rehabilitation of an artist associated with "otaku" subculture, but additionally so is how reevaluations of Azuma and Tezuka are so often linked. From February to May 2011, even as *Osamu Moet Moso* continued its travels across Japan, the histories of Azuma and Tezuka converged in exhibitions held at the Yoshihiro Yonezawa Memorial Library of Manga and Subcultures and Meiji University, a lecture series, and a book (figure 3.6).[15] In print and in person, Azuma, heralded as the "creator of cute eroticism" (*kawaii ero no sōzōsha*)—the very same aesthetic seen in Pop, which some international critics find problematic—regularly expressed his admiration for Tezuka, who he counted among his biggest inspirations. However seemingly outrageous the manga in question might be, from cat girls and cute eroticism to robot girls and tentacle sex, Azuma essentially said that Tezuka had done it first. And people close to Tezuka seemed to approve of that assessment. While Japanese thinkers were already tying Tezuka to lolicon in the early 2000s—positioning him "on the side of lolicon" (*rorikon gawa no hito*) (Azuma, Saitō, and Kotani 2003, 181)—by 2011, it was possible for Tezuka's own son to call Azuma both a "subculture pioneer" and one of his father's "legitimate successors" (*seitō-teki na kōkeisha*) (Tezuka Makoto 2011, 172).[16] In this way, in numerous venues, Tezuka, lolicon, and contemporary "otaku" subculture are connected (see also Morikawa 2003, 109–16; Honda Tōru 2005a, 116–22; Nagayama 2014, 27–32).[17]

By the time that *Osamu Moet Moso* was being planned, many were already starting to see moe in some of Tezuka's earliest works. For example, *Lost World* (Rosuto wārudo zenseiki, 1948) is a dark sci-fi narrative featuring cute characters (figure 3.7). Operating in a legal and ethical grey zone on an alien planet, a senior scientist uses plant matter to create two women, Ayame and Momiji. Scheming to sell these plant girls, the scientist gives them sexually attractive forms. While it is not surprising that Tezuka, an adult man, drew sexually attractive adult women, he also introduced ideas that complicate desire for them. Looking like adult women, Ayame and Momiji are newborn creatures that know nothing of the world, which is a combination of sexuality and innocence that design theorist Morikawa Ka'ichirō compares to contemporary moe characters (Morikawa 2011b). Manga/anime historian Helen McCarthy, author of an extensive catalogue of Tezuka's work, supports Morikawa's reading (McCarthy 2009a). Both

FIGURE 3.6
Azuma exhibition at Meiji University, April and May 2011.

Morikawa and McCarthy zero in on a key scene in which Ayame and a young scientist named Shikishima Ken'ichi, left stranded on the alien planet, decide to live on as "brother and sister." As McCarthy sees it, "This is essential moe—an innocent, literally budding, girl, a geeky young man with the heart of a hero and protective instincts to do any father proud, and a completely non-sexual relationship."

This key scene is completely nonsexual but at the same time completely sexual, given that Tezuka draws Ayame as half-naked and embracing Shikishima. The character interaction and relation are ambiguous: a brother holds his adopted sister the plant-girl and tells her that they will also be king and queen of their lost world; one wonders if this might even be a conjugal couple. The scene evokes all sorts of potential relationships of intimacy, but does not settle into stable and set familial or sexual forms; the terms

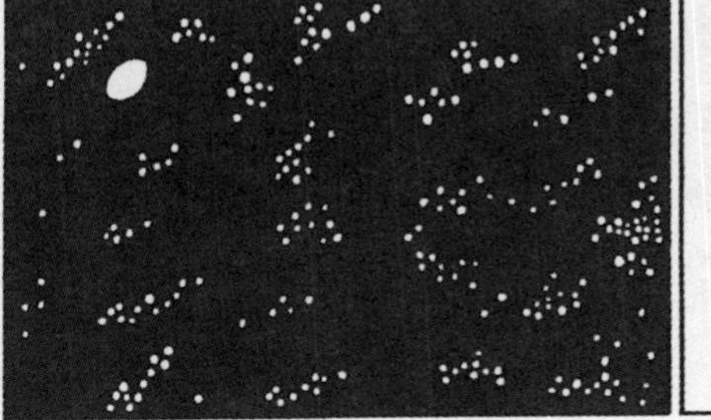

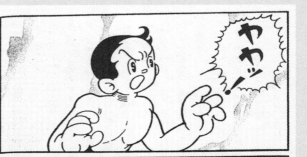

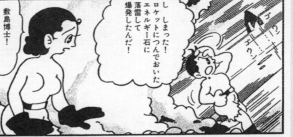

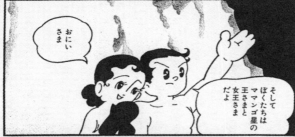

FIGURE 3.7
Tezuka's *Lost World*: moe?

of intimacy continue to move and, in their movement, transform; combinations of plant and human, adult and child, sexual and innocent contribute to an unsettled and unsettling relationship between characters and with them, which can have powerful effects. Media studies scholar Okuno Takuji underscores this in his discussion of moe: "Originally, *moe* referred to the affectionate feelings (*renjō*) that *otaku* held for female manga and anime characters. The objects of that affection were generally *bishōjo* . . . Although these characters were always intimates, their positions were quite separate, which meant that the affection could not be expressed directly. *Moe*, then, was that hazy (*moya moya*) feeling" (quoted in Condry 2013, 191). Affection for Ayame certainly fits this description. Further, as Morikawa stresses, the image of this bare-breasted plant-girl as sister-queen was stimulating enough that some manga artists today can still recall it from their childhoods (Morikawa 2011b).

As an added complication to its direct expression, desire is oriented toward fictional characters, or cute girl characters in manga and anime. For much of the postwar period, what Okuno and others call "two-dimensional desire" was thought to be taboo or unspeakable, something that needed to be suppressed, hidden, and denied; it could not be faced, let alone expressed, directly, which contributed to that "hazy feeling." Increasingly acknowledged is that manga/anime artists from Tezuka on were creating cute, cartoony characters that could become objects of desire. Like that senior scientist in *Lost World*, Tezuka gave Ayame and Momiji attractive forms to sell to buyers (of the manga), but the point is even more fundamental. For his part, Ōtsuka Eiji ties Tezuka to moe because Tezuka introduced the possibility that a cute, cartoony character had a body that could be hurt, feel pain, and die (Ōtsuka 2008, 121–22; also Azuma, Saitō, and Kotani 2003, 181). It follows, then, that this character body could also have sex and feel pleasure. As Ōtsuka sees it, Tezuka's attribution of "reality" to "unrealistic" forms allowed for, on the one hand, postwar manga and anime to explore literary themes, and, on the other, to "move in the direction of pornography associated with . . . moe" (Ōtsuka 2008, 121–22). Similarly, manga critic Itō Gō locates the origins of moe in using cute, cartoony characters to move readers to bodily response (Itō Gō 2005, 136).

After struggling with competition from more explicitly mature gekiga works targeting young adults in the 1960s (Gravett 2004), Tezuka was able to explore sexuality more freely from the end of the decade into the 1970s. Through it all, he never abandoned his cute, cartoony characters (Takeuchi Ichiro 2006, 91). It is thus not at all difficult for critics to find examples of "cute eroticism." In the opening years of the 1970s alone, Tezuka published *Apollo's Song* (Aporo no uta, 1970), which probes the psychology of sexual repression and violence; *Yakeppachi's Maria* (Yakeppachi no Maria, 1970), the story of a sexually frustrated schoolboy and the animated doll that helps him cope with adolescence; and *Marvelous Melmo* (Fushigi na Merumo, 1971–72), which tells of a young girl that can temporarily become an adult woman by ingesting pills. Envisioned by Tezuka as a form of sex education (McCarthy 2009b, 194) and adapted into a television anime, *Marvelous Melmo* is widely remembered for scenes of its girl protagonist transforming into an adult woman still wearing child-sized clothes. The adult Melmo has breasts that practically burst from her blouse, and any movement results in a peek at her panties beneath a too-short skirt. In 2008, a set of Melmo figurines went on sale at the Tokyo Anime Center (figure 3.8), placing the character in Akihabara and alongside contemporary examples of transforming girls and "fan service." Whatever Tezuka's intentions, some might agree with *Osamu Moet Moso* and see in his characters moe elements ripe for extraction. If nothing else, even if one does not go back as far as *Lost World* and *Astro Boy*, there is no shortage of what Azuma Hideo calls "erotic poses."

Contributing to her father's newfound fame by selecting two thousand pages of his manga representing its eroticism (Tezuka Osamu 2010a, 2010b), Tezuka's eldest daughter also drew attention to his own thoughts on the matter via a quote used to promote the project. The quote leads back to *Save Our Mother Earth* (Garasu no chikyū wo sukue, 1996), which Tezuka was writing at the time of his death in 1989. In this provocative book of fragments, Tezuka does not delve into the "Astro Boy is erotic theory," but does address eroticism in discussing his decision to make the character move in the trailblazing *Astro Boy* anime. To begin, Tezuka finds eroticism in "movement" (*ugoki*): "I feel a sense of eroticism in anything that moves, in things with movement. . . . The other way around, I hate things that are still. . . . Take a shape, for example, when a cloud changes from one shape to another, the process of that change is seductive. It's not good when the shape is fixed. . . . If I have to say why I feel eroticism, it's because I feel the power of life there" (Tezuka Osamu 1996, 166–67). The connection of movement, transformation, and "the power of life" (*seimeiryoku*) is striking, as is the connection of this movement to eroticism.[18] Frankly, Tezuka does not care if the body in motion is human, let alone male or female. In addition to nature, for Tezuka, there is eroticism in the movement of animated characters. Carried forward by the breathless momentum of his

FIGURE 3.8
Marvelous Melmo figurines in Akihabara. Photo by Adrian A. Lozano.

writing, Tezuka declares in no uncertain terms that he "started anime in pursuit of the eroticism of movement" (166–67).

And he continued this pursuit despite losing obscene amounts of money on production (Clements 2013, 129). Many working for Tezuka in the studio that he founded to produce *Astro Boy* argue that he could not stop, because "animation is like an addictive drug to the man" (Schodt 2007, 151). Put somewhat differently, Tezuka had an "obsessive desire" (Takeuchi Ichiro 2006, 87) to animate characters and see their bodies in motion. The desire was for a dynamic world, which Tezuka reportedly described as follows: "Visually or metaphorically, I like things always in motion. I have a longing for a world where nothing stays the same, where even reasons for existence change. It makes sense that everything keeps changing because life is about moving. By constantly changing, things are evolving and affecting other things. I like to observe such dynamic activities" (quoted in

Takeuchi Ichiro 2006, 89). What world is more dynamic than that of animation, where any form is possible (Eisenstein 1986, 21)? Where everything changes from one image to the next, even as movement from one to the next provides the illusion of stable form? Where every image thus pulsates with the energy of movement? Given his attraction to such a world, it is not entirely surprising that Tezuka did not, or could not, quit animation, even as it was not necessarily profitable for him to insist on maintaining the relationship. Animation was his love, his "mistress" (Schodt 2007, 56; Condry 2013, 103), that for which he burned.

Due to fierce competition from live-action and imported content, Tezuka committed to produce animation for television broadcast at a loss (Clements 2013, 116–27), with the understanding that he could recoup costs by franchising characters across media and material forms. The *Astro Boy* anime begins with synergy with the manga, which brought fans of one to the other and increased ratings and sales. As an extension of this, as media theorist Marc Steinberg documents, the anime was sponsored by confectionary company Meiji Seika, which offered consumers of its Marble Chocolates *Astro Boy* stickers with proof of purchase (Steinberg 2012, 45–48). Even as the manga/anime brought consumers to the chocolates, the chocolates brought consumers to the manga/anime, and *Astro Boy* characters brought media and commodity forms together. This model has come to be known as the "media mix" (*media mikkusu*), or a system of media and commodities in relation to one another, and it contributed to the spread of Astro Boy's character image. Even as children used the stickers to turn ordinary objects into character goods, and eventually such goods were produced for them by corporations, Astro Boy could be encountered "anywhere, anytime" (79). In other words, the character became part of everyday life. In the media mix model, worlds are created around characters, and consumers are in affective relations with characters in those worlds. While Tezuka's animation studio went bankrupt after only a decade in business, which might seem like an abject failure, he succeeded in inspiring imitators and rivals, kick-starting the domestic industry for television animation, and establishing character franchising. As characters proliferate across media and material forms and are designed to attract and hold attention in Japan today, Tezuka is said to be responsible for the nation becoming the "Empire of Characters" (41).

Not only are manga/anime characters an intimate part of everyday life for young people in contemporary Japan, but furthermore, with the rapid rise of mature works and audiences since the 1960s, one does not have to grow out of fandom. Responding to characters, fans contribute to shared and expanding manga/anime worlds by creating fanzines, figurines, and more. In such an environment, affection for manga/anime characters is encouraged. In a personal interview, manga/anime fan, critic, and writer Honda Tōru elaborated, with a familiar point of departure: "I think that we can blame Tezuka Osamu for moe culture. . . . For kids of all backgrounds, manga and anime are part of growing up. You get used to seeing cute characters. Many people learn to draw them. The presence of these characters and attention paid to them is unique. Nowhere in the world are there cuter characters in greater numbers than in Japan."[19] The impact of these characters is something that Honda knows firsthand. As a child, he watched reruns of the television anime *Princess Knight* (Ribon no kishi, 1967–68), an adaptation of Tezuka's manga, which features a cross-dressing heroine with both male and female hearts. Thinking the character was a boy, but then seeing her in a dress, Honda had a "proto-moe experience," as he puts it, that reverberates in the many stories he writes about androgyny and gender swapping. If characters such as Ayame, the plant-girl from *Lost World*, are described in the manga as "*obake*," or monsters, which in Japanese has the connotation of transformation, then Honda found them strangely attractive.[20] He is not alone. In Japan, many have come to interact intimately with manga/anime characters, which conjure forth "strange new desires" (Lamarre 2011, 121). For example, in a personal interview, Itō Gō recalled being drawn to and moved by Tezuka's characters, or responding to the "pleasure of lines" (*byōsen ni yoru kairaku*) in his early works.[21] Statements such as this speak to what Honda calls the unique attention paid to characters, and responses to their lines and movements, in Japan. He and others "blame" Tezuka for it, but this is just one way of looking at moe.

Perspective Two: Miyazaki Hayao and the Fireworks of Eros

Deified since his death in 1989, Tezuka Osamu laid the groundwork for manga and anime to become mass entertainment in postwar Japan. He is not, however, remembered as Japan's greatest animator, which is an honor more often bestowed on Miyazaki Hayao. Born thirteen years after "the God of Manga," Miyazaki came of age when manga was abundant, just about everyone wanted to draw, and Tezuka was the one to emulate. Recognizing the influence of Tezuka's manga on him and struggling to be rid of it—he is not as reverent as many of his peers (Miyazaki 2009, 193–97)—Miyazaki adopted the more realistic and gritty style of gekiga (McCarthy 1999, 27). However, in his final year of high school, Miyazaki abandoned gekiga, which he had come to associate with cynicism rather than maturity. In an essay about that time, Miyazaki writes, "I thought, Do I really want to draw *gekiga*? Don't I want to do something else? To be more specific, I thought it might be better to express in an honest way that what is good is good, what is pretty is pretty, and what is beautiful is beautiful" (Miyazaki 2009, 49).

The decision to be honest about what is good, pretty, and beautiful seems to have been intertwined with encountering a certain anime character. In his last year of high school, strung out and worried about the future, Miyazaki watched *The Tale of the White Serpent* (Hakujaden, 1958), Japan's first animated feature film in color. The story centers on Bai-Niang, the titular white serpent, and her love for Xu-Xian, a boy for whom she assumes human form and fights to be with. (Think *Romeo and Juliet*, but the forbidden romance is between a nonhuman and human, both animated characters.) In a stunning passage from an essay on the film, Miyazaki reveals just how much it meant to him:

> Japan's first true full-length color animated film, *Hakujaden* (The Tale of the White Serpent), was released in 1958. I first encountered it around the end of that same year, in a third-run theater in a seedy part of town, when I was in my final year of high school and busy studying for my college entrance exams. And here I have to make a somewhat embarrassing confession. I fell in love with the heroine of this animated film. I was moved to the depths of my soul and—with snow starting to fall on the street—staggered home. After seeing the dedication and earnestness of the heroine, I felt awkward and pathetic, and I spent the entire evening hunched over the heated *kotatsu* table, weeping. It would be easy to analyze this and write it off as the result of the gloom I felt over the exam-hell I then faced or my youthful immaturity, or to ascribe it merely to having seen a cheap melodrama. But, be that as it may, *Hakujaden* had a powerful impact on me. At the time I dreamed of being a manga artist, and I was trying to draw in the absurd style then popular [that is, gekiga], but *Hakujaden* made me realize how stupid I was. It made me realize that, behind a façade of cynical pronouncements, in actuality I really was in love with the pure, earnest world of the film, even if it were only another cheap melodrama. I was no longer able to deny the fact that there was another me—a me that yearned desperately to affirm the world rather than negate it. (Miyazaki 2009, 70)

Although Miyazaki cannot resist belittling *The Tale of the White Serpent* as "cheap melodrama," it moved him to tears, stirred up strange desires, and changed his life. Because of this experience, Miyazaki joined Toei Animation, which produced the film, and grew into an animator and director renowned for his ability to move audiences.

If Miyazaki seems to be confessing something in this vignette, which he has repeated many times over the years, then it is not just that he was deeply affected by "cheap melodrama." Rather, in his writings, Miyazaki draws attention to this: "I fell in love" (Miyazaki 2009, 70). While it gets subsumed under feelings for the animated film, Miyazaki does not hide that his love was primarily for Bai-Niang, the white serpent: "From personal experience, I can say that I first fell in love with animation when I saw *Hakujaden* (The Tale of the White Serpent), the animated feature produced by Toei Animation in 1958. I can still remember the pangs of emotion I felt at the sight of the incredibly beautiful, young female character, Bai-Niang, and how I went to see the film over and over as a result. It was like being in love, and Bai-Niang became a surrogate girlfriend for me at a time when I had none" (19). The rawness of this memory is almost painful: Bai-Niang is not merely an anime character, but also "incredibly beautiful"; the sight of her triggers "pangs of emotion"; for her, Miyazaki goes "to see the film over and over"; their relationship is "like being in love"; indeed, she is a "surrogate girlfriend." If one were to remove the qualifiers "like" and "surrogate" and simply say, "I was in love with Bai-Niang, who was my girlfriend," then Miyazaki sounds very much like contemporary manga/anime fans describing their moe relationships. It seems clear enough that he is highlighting the vague feelings and strange desires that others have tied to moe: much like Ayame in *Lost World*, Bai-Niang is both nonhuman and human, a serpent that transforms into a woman, Xu-Xian's ambiguous love interest; this is compounded by the fact that Bai-Niang is an anime character, Miyazaki's ambiguous love interest. Feelings of intimacy are combined with distance, in the sense that Miyazaki can never be with Bai-Niang, who exists in the world of animation that so attracts and moves him.

If seeing *The Tale of the White Serpent* changed his career path and inspired future creative activity, then some commentators follow Miyazaki in suggesting that Bai-Niang is key. By far the most influential of these is psychiatrist Saitō Tamaki, who authored a monograph on "otaku" that inspired a cadre of new academic critics in the 2000s. In that book, which focuses on the orientation of desire toward fiction and introduces moe, Saitō addresses Miyazaki's contact with "the incredibly beautiful, young female character, Bai-Niang" (Miyazaki 2009, 19) as "trauma":

> The young Miyazaki fell in love with the heroine of this film despite the fact that it was a work of animation. The experience itself may have been like a sweet dream, but he is still plagued by the fact that he had been made to experience pleasure against his will by a fictional construct. The heroine that becomes an object of love at that moment is an object of desire, but at the same time, because she is fictional, she also contains already within her the occasion for loss. . . . Why does he place so much importance on young girls? . . . I would argue this strangeness can be interpreted as the trauma and its repetition. . . . The trauma and its repetition, moreover, are intertwined with the history of anime, at least latently. . . . A generation traumatized by anime creates its own works that repeat the wound. That wound is taken over and repeated by the next generation. . . . As I have already pointed out in the case of Miyazaki Hayao, to love an anime is, in other words, to love (*moeru*) the beautiful girls in anime. An anime creator is born from the experience of *moe* as a trauma, and the next generation of anime fans finds *moe* in the heroines he creates. I am almost certain that this chain of *moe* as trauma underlines the currents of today's anime culture. (Saitō [2000] 2011, 88–89, 116)

Although few have stated it quite so strongly, Saitō's theory is familiar from discussions of Tezuka, whose attractive characters affected readers and the next wave of artists; these artists, for example, Azuma Hideo, explored the eroticism of manga/anime characters, and in the process generated even more attractive forms; the end result is character illustrations of the sort produced by Pop for *Osamu Moet Moso*. By Saitō's estimation, even as Miyazaki repeated his encounter with Bai-Niang in works featuring attractive female characters, his animation, like Tezuka's manga, affected a generation of young men, who went on to produce manga, anime, games, fanzines, figurines, and so on.

In this way, Miyazaki is reimagined as part of the history of moe and affective relations between manga/anime fans and characters, which seems to be supported by the record. After leaving Toei Animation and working on projects such as *Lupin III* (Rupan sansei, 1971–72, 1977–) and *Heidi, Girl of the Alps* (Arupusu no shōjo Haiji, 1974), Miyazaki captured the hearts of manga/anime fans in the late 1970s and early 1980s.[22] While female characters in the television anime had already stirred up vague feelings in male viewers (see Okuno in Condry 2013, 191), *Lupin III: The Castle of Cagliostro* (Rupan sansei: Kariosutoro no shiro, 1979) is significant in this regard. Marking Miyazaki's debut as a film director, *Lupin III: The Castle of Cagliostro* features Princess Clarisse, an original character that master thief Lupin met when she was a child and reunites with in her teens.[23] This shōjo character was popular enough to inspire *Clarisse Magazine*, a series of fanzines that sold like gangbusters (Takatsuki 2010, 102) (figure 3.9). The rise of *Clarisse Magazine* overlaps with Azuma Hideo's *Cybele*, and indeed Miyazaki's characters were often mentioned in magazines discussing the lolicon boom in the early 1980s (figure 3.10). Commenting on the popularity of Princess Clarisse in the June 1982 issue of *Animage*, however, Miyazaki divorces himself from the phenomenon:

> About Clarisse gaining popularity in terms of "lolicon," I think that this is entirely unrelated to me. It's probably just a matter of young people today using lolicon to mean "longing." It's an experience that everyone has in adolescence. In my case, there was a time when I longed for the character Bai-Niang from *The Tale of the White Serpent*. But I got over it a year later. (Laughs) I think it's something along those lines. That said, we didn't turn our longing into "play," and were embarrassed to talk about it openly. We had "shame," you know? Whether having shame is good or bad is a separate issue, but let me just say that I myself, now, hate men who use the word "lolicon."

On the one hand, in 1982, Miyazaki identifies with manga/anime fans, who, like he once did, experience a "longing" (*akogare*) for manga/anime characters; the very next year, these fans would be labeled "otaku." On the other hand, Miyazaki feels that these fans are crossing a line by turning their longing into "play" (*asobi*)—the sexual play of fanzines comes to mind—and is upset that they dare to speak of these things openly. While Miyazaki again alludes to Bai-Niang, his anime girlfriend, he is uncomfortable with fans that have no "shame" (*hajirai*) and use words such as "lolicon." And while he "got over" (*sotsugyō*, literally "graduate," as in "out of") it, these fans do not. (There is resonance here with critiques of "otaku" as men that insist on relations with cute girl characters and refuse to "grow up" and "get a life.") They are still in love, and they take it further than Miyazaki ever did—too far for his liking. However much he might have once shared their experience of longing, Miyazaki no longer sees himself as one of these fans, whom he "hates" (*kirai*).

FIGURE 3.9
Lupin III: The Castle of Cagliostro fanzine.

From his perspective, Saitō argues that these unexpectedly harsh words are telling of Miyazaki's own identity and investments (Saitō [2000] 2011, 88–89), and there are reasons to take this seriously. Consider Miyazaki's relationship with another character often mentioned in reports on the lolicon boom, Lana, the heroine of *Future Boy Conan* (Mirai shōnen Konan, 1978).[24] Marking Miyazaki's first turn as the solo director of a full series of television anime, *Future Boy Conan* pays special attention to Lana, to the

'81—'82アニメ総括と展望PART I

③新アイドル"アラレちゃん"の大活躍。"んちゃ""ばいちゃ"とアラレことばも大はやり。

昨年4月の放映開始以来『Dr.スランプ』の人気には目を見はるものがある。視聴率はかるく30%の大台を突破。キャラクター商品も700種と、いままで最高だった『キャンディ・キャンディ』の350種（'76～'81の実績）の倍。レコードでは『アラレちゃん音頭』が生まれ、某大手デパートのポスターには、イメージキャラクターとして登場。そして、中高生ファンのあいだでは「んちゃ」「ばいちゃ」とアラレことばで手紙を書くのが大はやりと、スーパーアイドルぶり。

なぜ、アラレちゃんがこんなにモテるのか!? キャラクター商品を手がけるメーカーに聞いてみると——。

うちのいちばんの人気商品（350種）は「アラレちゃん人形」で2300円から15000円まであります。その人形を、娘さんが2300円の物を買い、おかあさんが5800円の物というように、ファンの年齢層の幅が広いことが、アラレちゃんの人気をささえるひとつだと思います。

原作者の鳥山明さんは、自分が子どもになりきって描いています。だから押しきせでないやさしさが表われていると思います。それを、子どもたちが敏感にかぎつけて、これほどのブームになったともいえるのではないかと思います。

（ポピー開発部・上野和典）

④クラリス、ラナ……日本縦断"ロリコンブーム"。

『カリオストロの城』を上映すると、クラリス登場シーンで、かならず写真をとる30～40歳ぐらいのおじさんがいたとか、コミックマーケットでは手製の"ラナシール"が爆発的に売れているとか……いまや、クラリス、ラナに代表されるいたいけで、かわいらしく、愛くるしい美少女—いってみれば"守ってあげたくなるような女の子"のキャラクターに男性アニメファン（中心は16～25歳）の人気が集中している。

対象になるキャラクターは、先のクラリス・ラナのほかに『パンダコパンダ』のミミコ『ホルスの大冒険』のヒルダ『コナン』のモンスリー、『龍の子太郎』のあや『海のトリトン』のピピなどがあげられる。

ウラジミール・ナボコフの小説『ロリータ』に端を発し命名された「大人の女性に恋愛感情をもてず、少女のみに恋愛感情をいだく男性のコンプレックス」——ロリータ・コンプレックス（略してロリコン）のこのブームは、いまなぜ、おとずれたのだろう。

コミックマーケットの主催者であり、マンガ、アニメ状況にくわしい米沢嘉博さんに"いま、なぜ"を聞いてみた。

[illegible]

（マンガ評論家・米沢嘉博）

◀アラレちゃん音頭のふりつけ

▲某大手デパートのポスター

▲キャラクター商品

▶キャラクター商品

▲ラナちゃんはいつ見てもかっわゆーい!!

▶クラリスの魅力は、芯の強さと清潔感。

▶ペンギン村の住人たちこの明るさが魅力!?

◀『コナン』のモンスリー（少女時代）

FIGURE 3.10 Miyazaki and "the lolicon boom" in *Animage*, February 1982.

extent that richly animated sequences of her in episode 8 became legendary. When an interviewer brings this up in 1983, Miyazaki responds:

> Well, I think I put way too much of my own feelings into episode eight. I did everything I wanted to do my own way. . . . Some people have of course criticized me saying I went overboard. And when I put together the first scripts of the show I, too, frankly thought they were too embarrassing to produce. But by episode[s] five and six, I had grown fonder

> and fonder of Lana. And that made it possible for me to continue. I wouldn't have been able to make the show without feeling this way about her. . . . But I eventually resolved my feelings for Lana. In the beginning, I created her thinking that she was mine, but as we went along I came to see that she belonged to Conan. . . . It's a feeling of extraordinary longing and frustration, an awareness of another world that is out of reach. . . . I would have loved to run like Conan in the show, carrying a girl like that. I'm quite shameless about it. (Miyazaki 2009, 296–97)

What is being relayed here seems to align Miyazaki with lolicon, but it is worth noting the complexity and vagary of his desires. To begin, the character of Lana is eleven years old, as is Conan, the boy hero. Captain Dyce, the adult man that has Lana captive in the opening sequences of episode 8, is closer to Miyazaki's own age in 1983. When Miyazaki talks about his longing for Lana, however, he recalls the past, when he was around her age in elementary and middle school. And Lana exists in the world of animation, "another world that is out of reach," what "otaku" might call the two-dimensional. Although his feelings were intense enough to propel creative activity in difficult conditions, Miyazaki reminds the interviewer—perhaps defensively, perhaps mournfully—that it is "a world of pretend anyway" (296). After opening a space to discuss desire for fictional characters and worlds, Miyazaki reminds himself and others that it is all "pretend"—not "real"—and should not be taken too seriously.

In this context, it is worth zeroing in on the issue of shame. Although Miyazaki claims to be shameless in his desire to run with Lana in his arms, he was embarrassed to share this when planning the anime, which suggests a sense of shame. Likewise, he admits to falling in love with Bai-Niang, which changed his career path and life, but seems ashamed to take this as seriously as it obviously was for him at the time and mockingly describes the work featuring her as cheap melodrama. He got over it, or rather her, in a year. And in 1982, in the thick of the lolicon boom, Miyazaki recalls that he and other anime lovers had shame, which is troublingly absent from those attracted to Princess Clarisse and open and playful in their relationships with her and other characters. To a certain extent, it is precisely because manga/anime fans were no longer ashamed to share their relationships with characters that the discourse about "otaku" emerged in the early 1980s. In niche and minor publications, in fanzines and at special events, manga/anime fans expressed a shared affection for, and orientation toward, cute girl characters.[25] These platforms and spaces allowed for sharing without shame, or at least for shame to be shared in playful and pleasurable ways (more on this in the next section). Ironically, was Miyazaki not involved in exactly this sort of sharing with his confessions about Bai-Niang and Lana? He anticipates that others will dismiss these relationships, at times does so himself, and eventually says that he has given them up, but Miyazaki is still sharing experiences of being powerfully attracted to and moved by anime characters that he loved.

Given this, it is important to note that, in April 1983, Miyazaki offered a much more nuanced take on girl characters and the men that love them. Commenting on two short films by the Waseda University Animation Club, both focusing on shōjo, Miyazaki begins by declaring that he cannot reject such works, because, "I am also one of these filmmakers" (Miyazaki 2009, 131). Thus coming out and establishing connections, however obliquely, Miyazaki goes on to explain why some men focus on shōjo:

> At a certain period in life—that unbalanced time of transformation from boyhood to youth—young males with a certain tendency start to see a sacred symbolism in stories about girls. . . . Their repressed feelings are too deep to be dismissed by insisting that they just have a Lolita complex or that resolving it in role-playing games is perfectly fine. This type of youth begins to feed the girl within himself. The girl is part of him, and a projection of himself. . . . These girls express nostalgia for a self that was free of the detritus of life. The girl is not living outside of him; she is the very self that he has nurtured inside himself. As I stated at the start, I am one of these filmmakers. . . . What is the good of analyzing, negating, and suppressing the longings and feelings that exist as definite forms inside of me? (Miyazaki 2009, 130–31)

In that Miyazaki goes on to juxtapose the girl and masculine/adult world, his is an eloquent statement on "male" shōjo fandom. This girl, nurtured in one's self, could very well open up other ways of seeing and being (Itō Kimio 2010, 176). Miyazaki's words might also apply to many so-called lolicon artists, who, like Miyazaki himself in the early 1980s, focused on shōjo, or rather bishōjo, characters.[26]

Even as Miyazaki was coming to recognize his focus on girl characters, he was also adapting his successful manga *Nausicaä of the Valley of the Wind* (Kaze no tani no Naushika, 1982–94) into an animated feature film. Published in *Animage*, a major platform for manga/anime fandom in the early 1980s, Miyazaki's *Nausicaä* was a popular feature of the magazine, and regular articles kept readers apprised of the adaptation process. As a manga character admired in its pages and an upcoming anime character, Princess Nausicaä was often the cover girl of *Animage*. Directed by Miyazaki, the film version of *Nausicaä of the Valley of the Wind* (1984) became a touchstone of manga/anime fandom in Japan. Subsequently becoming one of the most beloved characters in manga/anime history, Princess Nausicaä was regularly voted to the top spot on rankings that *Animage* compiled from reader responses and prominently displayed. Put somewhat differently, in the early 1980s, *Animage* was printing images of Princess Nausicaä from the manga series and animated film, had her on its cover, and organized character rankings that encouraged fans to communicate their affection for her.

Albeit less direct than *Manga Burikko* and the like, *Animage*, which promoted and profited from affective relations between fans and fictional characters, also functioned as a "Two-Dimensional Idol Comic Magazine."[27] It should not be missed that Miyazaki was at the epicenter of this, or that he was at the very least aware of, if not courting, fan interest in cute girl characters such as Princess Nausicaä. Consider the following exchange in the *Nausicaä of the Valley of the Wind* companion book from May 1984:

INTERVIEWER "Nausicaä, the girl, is so attractive."
MIYAZAKI "Nausicaä's breasts are rather large, aren't they?"
INTERVIEWER "Yes. (Laughs)" (Miyazaki 2009, 338)

Published by Tokuma Shoten, the company behind *Animage*, this companion book targeted fans, who would certainly have been in on Miyazaki's joke. The interviewer laughs because Miyazaki directly says what many fans are thinking. The in-group communication and appeal does not stop there. Critics point out that the voice actress for Princess Nausicaä is the same as for Princess Clarisse—an icon of the lolicon boom—and that the character design in the animated film is more sexual than in the manga (Schodt 1996, 279–80).[28] In the companion book, Miyazaki draws attention to the eroticized figure, which attracted and moved others. For example, Yamamoto Naoki (aka Moriyama Tō), an influential artist known for pornographic manga featuring cute girl characters, recalls that Miyazaki's animated feature film awakened him to the possibility of shōjo characters with a more substantial bust (Azuma and Yamamoto 2011, 142). Drawing and redrawing the character so much that he "almost died," Yamamoto folded Princess Nausicaä into his own designs.

Much has been made of the shift from male to female protagonists in Miyazaki's work from the late 1970s into the 1980s (e.g., Lamarre 2009a,

77–85), and his own thoughtful analyses often support readings of social and political significance. However, if one pursues Saitō's provocation that the underlying issue for Miyazaki is his relations with the anime girl as "trauma," then other statements snap into focus. Consider the following one from 1994, which came in response to a question that had by then become familiar: "Why do you always have girls as your main characters?"

> It's not from any logical thinking. It just seems to me that when you compare a boy doing something with a girl doing that same thing, the girl is much more spirited. If a boy is walking with long strides I think nothing of it, but if a girl is walking boldly, I think she looks so full of vitality. That's because I'm a man; women might think a boy striding along looks cool. At first I thought, "It's no longer a man's world; no longer an age when just causes are relevant." But after 10 years, it seems silly to keep saying that. So now, when people ask me your question, I just respond, "Because I like girls." That answer seems more real. (Miyazaki 2009, 428)

Coming ten years after the release of *Nausicaä of the Valley of the Wind*, which is so pivotal to conceptualizations of the female protagonist in his work, there are a few things to underscore in this proclamation: first, the girl seems to Miyazaki to be "full of vitality"; second, Miyazaki is attracted to the girl as a man that feels the limitations of "a man's world"; and third, Miyazaki focuses on girl characters because he "likes girls." Given his previous comments on the subject, one might qualify this by saying that Miyazaki likes *animated* girls, who are full of vitality (what Tezuka Osamu calls the power of life) and whose movement suggests something beyond the world of men.

In reflective moments, Miyazaki speaks about this world as beyond not only men, but also that which is "real." Consider again, for example, *Future Boy Conan*. On the one hand, it is "a world of pretend," but, on the other, Miyazaki longs for this world in which he runs with Lana in his arms. This is another world, an animated one, what "otaku" might call the two-dimensional. Now, Miyazaki acknowledges his "extraordinary longing and frustration, an awareness of another world that is out of reach" (Miyazaki 2009, 296–97), but what is it about animation that attracts him so? In a particularly dense section of an interview about *Future Boy Conan* in 1983, Miyazaki concentrates on the power of animation to not only make things move but also transform (305). The possibility of other forms, of transforming, draws viewers in:

> I think that cartoon movies above all help our spirits relax, they make us feel happy, and they make us feel refreshed. And while doing so, they may also allow us to escape from ourselves. . . . I like the expression "lost possibilities." To be born means being compelled to choose an era, a place, and a life. To exist here, now, means to lose the possibility of being countless other potential selves. For example, I might have been the captain of a pirate ship, sailing with a lovely princess by my side. It means giving up this universe, giving up other potential selves. There are selves which are lost possibilities, and selves that could have been, and this is not limited just to us but to people around us and even to Japan itself. Yet once born there is no turning back. And I think that's exactly why the fantasy worlds of cartoon movies so strongly represent our hopes and yearnings. They illustrate a world of lost possibilities for us. (Miyazaki 2009, 306–7)

At face value, Miyazaki appears to be talking about his own "potential selves" (*arieta kamoshirenai jibun*) and "lost possibilities" (*ushinawareta kanōsei*). Knowing his feelings for the heroine, it is not much of an imaginative stretch to see the pirate that Miyazaki might have been as Captain Dyce with Lana at his side. Knowing that he "would have loved to run . . . carrying a girl like" (Miyazaki 2009, 296–97) Lana in his arms, it is also not much of an imaginative stretch to see that Miyazaki might have been Conan. And knowing that men such as he nurture a girl within (130–31), it is certainly not difficult to imagine that Miyazaki might also have been Lana.

Beyond this, however, lies something even more radical. Not only might he have been born in a different place and time and in different circumstances, been a different boy or man, girl or woman, but Miyazaki might also have been a nonhuman animal or plant, a machine or cloud. That is, beyond potential selves, lost possibilities include *forms* other than the one settled in. Animation brings forms to life, and those interacting with animated forms get caught up in their movements. Thus not only does animation allow for "escape from ourselves" (Miyazaki 2009, 306–7), as Miyazaki puts it, but also for escape from our form and world in frozen form—movement in "a freer, more open world" (*motto jiyū na, ōraka na sekai*). It is not only about imagining other selves, forms, and sets of relations, but also other worlds, which for Miyazaki means something beyond "Japan" and the "real world" (*genjitsu shakai*). Contrary to Miyazaki's words above, one does not choose a self, form, or world, but rather emerges in the actual out of the virtual, where other possibilities lie. In a way, then, animation approaches the virtual—drawing forms into the actual. Like Tezuka Osamu before him, Miyazaki Hayao sees and seeks in animation the world of "plasmaticness" (Eisenstein 1986, 21), "plasmatic possibility," and "the pleasures of the plasmatic" (Bukatman 2012, 20).

After the arrest of the "otaku" murderer (see chapter 2), Miyazaki again denounced lolicon and playing with characters in the November 1989 issue of *Animage*, but he nevertheless grants that eroticism is part of his creative process. For example, Miyazaki reportedly regards an essay titled "The Fireworks of Eros" by his friend and frequent collaborator Takahata Isao as the best evaluation of his work (McCarthy 1999, 30). In that essay, Takahata writes of Miyazaki, "his spirit of self-control and self-denial, and his sense of shame and embarrassment . . . far exceed that of most people, so that he sometimes tries to hide them, with the result that his way of expressing himself may occasionally come out twisted and tangled up" (Takahata 2009, 454). Cutting through this, Takahata describes Miyazaki as a man that "feels things in an unusually powerful way" (456), including the movements of his characters, which can bring him to tears. By Takahata's estimation, Miyazaki is a man that "possesses an imagination so vivid it verges on a hallucinatory vision" (457) a man that "fluffs up his fantasies using his powers of visual imagination, sees all sorts of illusions, thrills to the idea that they might actually come true, and is beside himself with anticipation" (459). In an example that suggests the complex, partial, and shifting positions of self and other in animated worlds, Takahata draws attention to Miyazaki's desire for girl characters:

> He wants to save beautiful young females from trouble, he wants a middle-aged "pig" to act cool, and he wants a young woman character to be so beautiful, sensible, action-oriented, and noble that he would like to suddenly embrace her. . . . And his feelings about his characters grow stronger and stronger, to the point where he finally becomes possessed by this or that young woman or monster that doesn't resemble him in the least. . . . He remains possessed by, and fuses with, his characters—to the point where the heightened fireworks of Eros that result actually transform his ideals into flesh and blood. (Takahata 2009, 456)

Note how Miyazaki gets caught up in the movements of his characters and becomes possessed by—no, *becomes*—them, man and woman, human and nonhuman, monster and other. And so the fiction becomes real, flesh and blood, brought to life by imagination and creativity. Key here, Takahata argues, is eroticism, because Miyazaki "can only accomplish what he does when propelled by Eros" and so turns "the creative process into an erotic adventure" (Takahata 2009, 458). For his part, Miyazaki agrees that he could not have made *Future Boy Conan* without feeling the way he did about Lana, and powerful feelings for characters seem to inspire his work more generally.[29] Indeed, if one follows Saitō, then Miyazaki's career begins with falling in love with an anime character. Turning to this love, we come to our third perspective on moe.

Perspective Three: Character Love, Love Revolution

From the late 1970s into the early 1980s, manga/anime fans began to approach manga/anime characters as objects of desire and affection. In personal interviews, manga/anime critics often emphasized the lolicon boom and growing visibility of fans of characters created by Azuma Hideo, Miyazaki Hayao, and others. Numerous characters were mentioned, but a persistent one was Lum from Takahashi Rumiko's *Urusei Yatsura* (Those Obnoxious Aliens, 1978–87). Lum is a bishōjo, or cute girl character, and like Azuma Hideo's bishōjo, she appeared in manga that mixed gags, science fiction, fantasy, absurdity, and sexuality. Conspicuously different from Azuma, however, Takahashi introduced elements of romantic comedy and drama, as the alien Lum tries to make a life with the earthman that has won her heart. Also unlike Azuma's more underground and niche works, Takahashi's manga was a breakout hit serialized in the mainstream *Weekly Shōnen Sunday* for a decade and adapted into a long-running series of television anime (1981–86), six feature films, and twelve straight-to-video releases. In Japan in the 1980s, straight-to-video releases were a new format that targeted fans willing to pay for content (Clements 2013, 167–71). *Urusei Yatsura* fans were willing to pay for this and more, it turns out, because of Lum, who is a bombshell. Dressed in a tiger-skin bikini and a consistent character image central to the branding and marketing of the franchise, it is perhaps not too much to say that Lum became manga/anime's first major pinup girl.

Given this, it is not so surprising that *Urusei Yatsura* is remembered as a key title in the history of moe. The memory is typically of, on the one hand, intensely personal feelings for Lum, which, on the other hand, were shared by a generation of manga/anime fans. Consider, for example, how Ichikawa Kō'ichi, who was forty-one years old when we met in 2008, talks about the franchise and its impact: "I was a normal Japanese boy. But then I saw

Takahashi Rumiko's *Urusei Yatsura*. It had the first harem, and the character Lum-chan. She was a super sex symbol in Japan, what movie stars are in France and America, and was my first love. Lum-chan is the source of moe, the queen. She's the first *tsundere* character. The show had everything, and I was really interested in comparing the manga and the anime, the anime and the movies, and eventually in getting my hands on things that weren't in stores."[30] The quote is teeming with connections, but a few things stand out immediately. First, note how Ichikawa describes Lum. While a manga/anime character, Lum is for him a sex symbol on equal footing with any movie star. In fact, she seems to mean more to Ichikawa, who crowns her "the queen." Second, note the relationship between Ichikawa and Lum. Encountering her as a young man, Ichikawa recognizes Lum as his "first love," a love before anyone else and anyone supposedly more "real." Having followed her in the manga, anime, films, and more for decades, Ichikawa affectionately calls the character Lum-chan, "-chan" being a suffix attached to the names of people that are familiar, intimate, or close. Third, note how Ichikawa treats his relationship with Lum as a life-changing one. Before Lum, Ichikawa was "normal," but he became something else after. It seems that Ichikawa is here flagging his desire and affection for Lum, which made him somehow "abnormal" (an "otaku").

Not only does he present Lum as a sex symbol, not only is she part of a cast of bishōjo that are an imaginary "harem" for the male protagonist and fan, and not only were these characters marketed in frankly sexual ways, but Ichikawa also pursued things "that weren't in stores," which refers to pornographic drawings produced by and for fans. Attending the Comic Market since 1983—the same year that Nakamori Akio started writing about "otaku"—Ichikawa went on to have a booth there and eventually take a leading role in the preparations committee. Although girls and women had dominated the event for much of the 1970s, *Urusei Yatsura* factored into increased male participation at the Comic Market in the early 1980s (Comic Market Committee 2014, 28). Fanzines by and for these male fans were everywhere, as cultural critic Azuma Hiroki recalled in a personal interview: "I first visited Tokyo's gathering for producers of fanzines, the Comic Market, in 1984 or 1985, and fanzines devoted to characters from manga and anime series such as *Urusei Yatsura* . . . were everywhere. The fans were responding to characters, without a doubt. Actually, to me, *Urusei Yatsura* is really an ancestor of bishōjo games and moe media—a completely useless male character is surrounded by all these cute girl characters, including Lum, an alien girl who wears a bikini and is in love with this male character."[31] This is again teeming with connections, but suffice it to say that Azuma sees much of what Ichikawa does in *Urusei Yatsura*, which has a male protagonist surrounded by bishōjo, including Lum, who is sexy in her bikini and madly in love. While Ichikawa associates this with a "harem" and Azuma with "bishōjo games," which allow players to interact with cute girl characters romantically and sexually (Clements 2013, 201–2), crucial here is that *Urusei Yatsura* is positioned as a model of "moe media." Similar to films that "appeal to the body" (Williams 1989, 5), moe media is meant to trigger an affective response, which it does through characters. If, as Azuma argues, contemporary manga/anime focuses on "moe elements" (Azuma [2001] 2009, 42–53), then *Urusei Yatsura* and its characters can retrospectively be seen as possessing them in spades. For example, Ichikawa characterizes Lum as "tsundere," a type that is cold or harsh to the protagonist but in time reveals a warm or soft side. Replicated in moe media and characters, tsundere has become a trope (Galbraith 2009b, 226–27).

In addition to official and fan-produced media, Lum also began to appear in material form. In a personal interview, Bome, who professionally sculpts figurines of manga/anime characters, reminisced about the explosive popularity of Lum in the 1980s: "At the time, the TV series was on and many people were making Lum-chan figurines, including me. We were all kind of like, 'My Lum-chan is better than yours!' There was a time when Lum-chan overwhelmed the Comic Market. People said when you put her on the cover, the book would sell. I believe that she was a revolutionary character. Before that, there were no manga or anime for boys that had female characters as the lead."[32] Ignoring the male protagonist, Bome sees Lum as the lead of *Urusei Yatsura*. If Princess Nausicaä inspired Yamamoto Naoki and others, it was Lum that inspired Bome to create. Again Lum is a familiar presence ("-chan"), and fans responded to her by producing fanzines and figurines. The character and relationship with her are thus personalized ("my Lum-chan") even as they are shared ("is better than yours"). As fan demands and activities fed back into the industry—Bome, for example, was hired by Kaiyōdō—figurines have become part of the manga/anime ecology and another standard way to encounter characters. Spreading out into the world, characters become part of everyday life. In the 1980s, some fans took this further by carrying material representations of Lum with them, which extended contact and copresence spatially and temporally, even as it introduced her into social interactions and relations.

Echoing Ichikawa, Bome also recognizes Lum as his "first love" (*hatsukoi*), which draws attention to how this manga/anime character became a lover for manga/anime fans. In many ways, Takahashi Rumiko, a female artist, seems to have been parodying male desire in *Urusei Yatsura*, which lingers on images of hoards of horny earthmen ogling Lum, a busty alien babe in a bikini. This was at least partially an elaborate joke, as anime historian Jonathan Clements (2016) points out, referring to a pinup girl popular in Japanese magazines in the 1970s. Photographs of pinup girls at the time were shot to present the viewer with a "virtual companion," or, as Clements puts it, "her company, her attention" in intimate settings, moments of exposure, and returning the gaze. Onto the scene came Agnes Lum, who was born in Hawaiʻi and became a sensation in Japan (figure 3.10):

> The fiercely attractive Lum was notable for her magnificent boobs, a feature less prominent in Japanese girls of the day, which soon lured her photographers away from urban fashion shoots and into the realm of swimwear, all the better to show them off. This, in turn, incentivised beach locations, and it was not long before the expense and exoticism of teen photo-shoots began to spiral upwards. Wouldn't *you* rather put a weekend in Hawaii on expenses? The male population's panting obsession with a pneumatic, bikini-clad foreigner was soon satirised by manga creator Rumiko Takahashi in *Urusei Yatsura* and its iconic Lum-chan, a green-haired, sexually aggressive devil girl in a tiger-skin two-piece. (Clements 2016)

While perhaps not intended to be entirely serious, foregrounding Lum's largely naked cartoon body served to highlight its distinct appeal. Indeed, as Ichikawa, Bome, and many others testify, the character Lum—and Clements, too, cannot help but call her "-chan"—was for her fans not a parody of the "real" Lum. Rather than referring to Agnes Lum, the character Lum was a separate existence and object of desire. She was a pinup girl in her own right (figure 3.11). Identifying this as a watershed moment, sociologist Yoshimoto Taimatsu argues that manga/anime characters had become "sensual" (*nikkan-teki*) and "sexual" (*sei-teki*) (Yoshimoto 2009, 169). From here, it is a short step to manga/anime characters as "two-dimensional idols" in *Lemon People* and *Manga Burikko*, and pornographic animation such as *Lolita Anime* and *Cream Lemon* (Kurīmu remon, 1984–2006), which presented, in progressive detail, the bodies of manga/anime characters as lovers.

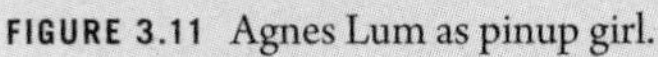

FIGURE 3.11 Agnes Lum as pinup girl.

FIGURE 3.12 "Lum-chan" as pinup girl.

Exchanges with devoted fans, however, make plain that Lum's appeal was not limited to sex. In *Urusei Yatsura*, Takahashi combines bodily exposure and bawdy humor with romance and drama. Formally, the manga/anime is an example of what media theorist Thomas Lamarre dubs "serial romance," in which tension remains between characters due to ceaseless interruptions and obstacles to a climax, be it sex or a stable relationship (Lamarre 2009b, 56). The core tension in *Urusei Yatsura* comes from Lum wanting to marry and settle down with the male protagonist, who is a would-be Lothario that chases after any and all women. (More parody of male desire?) In addition, an ever-expanding cast of humans, aliens, and others appear and pull the couple hither, thither, and yon. The result is that Lum and the male protagonist "remain in limbo, trying to work out how to live together, not as man and wife but as quasi-man and quasi-wife, as an off-kilter unmarried couple, one whose relationship is subject to potentially endless serialization (even if the series itself does not continue)" (55–56).

True to form, the relationship between Lum, her intended husband, and the rest carried on across manga, anime, films, straight-to-video releases, and, even after that all concluded, fanzines.

Over the course of the serial romance, Takahashi developed the character of Lum from a sex object into a full-fledged subject with interiority and depth. *Urusei Yatsura* features numerous scenes of the usually exuberant and always superpowered Lum looking vulnerable and emotionally devastated. For those watching closely, it was all too obvious that behind the gags and glamour shots was a young woman in love, who could be and was hurt by the male protagonist (Sasakibara 2004, 63–69). Even as they feel for Lum, fans fall for her. They want Lum to be happy, which seems to mean for her marrying the male protagonist, but what fan would approve of someone so insensitive? He is, frankly speaking, an absolute jerk that is unappreciative of her and at times outright abusive. They want better for Lum, to make her happy. Imaginatively, fans step in and become Lum's lovers, who will do right by her; imaginatively, they are the ones that marry her. ("Marriage" to favorite characters would become a meme in manga/anime fandom, as discussed below.) As fans fell in love with Lum, they extended relations with her into everyday life, aided by material representations, which proliferated without end. The serial romance thus shifted to Lum and her lovers in the three-dimensional, the climax interrupted by her absence, even as media and material made her present.

We have, then, Lum as lover. On the one hand, the bodacious alien, object of desire, and on the other, the leading lady of a romantic comedy and drama, object of affection. Initially attracted to the character image, over weeks, months, and years, fans grew to know Lum, if not also care about her. Indeed, fans such as Ichikawa and Bome say that they fell in love with the character, who was their first love. This brings to mind Miyazaki Hayao and Bai-Niang, his "surrogate girlfriend" (Miyazaki 2009, 19), but *Urusei Yatsura* fans did not qualify their relationship with Lum as anything less than real. Like the pinup girls that inform her design, Lum returns the viewer's gaze, which serves to establish a relationship. Even as "girlfriend experiences," or "the simple presence of a female making eye contact" (Clements 2016), transfer from pinup photography to manga and anime, the girlfriend or female is a manga/anime character. Fans responded, further bringing the character and relationship into reality. Put bluntly, even as Azuma Hideo's *Cybele* was sparking the lolicon boom, even as fans were rallying to Miyazaki's *Lupin III: The Castle of Cagliostro,* Takahashi created a manga/anime character as lover.

In the early 1980s, two-dimensional idols would become a mainstay in the pages of *Manga Burikko,* where an orientation of desire toward fiction was explicit enough to trigger debates about the imagined excesses and perversions of "otaku," but the discourse surrounding moe suggests a shift in perception. Consider how, for example, Azuma Hiroki defines moe: "In the original meaning, it was something only used when talking about characters—you didn't say you felt moe for a human being. Moe referred to a sort of perverse way of experiencing feelings of love—loving a fictional character as though it was a real person."[33] One hears reverberations of critiques of "otaku," who do not love like "normal people," but many manga/anime fans define moe without mentioning perversion. Moe is "an expression of affection for fictional characters"; "the expression of feelings for fictional characters"; "affection for a character"; "a feeling of love for fictional characters"; "a feeling like love, but a sort of bittersweet love"; "like falling in love for the first time"; "it means I love that character."[34] Taken together, these statements point toward a growing awareness and acceptance of character love in Japan.

The word "moe" first appeared as slang in the early 1990s, and the affective relations with characters that it indicates were to a certain extent normalized in that decade. Despite an economic crash and recession that led to social and political unrest (Leheny 2006b, 27–47), manga, anime, and games featuring manga/anime characters roared on in Japan in the 1990s. This was a time when manga magazines had circulations in the millions—*Weekly Shōnen Jump,* for example, circulated six million copies—and manga accounted for some 40 percent of all print publications (Schodt 1996, 19, 90). Around ninety anime were airing on television each week (Condry 2013, 86, 106), including smash hits such as *Dragon Ball Z* (Doragon bōru zetto, 1989–) and *Sailor Moon* (Bishōjo senshi Sērā Mūn, 1992–). Regardless of backlash against "harmful manga" and "otaku," cute girl characters were becoming increasingly mainstream (Akagi 1993, 231; Kinsella 2000, 122–23), most evidently through *Sailor Moon,* which includes the term "bishōjo" in its Japanese title. A magical girl series ostensibly for children, *Sailor Moon* also captivated adult men (Allison 2006, 133–34). Far from unexpected, some submit that the anime in fact played up the sex appeal of its characters through costuming and posing (Morikawa 2003, 93). Although not without critics, the Comic Market enjoyed skyrocketing attendance in the 1990s (Comic Market Committee 2014, 26), which speaks to an intense demand for fanzines dedicated to popular manga/anime characters.

Concomitantly, bishōjo games, which allow players to interact romantically and sexually with cute girl characters, transformed from the relatively basic pornography that they had been in the 1980s into a more mainstream and melodramatic genre in the 1990s (Kagami 2010, 136–38). These games overwhelmingly feature manga/anime-style characters, which announces a preference for something other than "real" (Morikawa 2003, 97–99). Possible links to *Urusei Yatsura* aside, bishōjo games are all about "virtual companions" and "girlfriend experiences" (Clements 2016). Viewed from a first-person perspective, the characters stare out of the screen and directly at the player, returning the gaze and establishing a relationship (Sasakibara 2003, 105, 107; also Greenwood 2014). The majority of game time is devoted to dialogue with characters, whom the player comes to know, if not care about, as the story advances over the course of hours and days. Blending romance and sex, Elf's *Classmates 2* (Dōkyūsei 2, 1995); Leaf's *Drops* (Shizuku, 1996), *Scar* (Kizuato, 1996), and *To Heart* (Tu hāto, 1997); and Key's *Kanon* (Kanon, 1999), *Air* (Eā, 2000), and *Clannad* (Kuranado, 2004) led to a renaissance in novelistic stories, compelling characters, and moving moments that brought players to tears (Galbraith 2014, 104–5, 124–25). This in turn fed back into the manga/anime ecology, as bishōjo games were adapted into series. Sex scenes were removed from releases for "general audiences" but still implied, and explicit content was at any rate part of the media mix, which as always centered on affective relations with characters. The situation was such in the 1990s that Konami's *Tokimeki Memorial* (Tokimeki memoriaru, 1994), a bishōjo game that focuses on simulated dating and targets general audiences, became a national phenomenon. The primary love interest of players, Fujisaki Shiori, was literally an idol. Her single "Tell Me, Mr. Sky" (Oshiete Mr. Sky, 1996)—officially sung by the character, not anyone more "real"—reached number 21 on the Oricon charts (Ōtsuka 2004, 18). Indeed, *Tokimeki Memorial* is said to have sparked one of the two big booms that contributed to the spread of moe (Galbraith 2014, 159).

The other is *Neon Genesis Evangelion* (Shin seiki Evangerion, 1995–96), a television anime produced by Gainax and directed by Anno Hideaki. Founded by fans that collaborated on amateur animation featuring cute girl characters during the lolicon boom, Gainax made a name for itself by catering to fans.[35] For example, in a particularly vibrant sequence in *Daicon IV Opening Animation* (1983), a buxom bishōjo in a Playboy bunny suit rotates sharply to face the viewer while raising her fists in triumph, and momentum leads to her breasts jiggling in ways hitherto unseen in anime.[36] In subsequent years, Gainax often focused on the bodies of cute girl characters to appeal to fans and sell straight-to-video animation such as *Gunbuster* (Toppu wo nerae, 1988–89). Struggling to make money, the scrappy studio also put out bishōjo games such as *Princess Maker* (Purinsesu mēkā, 1991) and *CYBERNETIC HI-SCHOOL* (Den'nō gakuen, 1989–91), the latter of which includes characters from its anime series in sexual situations. As Clements rightly argues, "Gainax's main advantages in the competition for consumer attention were quality of artwork and the ability to subvert their own characters" (Clements 2013, 201), but it was not until *Neon Genesis Evangelion* that the value of such subversion became truly apparent.

By the time of the concurrent manga publication and anime broadcast of *Neon Genesis Evangelion*, Gainax had completed its company website and was courting fans, which encouraged active engagement and helped the franchise catch on (Clements 2013, 2, 208). If manga/anime fans gathering online used the word "moe" as slang in discussions of characters in the early 1990s, then *Neon Genesis Evangelion* pushed this to new heights later in the decade. Indeed, the anime is often remembered for characters that trigger an affective response. Working on a tight budget, Gainax adopted techniques of limited animation, and illustrator Sadamoto Yoshiyuki needed to design characters that could attract and hold attention while remaining still (Lamarre 2009a, 201). Put somewhat differently, the characters were designed to suggest inner movement and to move viewers without necessarily moving themselves. In this respect, *Neon Genesis Evangelion* resembled bishōjo games, which focus on static character images that appeal directly to the viewer/interactor (Clements 2013, 201–2). Like *Sailor Moon* and bishōjo games, some critics argue that *Neon Genesis Evangelion* emphasized the sex appeal of its cute girl characters by design (Morikawa 2003, 93). Also like *Sailor Moon* and bishōjo games, *Neon Genesis Evangelion* featured the talents of professional voice actresses revered for their ability to produce manga/anime characters that move fans.

Although it has been implied that some fans were more interested in the cute characters than in the complex and cryptic story of *Neon Genesis Evangelion* (Azuma [2001] 2009, 36–38), the story in fact functions to make the characters more captivating and interactions between them more moving. A prime example of this is Ayanami Rei, perhaps the most beloved character in the franchise, who has been called a "goddess," an "icon of Japanese anime," and the "most iconic character of the 1990s" (Newtype 2010). Said to have become a character archetype, elements of Ayanami can be recognized in derivative forms throughout anime since

(Azuma [2001] 2009, 49–52). Even as pundits speculate, "There are probably a million men in Japan that are in love with Ayanami Rei" (Nikkei Net 2007), the producers of *Neon Genesis Evangelion* acted as matchmakers pushing fans to her with the story.[37] As things begin to unravel in the postapocalyptic world of the manga/anime, it is revealed that Ayanami is a clone, and the one that the viewer/interactor has come to know is not the first; there have been Ayanamis before her that died in various ways; dozens more are prepared in test tubes and wait to replace Ayanami, who is distinguished only by her social experiences. The clones are created using the DNA of the male protagonist's deceased mother, which makes Ayanami's position as a love interest that much more complicated. And Ayanami also seems to be somehow related to Lilith, a primordial creature and the mother of all humans.[38] This information all comes in bits and pieces, and the typically expressionless and quiet Ayanami remains a mystery for most of the series.

Even as it builds up compounding fascination with Ayanami, *Neon Genesis Evangelion* includes numerous scenes involving the character that powerfully affect the viewer/interactor. Consider, for example, episode 6, at which point the viewer/interactor still knows little about Ayanami other than her solitude, silence, and "special" relationship with the male protagonist's father. If anything, she has been cold to the male protagonist, whose fraught relationship with his father causes friction between them. When she and the male protagonist are tasked with defeating a giant enemy invader, however, Ayanami assures the terrified boy that she will protect him at all cost; if she dies in the process, the girl adds, there are replacements. Not yet realizing that Ayanami is a clone, the viewer/interactor takes this to mean that she is a disposable pawn for the father, much like the male protagonist. Ostensibly only fourteen years old and fighting on her own until now, it is painful to hear Ayanami flatly tell the male protagonist goodbye before the battle. The effect is amplified by voice actress Hayashibara Megumi's delivery of the Japanese "sayonara," which has a sense of casual finality. When Ayanami does indeed almost die, the male protagonist rushes to her side. Also fourteen and breaking down at the sight of her, the male protagonist weeps. After uncomfortably staring at the boy for a time, confused by his display of raw emotion, Ayanami finally seems to see him. Gently, she smiles. In this moment, a close-up of Ayanami almost seems to have her looking at the screen and the viewer, who becomes an interactor in relation with her, and a combination of visuals, sound, and direct appeal trigger an affective response (figure 3.13).

FIGURE 3.13
Ayanami smiles and fans melt.

A frustratingly convoluted work that is arguably open for interpretation, *Neon Genesis Evangelion* fired the imagination of fans, even as its characters captured their hearts. After a shockingly abstract but somehow hopeful wrap to the television series, director Anno brought the story to a crushing conclusion with *The End of Evangelion* (Shin seiki Evangerion gekijō-ban: Ea/magokoro wo kimi ni, 1997), which brutally killed off popular characters, including Ayanami, and fans responded by producing alternatives. In a more literal sense of Saitō's "trauma" (Saitō [2000] 2011, 88–89, 116), fans in love with characters were moved so violently that they joined the burgeoning ranks of manga/anime creators in Japan in the late 1990s (Galbraith 2014, 119).

For its part, Gainax seemed to anticipate fan activity from the beginning of *Neon Genesis Evangelion,* which is reflected in the franchise itself. Famously, in each preview for the next episode, one of the voice actresses promised viewers—in character—that there would be "service" (*sābisu*), which refers to the convention of including titillating content for fans. While director Anno undermined that promise and viewer expectations in the anime itself, Gainax in turn released content featuring its characters and appealing to fans. Azuma explains: "In the case of *Evangelion,* . . . there were no sequels and no plans to make sequels. Instead, the original creator's production company, Gainax, developed . . . derivative works . . . and at the same time created plans for related concepts; for instance, there are mahjong games, erotic telephone card designs using the *Evangelion* characters, and [so much more]" (Azuma [2001] 2009, 37). Even as anime lovers extended their relations with characters in fanzines, Gainax provided them with *Neon Genesis Evangelion: Ayanami Raising Project* (Shin seiki Evangerion: Ayanami ikusei keikaku, 2001), a bishōjo game that allows the player to virtually spend time with Ayanami and influence her development. Fitting in with the story as it does, the game invites fans to step into the world of *Neon Genesis Evangelion* and nurture their own clone character. This is very much fan art and fiction, but produced by Gainax. Indeed, official and fan production converge. Again, Azuma: "Anno Hideaki (the director of *Evangelion*) anticipated the appearance of derivative works . . . from the beginning, setting up various gimmicks within the original to promote those products. For instance, a scene from a parallel *Evangelion* world is inserted in the final episode of the television series. In that parallel world with a completely different history, an Ayanami Rei dwells with a completely different personality. But in fact the scene depicted there was already a parody of an image that had been widely circulated as a derivative work at the time of the original broadcast" (Azuma [2001] 2009, 38). The scene in question spotlights a hyperactive, talkative, and extremely expressive Ayanami, who arrives as a transfer student at the male protagonist's middle school in what appears to be a romantic comedy and drama in the making. This is Ayanami out of character, or rather a reimagining of the character along the lines of fan fiction and art. The scene, then, is an official fan parody, or a parody of fan works integrated into the original. Furthermore, it has been intimated that the scene is also a parody of Anno's initial idea for *Neon Genesis Evangelion* as something more typical—like *Urusei Yatsura*, perhaps—that would "make anime lovers happy" (Gwern 2012).[39]

Learning from previous experience to reserve rights and cash in on character media and merchandise (Takeda 2005, 132), Gainax ushered in a new era with *Neon Genesis Evangelion*. Responding to and reinforcing fan affection, the market for character figurines reportedly grew tenfold (Galbraith 2014, 159–60). Figurines of Ayanami especially—clones of clones, as it were, designed to attract and affect—"sold like wild fire" and "ignited a boom in merchandise unprecedented in a country already awash with such goods" (Fujie and Foster 2004, 98, 126). Beyond figurines, as commentators Kazuhisa Fujie and Martin Foster write, Ayanami "Rei's popularity soared in Japan, with books featuring her image on the cover selling like hot cakes. She was christened by the media, 'The girl who manipulates magazine sales at will,' 'The fastest route to the sold-out sign!' and even, 'The Premium Girl'" (39). Entire fanzine conventions were committed to the series and its characters, and mainstream bookstores nationwide had *Neon Genesis Evangelion* sections. In a sea of media and material representations, characters often compete for attention by appearing in fetish costumes and being posed provocatively, which brings to mind the design sense of *Urusei Yatsura* and subverts *Neon Genesis Evangelion* according to Gainax's plans. The service promised and denied in the anime proper does come, much to the delight of fans, who pay handsomely for it. While some may go "too far" (126), there is an undeniable demand for these media and material representations, which ground and expand fan relationships with characters through physical contact and copresence. There are figurines that reproduce voices, even life-sized versions (figure 3.14).

Called a "social phenomenon" (Takeda 2005, 166) and "estimated to have generated 30 billion yen" (Morikawa 2012, 147), *Neon Genesis Evangelion* intensified the business of media mixes, emphasizing affective relations with characters and inspiring countless imitators. Following the *Tokimeki Memorial* boom, *Neon Genesis Evangelion* touched off a subsequent explosion of anime focusing on cute girl characters, overlapped with the bishōjo game revolution, and accelerated content crossover. Amid all this, character love ceased to seem as strange as it once had. In a personal interview, Saitō updated his theory of trauma to describe something much more mundane: "It is my impression that if men come into contact with anime, manga, and games, a certain portion will become 'otaku.' This seems to have little to do with personal history, and more to do with social factors—if the encounter and attraction is allowed, even encouraged, by a certain environment."[40] While aware that there are also women that love manga/anime characters (Saitō 2007), "otaku" are stereotypically understood to be "men" (Kam 2013b, 163–65), specifically and historically those attracted to bishōjo, and Saitō argues that social factors are no longer discouraging this as strongly as they did in previous decades. In Saitō's opinion, the presence of attractive manga/anime characters, as well as an environment that supports rather than condemns relationships with them, is key to comprehending what is happening with moe. In a personal interview, Momoi Halko, a voice actress, singer, and producer long associated with bishōjo games and anime, agreed:

まさにサードインパクト!!

等身大

SCOOP

新世紀エヴァンゲリオン

綾波レイ

登場!!

身長1m59cm

•57

FIGURE 3.14 Life-sized Ayanami figurine for sale.

Basically, when "otaku" say that they feel moe for a character, they mean, "I love that character." Coming out and saying stuff like this became much more common in the 1990s, because of the success of the bishōjo game *Tokimeki Memorial* and the television anime *Neon Genesis Evangelion*. It used to be taboo to say that you loved a fictional character, but for people my age it was not so strange for someone's first love to be Fujisaki Shiori from *Tokimeki Memorial* or Ayanami Rei from *Neon Genesis Evangelion*. These characters were super popular and people were crazy about them. This was all the more true in Akihabara, where you could buy figurines of these characters. I've come to think that spending my youth in Akihabara, surrounded by anime, games, and idols, was a special sort of education. The feeling of moe seemed natural in such an environment.[41]

If the term "moe" emerged in discussions among manga/anime fans online in the early 1990s (Morikawa 2003, 30–32), then an environment of shared affective response was established offline in Akihabara, where bishōjo game retailers were clustered and stores targeting fans of cute girl characters with media and material representations opened later in the decade (Morikawa 2012, 151–52). Just as they had been shared objects of desire and affection in niche magazines, fanzines, and at special events, cute girl characters were now shared objects online and offline in Akihabara.

Although Saitō, Momoi, and others make the case for a new normal of falling in love with characters, the man most representative of that claim is Honda Tōru, who is something of a moe guru to his legions of fans. In a personal interview in Akihabara, Honda explained his problem with approaching character love as somehow compensatory: "People don't imagine a relationship with an anime character because they couldn't get a girlfriend, but rather they fell in love with a character in the first place. . . . We have grown up in a media environment where it is possible to fall in love with manga and anime characters. Some people never stop feeling love for them."[42] Quick to laugh, Honda is a funny guy, but his personal history reveals that the love he shares is not a joke. Depressed and besieged by suicidal thoughts in the 1980s, Honda found something to hold on to in anime, which he believes saved his life.[43] After a failed attempt to quit being an "otaku" and become "normal," a series of encounters in the 1990s—*Sailor Moon*, when he started producing fanzines; *Neon Genesis Evangelion*, which inspired him to make a website devoted to one of its cute girl characters and take up writing professionally; and bishōjo games—solidified his orientation.[44] Playing bishōjo games in the late 1990s, Honda fell in love with Kawana Misaki, a cute girl character in Tactics' *One: Toward the Shining Season* (One: Kagayaku kisetsu e, 1998). "I am married to her," Honda confirmed in our interview. "She is my wife." Committed to Kawana specifically and attracted to manga/anime characters generally, Honda does not mince words: "I have no interest in three-dimensional women. I'm not even interested in idol singers." Such a statement would undoubtedly earn him the label of "otaku" as it was conceived in 1983, but Honda sees this as an orientation or lifestyle and nothing to be ashamed of. He is not alone, as one gathers from the now-common practice of proudly identifying a favorite manga/anime character as "my wife" (*ore no yome* or *mai waifu*) and less common ones such as organizing weddings, honeymoons, and petitions for legal recognition of unions (Katayama 2009b; C. Smith 2010; Condry 2013).

When talking about his marriage, Honda makes the personal something explicitly political. Even as the booming manga/anime economy in Japan contributed to a revaluation of "otaku," who were reimagined as normal men that just needed to meet the right women (Freedman 2009), Honda seized the moment to publicize his counterclaims about loving fictional characters. In books such as *The Moe Man* (Moeru otoko, 2005), *The Lunatic Man* (Dempa otoko, 2005), and *Recommending Imaginary Love* (Nō'nai ren'ai no susume, 2007), Honda advocates what he calls a "love revolution" (*ren'ai kakumei*), which means embracing manga/anime characters as an alternative (Honda Tōru 2005a, 92, 142–43; 2005b, 205–6).[45] Rather than going along with the norms of "love capitalism" (*ren'ai shihonshugi*), which demand certain performances from men and women to successfully couple and achieve reproductive maturity (Honda Tōru 2005a, 23–24; 2005b, 43–46, 66–68), Honda says that manga/anime fans might instead choose to withdraw. Candidly, as Honda sees it, the norms have become toxic. Many men are made to feel like failures, which can lead to social isolation, psychological stress, and violence toward oneself and others (Honda Tōru 2005a, 321–22; 2005b, 74–77).[46] In our interview, Honda gave a particularly lucid summary of his position:

> Moe provides a low-cost, low-stress solution to this problem. It is love on our terms. Moe is a love revolution that challenges people's commonsense notions about the world. You don't need much capital to access moe, and you can do it in a way that suits you. Don't misunderstand me. I'm not saying that everyone should give up on reality. I'm just pointing out that some of us find satisfaction with fictional characters. It's not for everyone, but maybe more people would recognize this life choice if it wasn't always belittled. Forcing people to live up to impossible ideals so that they can participate in so-called reality creates so-called losers, who in their despair might lash out at society. We don't have to accept something just because people tell us that it is normal or right or better.[47]

Reacting to an angry young man that snapped and killed seven people in Akihabara in June 2008, Honda reiterates the need to let go of expectations and demands for a life that is "normal" (Honda and Yanashita 2008, 69, 72–73). His message: "take it easy" (*yuruku ikō*). Find something to love and hold on to and share with others. Perhaps, like Honda, that is anime, or bishōjo games, or a certain cute girl character. Not coincidentally, Honda locates himself in the history of Japanese men struggling with the "myth of masculinity" (*dansei-sei no shinwa*) (Honda Tōru 2005b, 153; see also Akagi

1993, 232–33; Kinsella 2000, 121–24; Nagayama 2003, 50–52).[48] This history overlaps with "male" shōjo fans seeking an alternative since the 1970s, as well as what feminist thinker Ueno Chizuko describes as a flight from reproductive maturity propelling the "sexual revolution of the 1990s" (Ueno 1989, 131).

The politics of moe are nested in a crisis of hegemony in Japan in the 1990s, or "lost decade," when many young people were set adrift by economic unrest and disintegrating institutions (Leheny 2006b; Allison 2006, 2013). Unable to transition from good schools to good jobs and start families, they seemed as lost as Japan itself. Even as the times were changing, success was still determined by the achievement of a narrow ideal of reproductive maturity; hegemonic masculinity remained particularly stubborn (Dasgupta 2005, 168; McLelland 2005, 97; Taga 2005, 161). A large number of men were thus perceived as failures. The 1990s was a time of winners and losers, with a widening gap between them, and those on the wrong side finding romantic prospects scarce (Honda Tōru 2005b, 74–75). Facing a "love gap" (*ren'ai kakusa*), people began to imagine and create alternatives. Just as Anne Allison observed the creation of virtual worlds, pets, and friends as a major trend in Japan in the 1990s (Allison 2006, 14, 91, 201), so too was the creation of virtual lovers. If moe draws attention to relations with characters, then these relations helped men such as Honda survive and live on with fictional and real others. In a personal interview, Maeda Jun, a producer of bishōjo games that entered the industry in the 1990s, assessed the importance of moe as follows: "Many people feel insecure. You go to school, but you might not be able to get a job, and even if you do it might not be a full-time position. Without a stable income, it's hard to start a family. There is a general move toward isolation. People don't have a direction or purpose. That is why I say that moe is a reason to live. Once people find something, they pursue it. Manga, anime, games, or whatever it may be provides a reason to live and a passion that can be shared with others."[49] For Maeda, moe is no less than "a reason to live" (*ikigai*), an opening to the push of life in interactions and relations with fictional and real others, which became imperative to those feeling abandoned and alone in the uneasy 1990s and beyond.

Sharing moe, a new reality was imagined and created in Japan. In *The Lunatic Man*, Honda portrays this as overcoming the common sense that "love is limited to the three-dimensional world" (Honda Tōru 2005a, 142), which was made possible by online and offline interactions and relations from the 1990s into the 2000s. Indeed, Honda's own books became something of a rallying cry for manga/anime fans opposed to "reality" and its perceived restrictions. In response to advertisements celebrating a "true love story" between a woman and "otaku," manga/anime fans in Akihabara posted a sign reading "Real Otaku Do Not Sexually Desire Three-Dimensional Women."[50] This was meant to push back against common sense about love and make room for alternatives, which is in the spirit of *The Lunatic Man*, although Honda might not appreciate the unmistakable edge of misogyny (Lamarre 2006, 381–84). (To be fair, the dismissal of women is not entirely absent from his writings.) And while Honda does not promote turning away from reality so much as embracing an alternative one of interactions and relations with characters, there are manga/anime fans that identify themselves against "*riajū*," which is slang for men and women satisfied in and with the "real."[51] In so doing, these manga/anime fans insist that an orientation toward fiction is not inferior to one toward reality, or even that it is superior. This is often as hyperbolic as it is polemical, and much of the time trumped up even more for both amusement and recognition. Meanwhile, in a series of personal interviews on moe, economic analyst Morinaga Takurō argued that "fundamentalists" (*genrishugisha*), or those oriented exclusively toward the two-dimensional, are the minority, and most manga/anime fans are two- and three-dimensionally "bisexual" (*baisekushuaru*).[52] The various problems and perspectives that emerge around moe demonstrate its success in opening up discussions of affective relations with characters, which are part of everyday, lived, social reality in Japan today.

Conclusion

Near the end of *The Moe Man*, Honda Tōru proposes a way to survive the compromised conditions of contemporary Japan. We must, he contends, imagine and create our own salvation. To illustrate the point, Honda turns to *Buddha* (Budda, 1972–83), a manga by Tezuka Osamu, and the story of a man in prison (Honda Tōru 2005b, 212–15). On the verge of madness, the man prays for aid, only to be told that a patch of grass in his cell is all he needs. As the man interacts with the grass, it transforms into a cute girl character. With the plant-girl (echoes of Ayame in *Lost World*), the man is soothed and at peace. The guards mock him, but the man continues to respond to the character and be moved, which keeps him alive and happy. The story is a striking one, as is Honda's reading of it: "An imaginary 'character' that saves a lonely and wounded soul—a 'character' born of a human that could only save himself by himself—that is the essence of 'moe.' . . . In other words, the moe man has the ability to discover 'god' inside himself. Moe is 'personal faith' and 'religion for one'" (Honda Tōru 2005b, 212, 215). Some might be outraged by the blasphemy, but Honda is not alone in describing characters as gods (Lamarre 2009a, 83–85; Steinberg 2012, 188–90; Condry 2013, 192). Unique, however, is his insistence on autonomy, which seems to underplay the social dynamics of religion and fandom. Moe does indeed teach us that one can imagine characters out of grass (Galbraith 2015a, 161–64), but most respond to those established in manga and anime, which are shared objects of desire and affection. Creators put these manga/anime characters into the world, and fans are moved by them to creative activity, which Thomas Lamarre argues contributes to the spread of media and material representations and "generates a world, a reality" (Lamarre 2006, 383).

While Honda dreams of the day when moe will be shared openly and freely (Honda Tōru 2005b, 215), the movement of manga/anime fans has already made that a reality for some. Despite his individualistic tendency to gesture to the future rather than fully embrace what is already underway, Honda agrees that moe has led to "a new shared fantasy" (*atarashii kyōdō gensō*), which at least has the potential to affect reality (173). This resonates with earlier discussions of manga/anime magazines, fanzines, and events becoming a "'platform' of shared fantasy" (Bessatsu Takarajima Henshūbu 1989, 3), namely a platform for the bishōjo as shared object of desire and affection, which allowed "otaku" to challenge the common sense that boys will grow into men, men will be men, and real men will be with real women and achieve reproductive maturity. This is a start, but, from Honda's viewpoint, true change would require a full-blown "moe revolution" (*moe reboryūshon*). "When the otaku population is over half," he speculates, "there will be a revolution in Japan" (Honda Tōru 2005a, 335). The "otaku" population increases with the proliferation of manga/anime characters and responses to them, which, like affect itself, can be contagious (Brennan 2004). Building on Honda, but emphasizing the social dimensions of moe, Ian Condry states that the shared movement of manga/anime fans is leading to the emergence of "alternative social worlds" (Condry 2013, 203).

If moe engenders new social worlds and realities, as Lamarre and Condry suggest, then it also threatens what religious studies scholar Joseph P. Laycock calls "commonsense reality" (Laycock 2015, 10–14), which can incite conflict. We are confronted again here with "otaku" and "reality problems," or the struggle with reality and for imagination. The next chapter explores aspects of that struggle in Akihabara, the "Moe City," where manga/anime fans gather and affection for bishōjo is more visible than anywhere else in Tokyo, Japan, or the world. If affective relations with manga/anime characters used to be something to be ashamed of, as Miyazaki Hayao, Momoi Halko, and others recall, then that shame is publically shared in Akihabara in ways that are both pleasurable and political. All the more so given that sexual desire for cute girl characters, often glossed over in discussions of moe, is centrally and clearly on display in Akihabara, even as the neighborhood has also become a manga/anime tourism destination and symbolic site in the government's "Cool Japan" branding campaigns. Based on extensive fieldwork, the chapter follows the moe, love, or sexual revolution that began in the 1990s into Akihabara in the 2000s, when various forces clashed over "otaku" and their performances in relation to characters and one another.

FOUR AKIHABARA

"Otaku" and Contested Imaginaries in Japan

March 24, 2015. Known in certain circles for my fieldwork in Akihabara, which began over a decade ago in 2004, I have been invited to a meeting of the Tokyo Cultural Heritage Alliance (Tōkyō bunka shigen kaigi).[1] The room is full of powerful men from the University of Tokyo, Japan's most prestigious institute of higher learning; Dentsu, Japan's largest advertising agency; the committee for the 2020 Summer Olympics in Tokyo; and more. We have come together in Kasumigaseki, the seat of the Japanese government. More comfortable in Akihabara, I feel somewhat out of place in Kasumigaseki, but, oddly enough, both are located in Chiyoda Ward. And my field site is never far away at the table, where the men discuss establishing a "cultural resource area" (*bunka shigen ku*) in Tokyo, which would include the neighborhoods of Ueno, home of national museums and galleries; Hongo, where many universities are clustered; Yanesen, famous for its preservation of old buildings and streets; Jinbōchō, a publishing hub and the heart of used book sales; and, yes, Akihabara.

While the selection may seem arbitrary, the academics have mustered historical evidence for the existence of a unified area. The door now open, various other connections are made. Linked as it is with contemporary manga/anime culture, someone mentions that Akihabara is also a site of traditional culture, given the proximity of Kanda-Myōjin, a Shinto shrine responsible for one of the three great festivals in Tokyo. Even as Akihabara attracts tourists from around the world, tie-ups with manga/anime franchises are bringing more and more young Japanese to the shrine. Characters seem to be key, and the men float the idea of having one represent the cultural resource area as a whole. I wonder if something along the lines of the cute girl characters popular in Akihabara would be acceptable, but the topic changes to getting a "big sponsor" such as Chanel, Louis Vuitton, or Hermes, which would make the proposed new—or newly rediscovered—area of Tokyo more "cultural" (*bunka-teki*) and add to its "brand" (*burando*).

For my part, I cannot help but wonder how appeals to culture in the sense of "tradition" or "the best and brightest" fit with what one member of the Tokyo Cultural Heritage Alliance describes as Akihabara's "underground culture" (*andāguraundo bunka*), by which he means "otaku" or manga/anime subculture. Then again, Louis Vuitton has already collaborated with Murakami Takashi, whose internationally acclaimed pop art is inspired by precisely that underground culture, even as it is also closely aligned with the "Cool Japan" image that the government is promoting in policy and public diplomacy initiatives.[2] As the meeting goes on, questions swirl in my mind: What happens when "otaku" subculture becomes a resource for the nation? When it is reimagined as part of national culture? And what of the critics in Japan and abroad that think the "otaku" happenings in Akihabara are crazy and creepy, if not criminal, rather than cultural or cool?[3]

This chapter focuses on Akihabara as the imagined center of the "otaku" world, or the "Holy Land of Otaku" (*otaku no sei'chi*). Hailed by design theorist Morikawa Ka'ichirō as the "Moe City" (*moeru toshi*) (Morikawa 2003, 25), Akihabara is the Holy Land of Otaku in the specific sense of "otaku" as manga/anime fans oriented toward the two-dimensional and responding to two-dimensional characters. In this neighborhood, media and material representations of manga/anime characters, first and foremost bishōjo, are not only inescapable but also overwhelming. As striking as the concentration of stores catering to "otaku" may be, Morikawa convincingly argues that the development was not planned, but rather occurred spontaneously after the manga/anime booms of the 1990s (14, 51–62). The movement of "otaku" to and in Akihabara, in relation to cute girl characters and one another, transformed the space. Put somewhat differently, in Akihabara, "otaku" imagined and created a space, which scales up the approach of men studies scholar Itō Kimio to shōjo fans opening their "own space by enjoying the commodified world through their own point of view, or by manipulating the commodified objects of consumption and adopting them to their own needs" (Itō Kimio 2010, 174). It has long been noted that media become "resources . . . for the construction of imagined selves and imagined worlds" (Appadurai 1996, 3), and in Akihabara "otaku" imagined and created selves and others, other selves and other worlds.[4]

Critics, however, see in Akihabara a space of imagined excess and perversion. For example, Okada Toshio, one of the founders of Gainax, fumes, "What you find in Akihabara today is only sexual desire. They all go to Akihabara, which is overflowing with things that offer convenient gratification of sexual desire, made possible by the power of technology and media" (Okada, Morikawa, and Murakami 2005, 170–72). The problem, Okada clarifies, is "virtual sexuality" (*bācharu seifūzoku*) and men that "reject the physical" (*nikutai-teki na mono wo kyohi suru*). In this Okada repeats the original critique of "otaku," but no longer are deviant manga/anime fans confined to the Comic Market, *Manga Burikko*, or even the internet. In the summer of 1983, writer Nakamori Akio sounded the alarm that "the city is full of 'otaku,'" but that is now literally the case in Akihabara. And as much as things change, they also stay the same. Survey results show that negative opinions about "otaku" in Japan dropped from 62 percent of respondents in 1998 to 42 percent in 2007, but still only 35 percent had positive things to say (Kikuchi 2015, 154–55).[5] In the 2000s, "otaku" were "increasingly connected to Akihabara" (147), but both were for many still associated with "a peculiar sexual preference" (*tokuyū na sei-teki shikō*) (Kikuchi 2008, 69).

For Okada and others, the Moe City is also problematic because affective relations with characters are so public there. Beyond the special events and marginal spaces of decades past, "otaku" were out on the streets of Akihabara from the late 1990s into the 2000s. In 1982, director Miyazaki Hayao described character love as something common, but also to be kept private and behind walls of shame. It was something adolescent, a love to mature out of and remember with embarrassment. Back then, Miyazaki was already haranguing manga/anime fans for their relatively unrestrained relations with characters, but things were on another level entirely from the late 1990s into the 2000s. In Akihabara, fans were openly sharing and celebrating relations with characters that they did not grow out of. And so, just as Miyazaki distanced himself from those that would be labeled "otaku" during the lolicon boom, Okada distanced himself from "otaku" during the moe boom. Even if Gainax profited in the 1990s by producing bishōjo characters, including some that were crucial to the moe phenomenon and transformation of Akihabara (Morikawa 2003, 56–62), Okada wanted nothing to do with the "otaku" there. Faced with them, he claims, "I can neither become an *otaku* myself nor understand *moe*" (Okada, Morikawa, and Murakami 2005, 170). Given that his career with Gainax, publications, and media appearances earned him the nickname "the Otaku King," Okada's statement calls into question what is meant by "otaku." It also highlights the positioning of "otaku" in Akihabara, the positioning of imagined and created selves and others.

Adding another layer of complexity here is the positioning of Akihabara as a symbolic site of Cool Japan, with "otaku" as its representatives, in the 2000s. Despite years of condemning "otaku" in Japan, the popularity of manga and anime abroad led to new imaginings of fans internationally and domestically. Negativity notwithstanding, as Akihabara emerged as a manga/anime tourism destination, "otaku" received positive spin there. The process was anything but smooth; worlds collided, images came crashing together. From my time in Akihabara, I have come to see it as a space of contested imaginaries of "otaku." In Akihabara, manga/anime fans are visible and recognized as "otaku," even as various imaginings of "otaku" clash. Furthermore, drawing on fieldwork from the mid- to late 2000s, I demonstrate how promoting "otaku" as part of Cool Japan coincided with policing "otaku" in Akihabara. The tension itself is not new, as can be gleaned from discourse about "criminal otaku" and "cool otaku" coexisting in Japan in the 1990s (Kinsella 2000, 126–31), but Akihabara offers a unique perspective on how such tension is managed in practice. In brief, with increased interest and investment in Akihabara, "weird otaku" (*hen na otaku*) came under scrutiny there. Disciplining "weird otaku," punishing "criminal otaku," was necessary to create "cool otaku." Concomitantly, even as "otaku" were in some sense redeemed, they were haunted by the specter of those other "otaku," which threatens to undermine normalization and nationalization. If, as media theorist Thomas Lamarre suggests, most discussions of "otaku" emphasize movement that levels hierarchies and crosses borders, but stop short of gender and nation (Lamarre 2006, 368, 387), then "weird otaku" challenge such discourse. These "otaku" are weird because they trouble the categories of "Man and Japan" (361), which are key to a normalized and nationalized identity.

In this chapter, I approach Akihabara as a space of "otaku" performance, or a space in which manga/anime fans perform as "otaku" with characters and one another, the media, and authorities. Manga/anime fans imagine and create Akihabara as a space of "otaku" by performing there, even as the media and authorities imagine and create Akihabara in their own ways, which are not always in harmony. For example, sociologist Kikuchi Satoru notes that Akihabara as the Moe City "is clearly at odds with the brand image envisioned by leaders of government and business who see Akihabara as a high-tech town or site of Cool Japan" (Kikuchi 2015, 155–56). As Akihabara became a symbolic site of Cool Japan, some "otaku" performances were promoted and others policed, which affects imaginaries. Anthropologist Arjun Appadurai argues that "the imagination . . . creates ideas of neighborhood and nationhood" (Appadurai 1996, 7), which casts into relief both the work of the imagination and its politics.[6] We cannot take for granted that those imagining and creating a neighborhood will do so in a fashion that aligns with those imagining and creating a nation. At stake are "worlds imagined by . . . different interests and movements" (23) and the people inhabiting those worlds. The work of the imagination is increasingly a struggle, in this case over Akihabara and "otaku."

A Space of Contested Imaginaries

Located in eastern Tokyo, "Akihabara" refers to a neighborhood composed of Soto Kanda and Kanda Sakumachō in Chiyoda Ward and Akihabara in Taitō Ward. "Akihabara," then, is a neighborhood imagined out of others. It is also a space of imagination, one associated with the imagination that excites it. In Japan, it is the most famous of the "electric towns" (*denkigai*), where stores selling home appliances and electronics bunch together. More than any other electric town, Akihabara is imaginatively linked to the "miracle" of the Japanese postwar recovery. Burned to the ground in the Second World War, Akihabara was a black market during the Allied occupation, when it gained a reputation for quality parts and expert knowledge concerning radios (Morikawa 2012, 150). As Japan was undergoing a period of rapid economic growth in the 1960s, Akihabara became a destination for washing machines, refrigerators, and television sets; at one point, it accounted for an estimated 10 percent of the national market for home appliances (150). Images of Akihabara were of the upwardly mobile family buying into the good life, a "family town" (135) that was in many ways a metonym for the "family-nation" (Kelly and White 2006, 66–68).[7]

At the cutting edge of personal computers since the 1970s (Morikawa 2012, 135–36; Kikuchi 2015, 148), Akihabara also became emblematic of the "made in Japan" brand with the rise of Japanese electronics globally in the 1980s. When the so-called bubble economy burst, recession and reform in the 1990s led to the disintegration of the Japanese postwar industrial regime (Leheny 2006b; Allison 2006; Allison 2013). In this new landscape, Akihabara stood for the potential of information technology, even as prominent stores selling manga and anime, which had reached unprecedented heights of production and distribution domestically and were increasingly successful internationally, also visually represented reserves of intellectual property. As politicians rallied behind Cool Japan policy and public diplomacy initiatives (Leheny 2006a, 218–28; Daliot-Bul 2009, 250–51; Iwabuchi 2010, 89–90), tourists started visiting Akihabara in greater numbers. Today, Akihabara is one of the most photographed, filmed, and talked about locations in Japan, where pundits propose that it is "a symbol of Japan's economic development as a whole" (NHK 2014). Despite being only a neighborhood in Tokyo, it is one of the few Japanese place names known outside the country. Akihabara is, quite simply, "one of the strongest place-brands in Japan" (Kikuchi 2015, 149).

Looming large in the imagination, Akihabara is surprisingly circumscribed geographically. The area typically understood to be Akihabara is only about one square kilometer (Morikawa 2012, 150). Its generally accepted boundaries are Kanda River to the south, Kuramaebashi Street to the north, Shōwa Street to the east, and Shōheibashi Street to the west. The usual point of access is Japan Railways Akihabara Station, and exiting from its Electric Town Gate, one enters the section most renowned as an "otaku" wonderland. Just west of the station is Chūō Street, Akihabara's main traffic artery, and down it along both sides and connecting streets are hundreds of stores selling comic books, cartoons, computer/console games, character figurines and costumes, music, fanzines, and other related merchandise. These stores range from basement rooms to massive eight-story buildings. Everywhere are media and material representations of cute girl characters, which disappear almost immediately when one crosses Kanda River, Shōheibashi Street, Kuramaebashi Street, or Shōwa Street.[8]

Given the clear limits of what is now called the "Holy Land of Otaku," one might assume some sort of official planning or zoning, but neither the government nor a large corporation pushed the electric town in this new direction. Rather, Morikawa asserts that Akihabara changed in response to those gathering there (Morikawa 2003, 14, 51–62). Dramatically stating his thesis, Morikawa writes, "For the first time in history a non-mainstream taste was driving urban development, independently from any political or corporate power" (Morikawa 2012, 134). Setting aside for now questions of precedence and power, "non-mainstream taste" here means a taste for cute girl characters, which was crucial to Akihabara's shift from an electric town to the Holy Land of Otaku. Beneath the surface of the broad historical narrative about a family town are the beginnings of Akihabara metamorphosing into something else entirely. By the 1980s, conveniently located box stores had drawn families away with discount home appliances and electronics, and Akihabara was primarily a hangout for computer enthusiasts, who were mostly men (Morikawa 2003, 42–44). Soon enough, bishōjo games were sold alongside computers.[9] Featuring manga/anime-style characters, these games appealed to men that had grown up in intimate relation to manga/anime characters, which were increasingly designed to be attractive and appeared in adult media. Put somewhat differently, bishōjo games focused on romance and sex with cute girl characters as opposed to anything more "real" (97–99). Even as computers became more widespread in the 1990s, bishōjo games became compatible with the Windows operating system, which expanded their reach, as did mainstream hits such as *Tokimeki Memorial*. As new players and producers came to bishōjo games, a renaissance in storytelling pushed the industry to new heights in the late 1990s and early 2000s.

Cute girl characters were the main sales point of bishōjo games, and advertisements presenting them to potential buyers appeared everywhere. With stores such as Messe Sanoh, Gamers, Trader, Getchuya, and Medio in competition, bishōjo became the face of Akihabara (Morikawa 2003, 1–2, 4–5, 95; Kagami 2010, 132). Writing in 2003, Morikawa portrayed the scene as follows: "The sheer density of anime imagery is intense, with posters cluttering walls, sidewalk signs, and life-sized cardboard cutouts. These images are particularly prominent in game-shop storefronts, which brazenly display posters of dating sims [= bishōjo games] while exhibiting the female characters as life-sized figures or body-pillow covers on the bustling sidewalks of Akihabara's main avenue" (Morikawa 2012, 152). Today, massive images of bishōjo are plastered on the sides of buildings (figures 4.1 and 4.2). The central role that bishōjo games played in Akihabara's contemporary formation accounts for its bias toward men attracted to cute girl characters. If Morikawa notes in the neighborhood a "sharing of sexual fantasies about characters" (*kyarakutā ni kan suru sei-teki na mōsō no kyōyū*) (Morikawa 2003, 48), then it is clear that the characters are predominantly bishōjo. Equally clear is the openness of shared sexual fantasies about them, which is remarkable in Tokyo, Japan, and the world.

A milestone in the increasingly emphasized appeal of characters in manga, anime, and games, *Neon Genesis Evangelion* and its cute girls drove

FIGURE 4.1 Bishōjo games advertised on an Akihabara street.

fans into a frenzy and amplified demand for fanzines and figurines. Seeing an opportunity in Akihabara and its established clientele hungry for bishōjo media and material, stores targeting manga/anime fans relocated or opened branches there in the late 1990s and early 2000s, which contributed to the neighborhood's transformation into the Holy Land of Otaku and Moe City. Again, computers are a significant factor in the story. As Morikawa explains, manga/anime fans turned moe into in-group slang through online discussions of characters in the early 1990s (Morikawa 2003, 30–32). These manga/anime fans were early adopters of computers and the internet, which allowed them to connect to one another and share their interests. Computers were also the chief platform for bishōjo games. There is thus convergence among early adopters of computers and the internet, manga/anime fans gathering online to discuss characters, and bishōjo gamers, which brings us to Akihabara. Computer enthusiasts were in Akihabara, as were bishōjo gamers, themselves also manga/anime fans; using computers, manga/anime fans connected online and were subsequently drawn to Akihabara and those that shared their interests. Notably, the *Neon Genesis Evangelion* boom has also been tied to the internet and fan activity, which again leads to Akihabara. It is not that Akihabara bears a superficial resemblance to online "communities of interest" (Morikawa 2012, 152), but

FIGURE 4.2 Bishōjo games advertised in an Akihabara building.

there is in fact a direct link between online communities of interest and Akihabara.

Even as manga/anime fans congregate in Akihabara, the neighborhood is prominently featured in manga, anime, and games. Many show their characters visiting Akihabara, and some are set there, for example, *Cyber Team in Akihabara* (Akihabara den'nō gumi, 1998), *Steins;Gate* (Shutainzu gēto, 2009), and *Akiba's Trip* (Akibazu torippu, 2011–).[10] These works are often characterized by an almost fetishistic attention to details of streets, signs, and stores, which serve to draw viewers into a space that is both imaginary and real. In addition to fantastic stories, there are also numerous other sources of information about the neighborhood. Not only does Akihabara have a dozen local magazines such as *Akibatsū* (2002–), but also its own newspaper, *Akiba Keizai Shimbun* (2006–).[11] Long before the spread of social media, Akiba Blog (2004–) was updating its readers multiple times a day with short posts and vivid photographs documenting Akihabara and events there.[12] On the website, images of manga/anime characters in advertisements for upcoming releases mix with photographs of streets, stores, and assembled masses. A neighborhood imagined out of others, Akihabara has been mapped over and over again, online and in print, most conspicuously by Akiba Map (2005–).[13] Giving a sense of not only the space and

FIGURE 4.3 Bishōjo game specialty store in Akihabara.

its boundaries but also what one might encounter there, these maps are decorated with manga/anime characters and dedicated for the most part to establishments selling related media and merchandise. The swirling clouds of images and information surrounding Akihabara contribute to the production of its locality.[14]

A concrete location where people gather, Akihabara is also more. In Akihabara, it is possible to "imagine and feel things together" (Appadurai 1996, 8), namely relations with cute girl characters. Given the prevalence of sex in these relations and its open display, Akihabara might well be counted as an example of what theorists Lauren Berlant and Michael Warner call "sex in public" (Berlant and Warner 1998). In certain times and places, outside the home, there "develops a dense, publically accessible sexual culture" (Warner 2000, 187). In public sex culture, Berlant and Warner continue, "Affective life slops over onto work and political life; people have key self-constitutive relations with strangers and acquaintances; and they have eroticism, if not sex, outside of the couple form" (Berlant and Warner 1998, 560). Shared movement in response to characters seems like a case in point. If there is pleasure in "belonging to a sexual world, in which one's sexuality finds an answering resonance . . . in a world of others" (Warner 2000, 179), then manga/anime fans imagined and created Akihabara as a world of "otaku." In the Holy Land of Otaku and Moe City, they belonged, and their sexuality resonated in a world of fictional and real others. No longer a "family town" (Morikawa 2012, 135), or even an electric town, Akihabara became something different, weird, queer. For those that did not imagine or feel that they belonged to it, this "otaku" world was disturbing, if not disgusting (Okada, Morikawa, and Murakami 2005, 170–72).[15] Antipathy was exacerbated because, in Akihabara, on the street, "otaku" performed in response to characters and one another.

A Space of "Otaku" Performance

Use of the term "performance" here does not indicate exaggerated behavior or something staged, but rather the process of carrying out an action, or, more simply, acting. Highlighting performance is in no way intended to cast doubt on whether or not someone is an "otaku," because I do not think that there is an "otaku" essence to begin with. As I approach it in Akihabara, "otaku" performance is the process of carrying out an action marked as "otaku," or acting as an "otaku." This opens up the field of relations, because rather than essentializing—that person is or is not an "otaku"—one observes who is performing in what way and context and how others are responding. While inspired by sociologist Howard S. Becker, I do not think that it is as straightforward as "otaku" being those to whom the label has been successfully applied (Becker 1963, 9), which leaves little room for the agency of performers. If "there is no such thing as an otaku," for example, then this often means that "otaku" have no say in the matter. Focusing on society and its rules, one sees objectifying judgments, as opposed to seeing moving subjects. In "otaku" performance, I consider not "the stylized repetition of acts through time" (Butler 1988, 520), which gives the illusion of stability, but rather the contingent act in its time and place.

So positioned, I perceive a limit to Morikawa's influential discussion of Akihabara as an "otaku" neighborhood. For Morikawa, Akihabara reflects "otaku" taste and personality (Morikawa 2003, 17; 2012, 152). It transformed because of a geographic concentration of "otaku," or more specifically "otaku" taste and personality. Essentially, Akihabara represents the taste and personality of "otaku," who are "otaku" because of their taste and personality. They just are "otaku." For this reason exactly, Morikawa distinguishes "otaku" from "performers" such as the *takenoko-zoku,* who made a scene on the streets of Tokyo's Harajuku neighborhood from the 1970s into the 1980s: "The takenoko-zoku were performers using Harajuku as their stage; they did not continue acting out their roles once they went home. The phenomenon in Akihabara, by contrast, represents the extension of private into public, personal rooms into cities. . . . The concentration of a marginal personality type in an urban district has exposed the previously hidden interests of otaku in Akihabara to the extent that it transformed urban space" (Morikawa 2012, 154). Insofar as the takenoko-zoku dressed in outrageous fashion to dance together on the streets of Harajuku, which they did not do elsewhere, it perhaps seems sensible enough to contrast them with "otaku," defined by taste and personality, regardless of place and time. The longer one considers the comparison, however, the more tenuous it becomes. Anthropological fieldwork reveals that many of those involved in the fashion subcultures of Harajuku change while there, but what might be seen as performance is nonetheless self-expression (Gagné 2008, 139–41). On the subject of "otaku," alongside the takenoko-zoku were the "Tominoko-zoku," or anime fans that costumed as characters from Tomino Yoshiyuki's *Mobile Suit Gundam* (Kidō senshi Gandamu, 1979–80) and appeared in Harajuku.[16] As important as *Mobile Suit Gundam* is in the history of anime fandom (Condry 2013, 123–27), it is difficult to discount such "otaku" performances.

Five years after the original publication of his book on Akihabara, Morikawa spoke directly to the topic of "otaku" performances in the neighborhood, which had become a source of controversy. On the grounds that a massive wave of media attention led to exaggerated behavior or something staged in Akihabara, Morikawa draws a line between "otaku" in the late 1990s and early 2000s and "performers" in the mid- and late 2000s (Morikawa 2008, 269–81).[17] In one fell swoop, Morikawa seems to affirm the existence of authentic "otaku" of the past and dismiss fake "performers" of the present, which to my mind is a problematically totalizing move. In the late 1990s and early 2000s, the rise of bishōjo games and anime was already encouraging "otaku" performances in Akihabara. On the street and in stores with others, openly sharing affection for cute girl characters was itself "otaku" performance. Back then, women were hired to wear character costumes and attract customers to events, and there were street performances, too. While it would be easy to assume that these women were not "otaku," such an assumption misses much. For example, Momoi Halko, a fan of *Tokimeki Memorial* and idols, produced her own cute girl character and began to perform in both Harajuku and Akihabara around 1997.[18] With deep ties to manga/anime and Akihabara, few would question Momoi's credentials as an "otaku," but she was, and is, also a performer.

For my part, I worry about the conceit of verifying the qualifications of others, which seems to place me above them and risks undermining their "otaku" performances. Meeting Momoi in Akihabara, it was immediately evident to me that she was comfortable and confident in her "otaku" performance, but this was not always so with others, for example, those I came into contact with for a book project called *Otaku Spaces*. During extensive interviews, I asked people, "Are you an otaku?" This seemed harmless enough, but it quickly became apparent that many felt that they were not performing adequately under scrutiny. For example, one young man answered, "It's really difficult. I feel I'm not qualified to be an otaku, but I have the tendency. I distinguish different otaku based on fields of interest. So using otaku as a general term is something that I don't really understand. I wouldn't call myself an otaku, but I would like to be known as one" (Galbraith 2012, 87). Reading this response now makes me cringe, because I see all too clearly that I was causing this young man a good deal of distress. In an instant, what had been a pleasant conversation about shared interests became an interrogation. Recording device and camera in hand, there I was in his room, generously invited into his personal space, asking something that seemed to call his "otaku" performance into question.

The parallels between this experience and conducting fieldwork in Akihabara are not lost on me. Entering this space of "otaku" performance with recording device and camera in hand, one might effortlessly slip into judging people as authentic or fake. At the same time, changing imaginings of "otaku," be they generated by the media, academy, or fans, affected the performances of everyone in Akihabara. When encountering "otaku" performances in the field, I was not considering authenticity so much as sincerity. On the difference between these terms, anthropologist John L. Jackson, Jr. writes, "Authenticity conjures up images of people, as animate subjects, verifying inanimate objects. Authenticity presupposes this kind of relationship between an independent, thinking subject and a dependent, unthinking thing. The defining association is one of objectification, 'thingification.' . . . Sincerity presumes a liaison *between subjects*—not some external adjudicator and a lifeless scroll. Questions of sincerity imply social interlocutors who presume one another's humanity, interiority, and subjectivity" (Jackson 2005, 15–16). I agree with Jackson that an anthropologist is not in the business of determining the authenticity of objects, but rather interacting with subjects. In Akihabara, I presumed the humanity of "otaku" performers, even as I performed alongside and with them. If, as Jackson argues, sincerity "demands its performance" (14), then I gauged the sincerity of others in their performances, as they did my own.

This occurred in an open-ended process of being there, which is fieldwork. After first arriving in Akihabara in 2004, I was soon coming to the neighborhood several times a week, then daily, for lengthier stays. Intensive fieldwork began in 2006, when street performances became more prominent. Wearing a character costume and joining "otaku" performances facilitated connecting with others, even as I also became a person of interest. To some I was "Gokū," a friend, while to others I was an "otaku" expert—no less than "Dr. Moe," a punch line for media personalities and proof of global interest in manga/anime and Japan—and to still others a "monstrous foreigner" (*monsutā gaikokujin*) illustrative of an increasingly out-of-control street.[19] What I could not be was uninvolved and unmoved; I was part of things, which I take to be a necessary component of participant observation. From 2007 onward, I also began providing regular tours of Akihabara, where visitors shared their thoughts on the neighborhood and "otaku" performances. I created the tour route and script by following others through Akihabara and listening to them talk about it. These "otaku" performers had been in Akihabara longer than I had and gave me the lay of the land as they saw it. Those I collaborated with were invested in stories that they wanted me to tell, and knowledge was thus negotiated. As an unexpected side effect, the tour raised my profile in Akihabara to the extent that I had access to local business owners and politicians, whom I interviewed. Although intensive fieldwork for this chapter ended in 2009, my engagements with Akihabara and people there are ongoing.

Like all anthropological writing, this chapter is partial (Clifford 1986), which comes from focusing on interactions with "otaku" performers on the street in the mid- to late 2000s. This means that I spend more time with their position that Akihabara is the Holy Land of Otaku and under attack from those that would incorporate it into Cool Japan. Others argue that these "weird otaku" are relative newcomers, disruptive outsiders, and have no place in Akihabara. In this chapter, "partial" also refers to the identities of "otaku" performers, who often exclusively used handles—or what some called "Akihabara names" (*Akiba nēmu*)—wore character costumes, and spun yarns about themselves.[20] While I might have forced the issue and demanded the truth, this seemed wrong. In subculture, one adopts disguises and disfigured origins "to escape the principle of identity" and dislocate oneself from a "parent culture" (Hebdige 2005, 366–67).[21] It seemed to me that pushing those I interacted with to expose their "true" identities would be to the detriment of their "otaku" performances. In Akihabara, it was often more productive to go with the flow. The continuous movement of people into, through, and out of Akihabara contributes to the excitement of a space populated by people from elsewhere, who are for the most part anonymous.[22] As much as being among others that share interests, this plays a part in the perceived freedom to perform as an "otaku," which became a problem for those working to develop Akihabara into another kind of space.[23]

Redevelopment of Akihabara, Revaluation of "Otaku"

Rather than positing a "pure-otaku" period and a compromised "post-otaku" Akihabara, let us consider the neighborhood as a space of "otaku" performance, where shifting relations of power allow and disallow certain acts. Against the backdrop of economic and political turmoil in the 1990s, it seems reasonable to suggest that the transformation of Akihabara into the Holy Land of Otaku was unplanned (Morikawa 2003, 14; 2012, 151). Transpiring in the wake of *Tokimeki Memorial* and *Neon Genesis Evangelion,* Morikawa argues, "The changes were not brought about by administrative policies. . . . It is worth noting again that there was no organized development by real estate or big-name investors" (Morikawa 2012, 151). In his book on Akihabara, originally published in 2003, Morikawa focuses primarily on the years from 1997 to 2000. If during that time there were no administrative policies or organized development projects by real estate companies or investors, then this changed drastically afterward. Stated somewhat more strongly, if the 1990s were characterized by "an absence of such power" (Morikawa 2003, 14), then the 2000s were characterized by its return. If "otaku" performances were relatively free in a corner of Tokyo that had become marginal in the 1990s, then they moved to center stage in the 2000s.

After the transformation of Akihabara into the Holy Land of Otaku in the late 1990s, which went largely unnoticed by the general population of Japan

(Kikuchi 2015, 151), redevelopment of the neighborhood began at the start of the new millennium. In *Tokyo Concept 2000* (Tōkyō kōsō 2000), then governor Ishihara Shin'tarō laid out a plan to make Akihabara into a base for the information-technology industry. The neighborhood was a natural choice, given its history as a famous electric town and subsequent association with computers. Part of *Tokyo Concept 2000*, "Urban Development Guidelines for the Akihabara Area" were released in 2001.[24] From 2002, the Crossfield Project, led by the Tokyo Metropolitan Government (Morikawa 2008, 256–57; Kikuchi 2015, 148) and including real estate companies such as Kajima, NTT Urban Development, and Daibiru, broke ground in Akihabara. In line with Governor Ishihara's vision, a report in March 2003 revealed that 742 software developers, internet ventures, and data processing companies were located within a one-kilometer radius of Japan Railways Akihabara Station (Fujita and Hill 2005, 30). By 2005, on one side of the station, the Akihabara Daibiru skyscraper was completed; the Akihabara UDX Building, a nearby structure that is monumental in scale, followed in 2006. On the other side of the station, in 2005, the Tsukuba Express line opened, connecting Akihabara to a major research hub and to suburban communities in Ibaraki Prefecture. Right above the Tsukuba Express terminal in Akihabara, Yodobashi Camera opened an eight-story megastore carrying home appliances, electronics, and more.

The edge of Akihabara's "redevelopment zone" (*saikaihatsu chi'iki*) falls right behind the stores lining Chūō Street, which have come to deal primarily in manga, anime, bishōjo games, fanzines, and related media and merchandise. Standing on Chūō Street in the old electric town, facing those stores and the redevelopment zone behind them, one sees the new electric town rising up. The architectural contrast is stunning: in the foreground, midsized buildings of inconsistent shape, which are marked by huge advertisements featuring colorful, cartoony, cute girl characters; in the background, the glassy fronts of the Daibiru skyscraper and UDX Building (figure 4.4). The new structures quite literally tower over, and overshadow, the Holy Land of Otaku. Further away from the redevelopment zone, on the other side of Chūō Street, are even smaller and more diverse stores located in side alleys, basements, and backrooms that are associated with the niche obsessions of "otaku." (For more on the contrast, see Kikuchi 2015, 150.)

Discussed as a social menace in the 1990s (Kinsella 2000, 126–29, 137–38), the redevelopment of Akihabara was contemporaneous with a revaluation of "otaku." Consider, for example, Seno'o Ken'ichirō, a professor of business and chairman of the Industry-Academia Collaboration Initiative, who was

FIGURE 4.4 Chūō Street, with "otaku" stores in foreground and redevelopment zone in background.

a major player in the Crossfield Project. In his book *Producing Akihabara: The Miracle of the Five-Year Redevelopment Project* (Akiba wo purodūsu: Saikaihatsu purojekuto 5 nenkan no kiseki, 2007), Seno'o factors "otaku" into Akihabara's status as a center for innovation.[25] In a paper for the Nomura Research Institute titled "The Otaku Group from a Business Perspective: Revaluation of Enthusiastic Consumers," Kitabayashi Ken agrees that "otaku" are a "driving force for bringing about industrial innovation" (Kitabayashi 2004, 1). Highlighting the active and creative participation of "otaku" in what excites them, Kitabayashi advocates that their movement be "integrated" and "used" to invigorate a range of Japanese industries (6–7). Beyond technology, Kitabayashi points to "otaku" driving innovation in the culture industries, which produce content such as manga and anime. The insight was increasingly shared at the time. The economic impact of franchises such as *Neon Genesis Evangelion*, which included "billions of yen in merchandise sales in niche markets," was widely reported in the mass media, and "it did not escape anyone's attention that the makers and supporters of hits such as *Neon Genesis Evangelion* were 'otaku'" (Kikuchi 2015, 152).

The revaluation of "otaku" came at a moment when many in Japan were thinking about manga and anime in not only economic but also political terms. In 2002, American journalist Douglas McGray's article on Japan's decline as an industrial nation and simultaneous rise as a producer of "cool" media and material culture made waves in Japanese policy circles (Leheny 2006a, 219–22). The concept of soft power, or the ability to attract and influence, gained currency. As a source of "cool," discourse about "Cool Japan," or a nation with soft power in reserve, began to form; eventually, the government would officially adopt the phrase and its underlying message. Among Japan's "cool" media and material culture, anime had made exceptional strides in global markets. The year following McGray's article, Miyazaki Hayao's *Spirited Away* (Sen to Chihiro no kamikakushi, 2001) won an Academy Award, even as anime appeared alongside Hollywood films and French fashion and music.[26] Soon after, reports indicated that Japanese "cultural exports" such as anime had "increased 300 percent since 1992 . . . while exports as a whole increased only 20 percent" (KWR International 2004). Perhaps the most shocking statistic bandied about was that Japanese anime accounted for as much as 60 percent of the animation shown in the world (JETRO 2005). The validity of such claims is less important than their consequence in spurring Cool Japan initiatives, which also affected the revaluation of "otaku." If "otaku" drive innovation in Japanese cultural industries, then they also play a role in creating content that goes global: "Japan's success in the world animation, comics, and games software markets derives from fierce firm competition inside of Japan for the attention of a large, demanding and diverse range of consumers. . . . Animators test their products in Tokyo first before marketing them in Japan and overseas. And animators look to Tokyo's participatory antenna districts for new product ideas and strategies" (Fujita and Hill 2005, 57). One such participatory antenna district, the authors of this report write, is Akihabara, where "otaku," those most demanding of manga/anime consumers, gather.

Now, revaluation aside, cool was not the first thing to come to most Japanese when asked about "otaku" (Kam 2013a, 2013b; Kikuchi 2015), but the situation was somewhat different abroad. That is, through association with anime and Japan, "otaku" were associated with cool for many people around the world. As anime grew in popularity in North America, for example, fans self-identified as "otaku" and looked to Japan as the cutting edge of cool (Lamarre 2006, 387–88). Speaking to intensifying international interest in "otaku," Morikawa Ka'ichirō organized an exhibition on the subject at the Venice Biennale in 2004, and Murakami Takashi an exhibition in New York in 2005. These exhibitions were not only highly praised, but also nationalized. Morikawa's exhibition was funded by the Japan Foundation, and a sign above the exhibition hall read, "GIAPPONE/OTAKU," or "JAPAN/OTAKU," where the slash brings and holds the terms together.[27] Funded by the Japan Society, Murakami's exhibition also linked Japan and "otaku," both seeming in equal parts crazy and cool, but at any rate fascinating and marketable.[28] By 2008, Sotheby's in New York was able to sell an anime-inspired sculpture by Murakami for US$13.5 million, which made it one of the most expensive pieces of artwork in history (Rushe 2008). The convergence of "otaku" and cool was made explicit by entrepreneur and media personality Danny Choo—son of fashion designer Jimmy Choo—in his book *Otacool* (2009), which introduced manga/anime culture from Japan as taken up by fans in over a dozen countries.

This all fed back into nascent discourse in Japan about an "otaku" culture celebrated overseas, and Akihabara became a key site to visualize it (Morikawa 2008, 264–65).[29] Consider the case of Asō Tarō, who made a name for himself as the minister of foreign affairs preaching about the triumphant global ascendance of Japanese popular culture. In a career spanning from 2005 to 2007, which notably overlaps with what would come to be known as the Akihabara boom, Asō often chose the neighborhood as a platform to deliver speeches, for example, in the Daibiru skyscraper in 2006.[30] Publically, Asō played up his manga readership and is rumored to have called himself an "otaku." Whether true or not, Asō did not deny the whispers, ostensibly because they did not bother him—and perhaps even made him seem a little cool.[31] Building on his career as minister of foreign affairs, Asō strove for greater heights, which included appealing to and as an "otaku." Campaigning to become prime minister of Japan, Asō held a rally in Akihabara on September 16, 2007. Addressing the crowd as well as the cameras, Asō said, "Thanks to otaku, Japanese culture, subculture, is undoubtedly being transmitted to the world. . . . Isn't this something that we should take more pride in?" (Tantei File News Watch 2007). The connection of subculture—in context, "otaku" culture—to Japanese culture is striking, as is the positioning of "otaku" as crucial to Japan's international success and something for the nation to be proud of. If Asō as a manga reader engaged in "otaku" performances, he was now performing with "otaku" on the streets of Akihabara, which was an explicitly political move.

Although he lost the election in 2007, Asō's association with "otaku" did not rule him out as a candidate, and even bolstered his reputation in certain sectors. One gets a sense of this from *The Day that Akihabara Swallows the World: On the Evolution of Akihabara Culture* (Akiba ga chikyū wo nomikomu hi: Akihabara karuchā shinkaron, 2007), a book published soon after

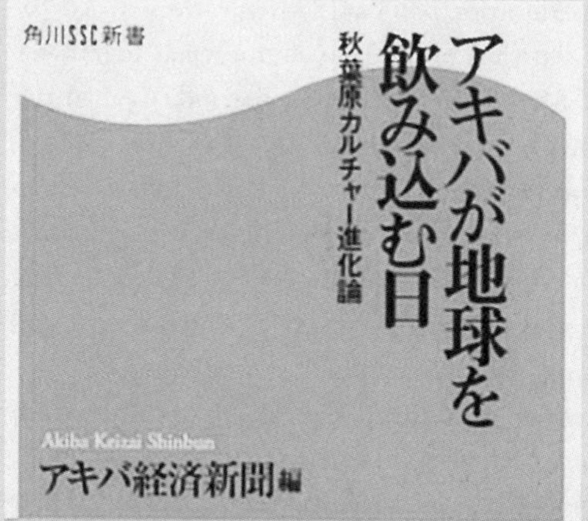

FIGURE 4.5
Asō: "Otaku culture is an asset for Japan."

Asō's rally in Akihabara. Edited by *Akiba Keizai Shimbun*, a newspaper dedicated to reporting on Akihabara, the book is advertised with a removable band that wraps around the lower half of the cover and features a photograph of Asō speaking into a microphone (figure 4.5). The accompanying text is breathless. The headline is in oversized black katakana script, which is used for foreign loanwords and in ways equivalent to italics: "Otaku = cool!" Then in red is "Mister Asō Tarō also gives high praise!" This is followed by what appears to be a quote from Asō: "Otaku culture is an asset for Japan. Let's spread it to the world with pride." Whether or not these are his exact words, Asō, who might have said this and certainly said similar things, became prime minister of Japan in 2008. On his path to the office, the politician delivered yet another speech in Akihabara, which was national news because "people cared that Asō was appearing in . . . the 'holy land of otaku'" (Kikuchi 2015, 149). In this way, the overheated discourse about Cool Japan resulted in more and more attention being paid to "otaku" performances in Akihabara. The "otaku" there, however, were not always "cool." Regardless of the revaluation, decades of concern about manga/anime fans as perverts and potentially dangerous shaded into critiques of "weird otaku," which I encountered in Akihabara. On the street, I observed friction between "otaku" performances categorized as "cool" and "weird," which was further aggravated by the inflated presence of media and tourists during the Akihabara boom.

The Akihabara Boom

As the Crossfield Project steadily advanced, Akihabara's profile rose rapidly in the media after *Train Man* (Densha otoko). Starting in 2004 as a string of posts on an online bulletin board, *Train Man* is the story of an "otaku" that meets a beautiful woman and solicits advice from others on the internet to become a man worthy of her. In 2005, *Train Man* was adapted into both a major motion picture and primetime television series, which cast "otaku" as romantic leading men. Specifically, the socially awkward protagonist is introduced as an "Akihabara otaku" (*Akiba-kei otaku*), or an "otaku" that hangs out in Akihabara, and he appears there in many scenes filmed on location. Reading like a parable of Japan's evolving relationship with its outcast sons, *Train Man*'s drama of falling in love with "otaku" unfolds on the streets of Akihabara. With the final episode of the television series reaching 25.5 percent of Japanese households (Freedman 2009) and the novelization selling one million copies (Morikawa 2008, 264), *Train Man* was a smash hit. Following a surge in domestic tourism—compared to September 2004, there was a 40 percent increase in people using Japan Railways Akihabara Station in September 2005 (Morikawa 2008, 263)—the media rushed to report on the "Akihabara boom" (*Akiba būmu*), which it helped create.

During the Akihabara boom, "otaku" performances were amplified, especially when the streets were most crowded. Since 1973, on Sundays, Akihabara had shut off vehicular traffic along the stretch of Chūō Street between Kanda River and Kuramaebashi Street to create a "Pedestrian Paradise" (*hokōsha tengoku*). It was not unique in this practice. For example, Harajuku was long known for its Pedestrian Paradise, which drew colorful characters and performative subcultures (recall the takenoko-zoku), but complaints from local residents and business owners ended it in 1998 (NTV 2010). At the Pedestrian Paradise in Akihabara in the mid 2000s, "otaku" seemed to be taking over the street. Being among others with shared interests contributed to an atmosphere that was not unlike a "festival" (*matsuri*), which is familiar to those that have attended anime conventions and experienced the collective effervescence of "otaku" performances there (Napier 2007, 149–67), but was happening weekly in Akihabara. With more "otaku" performers and attention, the festival blew up. After *Train Man*, on the streets of Akihabara, one could see amateur singing idols, dancing fans, costumed role-players, parked cars and bikes decorated with anime-character decals, and more. Performances drew cameras, which reproduced performances and spread them, in turn drawing others to Akihabara. As the cycle continued, the throngs of people during the Pedestrian Paradise were so dense in places that it was impossible to get past them.

The street culture in Akihabara and its connections to "otaku" were extensively reported in Japan and abroad, even in Lonely Planet guidebooks, which encouraged tourism. A Japan National Tourism Organization (JNTO) survey conducted in 2007 revealed that 8.6 percent of foreign visitors to Japan set foot in Akihabara, 69 percent for the first time (JNTO 2008a). According to JNTO's calculations, Akihabara was a more popular destination for foreigners than Tokyo Disneyland. Surprising as they are, these numbers are supported by contemporaneous research. For example, the television show COOL JAPAN: *Discovering Cool Japan* (COOL JAPAN: Hakkutsu kakko ii Nippon, 2006–), which introduces a panel of foreign guests to various aspects of Japan and polls them on whether or not these things are cool, conducted its own survey of visitors to Akihabara in 2007, which revealed that 5 percent of the total were from overseas (NHK 2007). Broadcast as enthusiastically as it was in the Japanese media, foreign fascination with Akihabara and "otaku" took on almost mythical proportions, as reflected in Ōkura Atsuhisa's *Moe USA* (2007) (figure 4.6). When asked about his intention with the manga, which was originally published in English and targets fans that it seems to also parody, Ōkura replied matter-of-factly, "Well, isn't that what you want? Foreigners want to come to Akihabara and see otaku, right?"[32]

While more attention was paid to foreigners, domestic tourism was at least as significant to the Akihabara boom. According to the same COOL JAPAN survey of visitors to Akihabara, 30 percent were Japanese tourists (NHK 2007). This is, incidentally, equal to the number reported to be coming to the neighborhood to pursue "otaku" interests. That these categories were made distinct in the survey should not be overlooked. During the Akihabara boom, there was widespread interest in "otaku," but domestic tourists did not necessarily share "otaku" interests, let alone consider such manga/anime fans to be cool. The link between "otaku" and cool that COOL JAPAN was making with and through its panel of foreign guests was not immediately apparent to many Japanese. Indeed, a Japan Travel Bureau book titled *Cool Japan: Otaku Japan Guide* (Cool Japan: Otaku Nippon gaido, 2008), originally published in Japanese, seems to have been an effort to introduce the foreign concept and stimulate domestic tourism. With Akihabara on the cover, the book's underscoring of the nation—appearing twice in the title, first as "Japan" in roman letters and then as "Nippon" in katakana—and its relationship with "otaku" is quite remarkable (figure 4.7). In this formulation, "Cool Japan" before the colon becomes "Otaku Japan" after it. The words "cool" and "otaku" both modify Japan and seem interchangeable. It turns out, however, that the association of "otaku" with not only cool but also Japan proved to be much more problematic on the streets of Akihabara.

Tension on the Streets of Akihabara

With so many eyes on Akihabara during the boom, "otaku" on the street had the potential to become minor celebrities. In May 2005, for example, representatives from Fuji Television, the station that was producing *Train Man,* came to the neighborhood and handed out fliers requesting "real otaku" to act as extras (Morikawa 2008, 280; also Freedman 2009). After the series became a hit, Fuji Television and other stations sent crews to Akihabara to film "otaku" and capitalize on the trend. On the street, the media regularly approached one Japanese man that I hung out with. Tall, sinewy, and missing teeth, this man did not immediately appear to be star material. The media was drawn to him, however, as an "otaku," specifically a huge fan of anime. When we first met, this man was especially into *The Melancholy of Haruhi Suzumiya* (Suzumiya Haruhi no yū'utsu, 2006), or rather its main schoolgirl character, so much so that he went by the handle "Haruhi" and wore her uniform. Put another way, Haruhi was engaged in "crossplay," or cross-gender costume play involving anime characters (in Japanese, *josō kosupure*). An "otaku" performer, Haruhi referred to his relationship with the media as "work" (*oshigoto*), which he did to earn pocket money and recognition from peers.

FIGURE 4.6 (left) *Moe USA* shows foreigners in awe of Akihabara. Image courtesy of Japanime Co. Ltd.

FIGURE 4.7 (opposite) *Cool Japan: Otaku Japan Guide.*

While at times working with the mainstream media, and working images of "otaku" and Akihabara, Haruhi's performances were not always welcome locally. In part, this had to do with the fact that he was not alone, and strange things happened when people gathered in Akihabara. For example, many of those watching *The Melancholy of Haruhi Suzumiya* not only dressed as its main schoolgirl character, but also learned the dance sequence that she and her friends perform during the end credits of each episode. The dance accompanies the song "Sunny Sunny Happiness" (*Hare hare yukai*), which could be heard in stores across Akihabara and became something of an unofficial anthem of the street culture. Expressing shared affection for *The Melancholy of Haruhi Suzumiya* and its characters, fans began to come together in Akihabara's Hōrin Park to practice and perform the "Sunny Sunny Happiness" dance sequence, or what was popularly known as the "Haruhi dance" (*Haruhi dansu*).[33] With progressively larger meet-ups organized online, "otaku" performances spilled over onto adjacent streets. So it was that my friend Haruhi and some fifty costumed accomplices temporarily took over Chūō Street to perform the Haruhi dance during the Pedestrian Paradise in the summer of 2007.[34] Similar to an anime convention, or a "media-saturated environment, in which fiction is actualized" (Lamerichs 2014, 270), the dancing characters of *The Melancholy of Haruhi Suzumiya* became moving bodies in Akihabara. Such were the "otaku" performances

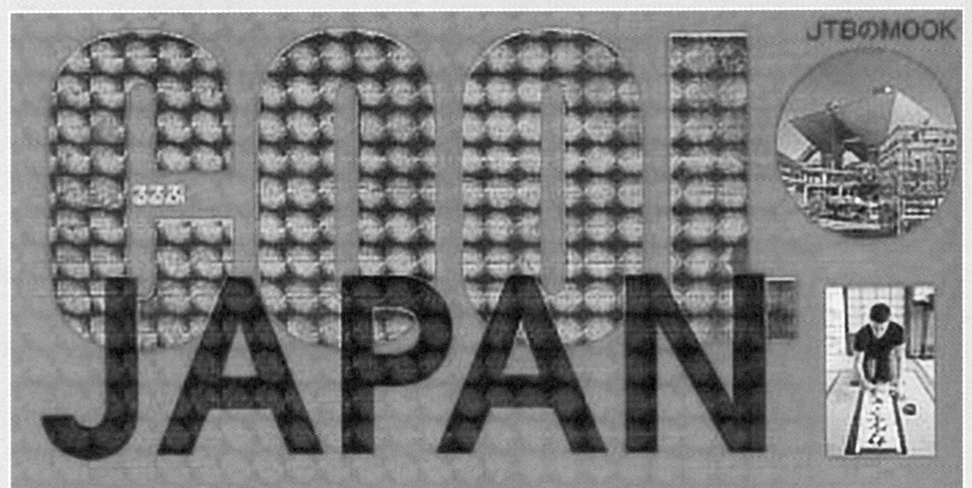

オタク ニッポン ガイド

OTAKU NIPPON GUIDE

メイドカフェ
コスプレ
アニソン
鉄ヲタ
廃墟萌え
秋葉原
中野
日本橋
大須
ガンダム
AKB48
乙女ロード
801
執事喫茶
コミケ
ワンフェス
KEI

どうしようもないこの国がどうしようもなく楽しい

of Haruhi, a man costuming as the cute girl character that he loved, and others like him.

Even as the temporary takeover of summer 2007 drew complaints from local residents and business owners, who requested police intervention, videos of the mass Haruhi dance in the middle of Chūō Street circulated widely and encouraged more "otaku" performances in Akihabara.[35] As the scene was repeated again and again, "otaku" performers and police clashed over Haruhi dances. Although the most notorious, Haruhi dances were not the only "otaku" performances thought by some in Akihabara to be a public disturbance or nuisance. On any given Sunday, dozens of fan groups swarmed around amateur idol singers and performed loud and wild cheerleading routines called *otagei* (literally "the otaku art"). All of this was reinforced by media—mass and niche, print and broadcast, online and social—representations of Akihabara, which positioned it as a place to observe "otaku" performances, if not participate in them. With police being dispatched and performances disrupted, "otaku" were at times making outright political statements by claiming the streets of Akihabara.

Amid growing concern about the chaos, the police became more aggressive in their attempts to reestablish order in Akihabara, even resorting to "public questioning" (*shokumu shitsumon*). While the media would stick a camera in the face of an "otaku" and ask "What's in your bag?" to provide the audience at home a tantalizing peek, police asked the same question during supposedly random searches on the street, which many performers saw as targeted harassment. For example, my friend Haruhi alleged that police would stop him on the pretense of suspicion of shoplifting; they of course knew who he was and found in his bag the schoolgirl character costume that they knew would be there, which led to probing about what he was planning to do with it (figure 4.8). They then reminded him, pointedly, that street performances are "forbidden" (*kinshi*) in Akihabara. Honestly, I initially had trouble squaring these narratives with the ubiquity of performance on the street, but the ordinance that the police were referring to was, in fact, as real as the harassment that I would later witness. Chiyoda Ward, the section of Tokyo where Akihabara is located—along with the National Diet, Supreme Court of Japan, Prime Minister's Official Residence, Imperial Palace, and more—does not permit "activities that disturb public order" (*zenryō na fūzoku wo gai suru katsudō*), and police made clear in handwritten signs placed around Akihabara from July 2007 that this includes street performances.[36] Performances might be overlooked in practice, but in theory they were against the rules. And some in particular, those

FIGURE 4.8
Haruhi is questioned by the police.

disturbing public order, were in the sights of authorities in Akihabara. At first Haruhi and other "otaku" performers perhaps did not know that they were running afoul of the ordinance, but with these police warnings, they could no longer plead ignorance as a defense.[37]

On the one hand officially forbidden, street performances were on the other hand a major aspect of Akihabara's media image. Indeed, media played a key role in presenting Akihabara as a space of "otaku" performance and drawing people to it. A Boss Coffee commercial from January 2008 offers a humorous parody of the scene.[38] A Japanese reporter stands on the street holding a microphone. In front of him is a film crew, and behind a Japanese woman in costume singing and dancing for a mass of Japanese men, who sing and dance along with her. "We've come to Akihabara," says the reporter. "There's a lot of excitement in the air!" After interviewing two performers, he concludes, "It seems that Akihabara is becoming like this." Although ambiguous, this statement nonetheless confirms that something is up on the streets of Akihabara, which viewers, of course, already know. This parody works because it is not far from the truth. In a personal interview, Sakuragawa Himeko, one of the costumed performers in the Boss Coffee commercial, admitted, "To be honest, I've never actually done a live performance on the street" (quoted in Galbraith 2009b, 106). This despite both the Boss Coffee commercial and her previous music video "Going to Akihabara!" (*Akiba ni iku non*, 2007), which was shot on the street and shows Sakuragawa alongside "otaku" performers.[39] If in the video Sakuragawa "wanted to capture a place that everyone knows" (quoted in Galbraith 2009b, 106), then she performed a certain way in Akihabara, or performed "Akihabara" in a certain way. Boss Coffee does the same (as do the less parodic examples discussed below).

Tension on the streets of Akihabara reached a boiling point in the summer of 2008. Vital to this was Sawamoto Asuka, a self-proclaimed "sexy idol" that wore a short skirt, climbed railings beside the street, and flashed her underwear as a form of "fan service." Although local residents and business owners denounced the indecency of Sawamoto's performances, reports about them appeared in numerous media outlets; her followers expanded into a mob, which moved around the neighborhood to avoid police. Some speculate that members of the media encouraged Sawamoto's performances (Akiba Blog 2008b), but she was nevertheless arrested for one of them on April 25, 2008. After this, programs such as *Information Live Miyane's Room* (Jōhō raibu Miyane ya), a talk show broadcast five days a week—which had earlier interviewed Sawamoto, no doubt titillating viewers—suggested that many street performers in Akihabara were dressed too provocatively. Performances such as Sawamoto's, combined with "otaku" performances and the hoards of cameramen there to film them, contributed to a growing consensus that Akihabara had descended into "a state of lawlessness" (*muhō jōtai*) (Akiba Blog 2008a). For their part, local residents and business owners took to the streets on April 28, 2008, to march with police and signs protesting performances (figure 4.9).

Still associated with Akihabara and promoted there, "otaku" performances increasingly needed to be brought under control. In a noteworthy example, on May 4, 2008, just over a week after Sawamoto's arrest and amid ongoing critique of the lawless street, the Akihabara Otaku Festival (*Akiba otaku matsuri*) was held. In advertisements, the event called for a new generation of "otaku" to join the festival in Akihabara (Raku Job 2008) (figure 4.10). Seeming nod to the street culture aside, the Akihabara Otaku Festival took place inside the UDX Building, where attendees were instructed not to dance rowdily or dress offensively. Beyond obeying the letter of the law and local ordinances, organizers also explicitly banned male-to-female crossplay and even "acts that are a nuisance to others" (*hoka no raijōsha ni meiwaku wo kakeru kōi*). Recognizable "otaku" performers such as Haruhi were thus not allowed to enter the Akihabara Otaku Festival, where a year

FIGURE 4.9 March against street performances in Akihabara.

before they had been the faces of the "otaku" festival on the streets of Akihabara. Inside the UDX Building, a landmark of the redevelopment zone, the Akihabara Otaku Festival shut out some "otaku" performances, even as it cultivated others and was itself an "otaku" performance.[40]

A short month later came the "Akihabara Incident" (*Akihabara tōrima jiken*), one of the worst mass slayings in postwar Japanese history. On June 8, 2008, Katō Tomohiro, a twenty-five-year-old dispatch worker stationed at a factory in Shizuoka Prefecture, drove a rented truck into the crowded Pedestrian Paradise in Akihabara and rampaged through the streets with a knife. By the time he was finally subdued by police, Katō had killed seven people and injured ten others. Taking this as the last straw, the Chiyoda Ward Council voted to discontinue the Pedestrian Paradise in Akihabara on June 12, 2008. This ushered in a period of reflection about what needed to change if the Pedestrian Paradise was ever to reopen, which was also more broadly about the present state and future direction of Akihabara. Among the things that needed to change, it turns out, were "otaku." Although Katō had very little if anything to do with the manga/anime fans congregating in the neighborhood (Slater and Galbraith 2011), in the wake of his arrest, many began to discuss problems associated with "otaku" performances in Akihabara. These problems, which had been building since the transformation of Akihabara in the 1990s, had to do with the neighborhood becoming "a playground for weirdoes" (*hen na hito no asobiba*) (Morikawa 2008, 288).[41] It was time, critics argued, to return to normal.

The Akihabara Liberation Demonstration

Walking from Chūō Street to Akihabara Station one afternoon in June 2007, I encounter a group of young Japanese men and women passing out fliers. In these heady days of activity on the street, it is not unusual to find people advertising some event or another, but this group on this day seems particularly earnest. In the brutal heat, the men are decked out in full business suits. I take a flier (figure 4.11), which is bright yellow and says at the top, "Rally at the Akihabara Liberation Demonstration (*Akihabara kaihō demo*) on June 30, 2007!"[42] A drawing below shows two men wearing helmets and sunglasses, the one on the left masking his lower face with a towel. Unmistakably resembling Japanese student radicals from the 1960s, these figures of resistance are aligned with "otaku" performances. Together they hold up a banner that reads, "Cosplay participation welcome," in which "cosplay" refers to the practice of manga/anime fans dressing in character costumes. Between the men at the center of the drawing are two bishōjo, whose eyes are covered by black bars but are obviously the main schoolgirl characters of *The Melancholy of Haruhi Suzumiya* and *Lucky Star* (Raki suta, 2007). The characters are dancing, as they do in their respective anime series, which famously inspired "otaku" performances on the streets of Akihabara. Even as they seem to be joining illicit "otaku" performances, the characters stand beside figures of resistance. Bold words are written across the drawing: "Let's start a revolution with the power of otaku!" Details of this revolution appear in a sidebar: "Make Akihabara a liberated zone! Otaku, moe, and the unpopular will occupy Akihabara." The notion of a "liberated zone" (*kaihōku*) has a history in Japanese protest politics (Sand 2013, 35, 39, 51), while the call to "occupy" (*senkyo suru*) resonates with more recent global movements (Hardt and Negri 2012).[43]

Going by the name "Shū-chan," the young man that handed me the flier is only too happy to elaborate on the reasons for the Akihabara Liberation Demonstration. As Shū-chan and his friends see it, Akihabara is a space for "otaku," who are outsiders that do not belong and are unwanted elsewhere. It is a marginal space for marginal people. All this stuff about the Crossfield Project and Cool Japan, the increased police presence, Shū-chan

FIGURE 4.10
The Akihabara Otaku Festival.

tells me that these are indicators of larger forces that would push "otaku" out of the neighborhood. Hence a demonstration against those in power, and a demonstration of "otaku" power, on the street. The official call-and-response of the Akihabara Liberation Demonstration speaks to its mission to keep Akihabara for "otaku:" "We'll make our future! We won't let anyone interfere in the things we love! For everyone's excitement and sparkle, we stand now!" Organizing the event are three groups—the Revolutionary Unpopular League (*Kakumei-teki himote dōmei*), the Revolutionary Otaku-ist League (*Kakumei-teki otaku-shugisha dōmei*), and the Revolutionary Moe-ist League (*Kakumei-teki moe-shugisha dōmei*)—two of which are allusions to the Japan Revolutionary Communist League, but dropping Japan and changing politics from anticapitalism to pro-otaku and pro-moe. Together they advocate a broad alliance:

FIGURE 4.11 The Akihabara Liberation Demonstration.

Calling all Akihabara otaku! Adult computer gamers and anime fans, trainspotters and military maniacs, net news junkies and those interested in communal production, Japanese and foreigners and aliens unite! The time has come to choose to live as we like or live restrained! People of the cosplay liberation faction! It doesn't matter if you are a man that dresses as a woman or a woman that dresses as a man! Maids also must rally now! Everyone, let's take on "weird forms" and liberate this darkened city! Unpopular men and women, virgins one and all! Love capitalism is shit! Let's reject love decided on physical appearance and money alone, which is ridiculous! People of heretical sexual orientation! There is nothing wrong with loving the two-dimensional! There is nothing wrong with loving boys! We will live honestly with our feelings! Those not in employment, education, or training, to the socially withdrawn! What entraps you is society at large! Society is wrong for

> being unable to save you! Everyone that is a minority! We have the right to live as we like without being held back by anyone! Let's fire the opening salvo and strike back at the many forms of violence of the majority![44]

Struck by the relationship between "otaku" and oppressed minorities spelled out in the flier, I ask Shū-chan if he believes that *Train Man* has improved things, which makes him grimace. Echoing Honda Tōru (Honda Tōru 2005a, 194–208), Shū-chan retorts that *Train Man* is a didactic message about an "otaku" that falls in love with a woman and "matures" as a man. By Shū-chan's estimation, this "otaku" performance does nothing to expand the imagination of an orientation toward the two-dimensional, which is still a "heretical sexual orientation" (*itan-teki sei-teki shikō*).[45] It does nothing to explore the possibility of relationships outside the model of "love capitalism." All it does, according to Shū-chan, is reinforce the mainstream stereotype of "otaku" as socially and sexually immature and in need of salvation. That this "otaku" performance takes place on the streets of Akihabara makes it all the more insulting to Shū-chan, who urges me to come to the demonstration and see for myself what is absent from *Train Man.*

Rather than dismiss this "otaku" performance in Akihabara (Morikawa 2008, 281), I accept Shū-chan's invitation on June 30, Saturday. Once again in my character costume, I arrive at the meeting spot, which is Rensei Park on the grounds of an abandoned middle school beyond Kuramaebashi Street. At 2:30 in the afternoon, the organizers use loudspeakers to prompt the assembled men and women, many in costume, to follow them and start walking. Although those at the head of the line shout slogans for us to repeat back, things are relatively quiet along Shōheibashi Street at the back edge of Akihabara. This changes drastically, however, as the demonstration turns down Kanda-Myōjin Street and moves toward Chūō Street. Where the two roads cross, at the heart of Akihabara, people pour off side streets and sidewalks to take part in the march, which was later estimated to have involved over five hundred people (figure 4.12). As numbers swell, the lengthening line of demonstrators becomes segmented. Up front, the organizers chant about keeping Akihabara for "otaku" and issues concerning redevelopment. They wear helmets, sunglasses, and towel masks, which are plainly references to Japanese student radicals from the 1960s, but the uniform has been appropriated by standard-bearers of the unpopular, "otaku," and moe in Akihabara (figure 4.13).

Meanwhile, further down the line are "otaku" performances that might not immediately seem as political. From specific characters such as Haruhi to more general types such as maids, many of the demonstrators are in costume. Crossplaying men are highly visible (figure 4.14). Signs identify groups formed online and at schools. Anime music blares from carted sound systems, which gets those within earshot singing and dancing. Not surprisingly, given its traction among manga/anime fans at the time, "Sunny Sunny Happiness" is a consistent choice. Becoming an impromptu choir singing and dancing along, the voices grow louder as the demonstration continues on Kanda-Myōjin Street across Chūō Street and into the redevelopment zone. The unofficial anthem of the street culture, "Sunny Sunny Happiness" reverberates off the windows of the UDX Building and Daibiru skyscraper. Some engage in a call-and-response distinct from what is happening at the head of the line: one person calls out "Suzumiya!," and many more respond "Haruhi!" The voices are insistent: "Suzumiya!" "HARUHI!" "Suzumiya!" "HARUHI!" "Suzumiya!" "HARUHI!" Against the backdrop of Haruhi crossplay and dances engendering conflict with authorities in the summer of 2007, these shared "otaku" performances are a significant aspect of the Akihabara Liberation Demonstration.

In many ways, Haruhi is an ideal symbol for "otaku" performances in Akihabara generally and the Akihabara Liberation Demonstration specifically. In part, *The Melancholy of Haruhi Suzumiya* is the story of an eponymous high school student unsettling the rhythms and routines of everyday life. At a time of strict discipline and control of youthful energy, the brilliant but eccentric Haruhi is bored with school and forms a club for extracurricular activities, which she hopes will lead to some excitement and something extraordinary; she dreams of time travelers, aliens, and superpowered individuals. Unbeknownst to Haruhi, she is a being capable of bending reality to her will—in fact, she is already doing so. In addition to a fairly normal classmate that she recruits, the three other members of Haruhi's club are secretly a time traveler, an alien, and a superpowered individual. Together, the ragtag group works to keep Haruhi busy and happy so that she does not will something terrible into a reality. Ultimately, rather than otherworldly encounters, it turns out that small group adventures are what transform an ordinary and boring world into something extraordinary and exciting.

The Melancholy of Haruhi Suzumiya is about coming together with others, which reaches out from the world of the anime to that of viewers. There are three facets to this. First, Haruhi forms a group, the "SOS Brigade" (*SOS-dan*), and is seeking members (figure 4.15). Using "otaku" slang such as "moe,"

FIGURE 4.12
The march grows as people pour into the street and walk together.

FIGURE 4.13
The front of the line, where demonstrators dress as student radicals. Photo by Danny Choo.

FIGURE 4.14
Further down the line, Haruhi cross-players. Photo by Danny Choo.

Haruhi appeals to manga/anime fans, who imaginatively join her and escape from the everyday. Second, the SOS Brigade is a bunch of weirdoes, and although Haruhi is unaware of just how weird they actually are, this is precisely what she is looking for in members. To Haruhi, the weirder one is, the better, which speaks to people that feel weird, marginal, like outsiders.[46] Third, fans are provided with ways to take part in the activities of the SOS Brigade. The original anime series ends each episode with Haruhi and the SOS Brigade dancing to "Sunny Sunny Happiness," and the choreography is realistic enough for fans to follow along. A version later released shows the bodily movements of characters in even greater detail, and is something of a guide to the Haruhi dance. It is thus entirely possible to dance with and as Haruhi, a dance that spread from private rooms to video-sharing sites to public spaces in Akihabara. With respect to fans of the cult film, one might dub this the "Rocky Horror effect," in which viewers are drawn to a world of weirdoes, want to participate in it, and are given ritual actions that allow them to do so. As with *The Rocky Horror Picture Show* (1975) and its infamous "Time Warp" sequence, Haruhi fans dance along with aliens and others, but they carry this outside theaters onto the streets.[47]

The Akihabara Liberation Demonstration is about making space for such "otaku" performances. The SOS Brigade stands for "Spreading Excitement All Over the World with Haruhi Suzumiya Brigade" (*Sekai wo ōi ni moriageru tame no Suzumiya Haruhi no dan*), which is also what the Akihabara Liberation Demonstration stands for. As noted in the official call-and-response, "For everyone's excitement and sparkle, we stand now!" Like Haruhi, the organizers embrace weirdoes—Japanese, foreigners, and aliens; bishōjo-oriented men and men crossplaying as cute girl characters; everyone that is a minority—including many from SOS Brigades formed by fans across the country (figure 4.16). They encourage "otaku" performers to take on "weird forms" (*hen na kakkō*). On the street, the message of the Akihabara Liberation Demonstration and those singing and dancing along with "Sunny Sunny Happiness" seems clear: we are "otaku" and we are in Akihabara; we are "otaku" and Akihabara is a space for us; we are weird and want to keep this space weird. Marching with them, the politics are palpable. If the proximity of "otaku" performances and figures of resistance—men crossplaying as Haruhi next to men wearing the uniform of Japanese student radicals—does not say enough, one demonstrator waves a Japanese flag upon which he has spray-painted the sign of anarchy. As it passes by Akihabara Station, where Asō Tarō would later in the year hold a political rally of his own and praise "otaku," as it passes through the redevelopment zone, the flag sticks out more

FIGURE 4.15 Haruhi seeks members for her SOS Brigade.

and more. Drawing the sign of anarchy over the rising sun and parading it alongside “otaku” performances, the demonstrator suggests that something is occurring in Akihabara that disrupts the order of the nation (figure 4.17).

In claiming the Holy Land of Otaku and Moe City, the Akihabara Liberation Demonstration is not only about pushing back against developers and authorities, but also about demonstrating “otaku” liberation in Akihabara. Among other things, “otaku” performers openly express affection for bishōjo from manga, anime, and computer/console games. This affection takes “weird forms,” for example, crossplaying as cute girl characters. If this affection had been shared at special events and in niche media, which supported it, then such is also the case in Akihabara, but in a more sustained and public way. The public sex culture in Akihabara, specifically the culture of imaginary sex in public, is part of a space imagined and created through “otaku” performances. As an example of such “otaku” performance, the Akihabara Liberation Demonstration announces that manga/anime fans do not have to “mature” into social and sexual roles defined and demanded by others. The official call-and-response: “We won’t let anyone interfere in the things we love!” Together, “otaku” performers imagine and create a space for shared orientation toward and affective relations with characters. A “utopian image of a spontaneous public appropriating common space”

FIGURE 4.16 SOS Brigades represent in Akihabara. Photo by Danny Choo.

(Sand 2013, 45), the Akihabara Liberation Demonstration is also a vision of the Holy Land of Otaku and Moe City.

If restrictive surveillance and law enforcement made spectacular "otaku" performances more difficult in Akihabara in the summer of 2007, then police are ironically required for the Akihabara Liberation Demonstration. To march on the streets, the organizers submitted a formal request and received a permit. As demonstrators shout, dance, and sing, officers walk in front, beside, and behind the line to direct traffic. Their presence is appreciated as we continue on Kanda-Myōjin Street, pass Yodobashi Camera, and turn onto Shōwa Street, where cars would otherwise be hurtling at us. After a brief stretch, we enter a side street and come to Izumi Park, our final destination. Exuberant at what feels like a victory in the revolution we imagine and create together, demonstrators flow into the park and begin engaging in improvised photo shoots, networking, and play. We can barely restrain ourselves enough to listen to the organizers perched at an elevated position and addressing us through a loudspeaker. Hardly paying attention, I emulate others in responding at appropriate moments with a raised fist and hearty cheer—until the police move in and order us to disperse. When I ask a nearby officer why this is necessary, he simply gestures to the school

FIGURE 4.17
The sign of anarchy over Japan in Akihabara.

next door, where curious students peer through a fence at our scruffy assembly and sweaty antics. The time of the Akihabara Liberation Demonstration has come to an end, right next to a space of discipline and control not unlike the one that Haruhi longs to escape in her anime world.

If parks were important for "otaku" performances in Akihabara, which meant occupying public spaces and transforming them into "otaku" spaces, then they have predictably enough been recuperated for other purposes. For example, Rensei Park, where the Akihabara Liberation Demonstration kicked off, is now attached to a fine art gallery, which opened in 2010. More illustrative is Hōrin Park, which is located near Chūō Street and was a staging ground for Haruhi dances. On one side of the park is an elementary school, and on the other side is Kamikaze Style, which caters to "otaku" with irreverent images of bishōjo, sex, and violence. Needless to say, some local residents and business owners had reservations about letting it be. In 2013, an imposing steel fence was erected around Hōrin Park, which is used to limit access but more generally signals that the space is not as open as it once was. Then, in 2014, Akihabara Park, which is right next to Akihabara Station in the redevelopment zone and had attracted the homeless as well as "otaku" performers, was closed and completely paved over. Still identified with a placard as Akihabara Park, it is in fact a smooth, clean walkway.

Even as some "otaku" performances replace others over time—*Train Man*, for example, shows its protagonist in a café adjacent to Akihabara Park, where "otaku" performers no longer gather—the management of parks points to something afoot in Akihabara more broadly.[48]

Managing Akihabara and Disciplining "Otaku"

In the wake of the Pedestrian Paradise being discontinued on June 12, 2008, many began to reexamine the relationship between "otaku," Akihabara, and Cool Japan. Chief among them was Kobayashi Takaya, a member of the Chiyoda Ward Council. As an established resident of Akihabara—detailed in his book, *Akihabara Ancestor* (Akiba genjin, 2006)—Kobayashi positions himself as the neighborhood's representative and describes his political function as its "management" (*kanri*).[49] In theory, Kobayashi sees the value of "otaku" as enthusiastic consumers and potential innovators (along the lines of Kitabayashi 2004), but in practice he is more ambivalent. For example, in January 2008, I attended a small event held in the Daibiru skyscraper in Akihabara's redevelopment zone, where Kobayashi was speaking. Addressing a roomful of entrepreneurs, Kobayashi adopted a long view of the neighborhood, starting from its past as Japan's premier electric town and highlighting its new direction with the Crossfield Project. Excised from the narrative were "otaku," and more specifically, bishōjo-oriented men. When queried about his thoughts on "otaku" performances, Kobayashi relegated them to a footnote in the history of Akihabara, the once and future Electric Town of Japan. On the street, however, Kobayashi seems a man caught between imaginaries of Akihabara. As the publisher of *Akibatsū*, a free magazine promoting businesses in Akihabara, Kobayashi makes bishōjo into cover girls, which appeals to "otaku" as do other media and material in the neighborhood. Next to Hōrin Park on the side of Kamikaze Style, Kobayashi's straight-faced campaign poster appears amid a sea of cute girl characters (figure 4.18).[50]

On April 21, 2009, I approached Kobayashi for a personal interview to clarify what had happened with the Pedestrian Paradise, which was still on hiatus. While the Akihabara Incident had been the direct trigger for discontinuing the Pedestrian Paradise, Kobayashi confirmed that larger concerns about "otaku" performances and the lawless street informed the decision. His constituents, Kobayashi explained, are local residents and business owners, who voiced strong opposition to performances and the

FIGURE 4.18 Politics in Akihabara: Kobayashi amid bishōjo.

crowds they drew. These were not customers putting coins into the coffers; if anything, his constituents felt that performances blocked customers and scared them off. Underscoring tension between people that live and own property in Akihabara and those that visit for fun, Kobayashi argued that the issue with the Pedestrian Paradise specifically and the neighborhood more generally was that "people coming to play turned it into a place of performance." To the key phrases "people coming to play" (*asobi ni kuru hito*) and "a place of performance" (*pafōmansu no basho*) Kobayashi added problematic "ways of using" (*tsukaikata*) the street. In short, some people were using the street in the wrong way during the Pedestrian Paradise in Akihabara, to play and perform rather than stroll and shop, which was unauthorized by Chiyoda Ward and unpopular among locals.

Although there had been street performances in Akihabara since at least the late 1990s (recall Momoi Halko), it was when "otaku" performances moved front and center that police intervention became necessary in the mid- and late 2000s. After the Akihabara boom, "otaku" performances increased in scale and frequency on the street, which local residents and business owners perceived as disruptive. According to Kobayashi, many thought that performances were ruining Akihabara's reputation. It is more accurate, however, to say that performances were giving Akihabara a reputation other than the one that local residents and business owners, specifically those with deep roots in the neighborhood and influential positions in community and commerce organizations, had hoped for. Indeed, Kobayashi's message at the Daibiru skyscraper resonates with his constituents, who remember Akihabara as an electric town and see its path forward with the Crossfield Project. What they do not see is Akihabara as the Holy Land of Otaku and Moe City, which puts them at odds with manga/anime fans and stores that rose to prominence from the late 1990s into the 2000s. In a certain sense, "otaku" performances were disruptive not just on the street, but also to the symbolic return of the Electric Town of Japan. Everyone around Kobayashi, he told me firmly, was against reviving the Pedestrian Paradise if it meant more performers, whom his constituents "do not like" (see also Morikawa 2008, 288–89). If the Akihabara Liberation Demonstration was about keeping space open for "otaku" performances, then Kobayashi's constituents wanted to keep Akihabara from such performers, who had colonized their streets.

In his management role in Akihabara, Kobayashi had dialed in on "otaku." On the one hand, he appreciated that "otaku" performances contributed to the perception of Akihabara as a hotspot, which attracted media and tourism and invigorated the neighborhood as a whole, if not always the businesses of his older constituents. On the other hand, "otaku" performances on the street were disruptive of not only public order, but also the reformed image of Akihabara and "otaku." In our personal interview, Kobayashi stressed that negative stereotypes of "otaku" persist in Japan. He then proceeded to draw a line between the newly improved image of "otaku" in Akihabara—epitomized by *Train Man*, of course—and that of what he called "weird otaku" (*hen na otaku*). If one follows the logic, then these "weird otaku" are a step backward. As Kobayashi defined them, "weird otaku" are the ones coming to Akihabara to play, or those turning it into a place of performance. To be fair, *Train Man* also turns Akihabara into a place of performance, as did Asō Tarō when he chose it as his platform to herald "otaku" as the avant-garde of Cool Japan. In singling out "weird otaku," those in the Akihabara Liberation Demonstration, for example, Kobayashi was saying that the stage needed to be better managed. The trick was to promote the newly improved image of "otaku" in Akihabara while at the same time policing "weird otaku" on the street. In envisioning Akihabara as a "showcase" (*shōkēsu*), Kobayashi saw no room for "weird otaku." (Recall the Akihabara Otaku Festival in the UDX Building similarly shutting them out.) For the success of what he championed as the project of "city-making" (*machizukuri*), Kobayashi understood that something must be done about "weird otaku."

In discussing "weird otaku," Kobayashi several times touched on issues of sexuality. Over the course of our interview, the target shifted from the risqué costumes of performers such as Sawamoto Asuka to the men coming to see them to crossplayers to imaginary sex and violence in bishōjo manga, anime, and games. On this last point of cute girl characters in adult content, which remains legal in Japan, Kobayashi suggested that some of it is "no good" (*dame*) and acknowledged that it has generated friction. If Akihabara is the Holy Land of Otaku and Moe City, where affection for fictional characters is shared more openly than anywhere else in Japan or the world, then Kobayashi professed that weird forms of affection are out of sync with the rest of Japan and the world.[51] Although Kobayashi's own *Akibatsū* has bishōjo as cover girls and seems to appeal to "otaku," he nonetheless distanced himself from sexuality associated with "weird otaku" while sitting with me. In retrospect, this is unsurprising, given that a bishōjo game featuring imaginary sex and violence involving underage characters had made international news in February 2009 (Galbraith 2017). Well informed about such things, and aware of the tradition of the United States critiquing sexuality in Japan, Kobayashi perhaps imagined that the American asking questions expected such a position from him. As Kobayashi seemed to fear, in the years following our interview, Akihabara did indeed become a symbol of "weird otaku" sexuality, if not also weird Japanese sexuality, for reporters and activists from around the world (Lah 2010; Adelstein and Kubo 2014; Ripley, Whiteman, and Henry 2014; Ostrovsky 2015; Dooley 2017).

It might be tempting to dismiss Kobayashi as an individual voice, but weirdness and sexuality come up quite often in deliberations about Akihabara and its future. I was reminded of this while participating in a panel during the Area Open Mini Symposium in Akihabara (*Chi'iki ōpun mini shinpojiumu in Akihabara*) on March 5, 2012. Organized by the Ministry of Economy, Trade, and Industry, the stated purpose of the symposium was to evaluate the place of Akihabara in ongoing Cool Japan policy and public diplomacy initiatives. There were five people on the panel: Suzuki Yū'ichirō and Migitaka Yasutomo, who own "moe businesses" catering to "otaku" in Akihabara; Ono Kazushi, president of Onoden, founded in 1951 and one of the oldest continually operating retailers of home appliances and electronics in the neighborhood; Seno'o Ken'ichirō, a major player in the Crossfield Project; and myself, possibly invited as an anthropologist with years of experience in the field, but more likely as a local tour guide and writer of books for manga/anime fans, and even more likely as a token foreigner that seemed to demonstrate the global influence of Japanese popular culture. I clearly stood out to the audience of bureaucrats, journalists, and curious others gathered at Mogra, a basement club on the outskirts of Akihabara that specializes in "otaku" music. While at first mostly celebrating the culture of Akihabara and Cool Japan, things veered in another direction when Ono introduced some of his concerns:

> Next to my store [on Chūō Street], there is a shop specializing in adult goods. When that store opened, it was nothing but adult goods from top to bottom, but recently it has been placing candies on display out front. Young people from China and Asia, to put it simply from the Confucian world, they find the displays interesting and enter that adult goods shop. Then they run out screaming. This is a little different from what's been said here today, but moral values differ so much from country to country. I know that Akihabara is an interesting place because everything is so mixed up, but if we don't straighten it out somehow there is a danger that people coming to Japan will leave thinking that Akihabara is awful. It would be terrible if, under the banner of Cool Japan, we instead became Porno Japan. Certainly every country has its own permissible range for that sort of thing [that is, sex]. If we don't control the interaction, and an interesting town is instead taken to be a weird town, I think we'll be in a lot of trouble. (METI 2012, 64–65)

One of those older residents and business owners in Kobayashi's constituency, Ono basically made the same point about needing to better manage Akihabara as a showcase. Now that the ice had been broken, Seno'o took the microphone: "To follow what Mr. Ono just said, we struggled with exactly that issue at the time of the project to redevelop Akihabara. . . . There was actually quite a debate then about the main street being dotted with stores that you wouldn't want children to go into, and school trips kept their distance from Akihabara. They thought Akihabara was a scary town, or a weird town" (METI 2012, 65; also Morikawa 2008, 288–89). With criticism of "otaku" and harmful manga/anime from the 1990s (Schodt 1996, 45–59) still simmering in the 2000s (Cather 2012, 233–37), it makes sense that Seno'o encountered some of this in Akihabara. If, however, the Crossfield Project was in part about improving a "bad image" (*warui imēji*), then it is significant that surveys conducted in Japan in 2005 show that over 80 percent of respondents saw Akihabara as an "otaku town" (*otaku no machi*), and roughly five times more associated it with moe than with the Crossfield Project (Morikawa 2008, 259–62). To be blunt, as Kobayashi and his constituents intimated, the brand image of the Electric Town of Japan had been disrupted by "weird otaku," who had made it a "scary town" (*kowai machi*) or "weird town" (*hen na machi*). At the symposium, Seno'o argued that members of the media exacerbated the problem by focusing on the weird, even as they also encouraged "otaku" performances.

Speaking for moe businesses, Suzuki advocated balance between the "underground" (*angura*) and "clean" (*kurīn*) aspects of Akihabara, but there was obvious anxiety about the potential impact on the image of the neighborhood and nation. For their part, Ono and Seno'o were explicit about the need to better manage bodies on the street, be they tourists that might be exposed to offensive things or "otaku" performers. At the end of the panel discussion, Ono took his case directly to officials from the Ministry of Economy, Trade, and Industry in the audience. "As representatives of the nation," he dramatically inquired, "what direction do you want to take Cool Japan using Akihabara?" (METI 2012, 74). Note Ono's rhetoric here: as a nation, the time has come to think about how to use Akihabara. Not only a showcase, but a showcase of Cool Japan, the neighborhood is a matter of national concern, and Ono's message was straightforward: unmanaged, it could give the impression of being a "weird town" (*hen na machi*); by association, Cool Japan could transform into what he called "Porno Japan" (*poruno Japan*), or, in keeping with the language of critique, Weird Japan. "Weird otaku" factor into the image of Akihabara as a weird town and, metonymically, the image of Weird Japan. In this way, "otaku" performance in Akihabara becomes a political issue.[52]

Back in 2009, debating what was to become of the Pedestrian Paradise in Akihabara, all eyes were on the street and "otaku." For their part, "otaku" performers were scrutinizing themselves and one another. Consider the example of AKIBA *Memory 2005~2007*, an exhibition held at Art Jeuness Akihabara in June 2009. Located on Chūō Street and selling bishōjo media and merchandise, Art Jeuness Akihabara was known as an "otaku" store. A series of black-and-white photographs of the Pedestrian Paradise in Akihabara, including many "otaku" performers, AKIBA *Memory 2005~2007* drew "otaku" performers, who could be overheard excitedly sharing past experiences. In many ways, the exhibition felt like a celebration of the street culture up to the year of the mass Haruhi dances. At the same time, organizers asked departing visitors to vote on reopening the Pedestrian Paradise, and an astonishingly large number were against bringing it back in the form that they had seen. Visitors unpacked their positions in comments written on sticky notes and posted on a message board for others to consider. At AKIBA *Memory 2005~2007*, I was struck by how many took it as an opportunity to reflect on "otaku" performances getting out of hand. A typical comment read that self-restraint was required if the street was to be free for everyone. Stating common sense to the collective, these posted comments hint at a kind of surveillance and policing internal to "otaku" in Akihabara, which was matched with external surveillance and policing. On January 26, 2010, Akihabara installed sixteen security cameras trained on the street, with neighborhood associations investing in another thirty-four (Japan Times 2010). In casual conversations, people joked that Chūō Street in Akihabara was probably better monitored than Kabukichō, which is a stronghold for organized crime in Shinjuku, Tokyo.

When the Pedestrian Paradise finally returned on January 23, 2011, it was emphatically said to be "experimental" (*jikken-teki*), and the test was carefully administered. Widely publicized new rules, which were just the old rules made explicit, included "no performances" (*pafōmansu kinshi*) (figure 4.19). Cooperation was requested to ensure that the street was "safe" (*anzen*) and available for "everyone" (*daremo*). That cooperation was ensured by the not-so-subtle presence of authorities. On Chūō Street during the Pedestrian Paradise experiment, uniformed police officers and volunteer citizen patrols were far more prevalent than "otaku" performers (figure 4.20). When a crossplaying "otaku" performer did appear, he was instantaneously surrounded by cameras and cops and escorted away (figure 4.21). Although this man was guilty only of wearing an anime character costume in public, when combined with media attention and causing a scene on the street in Akihabara, his "otaku" performance warranted swift disciplinary action. The next day, photographs of this negative "otaku" performance, and the positive police performance in response, were printed in nationally circulated newspapers (figure 4.22). In photographs of the street, one sees the estimated 100,000 people that visited Akihabara on January 23, 2011, but not a single one in costume (figure 4.23). People were performing on the street, but very visibly not in the ways that they had been before. Under strictly controlled conditions, they performed by using the street in the right way, which is to say for strolling and shopping.

Following this achievement, three years after it had been discontinued, the Pedestrian Paradise in Akihabara was reinstated in 2011, but the festival recalled in AKIBA *Memory 2005~2007* was increasingly distant. Aware of watching eyes and probable consequences, "otaku" performers did not stand out on the street, let alone attempt a takeover. As a company called Akihabara Town Management announces in slightly Orwellian signs, the neighborhood is "beautiful, peaceful, and happy," or has been made clean, calm, and consumer friendly (figure 4.24). From the perspective of historian Jordan Sand, what occurred in Akihabara is eerily familiar. When Pedestrian Paradises were first held in Tokyo in the 1970s, activists cautioned about "the new guise of power, appearing to offer a *hiroba* [= public space] to the citizenry, then ripping off its mask and revealing the reality of the police state at the moment that citizens sought to 'exercise true spontaneity'" (Sand 2013, 51). During the Pedestrian Paradise in Akihabara, the response to the spontaneity of "otaku" performances was police intervention. In Akihabara, as elsewhere, "the pedestrian paradise was thus revealed to be a new kind of openly policed public space built around limited free intercourse and controlled communication" (52), but what the space communicated is also crucial.

On the one hand, in Akihabara, "otaku" were claiming space with and for their performances, which was part of imagining and creating the Holy Land of Otaku and Moe City. Situating these "otaku" performances in the history of appropriation of public space after the student movement ended in the 1970s—and there were, at least for the organizers of the Akihabara Liberation Demonstration, connections—Sand does much to highlight their politics (Sand 2013, 52–53). On the other hand, in Akihabara, elected officials, developers, and locals were claiming space for the Electric Town of Japan and Cool Japan, where the place of "otaku" was tenuous at best. For critics, "otaku" performances were disruptive to the Electric Town of Japan and Cool Japan, at least potentially, but others saw them as necessary, if needing management. While Sand portrays Pedestrian Paradises in the 1970s as a way to capture the student movement's energy, which exposes "the system's power of co-optation" (51), things were a little less coherent in Akihabara. Even as policing "otaku" performances smothered movement on the street, promoters co-opted the "otaku" image. Important to various stakeholders, the struggle over Akihabara as "otaku" space led to conflicting and often confusing "otaku" performances after the crackdowns began in 2007.

Performing "Otaku" after the Crackdowns

The deluge of media devoted to Akihabara attracted tourists, but many were upset by what they discovered there. In fact, in 2007, Akihabara was the fifteenth most recommended place for foreign visitors to Japan, but the

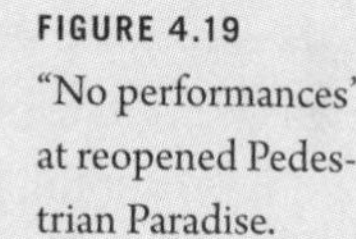

FIGURE 4.19
"No performances" at reopened Pedestrian Paradise.

FIGURE 4.20
Citizen patrols ensure that everything is in order. Photo by Adrian A. Lozano.

FIGURE 4.21
Crossplayer mobbed by cameras and authorities. Photo by Adrian A. Lozano.

FIGURE 4.22
Police performance reported in national papers.

東京新聞

2011年(平成23年) 1月24日

再び歩けるアキバ

10万人が来た！ ホコ天復活ルポ

安全な街願う

ルール厳しく

八ッ場 再計算なお疑問

国「流量3％減」 専門家「9％減」

全データ公開必要

宮崎インフル 41万羽殺処分

記者EV体験ドライブ

節分に小鬼巻きいかが

卓球男子単で水谷V5

国の「再計算」に疑問符

荒れ地変身29歳の挑戦

03-6910-2201

FAX 03-3595-6935

0120-026-999

03-6910-2556

FIGURE 4.23
Street packed with people, but none in character costume. Photo by Adrian A. Lozano.

FIGURE 4.24 Akihabara Town Management says, "Smile!"

eighth most disappointing (JNTO 2008b). There are a number of ways to interpret these survey results from the Japan National Tourism Organization. During my time guiding tours in Akihabara, I found that many foreign visitors were fans of director Miyazaki Hayao, mainstream manga/anime franchises such as *Naruto* (1997–), and Japanese game series such as *Final Fantasy* (1987–). These men and women often identified as "otaku" and came to Akihabara to find what they had heard was the Holy Land of Otaku, the beating heart of their global movement, their very own Cool Japan. In Akihabara, however, they came face to face with a local "otaku" movement with roots in adult computer gaming and tightly focused on affection for cute girl characters. While these visitors thought "otaku" meant manga/anime fans in general, in Akihabara, the Moe City, they saw men responding to bishōjo in adult manga, anime, and games; in pornographic fanzines; as provocatively posed figurines; and much, much more. However consistent with "otaku" in a certain historical sense, this was not what they had imagined as the Holy Land of Otaku. Visiting Cool Japan in Akihabara left many with impressions of "Porno Japan" (METI 2012, 64) or Weird Japan.

Foreign visitors to Akihabara might also have felt let down because they did not get the Holy Land of Otaku and Moe City that they had seen advertised. Visitors that associated Akihabara with affection for fictional worlds and characters spilling onto the streets were disappointed to learn that "otaku" performances such as Haruhi dances were nowhere to be seen. Promised by JNTO's English-language website "otaku tours" of the "Otaku Mecca," many visitors expected something that they did not get, especially after the discontinuation of the Pedestrian Paradise in June 2008 and stricter law enforcement that for all intents and purposes ended spectacular street performances.[53] One could conceivably imagine that JNTO was slow to respond to what was happening on the ground in Akihabara, but their promotional strategy remained unchanged years after the fact. In their Visit Japan Year 2010 Winter Campaign pamphlet, alongside entries for kabuki, sumo, and Japanese gardens, there is an entry titled "Pop Culture" (figure 4.25). Written in English, it reads in part, "Akihabara is where you will find all items related to animated cartoons and cartoon books, and is famous as the source of conveying *Otaku* culture to the world" (JNTO 2010, 7). The explanation is illustrated with a photograph of young Japanese men and women in colorful costumes on the street. Upon inspection, it turns out that the photograph is of a mass Haruhi dance on Chūō Street; checked against archival footage, the "otaku" performance can be traced to the summer of 2007. The photograph, then, is of an "otaku" performance denounced by local residents and business owners as disruptive and forbidden in Chiyoda Ward.

Focusing attention on costumed women, which resonates with the image of consumable femininity and male bias of Cool Japan policy and public diplomacy initiatives (Miller 2011), closer examination of the photograph reveals male-to-female crossplayers in the Haruhi character's schoolgirl uniform. They have been pushed to the margins, almost cut out, but there they are in Akihabara. In 2007, these were among the "otaku" performances that the Akihabara Liberation Demonstration encouraged: taking on "weird forms" and claiming the neighborhood as a weird space for weirdoes. These were also among the "otaku" performances that Kobayashi Takaya and others described as "weird," which were a disturbance to public order and the brand image of the Electric Town of Japan and Cool Japan. In fact, responding to complaints from local residents and business owners, authorities broke up Haruhi dances multiple times in the summer of 2007. By 2008, crossplay was explicitly banned from the Akihabara Otaku Festival, even as "otaku" performances taking place on a street were condemned as lawless and finally shut down by the Chiyoda Ward Council. In 2010, JNTO was employing a photograph of a shared "otaku" performance in Akihabara—an image from before crackdowns that policed them

Tokyo Art and Culture

Overview of Tokyo today

Kabuki

A classical performing art performed only by actors

Japan's classical theatrical performance of kabuki is well known throughout the world. Characterized by its rhythmical manner of elocution, colorful makeup and gorgeous stage settings, kabuki is best characterized by its all-male cast, with actors playing all female roles. Kabuki represents traditional culture passed on since the Edo Period where only men are permitted on stage. Performances are given almost every day at Kabuki-za Theater, and tickets can be purchased at its booking office or other locations.

Pop culture

Japan's pop culture that has impacted the entire world

Japanese culture is not restricted to traditional culture. Today, Japan's pop culture including cartoon books, animations and games are attracting worldwide attention. The Tokyo metropolitan area includes all the spots that tickle the minds of fans, particularly "Pokemon Center" in Hamamatsucho, Hello Kitty's "Sanrio Puroland," and "Ghibli Museum, Mitaka" (famous for Hayao Miyazaki's animated cartoons). Akihabara is where you will find all items related to animated cartoons and cartoon books, and is famous as the source of conveying *Otaku* culture to the world.

Sumo

Japan's national sport that gives importance to dignity and traditional manner

Sumo is a kind of sports performance peculiar to Japan that originated many centuries ago, where a bout involves two *rikishi* (professional wrestlers) engaging in various winning techniques on a ring called *dohyo*. As Japan's national sport backed by a long history, sumo is now internationally well-known, and recently more foreign *rikishi* have participated. In the sumo world, *banzuke* is a published listing of the power rankings of all *rikishi*". The highest division in sumo is called *maku-no-uchi* or *maku-uchi*, with the highest rank being *yokozuna*. Six official large-scale sumo tournaments (called *Hon-basho*,) are held during each year.

Ukiyo-e

Woodblock prints developed out of common people's culture in the Edo Period

Ukiyo-e depicts such motifs as kabuki actors, landscapes and other things popular among general people in the 17th to 18th centuries (Edo Period). The most famous *ukiyo-e* artists are Utagawa Hiroshige, who painted "Fifty-three Stations of the Tokaido," and Katsushika Hokusai, who is famous for his "Thirty-six Views of Mt. Fuji." *Ukiyo-e* can be appreciated at the Edo-Tokyo Museum and some other places.

Japan's largest fish market

Located on the River Sumida, Tsukiji market is well known as Japan's largest wholesale fish market. In fact, Tsukiji market is so famous for the assortment of tuna brought in from all over the world that the name "Tsukiji" immediately reminds us of tuna. The market is divided into two sections: the inner market where professionals conduct auctions, and the outer market where many retailers open their stores in rows.
There are many fresh fish stores, sushi restaurants and other shops in the outer market open to tourists and general visitors, and you may wish to visit such facilities during your tour of the market. While in the inner market, please be sure to watch your manners as a visitor.

Tsukiji market

Japanese gardens

Japan's traditional beauty existing in the heart of a city

Quite different from Western-style gardens, Japanese gardens are designed to convey a sense of beauty by carefully reproducing natural landscapes. In the central part of Tokyo, there are traditional gardens at the sites of former mansions of feudal lords, on the premises of Buddhist temples, hotels, and other places, as well as gardens now being well-maintained as public parks. "Rikugi-en" located in the northern part of the city is one such Japanese garden with many spots of interest, including a hilly mound and a large pond.

For further details, please visit the website. http://www.vjy2010.jp/cp

6

7

FIGURE 4.25 Akihabara in Visit Japan Year 2010 Winter Campaign pamphlet.

out of existence—to promote tourism to Japan. Visitors compelled by this image and coming to Akihabara looking for such "otaku" performances, or perhaps even to join them, were no doubt frustrated by their absence. If Akihabara is, as JNTO puts it, a place for "conveying *Otaku* culture to the world" (JNTO 2010, 7), then what is conveyed about it is often out of sync with the street. In this way, caught between promotional discourse and police discipline, "otaku" performances were partially incorporated into Cool Japan but not actually allowed in Akihabara, Japan.

Of course, JNTO was not alone in performing Akihabara as "otaku" space after the crackdowns. Made famous by artwork that invokes the imagination and creativity of "otaku," Murakami Takashi organized "otaku" performances at festivals such as his GEISAI#11, which included "a special exhibit on the subcultures of Tokyo's Akihabara district" (Design Boom 2008).

Held in September 2008, "otaku" performances at GEISAI#11 seemed to reference the street in Akihabara, but would not be permitted there. With the closing of the Pedestrian Paradise months before, "otaku" performances of this kind had been almost completely eradicated, but still appeared in this showcase of cool Japanese art. Even as artists expressed "otaku culture" (*otaku bunka*) in their works, GEISAI#11 set up its own "little Akihabara" (*puchi Akiba*) (Miyamura 2008). Noting visitors from around the world, and appealing to foreign judges, many artists took as their theme "Japanese culture such as schoolgirls and eroticism" (*joshikōsei ya ero to itta Nihon bunka*) (Miyamura 2008). The convergence of "Japanese culture," "otaku culture," and "Akihabara subcultures" should not be overlooked. In 2008, *Time* magazine named Murakami one of its one hundred most influential people, which suggests just how much he has done to popularize certain ideas about Japan, "otaku," and Akihabara.

So many took notice of Murakami's "Akihabara Majokko Princess," which was screened as part of the exhibition *Pop Life* at London's Tate Modern from October 2009 to January 2010.[54] Directed by McG and starring Kirsten Dunst, the video was filmed on location in Akihabara. An "otaku" performance in various ways, it chases a colorfully costumed Dunst as she dances through Akihabara. The video also performs "otaku" sexuality, displaying images of cute girl characters looking sexy or having sex; early on, the video cuts from these images to a Japanese man, who grins broadly and gives an enthusiastic two thumbs up. "Otaku" performances collide when Dunst vamps alongside idol singers on an indoor stage in Akihabara and is joined on the street by a group of masked "otaku" dancers. Blurring the line between fiction and reality, "otaku" performances attract a crowd of Japanese men and women, who photograph Dunst and the others, even as McG captures them all on film. Interspersed with images of bishōjo and sex and costumed characters, the dancing becomes more spastic as the video progresses. On the whole, it is a performance of Akihabara as an "otaku" space outside the norm.

As with most examples of Murakami's imaginings of "otaku," it is hard to tell whether "Akihabara Majokko Princess" is intended to be creepy or cool, silly or sexy, hilarious or horrifying, but viewers are nonetheless left with the impression that something is happening in Akihabara, Japan, over there. And as with most examples of Murakami's imaginings of "otaku," the video is subtly much more subversive than it at first seems. In lingering on the weird other, McG's gaze is exposed as an Orientalizing one (Said 1978), but also is set up by Murakami to present and sell "Japan," "otaku," and "Akihabara" to an international audience. "Otaku" performances are initiated and led by Dunst, a white American, who sings along with The Vapors' "Turning Japanese" (1980). That song, and the action of "Akihabara Majokko Princess," begins with an unmistakable "Oriental guitar riff." With this cue, one cannot help but spot how strange it is for Dunst to be "turning Japanese" by engaging in an "otaku" performance in Akihabara. How anything she or anyone does there is "Japanese" is debatable, because "Japanese culture," "otaku culture," and "Akihabara subcultures" merge into a murky mess, which is in any case seen through the lens of Orientalism. As an extra little jab, Murakami himself flails around in a character costume, but during a separate shoot in a space that has nothing to connect it to Akihabara except Dunst and the video. It all seems so empty, which is probably the point.

Despite layers and nuance, however, "Akihabara Majokko Princess" does not indicate that the street performances it celebrates are forbidden in the neighborhood it features. Filmed after the crackdowns in 2007 and 2008, the video should conclude with police intervention causing Dunst and her "otaku" dancers to disperse, but instead the viewer is left with an image of Akihabara as an "otaku" space.[55] The collaboration between Murakami and Hollywood thus contributes to the global imaginary of "otaku" performances in Japan, but does not reflect the reality of "otaku" performances in Akihabara. Fearing that this would be the case when solicited by email to assist the production of "Akihabara Majokko Princess," I declined, and was involved only as a spectator. If I had performed with Haruhi and the Akihabara Liberation Demonstration because their "otaku" performances seemed sincere, then I did not want to take part in something that seemed otherwise. It felt too much like co-opting the "otaku" image, and I was uncomfortable with a costumed American performing in Akihabara when Haruhi and others could not. Furthermore, I had seen the cost of promoting Akihabara with images of "otaku" performances, for example, when foreign visitors on tours I guided asked, "If this is Akihabara, where are all the otaku?" Demanding to see "otaku" performances that were long gone from the street, they were displeased and sometimes angry. Some even accused me of refusing to show them "otaku," as if I knew where they were hiding but would not divulge that secret. Whether observing them would confirm ideas about Cool Japan or Weird Japan, the absence of "otaku" performances was disappointing.

By 2010, I had stopped wearing my character costume when guiding tours in Akihabara, because I saw myself perpetuating the imaginary of "otaku" performances there. The "otaku" performers that I had joined in

Haruhi dances and the Akihabara Liberation Demonstration did not appear on the street anymore, and it seemed that I was standing in for them in front of cameras—not only those of foreign visitors, but also Japanese and international media. In sum, I began to see myself in Dunst, the costumed American performing in Akihabara when Haruhi and others could not. In the bigger picture, I saw that "weird otaku" from Japan were shut out of Akihabara even as "otaku" from abroad were invited in. And I saw the politics of not uncritically going along with it. Oddly enough, Murakami helped snap things into focus. Speaking at the Tokyo Institute of Technology on March 6, 2010, Murakami juxtaposed photographs of a white male model wearing an anime shirt and a stereotypical Japanese "otaku" in the same. Revealing biased views of cool and weird, Murakami also demonstrated the power of "weird otaku" to unsettle representations of "cool otaku." By insisting on "weird otaku," or less palatable "otaku" performances, Murakami drew attention to that which disturbs, and continues to disturb, regardless of what happens out on the street in Akihabara.

Conclusion

On March 22, 2009, the Live Park venue on Chūō Street hosted the World's Akihabara Festival (*Sekai no Akiba-sai*).[56] Planned by Akiba-kai, a nonprofit organization headed by Kobayashi Takaya with the goal of "energetic Akihabara-making" (*genki na Akihabara-zukuri*), the event was meant to invigorate the neighborhood after police crackdowns and discontinuing the Pedestrian Paradise. Those behind the World's Akihabara Festival hoped to channel the energy of "guerilla-like street performances" (*gerira-teki na rojō pafōmansu*) into events like this one—that is, to manage a series of "otaku" performances under controlled conditions. These performances would be "legal" (*gōhō*), Kobayashi insisted, and would occur with the approval of local residents and business owners, with whom he worked closely. Held off the street—inside the building housing Live Park—the World's Akihabara Festival featured costumed performers singing and dancing for fans, who were to remain seated throughout to avoid things getting out of hand. There were no cosplayers in attendance, let alone crossplayers, and clear lines were drawn between those on- and offstage. In prepared remarks, Kobayashi and many others appealed to everyone to participate in "energetic Akihabara-making," but the energy level at the event itself was depressingly low. Although marketed as a way to communicate Akihabara to the world, tourism had dipped, and the audience on March 22, 2009, was entirely Japanese. The numbers were small, the impact minimal. It was not long before Live Park had closed, future installments of the World's Akihabara Festival were cancelled, and Akiba-kai abandoned plans for regular events and "otaku" performances.

The World's Akihabara Festival shines a light on issues with attempts to capture the energy of "otaku" performances. In Akihabara and elsewhere, "otaku" are often associated with "subculture," which has specific valences in Japan (McKnight 2010, 125–28), but has been helpfully theorized in the United Kingdom. Foundational work on subculture defines it as "noise," or "interference in the orderly sequence" (Hebdige 2005, 355). This noise is generated in imaginative and creative engagements with media and material objects; subcultures subvert "original straight meanings" and transform objects into "fetish objects" (360). Troubling how "the social world is organized and experienced," noise has "considerable power to provoke and disturb" (356). Much of this is familiar from discussions of "otaku" and crossing gender/genre lines in the 1970s (chapter 1), manga/anime fetishism in the 1980s (chapter 2), and deviance and danger in the 1990s (chapters 2 and 3). What happened in the 2000s was a recuperation of "otaku" subculture, which was "trivialized, naturalized, domesticated" (Hebdige 2005, 358). For its part, the case of Akihabara casts into relief the tensions surrounding "otaku" performance at a time when subculture was being normalized and nationalized in Japan. In the promoting and policing of "otaku" in Akihabara, one sees how the noise of subculture is harmonized.[57] Aligning subculture and "parent culture" (367), "otaku" performances are not only trivialized, naturalized, and domesticated but in fact made trivial by naturalization and domestication, which does away with what is radically different and dissonant. The result looks something like the World's Akihabara Festival, where the noise of the street was tuned out, even as "otaku" performers appeared on stage and in framed photographs on the walls. Further tuning out the noise of subculture, "Akihabara" becomes a brand to sell "Japanese" media and popular culture to "otaku" from around the world.

Among its most enduring insights, foundational work on subculture draws attention to ideological recuperation, for example, the process of punks going from rejecting and threatening the family to being "a family affair" (Hebdige 2005, 358). In Japan, one can recognize this in *Train Man*'s depiction of an "otaku" maturing as a man in a romantic relationship with a woman, which is quite distinct from the noise of "otaku" subculture in the past. Following *Train Man* to Akihabara, visitors found trivialized, naturalized,

FIGURE 4.26
"Akihabara" as brand name for tourists in Haneda Airport.

and domesticated "otaku," but there remained what Kobayashi and others called "weird otaku." Radically different ones, whose performances were still disruptive: crossplayers taking on "weird forms," the "heretically sexually orientated," those positioned on the margins and marching in the Akihabara Liberation Demonstration. Ideological recuperation continued with politicians such as Asō Tarō coming to Akihabara to praise "otaku" for contributing to the spread of "Japanese culture" around the world, even as others worried that they were perverting Akihabara into a "weird town" and ruining the reputation of the neighborhood and nation. The story of "otaku" in Akihabara reveals a bifurcation of subculture into that which is recuperated and that which is not, the "good" and "bad"; one is associated with Cool Japan, the other with Weird Japan; one is promoted, the other policed.[58] If the story of "otaku" in Akihabara makes clear that ideological recuperation is never as absolute as the foundational literature seems to imply, then it also points to how the process does not mark "the subculture's imminent demise" (Hebdige 2005, 357). Just as the noise of "otaku" became that of "weird otaku," stopping movement on the street in Akihabara did not put an end to it in other spaces there. As an example, the next chapter turns to maid cafés, spaces between dimensions, and embodied interactions and relations with characters.

FIVE MAID CAFÉS

Relations with Fictional and Real Others in Spaces Between

On the cover of a pamphlet for the Japan National Tourism Organization's Visit Japan Year 2010 Winter Campaign stands a smiling woman in a kimono (figure 5.1). In the background is a stylized depiction of Mount Fuji and the rising sun. On the right, one sees the landmarks of Kyoto, the traditional capital, and on the left, Tokyo, the contemporary capital; the two are connected by railway, with a "bullet train" ready to shuttle passengers from one to the other. Against this background, behind the kimono-clad woman welcoming the viewer with open arms, stand eight individuals divided into two neat rows of four: to the right on the Kyoto side, a pilot, a tour guide, a fishmonger, and a geisha in training; to the left on the Tokyo side, an older woman in a kimono, a sushi chef, a younger woman in a maid costume, and a sumo wrestler. Part of a government-sponsored campaign, the pamphlet promises, "The Best of Japan Awaits You." Apparently, this includes not only sushi, sumo, and geisha, but also the maid, who is among the symbols of the nation and its culture. This might be a new brand of "made in Japan" (*meido in Japan*), which plays on the homonym of "made/maid" in English and Japanese pronunciation of borrowed English. Certainly the maid has come to be associated with Japanese popular culture, as evidenced by her appearance on everything from souvenir snacks to special issues of magazines devoted to the triumph of Cool Japan (figure 5.2 and 5.3). Even Hello

Kitty, described as an icon of "Japan's gross national cool" (McGray 2002, 49–50; also Yano 2013), finds herself posing in a maid costume in Akihabara, where many "maid cafés" are located (figures 5.4 and 5.5). Given introductions on Japanese television for domestic and international consumption, it is perhaps small wonder that visitors to Akihabara snap photographs of maids passing out fliers on the street or, when they cannot be found, signs advertising maid cafés in the station (figures 5.6–5.8).

Not everyone, however, is entirely happy with the prominence of maids in the imaginary of Akihabara and Japan. Some argue that a relatively minor aspect of "otaku" subculture was blown out of proportion by opportunistic media contributing to the Akihabara boom, which led to a drastic increase in the number of maid cafés and transformed them into tourist traps (Morikawa 2008, 254–56, 264–69).[1] Others find the use of maids in Cool Japan promotional material to be sexist, if not also catering to fetishists and the fantasy of sexually available Japanese women (Miller 2011, 18).[2] A few go further still, for example, Equality Now, which at one point reportedly considered maid cafés "a violation of the human rights of women" (Kagami 2010, 231). Representatives of the once and future Electric Town of Japan are also not pleased. When JNTO's Visit Japan Year 2010 Winter Campaign pamphlet came up at the Area Open Mini Symposium in Akihabara in 2012, Seno'o Ken'ichirō, a major player in the Crossfield Project, was critical of media drawing attention to maids, which he said disseminates an image of the neighborhood as "weird." In the media, Seno'o continued, Akihabara appears as a "weird town" where "everyone is dressed as a maid walking around on the street" (METI 2012, 65). Indeed, at the height of the boom, in addition to maids passing out fliers for cafés, there were also "weird otaku" crossplaying as maids to participate in Haruhi dances, the Akihabara Liberation Demonstration, and more (figures 5.9 and 5.10). And so, despite sharing the stage at the Area Open Mini Symposium in Akihabara with two owners of maid cafés—including Suzuki Yū'ichirō, president of Neo Delight International, which operates the fastest growing chain of them in Japan—Ono Kazushi, president of Onoden, asked bureaucrats in attendance, "As representatives of the nation, what direction do you want to take Cool Japan using Akihabara? To put it simply, I'd like us to decide whether it's all right for maids to be on the street" (74). If Seno'o and Ono seemed to be questioning the place of maids in Akihabara and Cool Japan, then Suzuki and others compared geisha in Kyoto to maids in Tokyo, which both appeal to tourists (63–64). For everyone, the issue was how to situate maids in "Japan," where they belonged or did not, factored into a positive or

ENGLISH
OFFICIAL GUIDEBOOK

VISIT JAPAN YEAR 2010
WINTER CAMPAIGN
The Best of Japan Awaits You.
Japan Tourism Agency
Japan National Tourism Organization

東京
地区限定発売
東京タワー
浮世絵
ハチ公
隅田川花火大会
国会議事堂
メイドカフェ
Cafe
GIANT
ペロティ

世界に広がる萌え文化・慰安婦日本の責任
ニューズウィーク日本版
400円
Newsweek
マンガ、アニメの
ブームを超えた
アキバ文化の国際化
萌える
世界
Service
Maid
Входи.
3·21

東京限定秋葉原バージョン
Hello Kitty
秋葉原めがねっこ
©1976, 2007 SANRIO CO., LTD. TOKYO, JAPAN Ⓢ

e cafe
http://www.cafe-athome.com/
ウエルカム
サマーキャンペーン!
7/1(水)~7/31(金)
更にお得に!!
ジャスト! 2,000円
@home cafe × Hello Kitty
コラボイベント
コラボグッズ
@home cafe

FIGURE 5.1 (opposite, top left)
Visit Japan Year 2010 Winter Campaign pamphlet cover.

FIGURE 5.2 (opposite, top right)
Maid cafés as Tokyo tourism destination in souvenir cookie set.

FIGURE 5.3 (opposite, bottom left)
Newsweek illustrates a piece on Cool Japan with a maid image.

FIGURE 5.4 (opposite, bottom right)
Hello Kitty in a maid costume.

FIGURE 5.5 (opposite, bottom right)
Hello Kitty with maids on the street in Akihabara.

FIGURE 5.6 (above left)
Maid cafés on Japanese television. Photo by Adrian A. Lozano.

FIGURE 5.7 (above right)
Hosts of a show intended for international audiences film in a maid café.

FIGURE 5.8 (right)
A woman photographs an advertisement for a maid café in Akihabara.

FIGURE 5.9 Maid crossplayers performing the Haruhi dance.

negative image, were cool or creepy. Listening, I could not help but think that we were missing something. Why are there maid cafés in Akihabara to begin with? Why disproportionately here? And why do some people not just visit, but visit regularly? I had been hanging out in maid cafés for years, and what I saw there did not seem to fit into the story of them representing "Japan." If anything, the men that I had come to know were interested in escaping "Japan." Then again, no one was talking about these men—only about the normalization and nationalization of maids. If "weird otaku" were pushed out of the picture of Akihabara inside the JNTO pamphlet, then they were also not part of the "maid in Japan" image on its cover.

This chapter focuses on relations in maid cafés in Akihabara. In these cafés, costumed waitresses called "maids" (*meido*) serve food and drink, pose for photographs, and play games with customers. When not filling orders, maids engage customers in conversation. Despite a huge amount of media exposure and subsequent tourism from the mid-2000s, many maid cafés rely on devoted patrons, or "regulars" (*jōrenkyaku*). Regulars come to cafés to interact with maids, who are paid to attract customers, ensure a fun and memorable experience, and keep regulars coming back. Regardless of the association of maids with sexual fantasy in Japan and beyond, in Akihabara, maid cafés do not sell sexual services.[3] Rather, what occurs in maid cafés seems part of the larger phenomenon that media and fandom

FIGURE 5.10 Maid crossplayers at the Akihabara Liberation Demonstration. Photo by Danny Choo.

scholar Henry Jenkins calls "affective economics," or building, developing, and maintaining relationships to shape desires and affect purchasing decisions (Jenkins 2006a, 61–62). The most obvious example of this is marketing, but there are wider implications for the service and entertainment industries, and things are not as clear-cut as a discussion of consumer manipulation. In Japan, anthropologist Akiko Takeyama argues that relationships in the "affect economy" satisfy "multiple players and institutions in mutual yet asymmetrical ways" (Takeyama 2010, 238). Key here is Takeyama's challenge to simple narratives about exploitation and "dichotomized views such as masculinity versus femininity, domination versus subordination, and subject versus object" (233). In the affect economy, lines are blurred and crossed, which requires a more nuanced approach. To this end, Takeyama turns to political philosophers Michael Hardt and Antonio Negri and their theorization of affective labor, or "labor that produces or manipulates affects" (Hardt and Negri 2004, 108). While acknowledging issues for workers and consumers, Hardt and Negri nevertheless do not lose sight of the fact that affective labor entails "the constitution of communities and collective subjectivities" (Hardt 1999, 89; also Negri 1999). Affective labor, and more broadly the affect economy, is productive of a dense meshwork of relations, which this chapter seeks to understand in maid cafés in Akihabara.[4]

In maid cafés in Akihabara, affect, specifically moe, is central to the experience. For example, hitomi, who has been a maid in Akihabara since 2004 and is routinely voted the most popular in the neighborhood, explains cafés as "moe space:" "It's like, the inside of your heart is pink. . . . When your heart is a bright, warm color, maybe that feeling is *moe*" (quoted in Galbraith 2009b, 136; see also Aida 2006).[5] This is affect in the general sense of change in a body resulting from an encounter with another body. Many members of the early generation of maid café regulars, however, are more explicit about the body they encounter and its affect. If moe is an affective response to fictional characters, then saying that maids trigger it suggests that they are fictional characters, even as they are also costumed waitresses. Of primary importance to the affective labor of women working in maid cafés is the production of characters, which are adopted while interacting with customers. That is, customers are interacting with characters—maid characters and moe characters. In contrast to those demanding something "real" from workers engaged in affective labor (Hochschild 1983; Flowers 1998; Lukács 2013), in maid cafés in Akihabara, one interacts with characters as characters, which are performed or "animated" by costumed waitresses (Silvio 2010). Regulars explain that maids are characters from the manga/anime world, or the two-dimensional world as opposed to the three-dimensional one. What makes maid cafés as they emerged in Akihabara stand out in the service and entertainment industries in Japan is the coming together of the two- and three-dimensional. It would be easy enough to critique the division of dimensions, but, in the spirit of the book overall, this chapter continues to explore how it works and what it does in practice. Like "low theory," which tries to find "the in-between spaces that save us from being snared by the hooks of hegemony" (Halberstam 2011, 2), maid cafés encourage us to think about spaces between dimensions, spaces that open between two- and three-dimensional worlds and bodies, between fictional and real others. This chapter is an attempt to imagine relations with and between fictional and real others, and to have the imagination it takes to move with others in spaces between. Where some see failure, I participate in the imaginative reworking of relations into new forms of possibility (McGlotten 2013, 12, 37–38). To do so is to carry on the struggle for imagination from the streets of the Moe City into maid cafés as "moe spaces" (*moeru kūkan*).

This chapter is based on fieldwork conducted in five maid cafés in Akihabara between 2004 and 2009. The first maid cafés in Tokyo, Japan, and the

おかげさまでご帰宅数
100万人突破!!

FIGURE 5.11 @home café: over one million served.

world cropped up in Akihabara in the late 1990s and early 2000s, and there are still more of them closer together in the neighborhood than anywhere else. My main site was @home café, which I frequented from 2004, shortly after it opened, until 2009, when it had expanded to five locations and served over one million customers (figure 5.11).[6] Although I also interviewed maids—who had their own reasons for being in cafés, where they earned as little as 850 yen (approximately US$8.50) an hour but nonetheless remained for months and years due to affective attachments (Galbraith 2011)—the bulk of my time was spent with fifty regulars, who visited a maid café at least once a week. In the sample specifically and in general, regulars range in age from late teens to forties. Many adopt handles and imagine and create other selves when in cafés, but they tend to be students and workers with enough economic security to come to cafés regularly and spend money. Some live alone, others with family, but most are not married and do not support dependents. Not all are single. There are female regulars, but I concentrated on male regulars, who were the vast majority. I thus refer to regulars as men ("he," "his," "master"), while arguing that masculinity is unsettled in maid cafés. All fifty regulars were born and raised in Japan. Given their positioning as basically "middle-class Japanese men," these regulars might be described as reluctant insiders seeking alternatives (Eng 2012, 99–100). Like the reluctant insiders discussed by Lawrence Eng in the United States, all fifty regulars were manga/anime fans that many would call "otaku." Not all maid cafés display this same bias in customers, and not all regulars are as acutely aware of their relations with characters as the ones that I came to know in Akihabara.[7] These men were looking for spaces to interact with the two- and three-dimensional in new ways, which they found in maid cafés.

Overview of Maid Cafés in Akihabara

An example of "concept cafés" (*konseputo kissa*), early maid cafés attempted to re-create the grandeur of Victorian mansions, but soon shifted to colorful décor and cute costumes that have very little conceptual connection to Europe and its past. When spoken of in general terms, all cafés with costumed waitresses in Akihabara, regardless of their actual concept, are called "maid cafés" (*meido kissa* or *meido kafe*). Similarly, when spoken of in general terms, all costumed waitresses are "maids." While the general terms can be confusing, this chapter follows their conventional use; explanations of specific concepts are provided as necessary. Categorized as "moe-style" (*moe-kei*) establishments, maid cafés such as @home are by far the most common in Akihabara today.

At a maid café, as at any other café, customers sit at tables or counters and order food and drink. Prices are notably inflated, which reflects the value of service (more on this below). In addition to conceptual décor, what differentiates a maid café is that the person bringing the food and drink is dressed in a distinctive costume, some sort of ritual is performed to personalize the food and drink, and the person in the costume and personalizing the food and drink interacts with customers in a stylized way. While there are male members of the staff on the premises, customers typically see only maids. In response to those that would linger, time can be limited to sixty or ninety minutes; there is often also a seating charge of about five hundred yen. Those wanting more leave and reenter the café, again paying the seating charge, or go to other cafés in the neighborhood.

In the case of @home café, there is a clear line between inside and outside, which marks for the customer a crossing over to a space that is something other than "normal." Before admittance to the café, a maid appears at the door and asks the customer, "Is this your first time coming home?" The question, as awkward in the original Japanese (*gokitaku hajimete desu ka*) as it is in translation, speaks to the ambiguity of relations between strangers and intimates, or relations in a "home" that is not one. If it is indeed one's first time, the maid relays the café rules, of which there are many: no touching or photography with a personal camera; no asking for personal information; each customer must order something; and so on. Made explicit, @home café has its rules printed on a laminated card for the uninitiated to read. After this, the maid ushers in the customer, rings a bell, and, depending on whether one appears to be "male" or "female," announces the return of the "master" (*goshujin-sama*) or "young miss" (*ojō-sama*).[8] All the maids on the floor turn, bow, and say in unison, "Welcome home, master" (*okaerinasaimase goshujin-sama*) or "Welcome home, young miss" (*okaerinasaimase ojō-sama*). This is a moment of ritual recognition of the customer as a master or young miss. After the customer is seated, the maid presents a menu and says, "Thank you for coming home today" (*gokitaku arigatō gozaimasu*). The stylized interaction then transitions into ordering as one would at any other café, but the customer is still called "master" or "young miss" until choosing a name. At @home café, this happens at the end of the initial visit, which means that the customer will have a name to recognize when returning.

At a maid café, one does not designate a preferred server, and can expect service from whichever maid is available and assigned to particular tables and counters. Returning another day, the maid might be different. Regulars, however, have favorite maids and anticipate interacting and talking with them during visits; they know their work schedules and show up for them. This is not an official designation, but rather something negotiated between maids and regulars. In practice, most maids have a number of regulars drawn and attached to them. Trying to establish this relationship or ensure service with tips or gifts is not allowed. There are also other boundaries to regulars interacting and talking with maids. In addition to being limited to cafés and allotted time, maids do not sit with masters. Even when interacting and talking with regulars, maids stand across or at an angle from them, often separated by a table or counter (figure 5.12). Bodies may be in close proximity—for example, when the maid leans in to be heard—but they do not touch. Furthermore, maids do not stay long in any one place; instead, they move around the café taking orders, serving, and chatting. When not interacting and talking with maids, regulars, typically seated alone, wait and occupy themselves otherwise.

FIGURE 5.12 A maid interacts with customers across a counter. Photo by Adrian A. Lozano.

While some maid cafés offer extensive menus, popular options include "omelet rice," Japanese curry, hamburger steak, sweet beverages, and parfaits. These items often come decorated or shaped into something cute, for example, hearts or animal faces. If this seems cloying and childish, the story at @home café is that maids prepare the dishes offered to their masters, which are full of love. (Everyone knows that orders come from a kitchen staffed mostly by men.) The quality of the food and drink is often less important than its presentation, which includes interactions with maids that can be quite elaborate.

For example, at @home café, when presenting an order of omelet rice, the maid requests that the master think of something for her to draw on it using ketchup (contained in a special bottle with a narrow nozzle) (figure 5.13). This preparation is done at the table or counter in front of the master. Once complete, the maid asks the master to join her in an incantation to make the food taste better. The most basic chant is "*moe moe kyun*," where "kyun" is onomatopoeia for tugging on the heartstrings and "moe" is an affective response (to fictional characters). Reinforcing the words, both the maid and master make heart shapes with their hands, which they hold over their left breasts and move toward the food as if shooting love beams (figure 5.14). Having successfully performed the ritual, the maid and master clap in celebration. This is repeated, with small variations, every time the maid

FIGURE 5.13
Food decorated with ketchup.

FIGURE 5.14
Maids perform the "*moe moe kyun*" ritual. Photo by Daniele Mattioli.

delivers an order. While the service is repetitive and may seem boring, regulars enjoy it as familiar interaction with the maid. There is a rhythm to it, and a pleasure to proximity and synchronized movement. Crucially, the service is part of what makes the maid recognizable as a maid. That is, repetition of key phrases and gestures invokes the maid character (Silvio 2010, 432–34), and what @home café calls "moe moe service" is productive of interactions with the maid character.[9]

Beyond what comes with food and drink orders, interaction at @home café also includes "entertainment menu" options such as playing tabletop or card games with the maid (500 yen for three minutes) and taking photographs with her (500 yen per shot). Each supports its own forms of interaction. For example, when the master purchases a photograph—called a *cheki,* a material object produced in an instant—he is summoned to the center of the room and poses with one maid while another operates the camera (figure 5.15). Although bodily contact is prohibited, there is a palpable excitement to being so close to the maid. This is amplified by the "to-be-seen-ness" of the interaction, which is witnessed by the maid behind the camera; others in the café at the time the photograph is taken; the maid in front of the camera, who poses with the master and later looks at the photograph as she personalizes the material object by drawing on it; the master that poses with the maid and later gazes at the photograph he receives from her; and others to whom he shows it. The interaction brings the master and maid together for a moment, which is seen and remembered. Some regulars order multiple photographs over the course of a single visit, while others collect and carry them in albums.

As is the case with taking photographs, interactions with maids can involve everyone in the café. For example, approximately once every hour at @home café, there is an event called "fun time" (*tanoshimikai*), when maids challenge the room to a collective game of rock-paper-scissors (figure 5.16). Like the moe moe kyun ritual, this game has special phrases and gestures that go with it, which customers learn and perform with maids and one another. The game continues until only one customer remains; the winner then joins the maids at the center of the room, answers a few questions for them and the audience, and accepts a small prize (for example, a personalized paper coaster).

Ultimately, more than a photograph or prize, regulars want to interact and talk with maids.[10] In the long run, they want a relationship with maids and to be recognized by them. On the one hand, each purchase in the maid café provides an opportunity for interaction; on the other, the more a

FIGURE 5.15
Example of a cheki, or instant photograph, decorated by maids.

regular comes to the café and purchases, the more time he spends with the maids and is recognized by them, which further facilitates interaction. For its part, the maid café can routinize interaction to the extent that it, as one regular put it, "feels like a game" (*gēmu mitai na kanji*). Simple, repetitive activities allow one to "level up" and be rewarded with recognition from maids and other regulars. Regulars rarely mention the cost of visiting a maid café, a minimum of 1,000 yen (seating charge plus one order), even if they come multiple times a week or day and very seldom spend the minimum amount. Over the five years that I conducted fieldwork in maid cafés in Akihabara, regulars continued to frequent their favorite establishments. Lest their devotion be doubted, many @home café regulars carried a black membership card, which indicates that they visited at least two thousand times (figure 5.17).

FIGURE 5.16 (above) Maids teach customers how to play together.

FIGURE 5.17 (left) The @home café customer ranking system.

Relations with Fictional and Real Others: The Circle

November 21, 2007. At the request of Mr. Yoshida, I have accompanied him and a group of his coworkers to @home café. We have known each other for years, but this is the first time that Mr. Yoshida is entering the "otaku" world, which is as foreign to him as I am. A high-ranking man at a Japanese chemical company during the bubble economy of the 1980s, Mr. Yoshida has cultivated a taste for the finer things in life, from exclusive wine and sushi bars in Ginza and Asakusa to bourbon and cigars in Shimbashi. In his late sixties and still at the same company, Mr. Yoshida has a habit of dragging younger colleagues to his favorite "snacks" (*sunakku*), or clubs where hostesses fawn over them while serving alcohol and lighting cigarettes. Included on occasion and probed by Mr. Yoshida, I talked to him about my research. Having seen maid cafés on television, Mr. Yoshida suggested that I lead him and a group of his coworkers on an excursion to one, which brings us to the present. It is dinnertime, and the men—and one woman—have come directly from the office (figure 5.18). They stick out in their suits and ties and as a group. New to maid cafés, they closely observe the moe rituals and even play along. When the maids leave and the initial shock wanes, however, Mr. Yoshida and his coworkers settle into silence. Tired from work and unmoved to talk, they curiously poke at the cute food and drink and wonder, as Mr. Yoshida puts it to me in a conspiratorial whisper, "When does this get fun?" The maid café does not function like the snacks that Mr. Yoshida knows and takes pleasure in, and he and his coworkers do not get it. The whisper is perhaps also a jab at me for seeming to have fun in contrast to everyone else. True, I have been coming to this café for years and like interacting with the maids, who this night are making a to-do about my upcoming birthday. Talking to Yume, a maid whose name means "Dream," I might have been lost in one myself until Mr. Yoshida pulled me back with that whisper. To reestablish rapport, I stand, travel to the seat of each member of the group, and inquire what they think of the maid café. Most are glad to have visited, but admit that they find it "weird" (*hen*) and have no plans to return. Those who do return are also weird, and I suspect that by this they also mean me. In the maid café, I am apart from their group and counted among the weirdoes. Later, as we leave, I see Mr. Yoshida linger for a moment looking back at some regulars seated by the door. He seems genuinely puzzled by these strange men and their peculiar enjoyment.[11]

This experience with Mr. Yoshida and his coworkers made clear to me that the maid café is not necessarily interchangeable with the snack or

FIGURE 5.18 A group of white-collar workers visits @home café.

"hostess club," which is a common feature of the landscape in Japan's robust service and entertainment industries. Given that the hostess club seems superficially similar to the maid café, comparing them is helpful to better understand relations in the latter. In particular, the way that Mr. Yoshida used hostess clubs with younger colleagues, which speaks to an older form of relations, throws those in maid cafés into stark relief. At a hostess club, as at a maid café, women are paid to interact and talk with customers. More specifically, as related by anthropologist Anne Allison in her account of a Tokyo hostess club in 1981, women are paid to sit with groups of men, attend to them, and facilitate conversation. In her fieldwork, Allison discovered that most of the customers in her club were groups of "salarymen," or white-collar workers, who visited at company expense (Allison 1994, 36). These men's employers budgeted for such outings not only as a reward for hard work, but also as a way to extend workplace relations into leisure time. Participation was semi-mandatory. By sharing time and activity with one another, men bonded as a group, which was framed by and in the service of the company (14). This group, Allison continues, was not merely defined by corporate belonging but also by gender performance. In the hostess club, the customer was a man among men gazed upon by women, who made him "feel like a man" (8). Being flattered by the hostess pumped up the male ego; men acted lecherously, which was accepted as part of their "nature" (19). Despite heavy flirtation and light fondling, interactions with hostesses at Allison's club did not end in sex and were not supposed to contribute to lasting relationships (i.e., as friends or lovers); men did not spend too much time there, which limited the potential for getting to know any given hostess (16). A visit to the hostess club, Allison explains, was intended to strengthen bonds among a group of workingmen, who came to the establishment together, experienced it together, and left together to find the next place. A respectable man did not come to the club on his own or to see an individual hostess. Interactions with hostesses did not take men away from roles and responsibilities at work and home; rather, hostesses were meant to recognize good men, who were productive members of companies and families. In Tokyo in the 1980s, Allison concludes, visits to hostess clubs propped up "corporate masculinity."

If hostess clubs of this kind in the 1980s were places for "good men," then maid cafés in Akihabara in the 2000s were places for "weird men." Separated by the socioeconomic flux of the 1990s (Allison 2006, 2013), almost all of what connected the hostess club to corporate masculinity is absent from the maid café. While visiting a specific hostess club alone and often might have been seen as a sign of failure to perform roles and responsibilities elsewhere, this is the norm for maid café regulars. Regulars spend an hour in the maid café, about the same amount of time on average that customers spent in Allison's club, but they return again and again; in fact, some leave after the time limit only to immediately come back. Rather than coming and going as a group, with hostesses facilitating communication and bonding among members of the group, regulars come alone, interact and talk with maids, and leave alone; visiting often facilitates interaction with maids; instead of strengthening group bonds forged outside the café, regulars develop bonds with maids—and, as we shall see, other regulars—inside the café. In further distinction from Allison's club, regulars are in many cases attached to one maid; while interaction still does not lead to sex, it does lead to lasting relationships. In the maid café, regulars are not affirmed as men fulfilling roles and responsibilities at work and home; rather, they work to imagine and create home in the café. Not only do maids not bolster the social identity of "good men," but they are also not targets for "natural" male advances. They maintain distance, refraining from sitting with masters, let alone indulging in petting. Physical and verbal harassment, including touching and even saying things that make maids uncomfortable, are forbidden. The master must master himself in the café, even as he engages in a kind of fantasy role-play as a master interacting with maids. The master, quite simply, is not made to "feel like a man" (Allison 1994, 8), be it a workingman or a virile sexual one. Reinforcing the disconnect from the institutional circuits in which the hostess club was embedded, in the maid café, regulars and maids avoid talking about home, school, and work, which might define them in certain ways; windows are blocked with curtains, and reflective surfaces removed. Set off from the outside world and "reality," regulars and maids imagine and create alternatives. It is precisely because the maid café appears to be an escape from reality—accentuated by ties to manga/anime—that it is associated with weird or failed men, "otaku," while the hostess club is considered "normal" (Kam 2013b, 160).[12]

Despite the apparent applicability of the "otaku" label, which in Japan strongly implies antisociality (Kam 2013a, 2013b), it is more accurate to say that maid café regulars are social in ways that challenge "common sense." To rephrase, maid cafés allow for emergent forms of relations with fictional and real others. An example from the field will ground this discussion. Dragon, age thirty-four, is an audio technician from suburban Tokyo.[13] He does fairly well for himself, but tells me that he feels like he has given up on his dream of becoming a musician. Single, he still plays the guitar. Dragon recalls that he started coming to @home café in 2005. On his first visit, Dragon met Ringo, a maid who wants to be a singer and is a member of @home's idol group, Complete Maid Declaration (*Kanzen meido sengen*). Soon Dragon was stopping by the café whenever he could. Fiercely loyal, Dragon says of @home, "This isn't just a place I eat. It's a place I belong. That's why I always come back here. I don't go to other cafés. This is where I want to spend my time." More specifically, Dragon wants to spend his time in the café with Ringo, whose work schedule he has memorized. In addition to regular café visits, Dragon also buys tickets to Complete Maid Declaration concerts, which take place at small venues around Tokyo, and boasts that he has never missed Ringo on stage. During Complete Maid Declaration concerts, Ringo's regulars, including Dragon, know the parts of each song where she is featured, at which time they call out and praise her loudly. This support is vital to Ringo's success. Indeed, Dragon explains that he wants to help Ringo fulfill her dream of becoming a singer. He is proud of her achievements, which affect his status as a regular.[14] Volunteering to use his trade skills and assist in setting up sound equipment for Complete Maid Declaration concerts, Dragon reports feeling his own sense of achievement. In the café, Dragon and Ringo speak of shared experiences at concerts and as musicians—a mutual recognition of dreams—which makes their relationship seem special. Driving together to a concert, Dragon informs me that he loves Ringo. This is not a revelation, he makes clear, because all of Ringo's regulars love her. There is no need to say these words to her or "confess" (*kokuhaku*). Dragon is content to skip the drama and be near Ringo in a continuation of their relationship as master and maid.

At a glance, Dragon seems like a stereotype of the maid café regular: failed dream, no girlfriend, paying for and fantasizing a compensatory relationship, cannot or will not make a move, a failed man. However, Dragon is only a failure if we evaluate him using commonsense measures of success, which are often based on reaching goals, most obviously in this case "getting the girl."[15] While queer theorist Jack Halberstam argues that failure can contribute to imagining "other goals for life, for love, for art, and for being" (Halberstam 2011, 88), Dragon and Ringo suggest that one does not need goals to live and love otherwise, which in any case is not necessarily the result of failure. The goal of Ringo becoming a singer is not the goal of their relationship, which is not a failed love relationship but a different one. Dragon, a regular and master, loves Ringo, a maid. As master and maid, there are boundaries to their relationship, but nothing is settled; with an ambiguous distance between them, there is room enough to move and be moved. The relationship is open-ended and ongoing; if it starts at some point, then any line from there is not vectored toward another point; the line is not straight, and not a path to follow, but rather the trace left by the movement of the relationship. Dragon loves Ringo, but their relationship is not vectored toward the goal of becoming a couple or family, which are the most socially recognized and valued forms.

Moreover, the relationship is not limited to Dragon and Ringo as a pair. As Dragon puts it, he is part of a "circle" (*sākuru*) of Ringo's regulars. As a form of relations, the circle is a loose association of people that support someone or something and are in turn supported by that someone or something. Not an "imagined community," nor a feeling of belonging to an abstract and homogenous collective (Anderson [1983] 2006), the circle is concrete and heterogeneous. "Membership," if it can even be called that, is voluntary, and one is in the circle to the extent that they are in love. Relations between a given person in the circle and what they support are not private or exclusive, because others are also in relations with that someone or something and with one another. Affection is promiscuous in the circle; all of Ringo's regulars, Dragon elucidates, are in love with her; they are all in the circle and in love. In not confessing to Ringo and trying to change their relationship into a private and exclusive pairing, Dragon maintains relations with her in the circle, as well as relations with the circle. Again, this is not a failed love relationship, but a different way of being in love and relation. As literary and social theorist Michael Warner (2000, 134) notes, alternative forms of intimacy—"a whole circle of intimacies"—go unnoticed in societies that recognize and value only intimacy in the couple or family. Those fixated on these "normal" or "natural" or "commonsense" relations can see Dragon only as a failure, which glosses over the texture and experience of his life and love.

Although not all of the relations between regulars and maids are commoditized, they can and do occur in the commoditized space of the café. Regulars pay to occupy a space with maids, and co-occupy it with others, but that does not make relations any less "real" or capable of affecting. Indeed, one of the key lessons of the affect economy is that there are different values to relations (Takeyama 2010), which cannot be reduced to the relations and values familiar to critiques of capitalism. Maid cafés support relations that exceed what one might generally expect of the service and entertainment industries. To give a mundane example, regulars are encouraged to spend special days in maid cafés. If a regular comes to @home on his birthday, the maids will sing to him, present a free dessert, and pose for a commemorative group photograph. In some cases, maids will send their regulars personalized messages (figure 5.19). Now, it is easy to dismiss this as a strategy to build customer loyalty, which it most certainly is, but what might it mean for someone that has few chances to feel special and wants to spend the day with the maid he loves, if not also a circle of @home café maids and regulars? Having sat alongside regulars for years as I conducted fieldwork in maid cafés in Akihabara, I personally cannot wave away what I observed and experienced as significant relations. Maids, like regulars, celebrate their birthdays in cafés. On these special days, regulars come together to interact and talk with maids. At times, the energy and excitement of an interaction draws others in, with more than one regular talking to a maid and then talking to one another. Participants are moved to share activity; relationships develop; the circle expands. Some special days generate so much interest that they become events planned and advertised by cafés, which sell tickets. Acknowledging the apparatus that captures some of the value of relations between regulars and maids does not, however, diminish the relations themselves, which go beyond the café and its walls.

Consider Ringo's "graduation" (*sotsugyō*) from @home café in 2006. "Graduation" is an affectively charged word in Japan, where it indicates

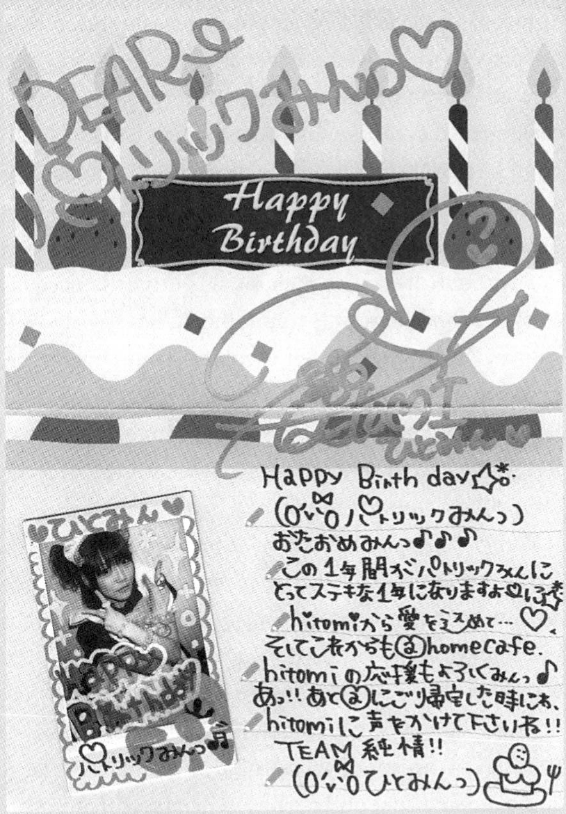

FIGURE 5.19
An example of a personalized message from a maid.

institutional and life transition. In the case of @home and similar establishments, "graduation" is a euphemism for leaving the café, which comes after quitting or being fired. The graduation event is often the maid's last time to be seen in costume and in the café, which serves to intensify interactions. Tickets are sold, and regulars line up for a seat. In such a way, on the night of Ringo's graduation, I find myself next to Dragon outside @home café. After waiting for an hour, we join the crowd inside. There is Ringo, teary eyed, thanking her regulars. She has one final performance, in which she sings a solo. Sitting and watching her, arms folded across his chest, Dragon nods in approval. The regulars in the maid café with Ringo that night are connected—to the place, to the moment, to one another. Recalling the experience in a later conversation, Dragon describes what we felt as "a sense of unity" (*ittaikan*), a coming together. Importantly, just as the circle does not disperse when Ringo leaves @home, coming together does not suddenly stop at that point. An example of how relations are enabled by the maid café but also exceed it, @home is where Dragon and Ringo met and developed a relationship, but even after Ringo graduates, Dragon continues to follow her blog, visit other cafés where she works sporadically, and attend her performances as an indie singer. These performances are so small that in effect only her circle attends. At one particularly intimate show, held in a spare room in an office building across the street from @home in Akihabara, Ringo sings for her regulars—and Dragon, beaming, accompanies on the guitar. The moment is touching, but not a conclusion to a story that is not limited to them. There is more to this relationship than Dragon and Ringo. Even as the circle persists in its support of Ringo, her expressed love for regulars supports them.

Crucial here is that the relationship between Dragon and Ringo is in some ways possible because of limits. As regular/master and maid, they are not "man and woman," and goals such as "getting the girl"—having sex, becoming a couple or family unit—are off limits. There are roles, but much else is in play. The relationship between regular/master and maid is ambiguous, even as it is also open-ended and ongoing. This role-play is more striking still because Dragon and Ringo, in their relations as regular/master and maid, produce and perform characters that both are and are not them. All this contributes to a relationship that has its limits, but does not settle into familiar forms and remains in motion. Thinking with Gilles Deleuze and Félix Guattari, literary scholar Ronald Bogue describes the maid as an "antifamilial" or "anticonjugal" type that offers "new passages of movement, new lines of flight" (Bogue 1989, 114). Applying this proposition to the relationship between Dragon and Ringo proves illuminating. First, although the relationship began in a café called @home, it is antifamilial, which is to say that it takes place outside the home and is not oriented toward the goal of "long-term domestic couplehood" (Freeman 2002, xi).[16] Second, the relationship is anticonjugal, which is to say that it is not oriented toward the goal of the couple's sexual union. Third, Dragon loves Ringo as a maid, which is to say that he loves both her and something other than her.[17] As a maid, Ringo is both a real person and a fictional character, and relations with the character are made possible by limiting exposure of the person. Every bit as much as relations like the circle that are not private or exclusive, relations with characters open new passages of movement and lines of flight in maid cafés in Akihabara.

Relations with Fictional and Real Others: The Character

You cannot have a maid café without maids, which does not mean simply waitresses in costumes, but rather characters. A key concept in maid cafés in Akihabara, "character" (*kyarakutā*) has at least three overlapping meanings. First, and most obviously, are the characters that waitresses produce and perform in maid cafés. In order to ensure privacy and safety, waitresses do not reveal personal information while working. Instead, they take on maid names (e.g., "Ringo") and backgrounds (e.g., "born in the land of dreams"), which are components of characters that they do not break when interacting with customers, even regulars. No one thinks that the names and backgrounds are "true"; rather, they interact with waitresses as characters. To ask for a "real" name or "real" personal details is a serious violation of the rules of maid cafés such as @home, which takes this to be a form of harassment and can and will kick customers out for it (Galbraith 2011). Complementing the characters of maids, regulars often adopt handles and produce and perform alternative versions of themselves in cafés (e.g., "Dragon").

For their part, regulars have their own rules against demanding more than the character, or even approaching a maid if she is recognized outside of the café and out of costume, which leads to the second meaning of character. Maid cafés come out of a culture of appreciation for fictional characters, which has its roots in Japan in the 1970s and 1980s. Consider, for example, Matsuda Seiko, who became a top singer and celebrity in Japan after her debut in 1980. As an "idol" (*aidoru*), or highly produced and promoted performer that appeals directly to fans for support, Matsuda was known for her affected cuteness, which led to descriptions of her as a "fake girl/child" (*burikko*) (Kinsella 1995, 235, 240). While intended as criticism (Miller 2004, 148), a subset of Matsuda's fans loved her precisely because she was a "fake girl/child." As sociologist Kijima Yoshimasa explains, Matsuda successfully fulfilled the "promises" (*yakusoku*) of the idol, who does not have to be "real" (Kijima 2012, 151–53). That is, the idol was celebrated as fiction, as something made, a production and performance of the cute girl. Indeed, the idol scene in Japan in the 1980s was such that commentators dubbed it a "fiction game" (Grassmuck 1990), which fans played along with. It perhaps comes as little surprise, then, that Matsuda inspired Lynn Minmay, a bishōjo singer and celebrity that appeared in anime in the early 1980s and became an idol in her own right, which reflects the culture of appreciation for fictional characters at the time (Ōtsuka 2004, 17–20, 126–28). Recall that *Manga Burikko* called itself a "two-dimensional idol comic magazine," even as readers attracted to cute girl characters were accused of having a "two-dimensional complex" and labeled "otaku" (chapter 2). Maid cafés build on the foundation of idols, as can be gleaned from waitresses claiming to be "eternally 17" (*eien no 17-sai*), dressing in frilly and colorful costumes, and fulfilling promises as fictional characters (figure 5.20). That some waitresses also perform in song-and-dance groups only reinforces the idol connection, even as it underscores an appreciation for fictional characters at odds with the demand for authenticity among celebrity watchers in contemporary Japan and beyond (Gamson 1994; Marshall 2014). Indeed, if the idol in the 1970s and 1980s was a fictional character, then the maid in the 1990s and 2000s was an even more explicitly fictional one, a maid idol, or, as @home café once put it, a "maidol" (*meidoru*).

In addition to what waitresses produce and perform and the idol as fiction, the third meaning of "character" in maid cafés is the manga/anime "maid." In maid cafés in Akihabara, costumed waitresses are called "*meido*," a Japanese sounding out of the English word "maid." Just as the borrowed English is distinct from Japanese words such as *kaseifu*, *jochū*, or *tetsudai*, the character is distinct from the reality of paid housekeeping and childrearing. Instead, this maid is associated with manga, anime, and games, as can be seen in introductions to maid cafés that juxtapose photographs of costumed waitresses and images of fictional characters drawn in the manga/anime style. Today there are dozens upon dozens of manga, anime, and games featuring maid characters, which appear with sufficient frequency to be counted as a trope (Azuma [2001] 2009, 42–47; also TV Tropes 2017c). Characters such as Multi from *To Heart* (Tu hāto, 1997–) and Mahoro from *Mahoromatic* (Mahoromatikku, 1998–2004) were some of the most popular among "otaku" in the late 1990s and early 2000s (Honda Tōru 2005a, 289, 307–11; 2005b, 140–41, 147–49; Azuma [2001] 2009, 75–77), even as both are also robots, which highlights how the maid combines with other manga/anime tropes (figures 5.21 and 5.22). Indeed, in the late 1990s and early 2000s, the unofficial mascot of "otaku" culture was Dejiko, a manga/anime bishōjo designed to trigger moe as a mash-up of affective elements such as "maid costume" and "cat ears" (Azuma [2001] 2009, 39–43) (figure 5.23). That Dejiko made her debut in advertisements for Gamers, a store headquartered in Akihabara since 1999, suggests some of the deeper history of the maid character. Cultural critic Azuma Hiroki traces the manga/anime maid back to *Black Cat Mansion* (Kuronekokan, 1986), an episode in the *Cream Lemon* series of pornographic anime (Azuma [2001] 2009, 42), but it was bishōjo games such as *Forbidden Blood Relatives* (Kindan no ketsuzoku, 1993, 1996, 1999), *Bird in the Cage* (Kara no naka no kotori, 1996), and *Song of the Chick* (Hinadori no saezuri, 1997) that established the character in the 1990s. Given that stores selling bishōjo games clustered in Akihabara and expanded rapidly in the 1990s (Morikawa 2003, 1–2, 4–5, 95; Kagami 2010, 132), images of maid characters were widely displayed in the neighborhood long before Dejiko.

Among the regulars that I spent time with in Akihabara, it was common knowledge that maid cafés emerged out of bishōjo games in the late 1990s and early 2000s. To hear them tell it, the direct inspiration for maid cafés was a bishōjo game called *Welcome to Pia Carrot!! 2* (Pia kyarotto e yōkoso 2, 1997). In this game, the player negotiates relationships with waitresses—not identified as "maids," although their uniforms look like those seen in maid cafés today; in fact, many of the highly stylized costumes in maid cafés do not resemble actual or even fantasy images of European maids, and would not be recognizable as "maid" costumes unless one had manga/anime in mind—in hopes of finding love. In August 1998, a temporary café with costumed waitresses popped up at an event called Tokyo Character Collection as a promotion for *Welcome to Pia Carrot!! 2* (figure 5.24). Women were paid to wear the uniforms of waitress characters from the game and serve customers. In July 1999, Gamers in Akihabara began hosting a Pia Carrot Restaurant, which continued sporadically into the next year. That Gamers was a destination for purchasing bishōjo games indicates that Pia Carrot Restaurant appealed to players by allowing them to interact with characters from the two-dimensional world in the three-dimensional one.[18] Even as interest in *Pia Carrot* began to wane, the first permanent maid café, Cure Maid Café, opened in Akihabara in March 2001. A fan of bishōjo games such as *Bird in the Cage* and *Song of the Chick*, the founder adopted the Victorian-style uniforms and mansion setting from them to Cure Maid Café (figure 5.25).[19] Here again the two-dimensional is brought into the three-dimensional, but not without differences. Even as the goal of dating and bedding the costumed waitresses in *Welcome to Pia Carrot!! 2* was derailed in maid cafés as they appeared in Akihabara, the sex acts in *Bird in the Cage* and *Song of the Chick* were ruled out, which contributed to "unconsummated erotics" (Freeman 2002, xv) in these spaces.

It should not be missed that maid cafés materialized in Akihabara in the late 1990s and early 2000s, which is to say in the wake of the *Tokimeki Memorial* and *Neon Genesis Evangelion* booms and blossoming of moe, or an affective response to fictional characters. Those without an interest in manga, anime, or games might not see the appeal (recall Mr. Yoshida and

FIGURE 5.20 (left) Introducing maids as fictional characters.

FIGURE 5.21 (above) Multi, the robot maid.

his coworkers), but, as formulated in Akihabara, maid cafés are spaces to interact with characters. Historically, this meant the maid character, but—even as maids began to increasingly show up in manga, anime, and games—maids began to draw on manga/anime characters to produce and perform their own in interactions with customers. That is, costumed as "maids," they act in ways that align them with character tropes familiar from manga, anime, and games. As with maids and robots and cat ears, tropes combine. More significantly, in Akihabara, it is entirely possible for maids to perform characters that exist in ways distinct to the manga/anime world, or to perform characters from the two-dimensional world as opposed to the three-dimensional one. An example is the "little sister" (*imōto*), which is a common character trope in manga, anime, and games associated with intimacy and devotion (TV Tropes 2017b). As a manga/anime character, the little

FIGURE 5.22 (above)
Mahoro, the robot maid.

FIGURE 5.23 (right)
Dejiko, moe maid mash-up.

sister is separate and distinct from any sort of reality of a younger sibling, which psychiatrist Saitō Tamaki unpacks and compares to the maid:

> There is a truism in *otaku* culture that those who feel *moe* for little sister characters in manga and anime don't have little sisters. If these men actually had sisters, then the reality of that would ruin the fantasy. If the object exists in reality, then it is not *moe*. So, you can feel *moe* for maid characters in manga and anime, but that has nothing to do with actual women who are paid to work as housekeepers. These men don't have maids, and if they did, the fantasy would be ruined. You see, the maid character in manga and anime is nothing at all like a real maid, so therefore desire for her is asymmetrical. (quoted in Galbraith 2014, 180)

FIGURE 5.24
Costumes from *Welcome to Pia Carrot!! 2*.

FIGURE 5.25
Bird in the Cage and *Song of the Chick* inspired Cure Maid Café.

By "asymmetrical," Saitō means desire for something that exists in the two-dimensional world as distinct from the three-dimensional one. In his influential writing on "otaku," Saitō argues that prolonged engagement with manga, anime, and games makes fans acutely aware of and sensitive to the difference between fiction and reality. To put it another way, they develop new forms of literacy. On the one hand, in his personal and professional encounters with "otaku," Saitō observes not only detailed knowledge of the fictional content of manga, anime, and games, but also the actual people involved in production, actual places used for settings, commentary on actual social issues, and so on. On the other hand, in what he perceives to be the defining characteristic of "otaku," they insist on the difference between fiction and reality in their attraction to fiction as such. Specifically, Saitō contends that "otaku" are attracted to "fictional contexts" (*kyokō no kontekusuto*), which are separate and distinct from reality, but can be related to it (Saitō [2000] 2011, 16–18). In what he describes as "straddling . . . layered contexts" (Saitō 2007, 227), Saitō suggests that "otaku" relate to fiction in reality and reality in fiction.

In a nutshell, this is what happens in maid cafés in Akihabara, which allow for embodied interactions with fictional characters. If a designer of games popular in Akihabara hyperbolically states, "A maid is a mythical being that all of us have heard about, but have never seen" (TV Tropes 2017c), then maid cafés make embodied interactions with such a being possible. Those familiar with maid cafés in Akihabara stress the importance of interactions with characters, for example, Hayakawa Kiyoshi, who writes, "The true charm of maid cafés is enjoying interactions with maids—who essentially exist only as 'moe characters' in manga, anime, and games—in a real space. In a maid café, an ambiguous space between reality and fiction, one can role-play the relationship between 'master and maid.' Many 'otaku' greeted the arrival of this role-play with shock and wildly enthusiastic joy" (Hayakawa et al. 2008, 26). Note first and foremost the insistence on the maid as a fictional character; second, interactions with this fictional character; and third, the affective response triggered by these interactions. It is as a fictional character that the maid triggers moe, or is a "moe character." Manga/anime fan and researcher Higashimura Hikaru, who has published extensively on moe, clarifies that to respond to a maid this way is to respond to a character, not a waitress in a costume producing and performing a character (Galbraith 2014, 140). The significance of the maid café, as Hayakawa and Higashimura see it, is facilitating embodied interactions with fictional characters, or role-playing interactions with two-dimensional beings in the three-dimensional world. Bodies come together, but in addition to that of the costumed waitress is the character—or, indeed, characters—layered onto her. Recognizing that characters are a crucial part of interactions, if not the most crucial part, is distinctive of maid cafés in Akihabara.

Insisting on the character affects relations in maid cafés in Akihabara. Consider the relationship that Hayakawa draws attention to, which is "between 'master and maid.'" As a maid café regular, Honda Tōru explains, "This is not a relationship between three-dimensional men and women, but a relationship between a maid and master" (quoted in Inforest 2005, 93). An explicit rejection of "a relationship between three-dimensional men and women" (*sanjigen no danjo no kankei*) allows for something else, namely a relationship with the two-dimensional.[20] Stated somewhat differently, Honda is not going to a maid café to feel like a man in relation to women—that is, the model of the hostess club (Allison 1994, 8)—but rather to perform like a master in relation to two-dimensional maids. Rather than affirming an essence, he is playing a role, which he does by bracketing out the common sense of relations between men and women. Strikingly, maids have complementary ideas. For example, hitomi, the longest-working and most beloved maid at @home café, says, "Our masters don't look at us as friends, but rather as maids. And we don't look at them as men, either. They are always masters in our eyes" (quoted in Galbraith 2009b, 134). Masters, not men, in relations with maids. The interlocking expectations of regulars such as Honda and maids such as hitomi are what make relations in cafés something other than those between men and women. The expectations are of an orientation toward the two-dimensional in the three-dimensional, the character in the café, which makes little sense unless one accepts the terms of manga/anime fandom in Japan.

Exploring how these terms work in practice allows one to see how a space is opened between the two- and three-dimensional, a space where relations defy common sense. Already Hayakawa (Hayakawa et al. 2008, 26) has hinted at the uniqueness of maid cafés: in bringing together the two-dimensional world of manga/anime and the three-dimensional world of humans, one can interact with fictional characters in a "real space" (*riaru kūkan*); the maid café is thus "an ambiguous space between reality and fiction" (*genjitsu to kyokō toga aimaimoko toshita kūkan*). Even more compelling here is Honda, who reflects on his attraction to maid cafés in Akihabara: "In a maid café, there are maids (waitresses costumed as maids), but the space is not three-dimensional (generally called 'reality'). It is also not two-dimensional. This special space should be called '2.5-dimensional.'

Think of it as a world positioned on the threshold of the two- and three-dimensional. Many ideas come out in the delicate atmosphere of the 2.5-dimensional. A vague 2.5-dimensional space such as a maid café is where the two-dimensional concepts and delusions in my mind can easily be brought into the three-dimensional world" (Honda Tōru 2005b, 18–19). The "delusions" (*mōsō*) of which Honda speaks are those of manga, anime, and games. In a maid café, two-dimensional characters are brought into the three-dimensional—as Honda puts it elsewhere, "The delusions of otaku are realized" (*otaku no mōsō ga genjitsu-ka shita*) (quoted in Inforest 2005, 93)—and one can interact with characters in new ways. From another angle, bringing the two- and three-dimensional together, maid cafés are a space to interact with others differently. As Honda sees it, relationships between and with manga/anime characters are "thought experiments," which he sometimes calls "'moe' thought experiments" (*"moe" no shisō jikken*) (Honda Tōru 2005b, 173). Such experiments, Honda argues, encourage thinking of relationships outside the common sense of men and women, and even outside the human; they may also help people avoid anger and resentment at perceived failure in commonsense relationships and contribute to personal and shared peace with imagined and created alternatives (Honda Tōru 2005a, 307–11; 2005b, 147–49).[21] Delusions about maids and master-maid relations demonstrate the power of manga/anime as "a platform of radical thought experiments simulating narratives of new relationality" (Honda Tōru 2005b, 140–41).[22] In turn, the maid café is a platform to role-play these experiments in "new relationality" (*arata na kankei-sei*).

What a maid café does, according to Honda, is permit the delusions of manga, anime, and games to be brought into and to affect "reality" (Honda Tōru 2005b, 173–74). The case of Dragon and Ringo has already shown how the relationship between master and maid can challenge commonsense notions of "couple" and "family" with alternatives such as "circle," but Honda is further drawing attention to the specific potential of the two-dimensional. Germane to the discussion is his conceptualization of "2.5-dimensional space" (*nitengo jigen kūkan*), or a space between the two-dimensional world of manga/anime characters and the three-dimensional world of humans. Positioned between the two- and three-dimensional worlds, the maid café is a space where the delusions of manga, anime, and games affect interactions and relations between masters and maids in reality; that is, the thought experiments of relationships between and with manga/anime characters come into the maid café; new relationality spills over from manga/anime characters to humans.[23] In such a space, one interacts with characters in human form, or humans in character form. From where he sits as a regular, Honda asserts that, in maid cafés in Akihabara, "a three-dimensional human puts on a two-dimensional character costume and becomes a character that exists only in the two-dimensional" (Honda Tōru 2005b, 174). In this transformative ritual, the character that exists only in the two-dimensional does in fact exist in the three-dimensional. What Honda seems to be suggesting here is that the maid, positioned between the two- and three-dimensional in the café, might be called a "2.5-dimensional being," or something between character and human (figure 5.26).

To better grasp this, it is productive to think with anthropologist Teri Silvio, who identifies cultural practices of animating characters (Silvio 2010, 433).[24] While, for example, some fashion subcultures in Japan speak of expressing their "true selves" (Gagné 2008, 141–42), manga/anime fans cosplay as characters, which are other than themselves but animated by their bodily movements (Silvio 2010, 436). It is telling that this word, "cosplay," is the one that Honda chooses to encapsulate what a maid does—"a three-dimensional human puts on a two-dimensional character costume and becomes a character that exists only in the two-dimensional" (Honda Tōru 2005b, 174)—even as he connects all this to moe.[25] Resonating with Honda and others, Silvio argues that moe elements are part of animation, in which "specific formal qualities stand for specific character traits" (Silvio 2010, 430). In Japan, this is buttressed by "role language" (*yakuwarigo*), or specific words and ways of speaking "associated with particular character types" (Teshigawara and Kinsui 2011, 38).[26] Focusing on simplified and exaggerated traits and types is what makes something "cartoony," and the maid appears as an example here (Silvio 2010, 430). However, at least in maid cafés in Akihabara, calling characters "cartoony" would not be a critique of performance, but rather praise of animation. If, as Silvio proposes, "Conventionalized poses are also a common way that manga and anime characters are invested with affect" (433), then the 2.5-dimensional being animates these characters and adopts their poses with her body. This is no less than "reanimating the characters by substituting the human body" (433), or the human body becoming a medium for character animation. By Silvio's estimation, how poses travel from manga, anime, and games to the "real world" and back is an ethnographic question (433–35), which can be asked in maid cafés in Akihabara. This is done out of more than mere curiosity. Not only is animation a "model for human action in the world," but for Silvio, as for Honda, it is also "a possible mode of performative (real, social) world making" (434). If the movement of humans and characters in

FIGURE 5.26
Maids between the two- and three-dimensional.

relation to one another contributes to "the emergence of alternative social worlds" (Condry 2013, 203), then the maid café is a site where these worlds dramatically intersect with and affect the "real world."

While the case of Dragon and Ringo emphasizes relations with a singular maid character—and involves various aspects of "reality," for example, a shared desire to become musicians—other regulars stress the importance of maid cafés for interacting with manga/anime characters animated by human bodies. One such regular is King, age thirty-two, a massive Japanese man who claims to be a professional wrestler. Although he visits habitually and attends all the special events, King is not an @home café regular in the same way as Dragon. Instead, King goes to many different cafés, and often. A jovial individual quick with a laugh, King has no problem spending money—sometimes lots of it—for a good time. When I inquire about his splurging and its aftermath, King replies, "I am not so old or weak. Things will work out." In a position where he apparently does not have to worry about his savings, King is able to indulge his passions, chief among which is interaction with a type of character called tsundere (icy-hot). Omnipresent in manga, anime, and games, tsundere indicates a character that is typically cold and mean, but then reveals their warm and sweet side (TV Tropes 2017f). There is often the added expectation of deep affection that cannot be directly expressed and remains hidden behind a bossy or bratty façade. Little sister characters, King tells me, are often tsundere.

In addition to watching anime and playing bishōjo games that feature such characters, King also gets his tsundere fix in maid cafés in Akihabara. When he is not at @home, King frequents a café called Nagomi, where costumed waitresses take on the role of little sisters. Despite assertions that cafés like this appeared to capitalize on the media boom in Akihabara (Morikawa 2008, 269), which implies a disconnection from "otaku" culture, little sister and tsundere characters are in fact some of the most ubiquitous in manga, anime, and games popular in the neighborhood. For his part, King is a regular at Nagomi not because it is trendy, but because it allows him to interact with a type of character that affects him, a moe character. At Nagomi, the brother-sister relationship is suggested by the waitresses speaking in plain or casual Japanese (i.e., without honorifics), which is usually reserved for those that are relationally close (and not widely used in the service industry in Japan), as well as calling all male customers "big brother" (*onī-chan*). There is also service described specifically as tsundere, which King says is to be expected—a "promise" or "trope"—of the brother-sister relationship. When a little sister sees King—who often stops by Nagomi in the early afternoon on weekdays, when it is least busy—she blocks him at the door and snaps, "Why are you here? Don't you have somewhere else to be?" Deflecting the criticism that he is a grown man and ought to be at work or otherwise get a life, King retorts that he has come to visit his little sister, and can think of no place that he would rather be. The little sister mutters, sighs, and calls him hopeless. Finally permitted inside, King has to find his own seat as the little sister grabs a bagged snack, which she unceremoniously throws at him. King did not order the snack, but he will be charged for it. He in fact does not want it, but nibbles on some seaweed-flavored chips anyway to avoid invoking the wrath of his little sister, who already seems put out by his presence and in no mood to cater to him.

During his visit to Nagomi, King is relentlessly bullied and belittled, up to the point of being called "gross" (*kimoi*). (It is hard to imagine something further from the hostesses at Allison's club stroking the egos of "good men." When first viewing it, the spectacle of a tiny woman berating the enormous man is jaw-dropping.) Unfazed and seemingly unoffended, King nods and continues the conversation with his little sister. When he does get up to leave, she is suddenly clingy: "Are you going already? It's too soon! Stay and talk to me." The shift from "icy" (*tsun*) to "hot" (*dere*) reveals her hidden, "true" feelings, namely love for her brother. In a later discussion, King explains the scenario as follows: because the visit was unexpected, his little sister was unprepared; this, in addition to being at home alone with a brother that she had not seen for some time, led to embarrassment; although she was honestly pleased to see him, she could not express that and ended up acting bossy and bratty. Reality check: any visit by a customer to a café is to some extent unexpected for waitresses, although King came to Nagomi enough that his appearance was somewhat predictable; the waitresses are in fact prepared for customers; King is not related to the waitresses; they were not at home together, had not been apart for any significant length of time, and were in any case not alone in the café. Perhaps King is delusional, but only in that he interprets the events of his visit in line with manga/anime delusions. Based on them, not only is the plain Japanese a sign of a close relationship, but the harsh words show how much his little sister cares for him. Indeed, as a tsundere character, the worse she treats him, the stronger her hidden, "true" feelings. (And the more powerfully they move when "revealed," because of the buildup and subsequent contrast.) Certainly not everyone called "gross" by a costumed waitress will respond to the experience as moe, but King does, because it is for him a tsundere character interaction.[27]

Beyond Nagomi, King seeks out the tsundere experience at maid cafés around Akihabara. At Cos-cha, it is a lesson in extremes. On the one hand, maids divide his cutely decorated omelet rice into small bites, which they spoon up, blow on to cool, and then feed to him. They smile and coo. On the other hand, maids pour a mountain of cayenne pepper on his food, mix fermented soybeans into his drink, and slap him across the face—hard—when he cannot choke it all down. They frown and pout. Reconciling the extremes requires some mental gymnastics, but they are provided at this same maid café in Akihabara for a reason. As King narrates it, the maids slap him because he does not appreciate the food and drink that they worked so hard on for him, failed to make delicious, and are embarrassed by. Imaginative explanation aside, King actually orders the intentionally nasty food and drink and slap as part of a "punishment game" (*batsu gēmu*), which costs 2,500 yen. King is attracted to the game, and willing to pay for it, because it is evocative of tsundere character interactions seen in the manga/anime world.

At more standard cafés such as @home, King gravitates toward what he calls "tsundere-type" (*tsundere-kei*) maids, who are bossy and bratty and often have pigtails. Of course, King does not refer to them as pigtails, but rather "twin tails" (*tsuin tēru*), which is jargon originally used to identify an aspect of character design in manga, anime, and games (TV Tropes 2017a). Characters with twin tails, King informs me, are typically tsundere, as are characters voiced by the actress Kugimiya Rie, including Shana from *Shakugan no Shana* (2005–12), Louise from *The Familiar of Zero* (Zero no tsukaima, 2006–12), and Nagi from *Hayate the Combat Butler* (Hayate no gotoku, 2007–13). This is a lot to absorb, but note how King, in pursuit of tsundere, reads hairstyle in a maid café in terms of the visual language of character design, which he then explains by bringing in an actress known for voicing characters in popular anime. This is clearly an example of straddling layered contexts (Saitō 2007, 227), but more importantly, this regular reads the layered contexts of manga/anime into and out of maid cafés in Akihabara. For their part, maids are not only aware of types of characters from manga, anime, and games, but in fact draw on them when producing and performing—or, rather, animating—their own. For example, Mei is an only child and by her own estimation not at all bossy or bratty, but when working at Nagomi she does her hair up in twin tails and becomes a tsundere little sister. When I ask about the inspiration for her character, Mei seems bewildered; as a fan of manga, anime, and games, she knows the types of characters, and tsundere is "basic knowledge" (*kiso chishiki*). It turns out that my question caused confusion because Mei assumed that it was obvious that her character was drawn from the manga/anime world; after all, one comes to maid cafés in Akihabara, or moe spaces in the Moe City, because of an attraction to the manga/anime world. Regulars such as King seek moe characters in cafés and read them in the mien of maids such as Mei, who share knowledge with regulars that undergirds interlocking expectations.

In his pursuit of tsundere, we observe King, a maid café regular, making connections to manga, anime, and games that animate characters and contribute to the affective force of their movement. Just as the relationship between Dragon and Ringo goes beyond @home, King's affection for tsundere characters begins before he enters a café and continues after he leaves. Unlike Dragon, King's relations are not with the character of a singular maid (Ringo), but rather a type of character (tsundere). That is, his relations are with a type of character seen in manga, anime, and games; this character is also seen in maid cafés in Akihabara, where one finds it produced and performed by people like Mei; her body is another medium for animating the character. If maid cafés are praised for approaching the manga/anime world—for example, regulars at Schatzkiste in Akihabara gush, "This is not a maid café. It's a work of three-dimensional animation" (figure 5.27)—then King might say of Mei, "She is not a costumed waitress. She is a three-dimensional tsundere character."[28] The case of King and tsundere provides an example of what cultural theorist Dominic Pettman dubs a "love vector," in which "distributed qualities [are] splashed across a multitude of people, characters, images and avatars" (Pettman 2009, 201). From another angle, we see that the character is always in excess of the individual: not only is the character other than the person whose bodily movements animate it, but in relations with maids such as Mei, King's relations are with a multitude of characters—all those that are tsundere, which extends across manga, anime, games, cafés, and more.

Fascinatingly, in maid cafés in Akihabara, characters do not have to neatly overlap with the physical bodies that animate them. At some cafés that I visit with King, men animate female characters, while at others women animate male characters. Regardless of if the person in the costume is a man or woman, many of these characters trigger moe in King. Despite being a man at times in relations with men in maid costumes, in my years hanging out with him, King never identifies as, or even gives the impression that he is, homosexual or bisexual. In cafés, his orientation is not toward men or women, but rather the two-dimensional, manga/anime, characters. Again, distinctive of maid cafés in Akihabara is the recognition that characters are an important, if not the most important, part of relations. As fictional and real others—others that are fictional, but real in their own right—characters move those interacting with them. An orientation toward the two-dimensional allows for relations with fictional and real others that do not always or necessarily map onto the common sense of relations between men and women.[29] Given that manga/anime characters that blur the line between male and female are popular enough to be counted as a trope (TV Tropes 2017e), they are also animated in maid cafés in Akihabara, which further factors into queer relations between bodies. Perhaps this is "weird," as Mr. Yoshida's coworkers reported to me, but that is not a problem for

FIGURE 5.27 Schatzkiste is "three-dimensional animation."

regulars such as King. Sitting alongside him in maid cafés in Akihabara, it does indeed seem that shared affection for manga/anime characters is at the heart of alternative social worlds. I feel a part of them. But I also wonder about those "affect aliens" (Ahmed 2010, 37) that are not moved in similar ways. Strangers with different passions, ones they cannot pursue, without passions; those that do have to worry about their savings and are not as confident as King that things will work out. Where do they go?

Conclusion

During a speaking engagement at Loft/Plus One on June 24, 2008, Okada Toshio commented on Katō Tomohiro's attack on Akihabara, which had occurred a few weeks earlier.[30] While some in the media were trying to brand Katō as an "otaku," reporting that he was interested only in "the two-dimensional world" (*nijigen sekai*) (FNN 2008), for example, Okada saw something else. True, Katō had said that he liked Akihabara, where he visited a maid café with a coworker, but Okada speculated that the experience had been an alienating one. Precariously employed at an auto-parts factory in Shizuoka Prefecture, Katō did not have the time or money to travel to Akihabara regularly and become a maid café regular. He visited, sure, but it was not his place to be. Maybe, Okada continued, being confronted by happy people there had only made Katō even more frustrated and angry, because he felt apart from it all. Hence the attack on Akihabara, a place that he supposedly liked but in fact resented. From where I sat that night, it seemed that many members of the audience agreed with Okada, shaking their heads at Katō, this pitiful man that could not become an "otaku."

For his part, however, Honda Tōru was not so sure that Katō was really interested in the two-dimensional world or relations with characters. There was talk about him possibly having an "imaginary little sister," but Katō nevertheless seemed fixated on being alone, or not being part of a (real) couple or family (Slater and Galbraith 2011). In a published dialogue, Honda argued that Katō did not want to become an "otaku," because he was firmly and deeply attached to middle-class masculine values concerning the good life. That is, he wanted to be one of the "good men," which is increasingly rare in Japan since the socioeconomic upheaval of the 1990s. The "good men" of the past are no longer the norm, but Katō thought that he could and should be one of them. Unable to shake a "normativity hangover" (Berlant 2007, 286) and constantly reminding himself of his perceived failure to achieve the normative status of "good man," Katō attempted suicide before finally turning his violence toward others in Akihabara. From Honda's perspective, Katō was living "a nightmare where he couldn't even participate in games" (Honda and Yanashita 2008, 72). Certainly time and money were also reasons, but Honda underscores that lingering middle-class masculine values and a desire to be "normal" contributed to Katō pulling back from an alternative lifestyle. Troubled by relations with the opposite sex and suicidal thoughts as a younger man, Honda identified to some extent with Katō, who "is basically the same as me" (69). The difference, by Honda's estimation, is that he embraced the two-dimensional world and relations with characters. While not for everyone, there is still something to learn here: "When I published *The Lunatic Man*, people came to me and said, 'I'm a similar kind of person, but I can't respond to fictional characters the way you do (*moerarenai*). What should I do?' I was really at a loss. . . .

But, you know, I wish that I had said, 'Just take it easy for now!' . . . I think he [Katō] was extremely prideful, so he couldn't put up with it [everyday life]. Probably since he was a kid. That's also probably why he couldn't take it easy" (69, 72–73). "Taking it easy" (*yuruku ikō*) suggests not getting hung up on hegemonic norms and values; it means not having to worry about growth or achievement.[31] Taking it easy suggests the possibility of alternative norms and values that do not demand so much; it means finding other ways to live, and live on, to live with oneself and with others.

Taking it easy is what regulars such as Honda, Dragon, and King do in maid cafés, where they imagine and create ways of life with fictional and real others. In contrast to the relative institutional stability of the 1980s, in contemporary Japan, Anne Allison notes both severe destabilization and emergent forms of affective relations that support life. Although not without reservations, she raises maid cafés as a case in point (Allison 2013, 97–99).[32] However, where Allison draws attention to social alienation leading to intimacy with "constructed realities" (Allison 2006, 83–88), I argue that maid cafés allow for affective relations that depend on sharing constructed realities.[33] This begins with distance from "moral norms" and "institutional power," which anthropologist Naisargi N. Dave proposes is "the *condition of possibility* for the creative practice of new, and multiple, affective relational forms" (Dave 2010, 373).[34] Such distance made possible the rise of maid cafés in Akihabara, even as it expanded inside them. In Akihabara, maid cafés evolved out of affective relations with manga/anime characters in the 1990s, or the blossoming of moe. In the two-dimensional world, or the constructed realities of manga/anime, character relations are a form of "'moe' thought experiments" (Honda Tōru 2005b, 173–74). The two-dimensional world is then brought into the three-dimensional one, with maid cafés being one of the most remarkable examples of a space between the manga/anime and human worlds, or "2.5-dimensional space" (18–19). In maid cafés, referred to as "moe space" (Galbraith 2009b, 136; also Aida 2006), waitresses not only wear costumes, but also animate moe characters. These characters are fictional and real others, and affective relations with them do not always or necessarily reproduce commonsense relations between men and women. In this way, in maid cafés, manga/anime delusions open into reality and disrupt common sense. Conversely, like the two-dimensional itself, maid cafés are a space for, as Dave might put it, "the imaginative labor of *inventing* formerly unimaginable possibilities" (Dave 2010, 373).

Relationships with characters as fictional and real others are associated with "otaku" stereotypes and considered antisocial in Japan (Kam 2013b,

159–61; 2015, 182–87), but it is more accurate to say that maid café regulars are social in different ways. This begins with escape from the "moral norms" of "reality," which not only limit the imagination, but have also become toxic. Responding to Katō's attack, Azuma Hiroki opined that, in contemporary Japan, those without any escape know "only despair" (*zetsubō shika nai*) (Azuma 2008). Honda agrees, but adds that we need to imagine and create lines of flight, ways out of reality, alternative realities, new constructed realities, which support living and moving on. For him, the lifeline is manga, anime, and games. In a personal interview, Honda elaborated on how the two-dimensional has kept him from despair over the years: "This fantasy time was important to me as an escape from home and school."[35] He repeated: "This was an important escape for me, because I was very unhappy at home and school." And then expanded out: "At work and in human relations, there is simply no way to be completely satisfied. You want to escape it. Moe provides a warmth and comfort that society does not." The struggle for imagination, to imagine and create alternative ways of seeing and being in the world, is a shared one. While he once advised at-risk youth to retreat into their rooms rather than hurting themselves or others (Honda and Hotta 2007), Honda also understands that "we go crazy if we live alone." The trick is to find ways to live and move on with others, both fictional and real, or imagine and create spaces in between for relations with fictional and real others.

Maid café regulars are ridiculed as highly irregular men, even failures, but I have come to see them as imagining and creating ways of life that are not oriented toward achieving the norms and commonsense good of reproductive maturity. In cafés in Akihabara, affective relations with maids are not private or exclusive, or even exclusive to the human; they instead spill over into alternatives such as the circle (in the case of Dragon and Ringo) and love vector (King and tsundere). Rather than pushing regulars to face "reality" and "get a life," which generates pressure that can be deadly, we might instead recognize alternatives that support life. This is not so much about "forgiving unsuccessful men" (Condry 2013, 194) as it is learning from those that live and move in the world otherwise. In maid cafés, I have at times thought that not insisting on self and depth might be what allows regulars to take on shifting positions as they move across layered surfaces. Inspired by Teri Silvio, I have thought that this might be "a vision of less violent and hierarchical interaction between self and environment, the human and nonhuman" (Silvio 2010, 435). Delusions, perhaps, but coming out of shared movement with others, and shared again now, as part of the struggle for imagination. In maid cafés and relations with fictional and real others, we can observe not only alternative social worlds, but also "more-than-human worlds" (Anderson 2012, 28). We can participate in those worlds, imagine and create them, together. At the very least, we can do better than accepting the "maid in Japan" image and discourse about maids as "Japanese culture," which smooths over what is distinctive about cafés in Akihabara and the people there. This, too, is part of the struggle for imagination. In lieu of a summary conclusion for the book, the next and final chapter is dedicated to a discussion of the politics of normalizing and nationalizing "otaku" in Japan and beyond. This is not just about government policy, but also journalists and academics who write about "otaku" and "Japanese popular culture."

CONCLUSION ESHI 100

The Politics of Japanese, "Otaku," Popular Culture in Akihabara and Beyond

People say a lot of things about Bamboo (aka Takeuchi Hiroshi), but never that he does not dream big. As chief representative of Overdrive, a bishōjo game company, Bamboo is proud of his work producing media, which affects and changes lives. "We are all influenced by media," Bamboo tells me at his offices in Asakusa, a historic temple and entertainment district in downtown Tokyo. "You wouldn't be here in Japan if it weren't for some media that influenced you."[1] I nod. He is not wrong, but being recruited and summed up this way is always a bit uncomfortable. Bamboo sees in me what he wants to see, which is a bishōjo fan from overseas. While many of his colleagues are concerned with growing criticism abroad (Galbraith 2017), Bamboo is dedicated to expanding the bishōjo game market outside Japan. With the conviction that there are "no borders" (he says this in English to underscore the point) in fandom, in 2008, Bamboo founded MangaGamer, a website with the mission of making bishōjo games from Japan accessible to players around the world.[2] Rather than any negative responses, Bamboo emphasizes feedback from those happy to finally get content that is too niche to make it into brick-and-mortar stores where they live. "The people that like bishōjo games are the same everywhere," Bamboo explains, laughing. "It doesn't matter where you are. When these fans are around, it's enough to make you think, 'Is this Japan?'"

Already something of an ambassador thanks to regular English-language interactions with bishōjo game players online and at conventions in North America, Bamboo dreams of more. He dreams, for instance, of cute girl characters welcoming foreigners to Japan, as they do in his *Go! Go! Nippon! My First Trip to Japan* (2011), a bishōjo game that is also a virtual tour of the country (figure C.1).[3] In the game, the player takes on the role of a white male "otaku," whose visit to Japan includes spending a week with two Japanese sisters. Exploring Japan with them, the player perhaps falls in love. Intended for general audiences, the content is relatively tame and even educational. In addition to manga/anime-style cute girls, the player spends time looking at landmarks and learning about them. Bamboo dreams of cute girl characters welcoming foreigners to Japan, but suggesting that something like *Go! Go! Nippon!* might be officially sponsored by the Japanese government as part of its ongoing public diplomacy efforts would no doubt be met with shock, incredulity, and disgust. After all, would that not be a shameful display of "sexist and creepy *otaku* products from Japan" (Miller 2011, 19)? That is, of bishōjo media? "Otaku" in Japan and elsewhere might expect "a pass" (19), but Japanese activists protest the government thinking that it is normal—as opposed to sexist and creepy—to use cute girl characters for campaigns (Aera Dot 2017). Nevertheless, Bamboo keeps on dreaming—as a mobile game, *Go! Go! Nippon!* could be handy for tourists coming to Tokyo for the 2020 Summer Olympics—and, available through his website, *Go! Go! Nippon!* continues to appeal to those dreaming of Japan and bishōjo.

In many ways, Bamboo's dream crystallizes tensions in "Cool Japan," or the range of policy initiatives under that banner promoting manga, anime, and other forms of Japanese popular culture. The international success of manga and anime generally, and reports of fandom in North America and Europe since the early 2000s specifically, represent for Japanese politicians not only the possibility of economic returns but also winning hearts and minds (Leheny 2006a; Daliot-Bul 2009; Iwabuchi 2010). The dream, then, is to turn manga/anime fans into "Japan fans" (Sugimoto 2013), or to translate affective attachments to media to the nation.[4] In bringing manga/anime fans to Japan, *Go! Go! Nippon!* seems like an ideal case in point, but there are issues in connecting cute girl characters with national interest(s). If Cool Japan seems to be selling the fantasy of cute girls (Miller 2011, 18–23; also White 2015), then *Go! Go! Nippon!* concentrates on relations with cute girl characters. Made an example for Cool Japan, its message might be that if "otaku" are attracted to bishōjo, then bishōjo can attract "otaku" to Japan;

FIGURE C.1
Go! Go! Nippon! My First Trip to Japan.

attraction to cute girl characters and attraction to Japan converge; one falls in love with bishōjo in Japan, and also falls in love with Japan interacting with bishōjo.

However, in relation to manga/anime images, it should be noted that the meaning of "Japan" is obscure. Even when it is as explicit as *Go! Go! Nippon!*, some bishōjo game players respond to "Japan" and others do not (Jones 2005a; Boas and Aoyagi 2015; Consalvo 2016); more broadly, the extent to which "Japan" matters to manga/anime fans, and how, is anything but straightforward (Newitz 1995; Hills 2002; Napier 2007). So while the rise in users of Bamboo's MangaGamer and other similar sites seems to indicate desire for cute girl characters around the world, or a global "otaku" movement, how this relates to Japan is an open question.[5] Just as Japan, as the source of manga and anime, can be "Cool Japan," as the source of bishōjo games, it can be "Weird Japan." It can also be both and neither, something else. Faced with bishōjo game players, Bamboo asks, "Is this Japan?" He means that anywhere bishōjo fans come together feels like "Japan," which implies that Japan is a nation of "otaku," even as it is not limited by national borders. This stands in stark contrast to persistent discourse about deviant others in Japan and Japan as deviant "other" (Hinton 2014, 65), but also undoes the nation as a bounded unit and associates it with "otaku" movement. Like the government with its Cool Japan policy, Bamboo's question comes in response to manga/anime fans abroad. Both Bamboo and the government imagine and create the nation and relations to it, but in different ways and to differing effect. Simply put, the extent to which one insists on "Japan," and what that means, is a matter of politics (Lamarre 2006, 385–91).

Returning to issues discussed throughout the book, this concluding chapter considers normalizing and nationalizing discourse about "otaku" as part of the struggle for imagination in contemporary Japan. The struggle increasingly confronts "inter-nationalism," which theorist Koichi Iwabuchi defines as a "reworking and strengthening of the national in tandem with the intensification of cross-border media flows" (Iwabuchi 2010, 89). One face of this is of course branding such as "Cool Japan," but, by Iwabuchi's estimation, journalistic and academic writing on "Japanese popular culture" in global circulation also reinforces the boundaries of the nation as they are crossed.[6] This is equally true of writing on "Weird Japan," which has exploded along with outrage that Japan has not followed Canada, Australia, and others in adopting a legal stance against cartoons featuring sexualized underage characters or explicit sex acts involving them (McLelland 2013).[7] If Japan has long been criticized for a perceived national interest in girls (Schoenberger 1989), then it has also emerged as an exemplary "other," which can be seen in widespread analysis of "Japan's Lolita complex" (Kinsella 2006, 65). While psychiatrist Saitō Tamaki pushes back against "attributing a given perverse tendency to an entire nation" (Saitō [2000] 2011, 6–7), this is precisely what happens in reporting on "a fascination with sexual interaction with young girls . . . in Japan" (Adelstein and Kubo 2014). Even as manga, anime, and other forms of "Japanese popular culture" gain visibility around the world, surveillance of "weird otaku" in Japan becomes surveillance of Japan as the source of deviant and dangerous images, a nation of "weird otaku."

Against this backdrop, this chapter focuses on the dynamics of imagining and creating "Japan" in relation to "otaku." With an eye for power at high levels, scholars of manga and the law have drawn attention to these dynamics (Cather 2012, 246; also Kinsella 2000), and we have seen them on the street in Akihabara (chapter 4). Here, on the foundation of theorist Stuart Hall, I develop a critical approach to the politics of "national-popular culture" (Hall 1998, 451), which in turn encourages a critical approach to "inter-nationalism" (Iwabuchi 2010, 93). The discussion is grounded by consideration of the work of bishōjo producers. Specifically, I dwell on *Eshi 100: Contemporary Japanese Illustration*, a manga/anime exhibition held annually in Akihabara since 2011. The vast majority of illustrations at *Eshi 100* are of bishōjo, which have their roots in "otaku" subculture in the 1970s and 1980s and became part of the landscape in Akihabara in the 1990s and 2000s. Founded by producers of bishōjo games, *Eshi 100* is officially sponsored by the Japanese government—exactly the sort of support that seemed scandalous in the theoretical case of Bamboo's *Go! Go! Nippon!*. To secure this support, relations between "Japan" and "otaku" are imagined and created at the exhibition. Parsing claims about "Japanese," "otaku," and "popular" culture made through and around *Eshi 100*, I argue that national-popular culture is best understood as "a battlefield" (Hall 1998, 451), where lines of alliance and cleavage are drawn. This is not only reworking and strengthening the national, but also struggling within to go beyond it. At *Eshi 100*, as in Akihabara, "otaku" play into and out of normalizing and nationalizing discourse in attempts to imagine and create other worlds.

"Popular Culture," "Japanese Popular Culture"

Manga and anime are routinely described as forms of "Japanese popular culture" (e.g., Schodt 1983, 16; Napier 2001, 11), but the meaning of those words is not as transparent as it might at first seem. In an influential essay, Hall deconstructs the concept of "popular culture" and argues against dominant approaches to it. These are, roughly, the market approach and the descriptive approach. The market approach assumes that whatever is consumed to a significant degree is popular culture. By Hall's accounting, there are two problems with this: first, mass and popular are conflated, and mass culture is frequently seen as base and manipulative, or simply corrupt; second, claims are often made about an authentic culture of the people in contrast to mass culture produced for the people.[8] "The danger," Hall explains, "arises because we tend to think of cultural forms as whole and coherent: either wholly corrupt or wholly authentic" (Hall 1998, 448). The market approach thus tends to ignore the nuances of "relations of cultural power" (447). This issue is not resolved by the descriptive approach, which considers popular culture as a distinctive way of life. From Hall's perspective, this approach problematically allows for anything to be included in "an infinitely expanding inventory," while at the same time missing "the structuring principle" determining what is included (448). That is, it misses relations of cultural power and the part of the one doing the describing in those relations. Popular or otherwise, nothing is given about "culture," which is not just out there waiting to be recorded. "The important fact, then, is not a mere descriptive inventory—which may have the negative effect of freezing popular culture into some timeless descriptive mould—but the relations of power which are constantly punctuating and dividing the domain of culture into its preferred and its residual categories" (449). On these categories, Hall comments that "a whole set of institutions and institutional processes are required to sustain each—and to continually mark the difference between them" (449)—over time.

This insight leads to Hall's approach, which might be called the process approach to popular culture. This approach, Hall writes, sheds light on relations of cultural power:

> It treats the domain of cultural forms and activities as a constantly changing field. Then it looks at the relations which constantly structure this field into dominant and subordinate formations. It looks at the process by which these relations of dominance and subordination are articulated. It treats them as a process: the process by means of which some things are actively preferred so that others can be dethroned. It has at its centre the changing and uneven relations of force which define the field of culture—that is, the question of cultural struggle and its many forms. Its main focus of attention is the relation between culture and questions of hegemony. . . . The important thing is to look at it dynamically: as an historical process. (Hall 1998, 449–50)

In examples of this historical process, "some cultural forms and practices are driven out of the centre of popular life, actively marginalized . . . so that something else can take their place" (443–44). The content of "popular culture" is thus not fixed and "will alter from one period to another" (448). This is a dynamic, ongoing process. It is also, Hall insists, a struggle. As Hall sees it, "the popular" is a "terrain of cultural struggle" (452). He elaborates, "There are points of resistance; there are also moments of supersession. This is the dialectic of cultural struggle. In our times, it goes on continuously, in the complex lines of resistance and acceptance, refusal and capitulation, which makes the field of culture a sort of constant battlefield" (447).

The stakes in this battle are high, because "just as there is no fixed content to the category of 'popular culture,' so there is no fixed subject to attach to it—'the people'" (Hall 1998, 452). Phrased somewhat differently, the struggle over "the popular" is also a struggle over "the people." In this struggle, "the people" are constituted, which Hall observes is crucial to "questions of hegemony" (449). Just as "we can be constituted as a force against the power bloc," Hall argues that we can also be constituted as "an effective populist force, saying 'Yes' to power" (453). Popular culture thus "is the arena of consent and struggle" (453). Here Hall underscores "national-popular culture" (450), where "national" and "popular" are brought together by the hyphen.[9] In this way, popular culture becomes national culture, and later tradition, which contributes to hegemonic ideas about "the people." If we resist the temptation of taking national-popular culture for granted, then we can see that there are those struggling for and against constitutions of "the popular" and "the people." Like the field of culture more generally, national-popular culture is "a battlefield" (451).

Adopting Hall's framework, we can see how media and material are selected and discussed as representative of "Japanese popular culture," which has a normalizing and nationalizing effect. Manga and anime are a case in point. Remarks about scale bring to mind what Hall identifies as the market approach, whereby what is consumed to a significant degree is treated as popular culture: more paper was used to publish manga than to make toilet paper in Japan in 1980, when manga publications outnumbered the Japanese population by a ratio of ten to one (Schodt 1983, 12, 17); manga constituted an estimated 40 percent of published material in Japan in 1995 (Schodt 1996, 19); between 40 and 50 percent of the output of Japanese film studios was animated in the 1990s (Napier 2001, 15); the highest-grossing domestic films of all time at the Japanese box office are animated (7); approximately ninety anime series were aired on television every week in the 2000s (Condry 2013, 86); and, being ubiquitous, manga and anime are part of "a total media environment" (Steinberg 2012, 166). In this way, much of the literature presents Japan as a nation in which manga and anime are popular culture. Somewhat more bluntly, the literature presents Japan as a nation of manga and anime. The point here is not that manga and anime are less prominent in Japan than statistics suggest, but rather that, as Hall insists in his intervention, we need to be aware of the process, relations of power, and politics of selecting and discussing media and material as "Japanese popular culture." Not everything that is consumed to a significant degree is held up as Japanese popular culture, which draws attention to the process of selection (often obscured by appealing to the supposedly apolitical facticity of "the market").

We can further observe this in collections of academic writing on Japanese popular culture, which are also collections of media and material representing "Japanese popular culture." Since these collections began to appear in English in the 1990s, manga and anime have been among the forms selected by scholars (Treat 1996; Martinez 1998; Craig 2000). As these collections continue to hit shelves (Lunning 2006; Craig 2017; Freedman and Slade 2017), a relatively stable set of forms discussed as Japanese popular culture has been established; manga and anime are conspicuous. Such collections resonate with what Hall calls the descriptive approach, and, as he argues, analysts should not overlook the structuring principle behind any inventory of "Japanese popular culture." Compiled by Japan experts, these collections highlight the institutional forces shaping national-popular culture. In addition to the obvious government agencies and national galleries, Hall reminds us that educational institutions also play a part in selecting "what is to be incorporated into 'the great tradition' and what is not" (Hall 1998, 450).[10] While easy to dismiss as trivial, the process is political. The descriptive approach tends to ignore these politics, along with the relations of power involved in selecting what counts as "culture," popular or otherwise, national or otherwise.

As Hall might have predicted, taken as popular culture, manga and anime feature in discussions of not only Japan but also the Japanese. From the observation of a vibrant market appealing to men and women of all ages (Schodt 1983, 15–17) comes the claim that "almost everyone in contemporary Japanese society reads *manga*," which thus "provides valuable insights into both Japanese society and culture" (C. Takeuchi 2015, 198, 201). Similarly, anime is "a useful mirror on contemporary Japanese society" because "anime in Japan is truly a mainstream pop cultural phenomenon" (Napier 2001, 7, 8). If manga and anime are mirrors onto Japan, then surely what appears in them is a reflection of Japan and the Japanese. In this way, discussions of manga and anime are also discussions of "Japan" and "the Japanese." While fragmented markets and fan activities mean that commercially successful media and material are not necessarily popular nationally, and in any case do not reflect profound truths about "the people" (Lukács 2010a, 421), the assumption that they do is common. This is not without consequence. On the one hand, those that celebrate manga and anime often celebrate "Japan" and "the Japanese," which aligns them with nationalizing discourse about Cool Japan. On the other hand, those that critique manga and anime often critique "Japan" and "the Japanese," which aligns them with nationalizing discourse about Weird Japan. In short, discussions of Japanese popular culture can serve to rework and strengthen "the national" (Iwabuchi 2010, 89). As a corrective, rather than uncritically accepting national-popular culture, researchers might instead examine it as a terrain of struggle.

Making Sense out of the Past

In the process of normalizing and nationalizing manga and anime as Japanese popular culture, a process that involves researchers and educators, striking historical connections are made. The most common version is to position manga—and, by extension, anime—in a lineage of Japanese popular culture beginning with the premodern, specifically the Edo period (1603–1868). Importantly, during the Edo period, Japanese authorities strictly controlled interaction with the outside world, and the existence of this isolationist policy allows for contemporary commentators to imagine the origins of a uniquely Japanese popular culture. During the "Edo boom" that rocked Japan from the 1980s into the 1990s, "the Edo period caught hold of the popular imagination" and became "the site of the lost-but-not-forgotten authentic Japan, the pre-Western 'outside' of modernity" (Steinberg 2004, 449; also Sand 2013). The point is not to say that the media and material culture associated with the Edo period did not exist, but rather to reveal the phenomenon of "making sense selectively *out of* the past," which, as historian James Clifford reminds us, is "political" (Clifford 1988, 267). In making sense of the Edo period in the present, we see a "selective tradition" (Storey 1997, 46; also Hall 1998), and it matters who is doing the selecting and to what effect.[11] That is, it matters who is doing what with history.

Even a cursory examination of discussions of Japanese popular culture turns up highlighted connections to the Edo period. Consider again the Japan National Tourism Organization's Visit Japan Year 2010 Winter Campaign pamphlet, which on its cover shows a woman dressed as a geisha and serving as a symbol of the past standing across from a woman dressed as a manga/anime character (the "Akihabara maid") and serving as a symbol of the present. Put somewhat differently, the Edo period is connected to the Heisei period (1989–2019), which is made explicit inside the pamphlet. Opening to a section titled "Art and Culture," the left-hand page is devoted to "traditional culture passed on since the Edo Period," and the right to "pop culture" such as "cartoon books, animations and games" (JNTO 2010, 6–7). This is clearly not an exhaustive inventory, but rather a selection of representative forms of "Japanese popular culture." Notable is the suggestive juxtaposition of Japanese traditional culture and pop culture, which had been going on for years prior to this pamphlet and at higher institutional levels. For example, addressing the National Diet in 2007, Prime Minister Abe Shin'zō said, "Japanese pop culture such as manga, animation, game[s], music, movie[s] and TV drama, as well as modern art, literature, theater arts and others are referred to as 'Japan cool.' It is gaining popularity among the younger generation around the world. . . . However, [it is not only] the attractiveness of Japanese [pop] culture transmitted and spread through cultural exchanges [that can] be classified as being 'cool.' As shown by the fact that Japan is the very country of the cradle of 'Japanimation,' Japanese contemporary culture's coolness is founded in and derived from its traditional culture" (Abe 2007). The revival of the largely dead term "Japanimation," which underscores the national origin of media and was used among fans of Japanese animation in North America in the 1980s and 1990s, by the prime minister should not go unnoticed. That, and his firm connection of Japanese traditional culture and Japanese pop culture.

Given the bald nationalism on display, it is somewhat troubling that the prime minister could just as well have been citing historian E. Taylor Atkins, who, introducing Japanese popular culture in a publication that same year, writes, "Edo period patterns of cultural commodification, production, and consumption portend what happens in the twentieth century" (Atkins 2007, 472). Similarly, historian William M. Tsutsui begins his introductory text *Japanese Popular Culture and Globalization* with a history chapter that states, "The origins of Japanese popular culture are often traced to the Tokugawa [= Edo] period" (Tsutsui 2010, 5). More germane to the discussion at hand, "Japan's long and unique cultural heritage, many observers have argued, is at the root of its postwar anime and manga" (Tsutsui 2010, 23; also Schodt 1983, 25, 28–37; Napier 2001, 4, 7, 21, 32; Atkins 2007, 463). So common is the move to link contemporary manga and anime to Japan's premodern past that media theorist Marc Steinberg dubs it "the return to Edo" (Steinberg 2004, 449). In emphasizing premodern history and national origins, there is a risk of deemphasizing the modern history and profoundly transnational hybridity of comics and cartoons in Japan (Ōtsuka 2013, 253–59), which allows for the past and present to collapse together in "Japanese popular culture."[12] This is an example of "selective uses of history" (White 2015, 111) in shaping national-popular culture.[13] That politicians, scholars, and others—both inside and outside of Japan—are resonating so strongly is reason for pause. Critics of Cool Japan discourse stress issues involving "national brand, the eradication of history, and cultural hegemony" (McLaren and Spies 2016, 26), but, in addition to being eradicated, history can also be ratified in ways that reinforce national brand and cultural hegemony.

Key to anchoring manga and anime in the Edo period and Japan are *ukiyo-e*, or woodblock prints. While often categorized as "traditional culture"

(JNTO 2010, 6), ukiyo-e can also be claimed as Edo-period "popular culture," or the manga/anime of their day (Schodt 1983, 32–37; Napier 2001, 21; Tsutsui 2010, 22, 24). In view of their shifting status over time, ukiyo-e are an ideal case in point of Hall's argument that the content of "popular culture" is not fixed and "will alter from one period to another" (Hall 1998, 448). During the Edo period, ukiyo-e were mass-produced images covering a wide range of subjects of interest to their consumers, including representations of women and sex that served as advertisements for the pleasure quarter and even masturbation material (H. Smith 1996, 26, 29; also Screech 1999). Ignored if not regulated, ukiyo-e were certainly not celebrated as Japanese culture (Schodt 1983, 33, 36; H. Smith 1996, 29, 32; Tsutsui 2010, 6).[14] Later, amid condemnation of Japan for perceived sexual indecency as it opened to the outside world (Buckley 1991, 168), authorities cracked down on ukiyo-e, which were poised to be swept into the dustbin of history. However, along with the import of Japanese merchandise, the discovery of ukiyo-e by artists in Europe and elsewhere led to the revaluation of woodblock prints (Schodt 1983, 34; Napier 2007, 21–50; Tsutsui 2010, 6).[15] From private collections, ukiyo-e eventually moved to public galleries. Ironically, even as ukiyo-e were representing Japanese popular culture and art beyond its shores, modern laws against obscenity meant that woodblock prints showing exposed genitals could no longer be displayed in Japan.[16] Today, most Japan experts accept these images, along with ukiyo-e more generally, as traditional Japanese popular culture and art. With Hall's intervention in mind, we can see in the case of ukiyo-e that policymakers and police, collectors and critics, experts and educators all played a part in shaping what came to be recognized as "Japanese popular culture." In different ways, all continue to "help to discipline and police" (Hall 1998, 450) the boundaries of national-popular culture.

Even as ukiyo-e are now well established as "Japanese," manga and anime are in the process of becoming Japanese culture, tradition, and art, which includes making connections to woodblock prints and Japanese history. Although there are arguably no formal or stylistic characteristics shared by ukiyo-e and manga/anime, connections are made anyway (for a review, see Steinberg 2004). Writing on his observation of Cool Japan branding, anthropologist Daniel White clarifies that "reconciling an obvious disjunction between the traditional high arts and contemporary popular culture by identifying the latter as originating from the former is the most obvious rhetorical strategy" (White 2015, 104). The persuasive force of such a claim comes from repetition and citation, which is true whether the imagined source of manga and anime is traditional high arts or traditional popular culture. Consider Katsushika Hokusai, an ukiyo-e artist whose masterpieces such as *The Great Wave off Kanagawa* (Kanagawa-oki nami ura, 1830–33) are internationally recognized. Over the course of a long and prolific career, the artist produced *Hokusai Manga* (1814–78, fifteen volumes). Again, this sketch work shares arguably no formal or stylistic characteristics with contemporary manga, but its suggestive title and existence do much to superficially anchor manga and anime in Japanese history. That is, Japan seems to be a nation of manga and anime because it has a long tradition of such popular culture and art, as evidenced by Hokusai. In this origin story of Japan as the manga/anime nation, manga existed then and it exists now.

This may seem reasonable enough, but specific examples of imagined and created connections between ukiyo-e and manga/anime expose a process of selection that is as problematic as it is political. Of his approximately 35,000 works, one of Hokusai's best-known is *The Dream of the Fisherman's Wife* (Tako to ama, 1814), a woodblock print depicting a woman being ravished by an octopus. The fact that this print is so infamous outside of Japan, and appears so often in discussions of Japanese popular culture, suggests a process of selection, but one in which Japanese authorities are no longer in even nominal control. In "inter-national" circulation, or the reworking and strengthening of the national as media crosses borders, the print comes to represent Japanese popular culture. Now, consider how it does so. While *The Dream of the Fisherman's Wife* could be chalked up as a remarkable print produced for a vibrant and competitive market in which "variation and originality were important" (Buckley 1991, 165)—a single piece in a massive body of work, itself only a small part of the larger output of a multitude of artists—it instead is taken as proof of a tradition of Japanese "tentacle porn" (Josephy-Hernández 2017, 178). Referencing Hokusai's print in the first English-language academic book on anime, literary scholar Susan J. Napier writes that one "cannot help but make a connection between that and the notorious 'tentacle sex' scenes occurring in some of anime's more sadistic pornography" (Napier 2001, 21).

That an academic introduction to anime would bring up "sadistic pornography" is interesting in itself, and speaks to a specific United Kingdom–United States historical encounter with Japanese animation ("Japanimation") as something radically different from domestic cartoons, which were ostensibly for children. Not coincidentally zeroing in on *Urotsukidōji: Legend of the Overfiend* (Chōjin densetsu Urotsukidōji, 1987–89) and *La*

Blue Girl (Injū gakuen La Blue Girl, 1992–94, 2001), which feature prominently in Napier's book, researcher Perry R. Hinton explains how the association of anime and sadistic pornography involving tentacles came to be highlighted:

> Controversy arose concerning adult anime in Western countries: in Britain the apocalyptic anime *Legend of the Overfiend* was severely cut on release in 1993, and in 1996 *La Blue Girl* was given an outright ban by the British Board of Film Classification amid concerns about the importation of cartoon "sex and tentacles." This had two results: a focus on a particular type of anime in the popular press and the association of anime with sexual violence against women and girls. Yet . . . this form of anime was a relatively small part of the Japanese anime output . . . chosen as a relatively large proportion of the anime imported by Western distributors at the time. Westerners viewing this content as "typical" Japanese anime output were potentially misinterpreting a Western selective interest, and inappropriately attributing it to a misperceived prevalence of "sex and tentacles" anime in the Japanese output, leading to the negative reputation of adult anime in Britain. (Hinton 2014, 55–56)

Plainly visible here are the forces shaping anime into a representative form of "Japanese popular culture" as it crosses borders, and Hinton is right to draw attention to selection bias. In the United States as well, adult anime was imported at a disproportionate rate because, as one distributor summarizes, licenses were comparatively easy to obtain, there was little competition, and sales were strong (Patten 2004, 110–18). There was not anything like this adult anime in domestic cartoons, seen as primarily for children, and this struck a chord. This seems, then, to be less a story about Japan than about supply and demand—the response to niche content—in the United Kingdom and the United States (Hinton 2014, 57). That tentacle porn would, on the contrary, be tied to Japanese history and tradition is striking, but, as Napier suggests, it seems difficult to resist. Placing the images side by side seems to reveal so much. The connection between Hokusai, tentacle porn, and manga/anime has since been made—and made often—in not only journalistic writing but also academic writing (Ortega-Brena 2009, 20; Briel 2010, 203; Brown 2010, 93–95, 170; Kang 2010, 112; Josephy-Hernández 2017, 175, 178).[17] In this way, an obscure premodern print is held up as the origin of an obscure subgenre of contemporary pornographic manga/anime, and both represent "Japanese popular culture."

Repetition and citation make the tenuous connection between ukiyo-e, manga/anime, and tentacle porn seem like fact. Further, because popular culture is taken to be a mirror onto "Japan" and "the Japanese," this "fact" becomes a revealing one about that nation and its people. By now a trope (TV Tropes 2017d), sex and tentacles appear in jokes about Japan and the Japanese, for example, in an episode of the American adult cartoon *Family Guy*:

[On a neon-lit street in a Japanese city]

JAPANESE GUY #1	"Hey, you want to go watch a movie?"
JAPANESE GUY #2	"Nah, we're Japanese. Let's go watch a schoolgirl bang an octopus!"

(*Family Guy* 2012)

The punch line is that Japanese are into sex and tentacles; viewers laugh because of a shared understanding that Japan is, after all, the nation of tentacle porn and the Japanese are, after all, a bunch of perverts. (Note the confirmation of established Orientalist tropes about "Japan," as well as fascination with its perceived sexual difference and deviance.) Never mind alternative explanations for the "sadistic pornography" we all know about—for example, that the modern obscenity laws that made ukiyo-e showing exposed genitals legally dubious in Japan also encouraged experimental depictions of sex in manga/anime such as replacing the penis with tentacles (Kimi 2015, 18)—or that, in any case, such media is minor (Nagayama 2014, 348). Never mind that viewers know about the schoolgirl and octopus due to the selection bias of manga/anime importers and consumers.

The existence of *The Dream of the Fisherman's Wife* and so-called tentacle porn is not in question. What matters is the selection of these things in discussions of Japanese popular culture and Japan, which is as problematic as it is political. The inevitability of certain ideas about "Japan" and "the Japanese"—one "cannot help but make a connection" (Napier 2001, 21)—is an effect of an ongoing process and of relations of cultural power. That media personality Anthony Bourdain, visiting Japan for a travel show, would devote a significant percentage of the episode to an interview with *Legend of the Overfiend* and *La Blue Girl* creator Maeda Toshio demonstrates just how entrenched this topic has become (Bourdain 2013). Selection, memorialization, and (re)presentation turn ukiyo-e, manga/

anime, and tentacle porn into Japanese culture, tradition, and art, which feeds into normalizing and nationalizing discourse about Cool Japan and Weird Japan. While some may imagine and create connections between the Edo period and the Heisei period that bring tradition to Cool Japan, others imagine and create a lineage of tentacle porn that brings tradition to Weird Japan. This is an example of not just "national cultural logic" (White 2015, 105), but also of inter-national cultural logic. As anthropologist David Novak argues, "Japan" emerges from the noise of inter-national circulation and feedback (Novak 2013, 10, 24). Similarly, in contradictory and complementary ways, "otaku" have come to be associated with Japanese popular culture and Japan.

Otaku Nippon: Manga/Anime Fans and Japan

The politics of popular culture in contemporary Japan continue from manga/anime to manga/anime fans, or "otaku." Long decried as perverts, if not also pedophiles and potential predators, the rise of the "otaku" market in Japan in the 1990s overlapped with the discovery by Japanese critics of manga/anime fans in North America and Europe, which encouraged normalizing and nationalizing discourse (Lamarre 2006, 387–91). This underpinned revaluation of "otaku" in Japan in the 2000s, but it was reformed "otaku," normalized and nationalized, not "weird otaku," who were folded into Cool Japan. Reformed "otaku" and "weird otaku": if one is associated with "counter—but still national—culture" (White 2015, 108), then the other is just that, other, threatening the norm and nation. By now a stock character in discussions of Japanese popular culture and Japan at home and abroad, the focus of "repetitive academic attention" (Kinsella 2014, 18) and even more repetitive journalistic attention, "otaku" represent for critics the worst of the nation (Kinsella 2000, 129), while "otaku" are for defenders active in and participatory fans contributing to the creative culture of manga/anime, which is winning hearts around the world (Leheny 2006a, 219–23).

In their association with Japan in increasingly "inter-national" discourse, startling links are made between "otaku" and Japanese culture, history, and tradition. For example, in the 1990s, producer Okada Toshio, who published numerous articles and books on manga/anime fans and even taught about them at the prestigious University of Tokyo, argued that "otaku" have inherited the urban consumer sensibilities and connoisseurship of the Edo period (Okada [1996] 2015a, 95–97). For Okada, "otaku" are "the legitimate heirs of Japanese culture," which "is alive in *otaku* culture" (95). "Otaku" culture is thus Japanese culture—in fact, an even more legitimate form rooted in "the pre-Western 'outside' of modernity" (Steinberg 2004, 449). Pop artist Murakami Takashi also juxtaposes manga/anime and Edo period art, "otaku" and Japan (Murakami 2000, 2005). In his work, "otaku" culture and art are also Japanese culture and art. Appealing to a global audience eager for Cool Japan in the 2000s, Murakami went on to be identified by *Time* magazine as one of the most influential people in the world. In his analysis of Okada, Murakami, and others, media theorist Thomas Lamarre traces the contours of a shared discourse, which is meant to "define a historical moment, promote a set of objects, or establish an identity" (Lamarre 2006, 365). In this discourse, the identity being established is not only that of "otaku" but also of "Japan."

In addition to producers and pop artists, government agencies and actors are also playing a role in connecting "otaku" with Japanese popular culture, or what Hall calls "national-popular culture" (Hall 1998, 450). Recall, for example, the "GIAPPONE/OTAKU" sign marking the Japan pavilion, funded by the Japan Foundation, at the Venice Biennale in 2004 (chapter 4). Even more directly, recall Asō Tarō, who would become prime minister of Japan, associating "otaku" subculture with "Japanese culture" in a speech in 2007 (chapter 4). The nation should take pride in and promote its "otaku" culture, Asō opined, pointing to the global successes of manga and anime. Clearly frustrated by the situation, cultural critic Ōtsuka Eiji summarizes, "We've reached the point where officials in the Ministry of Economy, Trade, and Industry have taken notice of the foreign approval of otaku culture, and contemporary artists intent on self-promotion have jumped on the wagon, insisting, quite arbitrarily, that otaku . . . are representative of Japanese pop culture" (Ōtsuka 2013, 252). With Hall in mind, note the emerging alliances between public and private interests in this revaluation of "otaku."[18] Such alliances make possible formulations such as *Cool Japan: Otaku Japan Guide*, in which "otaku" and cool are interchangeable modifiers for Japan and its popular culture (chapter 4).

These alliances, however, are shifting and uncertain (Strategy 2012). Take, for example, an obscenity trial against pornographic manga, which raised the specter of "otaku" and took place at the same time that Cool Japan policy initiatives gained traction in the 2000s. Going all the way to the Supreme Court of Japan, the defense asserted that manga, including adult content, are not only "otaku" culture, but also Japanese culture; they compared the manga on trial to ukiyo-e, and pointed out that, like ukiyo-e in the past, manga are celebrated abroad; they warned that interfering with freedom of expression would undermine the creativity of manga and hence its status as a vital economic and political resource (Cather 2012, 244–49). In the defense's case, "otaku" appeared as representatives of manga/anime culture in Japan and overseas; indeed, they were representatives of Japan; information concerning the Venice Biennale and its vision of GIAPPONE/OTAKU was submitted as evidence (244). In handing down a guilty verdict, the court decided that ukiyo-e showing exposed genitals are "canonized" (258), or have entered the realm of tradition, while manga showing exposed genitals are criminal. Despite the attempt to tap into the revaluation of "otaku," there were lingering concerns about them as perverts and potential sex offenders. Moreover, arguing that manga and "otaku" are Japanese culture and represent Japan on the world stage apparently backfired. In her review of the trial, legal scholar Kirsten Cather explains that "the fact that manga (and *otaku*) were symbols of national importance only fueled the state's desire to police them" (246). To rephrase, the more prominent manga and "otaku" have become as national-popular culture, the more investment is made in them and the more they are regulated. In the process, some forms are pushed out so that "something else can take their place" (Hall 1998, 443–44).[19]

As illustrated by manga/anime and "otaku," it is clear that Hall's approach sheds a great deal of light on the politics of popular culture in contemporary Japan, but it also needs to be updated to account for "changes in cultural production, circulation, and consumption" (Harsin and Hayward 2013, 203). In addition to the social media and technologies that communication scholars Jayson Harsin and Mark Hayward highlight, the "internationalism" (Iwabuchi 2010) that Iwabuchi calls attention to in the global circulation of media and material culture seems key. Addressing this, we still consider popular culture in terms of struggle, but also in terms of how cross-border flows of culture are, as anthropologist Rosemary J. Coombe puts it, "regulated, imagined, managed, and contested" (Coombe 1998, 39). This includes the imagination and regulation of self and other, normal and deviant, us and them, but not only in the familiar guise of Orientalism. Rather, we must also examine the internal dynamics of imagining "Japan": imagining it against others, reconciling some but not others into the imagined nation, imagining it otherwise. In the field, we can observe the various powers at play in not only imagining and regulating, but also managing and contesting "Japanese popular culture" and "Japan" in relation to "otaku" and manga/anime subculture. We have already started thinking this way on the street in Akihabara, which is heralded as "the source of conveying *Otaku* culture to the world" (JNTO 2010, 7), but is also a site of ongoing struggle. Revisiting Akihabara once more, we now turn to *Eshi 100*.

Eshi 100: From Akihabara to the World

Eshi 100: Contemporary Japanese Illustration (Eshi 100 nin ten) is an exhibition dedicated to manga/anime, specifically manga/anime-style characters, which appear in comics, cartoons, and certain forms of computer/console games and novels in Japan (figure C.2).[20] Since the inaugural event in May 2011, *Eshi 100* has become an annual affair with increasing name recognition and attendance records (Tokyo Otaku Mode 2013). Under the auspices of Sankei Shimbun, a Japanese media company with national reach and somewhat conservative leanings, *Eshi 100* is understood to be promoting manga/anime as Japanese popular culture, which is spreading around the world. The exhibition counts among its official sponsors the Japan Tourism Agency, the Ministry of Foreign Affairs, and the Ministry of Economy, Trade, and Industry. It is held in the UDX Building in Akihabara, a neighborhood in Tokyo that has become a destination for manga/anime tourism and a symbolic showcase for Japanese popular culture. All of this, but most significantly the sponsorship, points to *Eshi 100* aligning with Cool Japan policy initiatives. As if to strengthen connections to the nation, the exhibition has from its beginnings had organizing themes such as "Japan" (*Nihon*) in 2011, "Japan's Four Seasons" (*Nihon no shiki*) in 2012, and "Japanese Scene" (*Nihon no ikkei*) in 2013.

As prominently as Japan features in *Eshi 100*, however, cute girl characters feature even more prominently. In fact, since the inception of *Eshi 100*, bishōjo have appeared as the central figures in almost every single illustration displayed. In many ways, the exhibition seems like an extension of Akihabara, which was transformed by a concentration of stores selling bishōjo games that later drew in stores dealing with manga, anime, and related media and material featuring cute girl characters (Morikawa 2003, 42–44; Kagami 2010, 132). Although manga/anime stores are today more densely clustered in Akihabara than anywhere else in Tokyo, Japan, or the world, the neighborhood is still biased toward bishōjo and those attracted to them, as is *Eshi 100* (figure C.3). It turns out that this shared focus on cute girl characters is not a coincidence. *Eshi 100* was founded by Hattori Michisato, president of Greenwood, which is a bishōjo game production company. In a personal interview, Hattori explained that *Eshi 100* was conceived in part as a way to generate

FIGURE C.2
Eshi 100: Contemporary Japanese Illustration thematically evokes "Japan."

positive publicity for the bishōjo game industry, which is facing declining sales in Japan, criticism from abroad, and threats of increased regulation.[21] With the knowledge that Hattori is responsible for organizing the exhibition in practice, it is perhaps not so surprising that many illustrators—Watanabe Akio (under the pen name Poyoyon Rock), Nishimata Aoi, Hinoue Itaru, Itō Noizi, and others—working in the bishōjo game industry present at *Eshi 100*.[22] In Akihabara, fliers for the exhibition are distributed alongside fliers for upcoming bishōjo games in specialty shops such as Getchuya (figures C.4 and C.5). Although the explicit sex of bishōjo games is absent from the illustrations on display at *Eshi 100*, the exhibition clearly has overlapping contributors and fans, which aligns it with "otaku" and manga/anime subculture.

What we have with *Eshi 100*, then, is a deeply "otaku" exhibition that is heavily sponsored by the Japanese government, which throws into

FIGURE C.3 *Eshi 100* attracts bishōjo fans in Akihabara.

sharp relief many issues related to the politics of popular culture in contemporary Japan. Most obviously, Hattori, in response to criticism of bishōjo media and fans in Weird Japan discourse, attempted to align them with celebration of manga/anime and their fans in Cool Japan discourse. In the process, in response to escalating inter-national discourse, claims were made about Japanese, "otaku," and popular culture of the past and present. Of course, Hattori did not do this on his own, but rather worked to bring together an alliance of public and private interests to imagine and create relations between "otaku" and "Japanese popular culture." *Eshi 100* is possible because of this alliance, as are the claims made through and around it. At *Eshi 100*, we can see how connections to Japan are forged and positions staked and fought over on the battlefield of national-popular culture (Hall 1998, 450–51). Precisely because the positions are so boldly stated, the claims so rough and raw in their partial development, they reveal that there is nothing given about "culture"—national or otherwise, popular or otherwise. Not as taken-for-granted as usual, "Japanese popular culture" is open to interrogation as a contingent, contested formulation.

Described on its official English-language website as an exhibition to introduce original art by "100 eshi active on the front lines of popular

FIGURE C.4
Eshi 100 advertised at bishōjo game specialty shop.

culture," the men and women that produce bishōjo illustrations for *Eshi 100* are tied not only to popular culture, but specifically Japanese popular culture. This begins with the name that they are given, "eshi," a Japanese term that remains untranslated. In distinction from titles such as "illustrator" (*irasutorētā*), "artist" (*ātisuto*), or "character designer" (*kyarakutā dezainā*), which could equally apply to the contributors to *Eshi 100*, "eshi" was initially used to refer to creators of woodblock prints in the Edo period. Connections to Japanese history are made explicit in the promotional discourse of *Eshi 100*, for example, the written introduction to the exhibition, which is posted on a wall at the entrance to greet visitors:

> In recent years Japanese manga, anime, games, illustrations for light novels and other aspects of graphic pop culture have been the subject of increased attention from countries around the world, but their appreciation is even greater in Japan. The high degree of technique possessed by the artists who create these beautiful illustrations has been likened to that of the eshi, the artists who produced the famous woodblock prints during the Edo period, in the 18th and 19th centuries, leading them to also be referred to as eshi and winning them a large following of fans. The work in "Eshi 100" differs from the conventional image of art, but

FIGURE C.5
Eshi 100 advertised at bishōjo game specialty shop.

in the same way that woodblock prints appealed to the general public of the Edo period, these works capture the hearts of the contemporary people. (Sankei Shimbun 2013, 3)

Bear in mind that the beautiful illustrations in question are overwhelmingly of manga/anime-style cute girl characters. Analogous to those producing ukiyo-e in the Edo period, those producing bishōjo illustrations in the Heisei period are "contemporary eshi" (*gendai no eshi*). While much of the content of manga/anime—including pornographic varieties—might be considered trashy by critics (Schodt 1983, 16; Kinsella 2000, 168; Napier 2001, 3), *Eshi 100* suggests that so too were woodblock prints. They were nonetheless the culture of the people of Japan, which became famous in global circulation. As with woodblock prints, so too with manga/anime and bishōjo illustrations.

Now, if it seems that an alliance of public and private interests is positioning manga/anime generally and bishōjo illustrations specifically as the culture of the people of contemporary Japan, it is because that is exactly what is happening. What might be cast as "otaku" culture and art is being positioned as Japanese culture and art. No matter how much manga/anime and bishōjo illustrations are celebrated overseas, the visitor to *Eshi 100* is told that they originate in Japan and are more appreciated there. They are, quite simply, Japanese popular culture. Some go further still and claim, as one writer does in a piece for *Eshi 100*'s catalogue, "an unbroken line of . . . culture" (Sakata 2015, 222) from the Edo period to the Heisei period. Manga/anime and bishōjo illustrations are Japanese popular culture and art of the present, and, like ukiyo-e, will be traditional in the future. If woodblock prints of beautiful women—often geisha—did much to emblazon a particular inter-national image of Japan, which persists to this day and with which nation branding is complicit (JNTO 2010; Allison 2012; METI 2012), then manga/anime and bishōjo illustrations are contributing to a new image of Japan.[23] And while the Japanese government was late to respond to global praise and promote ukiyo-e, *Eshi 100* demonstrates that they are more proactive with manga/anime generally and bishōjo illustrations specifically, which are caught up in Cool Japan policy initiatives.

This is not without friction, however. When considering the alliance, it is important to remember that an imaginary Japan filled with bishōjo, or a Japan in which the people love cute girl characters, attracts some and repulses others. This engenders complicated positions, for example, those of Mihara Ryōtarō. Alongside study at Cornell and Oxford, Mihara worked for the Ministry of Economy, Trade, and Industry on Cool Japan policy initiatives. From firsthand observation of the spread of *The Melancholy of Haruhi Suzumiya* in the United States (Mihara 2010) to a review of the promises and pitfalls of Cool Japan (Mihara 2014), Mihara has emerged as a leading voice in the ongoing discussion of Japanese popular culture and politics. Commenting on *Eshi 100* in a piece published in its catalogue, Mihara states that manga and anime are part of the Japanese "character" (Mihara 2013). This is not itself a new claim, but Mihara takes it further by arguing that part of the Japanese character is an understanding and appreciation of, if not affection for, bishōjo (224). Identifying as Japanese and an "otaku," Mihara reflects on his time in the United States, where he encountered people that responded to manga/anime featuring bishōjo in a way shrilly foreign to him: "To the Americans it was overtly 'sexual' and simply appeared pedophilic. (The Heisei bishōjo style!) The 'charm' and 'artistry' incorporated into the Heisei bishōjo style were negated by the immorality of the 'Lolita complex' and 'sexual' elements. . . . I think that it requires quite a special ability to be able to concentrate dispassionately on the appreciation of the 'Japan,' 'Japanese seasons' or 'Japanese scene' that are expressed, while putting aside the powerful figure of the young girl in the foreground and remaining unmoved by the sexual implications" (224). By Mihara's estimation, it takes something special to look at bishōjo illustrations and see more than cute girls and sex, which can be offensive (see, for example, Adelstein and Kubo 2014). Coming from a former bureaucrat educated in the United States and United Kingdom, the claim is to a shared sensibility that develops in those growing up with manga/anime and its characters. At first blush, this sensibility seems to be shared nationally; in Mihara's experience, the Japanese have it, while the Americans do not.

There is, however, the possibility that those with an intimate relation to manga/anime outside of Japan might develop an understanding and appreciation of bishōjo—think fans of *The Melancholy of Haruhi Suzumiya* (Mihara 2010)—just as there are those in Japan that remain highly critical of them (Aera Dot 2017). As *Eshi 100* gathers attention online and travels internationally, it factors into the proliferation of manga/anime and invigorates manga/anime fandom. In this, Mihara confirms, the aims of *Eshi 100* "correspond with those of the 'Cool Japan' policy to promote the spread of the Japanese cultural industry (including that of the Heisei bishōjo style)" (Mihara 2013, 224). The government sponsors the exhibition for that very reason. Importantly, Mihara includes in the output of the Japanese culture industry not only manga/anime but also bishōjo. They are what is selling, or rather what is appealing to "otaku" in Japan and around the world; no matter how niche the industry producing them may appear, cute girl characters are crucial to the manga/anime economy in Japan, and the global economy of desire for "Japan."

Given this, Mihara offers his support to the alliance of public and private interests promoting manga/anime generally, and bishōjo illustrations specifically, as Japanese popular culture. Aware of opposition, Mihara addresses it head on: "There exists a large body of opinion at home and abroad that claims the aforementioned Heisei bishōjo style is nothing but child pornography and that proudly spreading this kind of Japanese 'character' around the world is simply exposing the country to shame. Moreover, there remains a strong unease at the idea of naively introducing the culture represented by the Heisei bishōjo style to the wider 'public' through Japanese backing" (224–25). At home and abroad, there are lingering associations between cute girl characters and the imagined perversion of "weird otaku." When the government normalizes and nationalizes "otaku" culture and art as "Japanese," it risks being seen as normalizing and nationalizing that perversion. A Japan awash with manga/anime and bishōjo illustrations could be seen as a nation with "a fascination with sexual interaction with young girls" (Adelstein and Kubo 2014). The problem, these reporters assert, is "cultural." This statement comes in an article illustrated with a photograph of a Japanese man browsing a display of bishōjo games at a store in Akihabara (see figure 2.5)—that is, the very same environment that extends to *Eshi 100*. A government that sponsors the exhibition of bishōjo illustrations as part of Cool Japan policy initiatives targeting overseas fans might be accused of selling the fantasy of sexual interaction with girls (Miller 2011, 18). Forget Weird Japan—for critics, this is Porno Japan, Japan as the Empire of Child Pornography, Child Porn Pimping Japan.

Ironically, it was after *Eshi 100* moved past Japan as its explicit organizing theme that this tension became most palpable. Well, moved past the word "Japan," anyway, while still seeming to insist on national-popular culture. Following "Japan," "Japan's Four Seasons," and "Japanese Scene," in 2014, the fourth installment of *Eshi 100* took as its theme "Cute" (*Kawaii*), said to be "synonymous with Cool Japan" (Sankei Shimbun 2014, 3). The welcoming message declares that "cute" in Japanese—*kawaii*—is not the same as "cute" in English, because there is a "uniquely Japanese nuance" (3). "Cute" in Japanese, the message continues, used to refer to "people who were in a weaker, subordinate position, or loved ones" (3), but now means something closer to "good." Putting aside the connection between weaker/subordinate people and loved ones and the relativity of judging something to be good, at *Eshi 100*, Japanese cute seems to indicate something other than "cute." What this might be is unclear, but it is in any case illustrated with bishōjo. "Moment to Make Kawaii," for example, focuses on a geisha, associated with the Edo period and woodblock prints, but mixes this image of Japanese culture with a magical girl, associated with manga/anime and "otaku" culture since the early 1980s (figure C.6). Meanwhile, "kawaii?!NIPPON" is a smorgasbord of characters drawn in styles ranging from girls' comics to fetish magazines (figure C.7). The result is jarring juxtaposition and colorful confusion. The title of the piece questions Japanese cute, but one infers that the capitalized NIPPON—that is, Japan—is also up for grabs. Not all the bishōjo here look like typical manga/anime characters, or what is at times considered the "Japanese" style, and seeing "Japan" in all this takes work as imaginative and creative as the piece itself.

FIGURE C.6
"Moment to Make Kawaii" shows geisha magical girl.

One of the standout pieces at the fourth installment of *Eshi 100* was "Duck Festival," which takes as its subject a young girl in thigh-high stockings and a school-issued swimsuit carrying a type of hard-leather backpack that is used only through primary school in Japan (figure C.8). It is easy to see why so many visitors to the exhibition stopped in front of this image, captivated and compelled to discuss it. The image is both cute and sexual, and responses to it will vary from attraction to repulsion—the latter perhaps more likely when the image is removed from the original context of encounter in Akihabara and reproduced for discussion elsewhere. Drawing under the pen name Poyoyon Rock, the man behind "Duck Festival" is Watanabe Akio, who has strong ties to the bishōjo game industry dating back to the 1990s. Today, Watanabe is revered as one of the greatest living

FIGURE C.7 "kawaii?!NIPPON" shows colorful confusion.

bishōjo illustrators—his work appears in the *Monogatari* series (2009–), among the best-selling anime franchises of the 2010s—but his contributions to bishōjo games and *Eshi 100* highlight thorny issues.[24] "Duck Festival" clearly has its roots in "otaku" culture since the late 1970s, which saw the emergence of what some art historians call "the contemporary Japanese aesthetic of 'cute eroticism'" (Azuma and Yamada 2011, 10). Occurring alongside the inaugural *Eshi 100*, note how this revaluation of "otaku" culture makes "cute eroticism" (*kawaii ero*) into a "Japanese aesthetic" (*Nihonteki bi'ishiki*), which might invite criticism of Japan for sexualizing youth. This is a problem with bishōjo illustrations at *Eshi 100* generally and "Duck Festival" specifically, and it shows how the imagined perversion of "weird otaku" haunts Cool Japan.[25]

FIGURE C.8 "Duck Festival" shows "cute eroticism."

Although beloved by fans around the world and participating in an exhibition that is apparently aligned with Cool Japan policy initiatives to spread manga/anime and stimulate global fandom, Watanabe sees himself as someone aligned with "otaku" and manga/anime subculture, which makes him anxious about having a higher profile and inviting outside criticism. In a personal interview, Watanabe explained, "In truth, I don't want Americans to express interest. I don't want these [bishōjo] games to be known. That's why I've refused all interviews."[26] Despite being one such American, I was granted this interview because of my ties to people in the industry, and because Watanabe had something that he wanted to say to me. "If these games come out into the open, we can't moe," he said, flustered but adamant. "We can't moe. If otaku culture is too open, then the power of imagination will decline." This last phrase, "power of imagination" (*sōzōryoku*), could also mean "power of creation," which suggests the power to both imagine and create manga/anime characters and worlds. Too much exposure jeopardized the ability of Watanabe and others like him to freely imagine and create bishōjo, which in turn compromised their ability to freely experience and share affective responses to them. I was caught off guard by the intensity of Watanabe's words: "we can't moe" (*moerarenai*), "moe" as a verb, conjugated to mean "not possible to moe," stated twice to underscore its significance. The tone, chilling: it was as if I was physically hurting this man, attacking him and threatening to take away his life. I was an outsider, a harbinger of forces that could disrupt moe and "otaku" culture. If Mihara's experiences have led him to think that an understanding and appreciation of bishōjo is part of the Japanese character and notably less so the American one, then Watanabe sees it as something "otaku," which is being publicized by alignment with Cool Japan and which American criticism and Japanese normalization and nationalization will ultimately destroy.

For his part, however, *Eshi 100* founder Hattori imagines a world in which affective relations with fictional characters generally and bishōjo specifically are shared and not associated with national borders and interests. That is, while still strategically aligned with Cool Japan policy initiatives and promotional discourse, Hattori is actively endeavoring to foster forms of transnational collaboration and hybridity that would undo "internationalism." Of course, having organized overseas editions of *Eshi 100*, Hattori is acutely aware of limits. If visitors in Taiwan and Vietnam were extremely receptive, other countries remain impossible for "cultural or religious reasons" (Hattori 2014, 227).[27] He elaborates no further, but one gathers from context that the issue is the sexuality of bishōjo, which can be "shocking"; in this way, the global spread of bishōjo illustrations causes "friction" among "those who do not understand" (226). It would be simple enough here to pit Japan against its "others," but Hattori resists such nationalizing discourse. Instead, as he lays out in a discussion of the theme of the fifth installment of *Eshi 100*, "The World of Eshi" (*Eshi no sekai*), Hattori imagines that bishōjo illustrators will open up worlds of creativity that transcend "Japan" (Hattori 2015, 218). This is visualized by the words "Japan," "Eshi," and "World," in that order, connected in a series of bidirectional arrows (figure C.9). In feedback loops with "Japan" and the "World," relations between eshi and one are as vital as relations between eshi and the other. Or rather, as Hattori goes on to clarify, others, as in other worlds, which eshi imagine, create, and share, and which affect

FIGURE C.9 Hattori imagines eshi going beyond Japan.

them and Japan. And just as there are multiple possible worlds, so too is "Japan" plural and potential.

In subtly differentiating the missions of Cool Japan and *Eshi 100*, Hattori develops a remarkable perspective. On the one hand, he sees that those imagining, creating, and sharing manga/anime worlds may be located in Japan, but they are also positioned in certain ways and struggling with those positions. This means that manga/anime are not purely and unproblematically "Japanese," but rather come from individual and collective struggles to imagine, create, and share worlds. On the other hand, Hattori sees a future in which more people outside of Japan will become artists and participate in imagining, creating, and sharing manga/anime worlds. A world full of eshi, even as these eshi all imagine and create and share worlds, moving in and beyond "Japan." In the future that Hattori envisions, these emergent worlds would be anchored by affection for manga/anime characters, and implicitly bishōjo, but they would no longer be recognized as strictly or solely "Japanese." That is, they would not necessarily need to come from and lead back to "Japan," the celebrated or critiqued national origin.[28] If "inter-nationalism" is the "reworking and strengthening of the national in tandem with the intensification of cross-border media flows" (Iwabuchi 2010, 89), then Hattori imagines undoing it. In this way, below the surface of *Eshi 100* as a tool for Cool Japan public diplomacy, there is a struggle with the nation and a desire to go beyond it. Rather than seeing manga/anime characters and worlds and falling back into the familiar inter-nationalism of talking about "Japan" and "Japanese popular culture," we might instead consider the terrain of struggle. If we take a position at *Eshi 100* and listen, Hattori, Watanabe, Mihara, and others will tell us about their struggles. Their words may invite us to imagine Japanese, "otaku," popular culture, and to do so again, and otherwise. This is no less than a struggle for imagination, and, whether acknowledged or not, we are involved in it.

Conclusion

Among the many issues that Koichi Iwabuchi highlights in response to journalistic and academic writing on Cool Japan, he argues that a focus on "inter-national" relations draws attention away from transnational collaborations, hybridity, and divisions within nations as assumed units of analysis (Iwabuchi 2010, 89, 91–94). Even as it ignores the meshworks that connect people across borders, "inter-nationalism" flattens internal differences and struggles.[29] In the study of popular culture, Iwabuchi proposes, "We need a serious consideration of the sociohistorical contexts in which people passionately consume/appropriate media texts, and of the cultural politics and cultural economy involved in their active consuming practices. We must consider issues such as self-empowerment in terms of marginalized identity politics (gender, sexuality, race, ethnicity, class, nation, and so on), coping with the tyranny of everyday life in the neoliberal world, the manifestation of a more participatory media culture, and the transnational audience/fan alliance against the control of media culture production and distribution by global media culture industries" (88). To my mind, Iwabuchi is advocating an approach to "Japanese popular culture" that takes into account Stuart Hall's intervention (Hall 1998). That is, something closer to the process approach, as distinct from the market and descriptive approaches in vogue.

In its discussion of "otaku" and the struggle for imagination in Japan, this book has touched on "the sociohistorical contexts in which people passionately consume/appropriate media texts" (chapter 1), "the cultural politics and cultural economy involved in their active consuming practices" (chapters 2 and 3), "marginalized identity politics (gender, sexuality, race, ethnicity, class, nation, and so on)" (chapter 4), and "coping with the tyranny of everyday life in the neoliberal world" (chapter 5). This concluding chapter concentrated on the (inter-)national politics of popular culture, or what Hall calls national-popular culture and describes as "a battlefield" (Hall 1998, 451–52). Elsewhere, Hall and his colleagues refer to their writing as "an intervention in the battleground of ideas" (Hall et al. 1978, x). In its own small way, this book is also intended as such. Following Hall, we can see that policymakers and police certainly deserve "a more 'honoured' place in the history of popular culture than they have usually been accorded" (Hall 1998, 443), but so do journalists, academics, and Japan experts, who "help to discipline and police" (450) what comes to be known as "Japanese popular culture." I agree with Iwabuchi that journalists, academics, and Japan experts are at times not only complicit in branding and marketing "Japan" and its popular culture, but also in homogenizing "Japan" as a nation in relation to others. While Iwabuchi's emphasis is celebratory discourse about Cool Japan, the same can be said of critical discourse about Weird Japan. If, as Iwabuchi suggests, imagination is crucial to inscribing exclusive national boundaries (Iwabuchi 2010, 94), then journalists, academics, and Japan experts play a part in that imagination and struggles over it.

Returning to *Eshi 100* and thinking with Hall and Iwabuchi, we see alliances being forged and broken within and beyond the nation. At *Eshi 100*, public and private interests align in exhibiting bishōjo illustrations as Japanese popular culture. The *Eshi 100* alliance may well bolster claims about national-popular culture and the people, whereby, for example, "Japanese" understand and appreciate bishōjo, while "Americans" do not. Importantly, such alliances are shifting and uncertain. Popular culture, Hall reminds us, is always a complex play of forces—"Lines of 'alliance' as well as lines of cleavage" (Hall 1998, 443). In the story of Hattori bringing the Japanese government and bishōjo game industry together, we can see the tension. Meanwhile, at *Eshi 100*, under the banner of Cool Japan, bishōjo illustrators reimagine and re-create "Japan." Consistently playing with national symbols—mixing the geisha and magical girl, for example—the result is a Japan that both is and is not "Japan," an "otaku" Japan, a weird one. This is not necessarily Cool Japan or Weird Japan, but rather "Japan" as part of the alternative worlds imagined, created, and shared by "weird otaku." Even as the movement of "weird otaku" crosses boundaries, blurs them, and opens up "Japan," attempts are made to control and channel it. Popular culture, Hall insists, is characterized by "the double movement of containment and resistance" (443), which also applies to the relation between "otaku" and "Japan." For Hall, cultures are "ways of struggle" that "constantly intersect" (451), which is truer still of popular culture in a connected world in motion. By carefully considering ways of struggle, we can transcend approaches that "uncritically regard the nation as the unit of analysis" (Iwabuchi 2010, 93) and reinforce borders as they are crossed. Researchers will then see lines of alliance and cleavage that are rarely coterminous with the lines drawn around nations.

If Hall approaches "the popular as a historically contingent space for the constitution of collective agency" (Harsin and Hayward 2013, 204), then the stakes in the struggle over it are all too clear. Again, this also applies to "otaku" in Japan. Some seek to normalize and nationalize "otaku" and manga/anime subculture, while others imagine, create, and share worlds beyond "Japan." For his part, *Eshi 100* founder Hattori Michisato imagines undoing inter-nationalism in shared affection for manga/anime characters, transnational collaboration, and hybrid forms (Hattori 2015, 218). As Hattori sees it, an open collective is possible—other worlds are possible—even as artists employ national symbolism. While some scholars note that affective alliances can reinforce national boundaries (Lukács 2010b, 23–24), others underscore a struggle between "naturalized familial community" and "alternative collective" (Aalgaard 2016, 50–52). If the line "separating the fascistic from the critical" can be "agonizingly thin and easily breached" (52), then this is why we struggle over it. If we are reflexive, then questions about what we discuss as "Japanese popular culture," or "otaku" culture, or "manga/anime," reveal power relations and our own relations of and to power. If we are not, we "might end up creating another depoliticized, contained image of Japan" (Iwabuchi 2010, 95). We might also end up creating another politicized, contained image of Japan as a source of sexual deviance and danger (Hinton 2014, 56). Instead of aligning ourselves with or against "Japan," which is a dubious proposition (Harootunian and Sakai 1999, 638), we may well think about the situated politics of "weird otaku" struggling to imagine, create, and share worlds. One need not be moved to join them to consider their positions.

Rather than accepting the nationalization of popular culture, which connects and divides in specific ways, researchers can take a position on the battlefield and fight for shared worlds organized otherwise. When conflating "otaku" culture with Japanese popular culture, we miss the movement of manga/anime fans imagining and creating alternative social worlds in Japan, as well as responses to imagined excesses and perversions. We miss the struggle. The fact that some manga/anime fans are still "weird otaku," despite normalization and nationalization, should clue us in to this oversight. If, as Iwabuchi contends, we need to move past discourse about the nation to see more nuanced relations within and beyond it (Iwabuchi 2010, 88), then this book has tried to pry open the space to do so. This has been part of my own struggle for imagination, which took me through not only *Eshi 100* in the 2010s, but also maid cafés and the streets of Akihabara in the 2000s, the moe phenomenon in the 1990s, niche media such as *The Book of Otaku* and *Manga Burikko* in the 1980s, and fanzines and events for "male" shōjo fans in the 1970s. While there are those that take "otaku" and "Japan" for granted, I hope that this book makes room for future studies of contingent articulations in the ongoing struggle for imagination.

NOTES

Introduction

1 On July 7, 2017, Vinclu changed its company name to Gatebox. For issues of clarity, and reflecting my writing about the company before its change, I have decided to retain Vinclu. The advertisement can be viewed online. Gatebox Lab, "Gatebox Promotion Movie: 'Okaeri' (English)," YouTube, December 13, 2016. https://www.youtube.com/watch?v=mMbiL8D6qXo.

2 "Profile," Azuma Hikari Official Site. https://web.archive.org/web/20180224114320/https://gatebox.ai/hikari/en/ (last accessed on April 20, 2018).

3 Gatebox Official Site. http://gatebox.ai/ (last accessed on February 12, 2019).

4 If it facilitates better understanding, we can translate this into anthropologist Shaka McGlotten's terms: on the one hand, responses to forms of intimacy perceived to be "less real than others," "dangerous," and "failed," and, on the other hand, "the labors, perverse and otherwise, that animatedly rework categories of intimacy" (McGlotten 2013, 12). For a complementary discussion of "otaku" and the labor of perversion, see Lamarre 2006, 375–85.

5 I am inspired by comics scholar Christopher Pizzino, who writes, "I am skeptical of the tendency in literary and cultural studies to assume that binary thinking is perforce a transgression that must be corrected before it is well understood" (Pizzino 2016, 67–68).

6 Also in the United States, but separate from anime fans, one might further consider "bronies," or adult men attracted to *My Little Pony: Friendship Is Magic* (2010–), who have been presented in similar ways as seeking alternatives to hegemonic masculinity by

consuming and appropriating a cartoon originally intended for young girls (Malaquais 2012).

7 Reflecting on his observations of manga/anime fandom outside of Japan, critic and editor Ōtsuka Eiji conjectures that "otaku" movement might be related to "mending social, cultural and mental identity for those who are somehow minorities in a given society" (Ōtsuka 2015, xxv).

8 Here I am thinking of the work of philosopher Gilles Deleuze and psychotherapist Félix Guattari, who argue that "we are composed of lines" (Deleuze and Guattari 1987, 202). Some lines are imposed from the outside, while others sprout up by chance. "Others can be invented, drawn, without a model and without chance: we must invent our lines of flight, if we are able, and the only way we can invent them is by effectively drawing them, in our lives" (202). To my mind, the lines of manga/anime characters can often be understood as lines of flight invented and drawn in the lives of artists and fans.

9 Women's studies scholar Sherrie A. Inness describes comics as a potentially "revolutionary" medium, because they create "alternative worlds in which gender operates very differently than it does in our own real world" (Inness 1999, 141). Feminist psychoanalyst Setsu Shigematsu points in a similar direction when arguing that comics open up "alternative sites and different dimensions of what is typically conceived of as sex and sexuality" (Shigematsu 1999, 128).

10 In fact, theorist Scott Bukatman positions animation as the antithesis of film: "Rather than recording a moving world as a series of still images, a series of still images is projected in sequence to produce movement where none existed. As if in recognition of this signal difference, cartoon logic reverses, in fact *rejects*, the logic and physics of 'the real world'" (Bukatman 2012, 47). Building on this insight, Bukatman proposes that animation offers resistance to the instrumental rationality of the world or "reality" as we know it. Carrying this over to viewers/readers in ways familiar from McCloud, Bukatman suggests that, in animation, "identification crosses gender boundaries to permit all to partake of these performances of disobedience and resistance" (25). It is worth noting that Bukatman draws attention to how artists and viewers/readers get caught up in the movements of characters, as well as the eroticism of movement (198–200). Bukatman shares with many critics in Japan the perspective that the "exuberant energy" of animation is related to "its only partially submilated sexuality" (19).

11 In fact, Bukatman uses this very word to describe animation (Bukatman 2012, 3). As I see it, comics and animation are marginal media of imagination in contrast to more mainstream entertainment and its "realism," which theorists Max Horkheimer and Theodor Adorno argue "denies its audience any dimension in which they might roam freely in the imagination" and leads to a "withering of imagination" (Horkheimer and Adorno 2002, 100). Marginal media unsettle reality, leave room for imagination, and contribute to its flourishing. Horkheimer and Adorno seem to recognize this potential of cartoons (106, 110).

12 Like comics, but in its own way, "animation allows the viewer to enter into other worlds and other formulations of this world" (Halberstam 2011, 181). So Halberstam perhaps overstates things somewhat when asserting, "It is *only* in the realm of animation that we actually find the alternative" (23). One might also question his preference for computer-generated animation and critique of "two-dimensional cartoons" (176).

13 The Japanese word for imagination is *sōzō*, which is also a homonym for "creation." The two are distinguished by the modified Chinese characters used to write them, and told apart in spoken conversation through context, but to say "I imagine a world" can also mean "I create a world."

14 Even as I write this in 2018, the University of Toronto Press has started an innovative new series called ethnoGRAPHIC, which, according to the official website, "realizes ethnographic research in graphic novel form." This gets at the issues that I am raising here, but also quite literally makes the deliberately juxtaposed images into sequential art, rather than images in text. We shall have to see if this experiment in ethnographic representation will catch on, but I have high hopes. "ethnoGRAPHIC," University of Toronto Press Official Site. https://utorontopress.com/us/books/by-series/ethnographic?dir=desc&order=publish_date (last accessed on February 12, 2019).

15 "Really imaginative ethnographies," writes Halberstam, "depend upon an unknowing relation to the other. To begin an ethnographic project with a goal, with an object of research and a set of presumptions, is already to stymie the process of discovery; it blocks one's ability to learn something that exceeds the frameworks with which one enters" (Halberstam 2011, 12). Well said. One can see here connections to Halberstam's conception of "low theory," or "theorization of alternatives within an undisciplined zone of knowledge production" (18).

Chapter 1. Seeking an Alternative

1 If "shōjo culture is notable for its rejection of anything excessively masculine" (Mackie 2010, 194), and if the shōjo is "a vision of alternative forms of sociality and alternative kinds of affective relationships that are not bound by the structures of the heteronormative nuclear family" (198), then there is no reason to assume that this appeals exclusively to girls and women. Feminist thinker Ueno Chizuko, for example, links shōjo deferring or avoiding sexual maturity with "male" shōjo fans doing the same (Ueno 1989, 131–32; for more, see chapter 2). It is not entirely helpful to propose a dualism between the "male, stuck in an immature sexuality that sees its object as the defloration of the innocent Lolita figure, and the Lolita who desperately tries to hang on to this innocence" (Mackie 2010, 200). For a discussion of men identifying with fictional girl characters in complex and contradictory ways, see Kinsella 2000, 121–24, 137–38.

2 This interaction took place at a meeting of the British Association for Japanese Studies (Japan Chapter) hosted at Chiba University on May 27, 2017.

3 Researcher Perry R. Hinton suggests that "the term 'Lolita' has a culturally specific meaning and that it has a different meaning in Western culture to that in Japan" (Hinton 2014, 54). Drawing attention to shōjo as crucial to the phenomenon in Japan, Hinton argues that "lolicon" might better be translated as "shoujo [*sic*] complex" (59). Insofar as it entails a refusal of or resistance to "growing up," lolicon is associated with "a Peter Pan complex rather than a Lolita complex" (62). On the whole, Hinton concludes that "the term 'Lolita complex' is an inappropriate rendering of rorikon [lolicon] given the Western popular representation of Lolita" (65) and its different meanings in Japan.

4 For an English-language discussion, see Shigematsu 1999, 129–32.

5 Manga critic Takekuma Ken'tarō explains, "One of the things that you cannot overlook when talking about manga at this time is that, after all, 'men started reading shōjo manga.' The 1970s were more than anything the era of shōjo manga. At the time, a man who identified as a manga fan, but didn't read shōjo manga, was basically considered to be unqualified" (quoted in Nagayama 2014, 56). Manga critic Nagayama Kaoru elaborates, "For men who identified as manga fans, works by the Magnificent 49ers [Hagio, Takemiya, and so on] were an absolute must, but if you were a real fanatic, then you would get into Okada Fumiko, who published in COM; Asuka Yumiko; Kimura Minori; Yashiro Masako, a precursor of the Magnificent 49ers; or, even beyond that, Mizuno Hideko, the great mother of contemporary shōjo manga who was also a member of the Tokiwasō group [of young artists close to Tezuka Osamu] and whose *Fire!* (1969) earned her many male fans in the 1970s; the more decorative Kihara Toshie; Kishi Yūko; Mutsu A-ko, known for her 'girly love comedy' and 'preppy manga'; Tabuchi Yumiko; there were even some who went all the way to Iwadate Mariko and the like" (Nagayama 2014, 233–34).

6 The work of still animation that inspired Harada was an adaptation of *Golgo 13* (Gorugo 13, 1971).

7 Although there is insufficient space in this chapter to pursue these connections, Labyrinth counted among its members and supporters Sagawa Toshihiko, founder of *June*, a specialty magazine for boys love manga, and Kawamoto Kōji, founder of *Peke*, a specialty magazine in which Azuma Hideo published bishōjo manga. Furthermore, Ōtsuka Eiji, under the pen name Ōtsuka Ēji, submitted to the reader response column of Labyrinth's fanzines, which were mainly focused on shōjo manga. For more, see Yonezawa 1989, 79; also Shimotsuki 2008.

8 The assertion is not uncommon in his influential writings and dialogues in the early 1980s. See for example page 60 in "Comic Live Discussion, Part II: Azuma Hideo vs. Yonezawa Yoshihiro," *Gekkan Out*, March 1982, 56–61.

9 In 1981, Azuma worked with Hagio on a publication (Azuma and Yamada 2011, 18).

10 The motivations of *Cybele* contributors are discussed in the April 1981 issue of *Animec*. For his part, in 1979, Azuma published *Soar Donkey* (Tobe tobe donkī) in *Gekkan Princess* (Azuma and Yamada 2011, 32). Such were his associations with shōjo manga that Azuma is discussed in manga critic Hashimoto Osamu's groundbreaking series *The Blooming Maidens' Stewed Roots* (Hanasaku otome-tachi no kinpiragobō, 1979–81) (Azuma and Yamamoto 2011, 148–49).

11 These quotes come from page 60 of "Comic Live Discussion, Part II: Azuma Hideo vs. Yonezawa Yoshihiro," *Gekkan Out*, March 1982, 56–61.

12 This resonates with discourse about boys love manga and yaoi fanzines as "pure fantasy" (Galbraith 2015a, 156), and such works as an opportunity for readers to "play sex/uality" (Fujimoto 1998, 196; also Fujimoto 2015).

13 For more on the reaction of gekiga artists to Azuma, see page 60 of "Comic Live Discussion, Part II: Azuma Hideo vs. Yonezawa Yoshihiro," *Gekkan Out*, March 1982, 56–61.

14 Sasakibara Gō, interview with the author, August 31, 2014.

15 It is worth noting how the bishōjo heroine of *Urusei Yatsura*, Lum, is situated in the lolicon boom. Although an alien whose age is somewhat of a mystery, Lum is most often

estimated to be about seventeen years old, which is equivalent to the age of the male protagonist of the series. In Lum's case, secondary sex characteristics are well established; she has a developed chest and hips. In short, Lum does not appear particularly "young," although she is an iconic manga/anime-style, cute girl character. Given this, it is interesting to see Kuribayashi, a male teacher that becomes infatuated with Lum, described as suffering from "the Lolita Complex, commonly called lolicon." Coming in episode 16, this is the first use of the term in the anime adaptation of *Urusei Yatsura*. The episode was originally aired in February 1982, which is to say amid growing awareness of lolicon. (For example, this is the same month that a discussion of the lolicon boom appeared in *Animage* magazine.) As is clear from its full glossing, it is possible that some viewers might not have known the term at the time. However, by the second reference to the "Lolita complex" in the series, which comes in episode 27, aired in May 1982, Count Dracula pursues Lum while proclaiming simply, "The Lolita blood is clamoring." This suggests that the term had become more established, or at least that understanding could be assumed among regular viewers of *Urusei Yatsura*. Both Kuribayashi and Count Dracula are portrayed as older men attracted to Lum, which could also be said of many fans of *Urusei Yatsura*, and this dynamic is highlighted as lolicon. A cute girl character such as Lum is perhaps not the first thing that comes to mind when one thinks of the Lolita complex in the anglophone world today, which serves to spotlight the specific usage of lolicon at this moment in the manga/anime movement in Japan.

16 While a startling case, Yuzuki speaks to the larger cross-gender/genre influence of shōjo manga generally and *Ribon* specifically. For example, in the September 2014 issue of *Da Vinci* magazine, which is devoted to *Ribon* and its impact, acclaimed bishōjo illustrator "Eguchi Hisashi" states unequivocally that he was influenced by Mutsu A-ko's shōjo style. (Perhaps the reason that he, like Azuma Hideo, is discussed in Hashimoto Osamu's *The Blooming Maidens' Stewed Roots*.) Moreover, Eguchi recalls seeing issues of *Ribon* lying around the offices of the boys' manga magazine where he was publishing in the late 1970s, as well as promotional giveaways emblazoned with Mutsu's designs hanging on the walls.

17 Uchiyama Aki, interview with the author, July 5, 2011. Uchiyama was not alone in idolizing Azuma, who was at the center of a cult fandom in the early 1980s (Sasakibara 2003, 122). In addition to his attempt to publish in *Ribon*, it is worth noting that Uchiyama at times drew images resembling those of Mutsu A-ko, whose star rose in that very same shōjo manga magazine. For example, despite its content, Uchiyama's "Cinderella in a Diaper" (Omutsu wo haita Shinderera, 1981) appears almost as if drawn by Mutsu (Nagayama 2014, 234). Playing on the imaginative associations of *Cinderella* this way resonates with Wada Shinji's take on *Alice in Wonderland* and Azuma Hideo's take on *Little Red Riding Hood* in the previous decade.

18 Satō Toshihiko, interview with the author, July 28, 2010. Unless otherwise indicated, all quotes from Satō come from this same interview.

19 There are numerous indications to the contrary, however, including episodes dedicated to what looks like intergenerational love (episode 36), as well as Minky Momo's own tragic love as someone stuck between child and adult (episode 35). Spot-on parodies of classic films, television, and anime were produced by and appeal to an older audience of male fans, not five-year-old girls (episodes 30, 47, and 48, with the first of the three

including a reference to *Alice in Wonderland* and, obliquely, lolicon). At least some in the production were more aware than Satō lets on.

20 Itō Noizi, interview with the author, December 18, 2009. Itō continues, "I think men who are into moe have a similar sensibility as girls."

21 Nunokawa Yūji, interview with the author, July 19, 2011.

22 Theorist Honda Masuko argues that this is characteristic of shōjo movement: "By its constant association with 'another world to be dreamed,' it blurs the border between ordinary reality and the world of imagination" (Honda Masuko 2011, 35). Seeking alternatives, "male" shōjo fans were attracted to magical girls and their world of imagination. Furthermore, if magical girls "disrupt traditional expectations about gender and sexuality" (Hinton 2014, 65), then this makes them all the more appealing to those seeking alternatives.

23 Even more successful than these was the *Cream Lemon* (Kurīmu remon, 1984–93) series, the title of which brings to mind *Lemon People* and *Creamy Mami, the Magic Angel*.

24 Uchiyama Aki, interview with the author, July 5, 2011.

25 At the time, the phenomenon of "male" readers of shōjo manga was still prominent enough to be a topic of social, media, and critical commentary (Schodt 1983, 17). It is telling that manga translator and historian Frederik L. Schodt, writing in the early 1980s, observes that "many grown men have recently confessed that they love to read comics created especially for girls" (17). Later, Schodt explains, "males, bored with overworked action and sex themes in boys' and men's comics magazines, have found themselves attracted to the girls' comic magazines they used to scorn. Some read girls' comics in order to learn how women think. Others find the emphasis on emotion and psychology refreshing" (103–5). By Schodt's estimation, the increased emphasis on relationships and romance, as well as the increased size of eyes, in manga overall demonstrates the influence of shōjo manga. Sociologist Sharon Kinsella refers to this as the "universalization of girls' culture," which became a cause of concern in Japan: "Hordes of teenage Japanese boys . . . who adore girls' manga, or who fetishize images of young girls from afar in their own boys'-girls' manga, have been met with shock and incomprehension" (Kinsella 1998, 316). Note the collapse of gender/genre boundaries in the neat phrase "boys'-girls' manga."

26 Although there is insufficient space in this chapter to pursue the issue, shōjo and bishōjo manga and the lolicon boom are not entirely disconnected from adult gekiga. The inclusion of female artists drawing shōjo manga in COM magazine influenced adult gekiga (Nagayama 2014, 36). Unattributed or using pen names, female artists such as Takano Fumiko submitted work to pornographic or "vending machine" manga magazines before becoming famous, and the presence of shōjo-style images would not have escaped the notice of those producing adult gekiga (Nagayama Kaoru, interview with the author, September 15, 2014). One well-known story has it that Nakajima Fumio, known for his adult gekiga, lived in the same apartment complex as Yamagishi Ryōko, often counted among those that revolutionized shōjo manga in the 1970s, which Nagayama Kaoru presents as evidence of these young artists occupying the "same battlefield" (Nagayama 2014, 57). During this decade, Nakajima read shōjo manga, took in elements of it, and became an influential lolicon artist whose work was featured in *Manga Burikko* and *Lolita Anime* (Nagayama Kaoru, interview with the author, September 15, 2014).

Even Uchiyama Aki, the "King of Lolicon," at times drew fleshy, physically present bodies in a style reminiscent of adult gekiga. This is not to diminish the influence of shōjo manga on Uchiyama (Nagayama 2014, 233–35) but rather to underscore connections and challenge simple binaries. Boundaries between male and female, child and adult, shōjo and gekiga were becoming fluid at this time.

27 While a significant departure from adult gekiga in its "cute style" (*kawai-rashii egara*), *Lemon People* originally included sections of glossy photographs of "shōjo models" but later transitioned to focus primarily on manga and anime. This preference for an unreal, cute, or manga/anime aesthetic, along with a move away from the "real thing," is an important aspect of lolicon, which was repeated in the pages of *Manga Burikko* (Galbraith 2015b, 24–26).

28 Nagayama Kaoru, interview with the author, September 15, 2014. More broadly, Nagayama states with absolute confidence, "There is no doubt that fans of lolicon manga basically all read shōjo manga." For more on Ōtsuka Eiji's recruitment of Nakata, see "Nakata Aki," Wikipedia. https://ja.wikipedia.org/wiki/%E4%B8%AD%E7%94%B0%E9%9B%85%E5%96%9C (last accessed on February 12, 2019).

29 Information on the readership of *Manga Burikko* comes from survey results published on page 193 of its November 1983 issue, which show that 80 percent of respondents were male, 15 percent were female, and 5 percent were undisclosed.

30 The example of Hayasaka Miki speaks to the blurred positionality of "male" shōjo artists more broadly. In an interview with the author on May 5, 2018, Noguchi Masayuki, better known as Uchiyama Aki, explained that his pen name came from an editor that found his art style to be "feminine" (*josei-teki*). According to Uchiyama, the editor decided to call him Aki because "it would be interesting to have adult comics drawn by a woman." The name Aki, then, was intentionally chosen to make Uchiyama appear to be a woman, or at least to suggest the possibility, which some would pick up on from his art style. As the pen name caught on, Uchiyama became almost entirely dissociated from the identity "Noguchi Masayuki." Even today, Uchiyama stated, many are unsure of his assigned sex and gender identity and just assume that he is a woman. In a particularly memorable vignette, Uchiyama recalled a shōjo manga artist looking at his drawings and insisting, despite evidence to the contrary, that they simply could not have originated from a man. As Uchiyama sees it, this marks the beginning of blurred lines between "male" and "female" creators drawing in exclusively "male" or "female" styles, which is an ambiguity that is characteristic of contemporary manga and anime.

31 Manga and sexuality scholar Nagaike Kazumi writes an entire academic article on the complexity of female fans' engagements with boy characters but then in a footnote closes off that possibility for male fans: "The analytical features of yaoi [= boys love manga] and *rorikon* [= lolicon] should be explored separately. Rorikon does not involve people fantasizing about themselves as the opposite sex; rather, it is a straightforward male-looking-at-female pornography" (Nagaike 2003, 100). As we have seen, there is nothing straightforward about lolicon, which may in fact involve men fantasizing about themselves as the opposite sex. Indeed, many have compared yaoi and lolicon and argued that they should be considered together (Ueno 1989, 133; Kinsella 2000, 124; Thorn 2004, 183).

32 In an interview with the author on March 19, 2010, manga critic Itō Gō explained, "Readers do not need to empathize with the rapist, because they are projecting themselves on the girls who are in horrible situations. It is an abstract desire and does not necessarily connect to real desires. This is something I was told by a lolicon artist, but he said that he is the girl who is raped in his manga."

Chapter 2. "Otaku" Research and Reality Problems

1 Although it includes dramatic statements about "otaku," this article—published in *positions: asia critique*, a leading academic journal in North America—is hardly an outlier. For other examples of statements about "otaku" as an object of analysis, see Hinton 2014, 62.

2 For Kinsella's thoughts on this, see Kinsella 1998, 314–16; Kinsella 2000, 123–24, 137–38.

3 This revelation comes on pages 193 and 195 of the November 1983 issue.

4 His pen name, Nakamori Akio, is a homage to Nakamori Akina, an idol that debuted in 1982. While infamous for "'Otaku' Research," Nakamori has written about idols for much of his career as a critic, including books such as *Idol Japan* (Aidoru Nippon, 2007).

5 Nakamori identifies his girlfriend as a second-year high-school student, which suggests that she is sixteen or seventeen years old. In places that legally recognize adults at age eighteen, Nakamori's girlfriend would be a minor. At the time, he was in his mid-twenties. For Nakamori, lolicon is apparently more an issue of desiring manga/anime characters than an older man with an underage girl.

6 In addition to this new imagery of "otaku" as subhuman, Nakamori maintains the old imagery of "otaku" as failed men that are "strangely faggy." At the end of this installment of the column, Nakamori writes that he and his girlfriend visited a park in Shinjuku at night, where they saw "otaku" and okama (men dressed as women) side by side.

7 In North America, this way of referring to "otaku" as "boys" might bring to mind "fanboys," who are also stereotyped as socially and sexually immature.

8 That Nakamori's circle is identified as belonging to *Tokyo Adults Club* drives the point home. Eji Sonta ends the column with an invitation to "otaku" readers of *Manga Burikko* to join the adults club.

9 This comes from an interview with Azuma published on pages 39 and 40 of a special report on lolicon. "Tokushū! Anime/manga ni bishōjo wo motomete: 'Ro' wa Rorīta no 'ro,'" *Animec*, April 1981, 21–45.

10 "Comic Live Discussion, Part II: Azuma Hideo vs. Yonezawa Yoshihiro," *Gekkan Out*, March 1982, 56–61.

11 In a neat turn of phrase, design theorist Morikawa Ka'ichirō dubs this the "fictionality of sexuality" (*sekushuariti no kyokōsei*) (Morikawa 2003, 94). For Morikawa and many others, issues of sexuality are central to discourse about "otaku."

12 Add to this that Miyazaki reportedly owned a copy machine, camera, and computer, and the image of a man lost in "virtual reality" became all the more convincing (Treat 1993, 353–55).

13 Again, the accuracy of this is questionable, as the identifiable adult manga in the photograph appears to focus on housewives (Ōtsuka 2004, 74).

14 Writing of Japan in the 1990s, Kinsella notes that the sense that "otaku" were "multiplying and threatening to take over the whole of society was strong" (Kinsella 2000, 129). This is a version of what anthropologist Gayle Rubin calls the "domino theory of sexual peril" (Rubin 2011, 151).

15 For Ōtsuka and Nakamori, see "Miyazaki Tsutomu-kun no heya wa bokura no sedai kyōtsū no heya da," *Spa!* September 1989, 98–99. For Miyazaki and Murakami, see "Kinkyū taidan: Misshitsu kara no dasshutsu," *Animage*, November 1989, 17–18.

16 Otakon Official Site. https://www.otakon.com/ (last accessed on February 12, 2019). Otaku USA Magazine Official Site. http://www.otakuusamagazine.com/Main/Home.aspx (last accessed on February 12, 2019). Danny Choo, "Otacool," Culture Japan, July 16, 2009. http://www.dannychoo.com/en/post/21664/OTACOOL.html.

17 For more on this approach to labeling, see Kam 2015, 190–92.

Chapter 3. Moe

1 Gail Mancuso, director, season 4, episode 6, "Klaus and Greta," NBC, aired January 14, 2010.

2 Although Franco's at times bizarre behavior "in real life," which regularly attracts attention on social media and is run through the gossip mill in the United States, makes the performance just plausible enough to be funny for celebrity watchers in the know, too.

3 Or to describe Japan as a land of "nudity, rudity, and crudity" (Dore 1958, 159).

4 Given that the United States was at war with Japan, Benedict could not conduct fieldwork when she was commissioned by the US Office of War Information to study this "most alien enemy" (Benedict [1946] 2006, 1). Instead of long-term immersion and engagement, Benedict drew on interviews with Japanese-Americans, as well as literature and film. This pattern of analyzing "Japan" at a distance is in many ways paradigmatic.

5 Ōtsuka Eiji, interview with the author, October 2, 2009. Unless otherwise indicated, all quotes from Ōtsuka in this and the following two paragraphs are from the same interview.

6 The Japanese definition makes this much clearer: *eikyō wo oyobosu*, to have an influence; *sayō suru*, to act on; *kandō saseru*, to move. "Affect," Weblio. http://ejje.weblio.jp/content/affect (last accessed on February 12, 2019).

7 Unsurprisingly, the precedent is shōjo manga (Takahashi 2008, 124).

8 Media theorist Thomas Lamarre defines "moe" as "an affective response to images" (Lamarre 2006, 380), but, as I have observed it in use in Japan, characters are more significant than images. Few said an image was moe unless it depicted or brought to mind a character.

9 This is according to the official website. "News: Osamu Moet Moso," Tezuka Osamu Net, September 16, 2010. http://tezukaosamu.net/en/news/?p=2503.

10 Note that *Osamu Moet Moso* does not exactly use the term "moe" in its title. "Moet" (*moetto*) sounds slightly foreign, as does "Moso" (*mosso*), although it is clear that the latter is intended to suggest *mōsō*, meaning a "delusion" or "wild idea." In context, the appeal to moe is hard to miss, and is confirmed in promotional material.

11 A roster of the twenty-six artists involved is available online. "Osamu Moet Moso," Wikipedia. http://ja.wikipedia.org/wiki/Osamu_moet_moso (last accessed on February 12, 2019).

12 This quote comes from a response to an online post. "Tezuka Moe Gallery," Astro Boy World, September 20, 2010. http://astroboyworld.blogspot.com/2010/09/tezuka-moe-gallery.html.

13 Taking this even further, Sakurai Tetsuo argues that "Astro Boy was originally envisioned as a girl robot, but he was redesigned as a male robot, so it could be assumed that Astro Boy is not really a boy but a hermaphrodite or of a third sex" (Sakurai 2006, 72).

14 These quotes come from page 60 of "Comic Live Discussion, Part II: Azuma Hideo vs. Yonezawa Yoshihiro," *Gekkan Out*, March 1982, 56–61.

15 The names of these exhibitions were *Azuma Hideo Maniacs* (Azuma Hideo maniakkusu) at the Yoshihiro Yonezawa Memorial Library of Manga and Subcultures (February 4 through May 29) and *Azuma Hideo Bishōjo Laboratory* (Azuma Hideo bishōjo jikken shitsu) at Meiji University (April 23 through May 23).

16 Building on his statement, psychiatrist Saitō Tamaki clarifies, "Tezuka is a person that, in an extremely frank way, brought sex and death and violence to Disney-like things" (Azuma, Saitō, and Kotani 2003, 181). In dialogue with Saitō, cultural critic Azuma Hiroki connects Tezuka, Azuma Hideo, shōjo manga, and lolicon (Azuma, Saitō, and Kotani 2003, 180).

17 Design theorist Morikawa Ka'ichirō claims that Tezuka felt for his characters what would now be called moe, and went on to develop nearly all of the character types popular today (Morikawa 2003, 116). Taking this even further, manga/anime writer and critic Honda Tōru states outright that Tezuka established the style beloved by "otaku," contributed to the formation of a world of "infantile sadism" (*yōji-teki na sadizumu*), and desired and created "eternally pure girl-children" (*eien ni muku naru yōjo*) (Honda Tōru 2005a, 117, 119; also Nagayama 2014, 27–32). Tracing the roots of practically everything back to Tezuka, Honda writes, "If Tezuka hadn't been there, Japan's otaku world might not even exist" (Honda Tōru 2005a, 121). Resonating with *Osamu Moet Moso*, Morikawa, Honda, and others see Tezuka in moe media in stores in Akihabara, the center of a particular kind of "otaku world."

18 The connection is also a theoretical one. In their discussion of the disorganized and transforming body, philosopher Gilles Deleuze and psychotherapist Félix Guattari, like Tezuka Osamu, draw attention to the "power of life" (Deleuze and Guattari 1987, 499).

19 Honda Tōru, interview with the author, September 26, 2009.

20 So, too, did Tezuka. Consider Tezuka's rabbit character, Mimio, who appears not only in *Lost World*, but also *The Mysterious Underground Men* (Chitei kuni no kaijin, 1948). On Mimio's prevalence in his early works, Tezuka is quoted as saying, "I had a strong attachment to the rabbit character so I wanted to draw him over and over again" (Itō Gō 2006, 112). Especially in *The Mysterious Underground Men*, Mimio is a "proto-character" (Itō Gō 2005, 94–97), or a character body that is not entirely organized and contained in the narrative world or its reality. Moreover, Mimio is singled out as unnatural and called a "rabbit obake" and even a "manga obake." True to the meaning of the word "obake," throughout *The Mysterious Underground Men*, Mimio takes on different guises and

appears to cross between human and animal, boy and girl, child and adult. This monstrous aspect of Mimio seems to be one of the reasons why Tezuka liked him/her/it.

21 Itō Gō, interview with the author, March 19, 2010.

22 *Heidi* achieved ratings of 15 percent (Clements 2013, 150) and attracted many male fans (Yoshimoto 2009, 106). It is often employed as an example to explain the appeal of anime, whether it be Okada Toshio saying that the character interactions are more mature than Western counterparts (Galbraith 2009b, 174) or Morikawa Ka'ichirō using the characters to introduce the concept of moe (Morikawa 2003, 29).

23 In *The Castle of Cagliostro*, Miyazaki has Lupin, a lecherous middle-aged thief, save Clarisse, a sixteen-year-old princess, from a forced marriage to the middle-aged Count Cagliostro. The film features tender scenes between Lupin and Clarisse, who met when they were much younger, and a finale where the thief goes against his instincts and refuses to embrace the princess or kiss her on the lips. If Lupin leaves Clarisse to be a pure and innocent memory, the Count would defile her. As Lupin crashes their wedding, Miyazaki pointedly has the thief identify the Count as someone suffering from "lolicon."

24 Many viewers missed *Conan*, which was broadcast on NHK, but discovered it in the wake of *Lupin III: The Castle of Cagliostro*. Sasakibara Gō, interview with the author, August 31, 2014.

25 While Miyazaki and others focused on men, something similar had been happening among girls and women interacting with boy characters since the 1970s (Sasakibara 2004, 21; Shimotsuki 2008, 18; Morikawa 2011a, 181–82; Clements 2013, 148; Comic Market Committee 2014, 21–22).

26 Writing about lolicon artists and fans, sociologist Sharon Kinsella argues that "the infantilized female object of desire held so close has crossed over to become an aspect of their own self-image and sense of sexuality" (Kinsella 2000, 122; see also Yomota 2006, 155).

27 In addition to *Animage*, Tokuma Shoten also published *Petit Apple Pie* (Puchi appuru pai, 1982–87), which was an anthology series edited by Ōtsuka Eiji and featuring artists such as Shirakura Yumi, Kagami Akira, and Hayasaka Miki, who are familiar from *Manga Burikko*. Although it did not include anything sexually explicit, *Petit Apple Pie* is remembered as a lolicon series. *Petit Apple Pie* also included contributions by "male" shōjo artist Wada Shinji, who is credited with introducing the term "Lolita complex" to manga in 1974, and Azuma Hideo, who pioneered bishōjo manga in the 1970s. Part of the larger cultural moment when men turned to shōjo manga and cuteness in Japan, *Petit Apple Pie* demonstrates the broad appeal of bishōjo characters at the time. Needless to say, Miyazaki was embroiled in this moment.

28 "Commercial animation in Japan puts a heavy emphasis on 'prepubescent female cuteness,' and . . . Nausicaä speaks in a high voice and is increasingly the victim of camera angles that show her short skirt fluttering in the wind as she takes off in her glider (leading to debates on the Internet as to whether or not she wears panties)" (Schodt 1996, 279–80).

29 In this sense, Miyazaki is again like Tezuka, who "started anime in pursuit of the eroticism of movement" (Tezuka Osamu 1996, 166–67) and continued that pursuit despite everything.

30 Ichikawa Kō'ichi, interview with the author, July 19, 2008. Also Galbraith 2009b, 46.

31 Azuma Hiroki, interview with the author, October 16, 2009. Also Galbraith 2014, 175–76.

32 Bome, interview with the author, November 7, 2008. Also Galbraith 2009b, 75–76.

33 Azuma Hiroki, interview with the author, October 16, 2009. Also Galbraith 2014, 172.

34 For more examples, see Galbraith 2009a, 2014.

35 The amateur animation in question is the *Daicon III Opening Animation* (1981), which features character designs by Akai Takami that might well be a homage to Azuma Hideo and fit right into the lolicon boom. Originally screened at a fan gathering, Gainax turned a profit by producing model kits of their main cute girl character and selling them to fans. The video can be viewed online. Oshan Ruiz, "Daicon III Opening Animation," YouTube, February 8, 2017. https://www.youtube.com/watch?v=gXwGIMCYkk4.

36 The video can be viewed online. Cracrayol, "Daicon IV Opening Animation," YouTube, August 3, 2009. https://www.youtube.com/watch?v=-84okeiiFDE.

37 In an interview with the author on August 26, 2009, economic analyst Morinaga Takurō agreed: "Ayanami Rei is the type that Japanese fans prefer."

38 Fittingly for Ayanami, beloved by a generation of fans, Lilith is said to be an "oneiric temptress, who makes men fruitlessly spill their seed and whose love, once tasted, prevents them from ever finding satisfaction with a human woman" (Ortega 2007, 227).

39 Conversely, Lamarre argues "Anno thought of *Evangelion* as a critique of *otaku* fandom" (Lamarre 2006, 378).

40 Saitō Tamaki, interview with the author, February 26, 2010. Also Galbraith 2014, 181.

41 Momoi Halko, interview with the author, November 12, 2009. Also Galbraith 2014, 74–75.

42 Honda Tōru, interview with the author, September 26, 2009. Also Galbraith 2014, 125. Unless otherwise indicated, all quotes from Honda in this paragraph come from the same interview.

43 The story is striking but not uncommon (Galbraith 2014, 146).

44 For his part, Honda suggests that his *Neon Genesis Evangelion* website was an influential platform for the moe phenomenon (Honda Tōru 2005a, 96).

45 Literally meaning "electromagnetic or radio wave," *dempa*, when used to describe a person, is slang for one that is not altogether there or rambles nonsensically.

46 The focus is exclusively on men, but something similar can and has been said about female fans of manga and anime (Sugiura 2006a, 2006b).

47 Honda Tōru, interview with the author, September 26, 2009. Also Galbraith 2014, 122.

48 Honda is not alone in this assessment. For example, manga editor and critic Akagi Akira approaches lolicon as a form of self-expression for those oppressed by the principles of competitive society, which limit and compel gender/sex performances (Akagi 1993, 232–33). Escaping the "male" position, Akagi submits, allows lolicon fans to access the "image of kindness and love of the girl" (*shōjo no ai to yasashisa no imēji*). Similarly, Honda argues that caring for fictional characters is a way to indulge feminine traits that are suppressed by hegemonic masculinity (Honda Tōru 2005b, 66–81). He uses various metaphors to get at this, including men installing their own "maiden circuits" (*otome kairo*) (16–18). Manga artist and activist Akamatsu Ken draws attention to a "maternal love" (*boseiai*) latent in men, which can be cultivated and expressed in relationships with fictional characters (Akamatsu 2005). All of these comments resonate

with Miyazaki's insight about nurturing the girl within, who is threatened by the pressure to face reality, grow up, and take on the roles and responsibilities expected of an adult man in Japanese society (Miyazaki 2009, 130–31).

49 Maeda Jun, interview with the author, December 18, 2009. Also Galbraith 2014, 106–7.

50 The Japanese is "*Somo somo shinjitsu no wota wa, 3D ni yokujō shimasen.*" Photos are available online. "DVD 'eiga densha otoko' hatsubai: 'Somo somo shinjitsu no wota wa, 3D ni yokujō shimasen,'" Akiba Blog, December 9, 2005. http://www.akibablog.net/archives/2005/12/dvd_3d.html.

51 Of course, not everyone agrees. For example, a collection of Azuma Hideo's manga carries the subtitle "For the Post Non-Riajū Generation" (Azuma and Kikichi 2012). The message seems to be to stop hating, because we are also satisfied with our reality of living with characters.

52 Morinaga Takurō, interviews with the author, August 26, 2009, and March 31, 2010.

Chapter 4. Akihabara

1 Although *shigen* means "resource," the official English name of the group translates it as "heritage." Information is available online. "Homepage," Tokyo Cultural Heritage Alliance Official Website. http://tohbun.jp/ (last accessed on February 12, 2019).

2 Examples of Murakami's collaborations with Louis Vuitton can be viewed online. Maude Churchill, "7 of Our Favorite Louis Vuitton and Murakami Pieces as the Collaboration Comes to an End," Highsnobiety, July 18, 2015. http://www.highsnobiety.com/2015/07/17/louis-vuitton-murakami-pieces/.

3 In later publications, for example, issue 4 of their newsletter, the group seems to suggest an answer. There a project is introduced to shift the perception of Akihabara from a "town of otaku" (*otaku no machi*) by connecting it back to Japanese cultural and historical developments since the Edo period (1603–1868). This, the architects of the plan suggest, will make room for the "next transformation" (*tsugi no henka*), which will be into something other than a "town of otaku." As late as June 2018, materials that I was presented scrupulously avoided talk of desire and affection for cute girl characters and the very public orientation toward them in Akihabara. The strategy, then, seems to be ignoring or working around more troubling aspects of "otaku."

4 Taking a cue from theorist Michel de Certeau, I am interested here in how places can "become liberated spaces that can be occupied" (de Certeau 2005, 459). I am also thinking with historian Jordan Sand, who highlights the possibility of imagining and creating space out of "fragments and deviations" (Sand 2013, 108). He helpfully draws attention to "the work of the imagination" in spaces "divorced from the monumentality of the public square and national politics" (45), but national politics return in Akihabara, where different imaginations collide.

5 The 1998 survey on opinions of "otaku" showed 62 percent negative, 17 percent positive, and 21 percent other, compared to the 2007 survey, which showed 42 percent negative, 35 percent positive, and 23 percent other (Kikuchi 2015, 154–55). For complementary results based on qualitative interviews with Japanese university students in the mid 2000s, see Kam 2013a, 2013b.

6 Specifically, Appadurai writes that "the work of the imagination . . . is deeply connected to politics, through the new ways in which individual attachments, interests, and aspirations increasingly crosscut those of the nation-state" (Appadurai 1996, 10). Imagination can thus become "a space of contestation" (4). What Appadurai calls "a battle of the imagination" (39) dovetails with my discussion of the struggle for imagination. Relevant to the case of Akihabara is tension between local "times and places for congregating and escaping" and "the needs of the nation-state for regulated public life" (191). In local spaces that become tourist sites, the state smooths out "internal, local dynamics through externally imposed modes of regulation . . . and image production" (192).

7 Among others, anthropologists William Kelly and Merry White underscore the ideology of Japan as a "family-nation" (*kazoku kokka*), which they define as an idealized relationship between the state, corporations, and families centered on (re)productive roles and responsibilities (Kelly and White 2006, 66–68). Although this ideology is weakening, it persists and makes itself known in times of crisis. As political scientist David Leheny convincingly argues, youth problems in Japan in the 1990s were often framed in terms of a selfish generation refusing adult roles and responsibilities that reproduce the family, society, and nation (Leheny 2006b, 40). In a reactionary response, the *Yomiuri Shimbun*, among the nation's most widely circulated daily newspapers, recommended that a clause be inserted into the preamble of the Constitution of Japan proclaiming that the family is the "foundation of Japanese society" (183).

8 Tolerance for images of cute girl characters is also spatially limited to the area. In a public talk on November 22, 2008, Morikawa relayed his experience trying to place a bishōjo on a banner for an exhibition at the Tokyo Metropolitan Museum of Photography in Ebisu, a posh Tokyo neighborhood, only to be asked to choose a more appropriate image. Ironically, the exhibition was on Akihabara and "otaku," so there could be no more appropriate image, but what the hosts ostensibly meant was something less offensive.

9 For example, Messe Sanoh on Chūō Street began to stock bishōjo games around 1987.

10 More examples, including comparative images, can be found online. Rilakku Lina, "Anime in Real Life: Akihabara, the City of Anime," MyAnimeList, September 3, 2015. https://myanimelist.net/featured/193/Anime_in_Real_Life_Akihabara_the_City_of_Anime.

11 "Homepage," Akibatsū Official Website. https://web.archive.org/web/20110203095605/http://www.a-s-p-a.jp/akiba2/ (last accessed on February 3, 2011). "Homepage," *Akiba Keizai Shimbun*. http://akiba.keizai.biz/ (last accessed on February 12, 2019).

12 "Homepage," Akiba Blog. http://blog.livedoor.jp/geek/ (last accessed on February 12, 2019).

13 "Homepage," Akiba Map Official Website. http://www.akibamap.net/ (last accessed on February 12, 2019).

14 The virtual, Appadurai submits, is "a significant new element in the production of locality" (Appadurai 1996, 197). Local, national, and international flows of images "add to the intense, and implosive, force under which spatial neighborhoods are produced" (197). Resonating with the case of Akihabara, Sand shows how various factors contributed to Tokyo's "Yanesen" area being "invented as a place with a single identity" (Sand 2013, 55). While Akihabara perhaps does not have a single identity, instructive is Sand's

suggestion that cameras, local publications, and maps are part of "the inscription of locality" (80). Focusing primarily on a single magazine, Sand draws attention to "a virtual community in print" and "imagined community" (87). As Sand writes, the magazine "*Yanesen* constructed a community that was simultaneously geographical and virtual, founded on the *idea* of the locality called 'Yanesen' but not bounded by its actuality. Elective solidarity around an invented place fit an era in which all urban experience was mediated and organic community existed more as a utopian image than a functioning reality" (84). Rather than seeing this as somehow deficient, however, one might instead concentrate on the simultaneously geographical and virtual community of elective solidarity and "its many social possibilities" (87).

15 If Akihabara and "otaku" are characterized by "a peculiar sexual preference" (Kikuchi 2008, 69), then philosopher Slavoj Žižek explains that "what gets on our nerves, what really bothers us about the 'other,' is the peculiar way he organizes his enjoyment" (Žižek 1991, 165).

16 Reports on these activities, including photos, are available online. "70 nendai," Kosukamekai no rekishi-teki haikei. http://coseve.com/History/1970.html (last accessed on February 12, 2019).

17 More concretely, Morikawa argues that the mass media was playing "otaku," even as "otaku" were playing the mass media, and this elaborate coperformance fed into the Akihabara boom (Morikawa 2008, 267, 280–81). Keywords here are "material for discussion" (*neta*), "production or direction" (*enshutsu*), and "faked situations or prearranged performances" (*yarase*). For example, Morikawa reveals how people on the street in Akihabara were interviewed by the media and encouraged to give "otaku-like comments" (*otaku-teki na komento*) (270). While Morikawa is exposing a very real phenomenon, and grounds his analysis in an enlightening, long-form interview with an "otaku" performer, he moves too quickly to dismiss all "otaku" performances. So it is that the "otaku" performers involved in the Akihabara Liberation Demonstration are situated on the side of the fakes, while authentic "otaku" observe their antics and are upset (281). I am not comfortable dismissing all "otaku" performers, just as I am uncomfortable leaving unquestioned the performance of the "otaku" that watches and is upset.

18 Momoi Halko, interview with the author, November 12, 2009. More information is available online. "Profile," Momoi Halko Official Website. http://rg-music.com/momoi/prof/ (last accessed on February 12. 2019).

19 For example, appearing on NHK's *Tokyo Eye* in October 2009, *Shin chishiki kaikyū Kumagusu* in December 2009, and in *Spa!* magazine in February 2009.

20 Consider, for example, Akiba Prince. "Akiba ōji," Ameba Blog. http://profile.ameba.jp/akibaprince (last accessed on February 12, 2019).

21 I am thinking here about how the movement associated with "subculture" can be a means of getting out of one's social location, or where one is known and knows their place. In this way, a subculture can be a "decisive break not only with the parent culture but with its own *location in experience*" (Hebdige 2005, 367). I am also thinking about how subculture can be a "voluntary assumption of outcast status" (363), which echoes approaches to "otaku" (Eng 2012, 100). There is, of course, a danger to calling "otaku" a subculture, which might seem to indicate something coherent and consistent (Kam 2013b, 153–55). Perhaps the "homology" (Hebdige 2005, 364–65) identified in

foundational work on subculture could instead be seen as "relative homologies" (Hills 2002, 13), where "otaku" identify with and against others based on imagined similarities and differences. Different people bring different levels of commitment to a subculture, which can be a major part of life or a slight distraction. "It can be used as a means of escape, of total detachment from the surrounding terrain, or as a way of fitting back in to it and settling down" (Hebdige 2005, 367). In subcultures, there is the possibility of change in "performance" (363), which is why we should pay attention.

22 Akihabara is located in Chiyoda Ward, where the population fluctuates 2,047 percent daily (Tanimura 2012, 111).

23 According to Appadurai, local spaces are "contexts in the sense that they provide the frame or setting within which various kinds of human action (productive, reproductive, interpretative, performative) can be initiated and conducted meaningfully" (Appadurai 1996, 184). Certainly Akihabara is a context providing the frame for meaningful human action, namely "otaku" performances. Local spaces, Appadurai continues, can also become "subject to the context-producing drives of more complex hierarchical organizations, especially those of the modern nation-state" (198). In the mid- to late 2000s, the context-producing drive of the Japanese state was to make Akihabara a site of Cool Japan, which promoted certain "otaku" performances. On the one hand, "otaku" were "increasingly prisoners in the context-producing activities of the nation-state, which makes their own efforts to produce locality seem feeble, even doomed" (186), but this is, on the other hand, part of an ongoing struggle for imagination in contemporary Japan.

24 "Outline of Activities," Akihabara Crossfield. http://www.akiba-cross.jp/english/ (last accessed on February 12, 2019).

25 For an example of how Seno'o's theory of innovation and the revaluation of "otaku" can be integrated, see Kikuchi 2015, 148–49.

26 In 2003, pop artist Murakami Takashi created the animated *Superflat Monogram* as a commercial for fashion brand Louis Vuitton, the techno-music duo Daft Punk released an anime music video called *Interstella 5555*, director Quentin Tarantino included an anime sequence in his *Kill Bill: Volume 1*, and the Wachowskis produced *The Animatrix*, a series of anime shorts meant to flesh out the world established by their celebrated film *The Matrix* (1999), which was itself pitched as a live-action adaptation of anime. Video clips are available online. Nudist Island Girl, "Japanese Commercial: Superflat Monogram," YouTube, May 5, 2007. https://www.youtube.com/watch?v=zkQUFb4SswY&t=7s. Emi Music, "Daft Punk: Aerodynamic," YouTube, March 7, 2009. https://www.youtube.com/watch?v=L93-7vRfxNs. Kevin Sandor, "O-Ren Ishii Story Kill Bill," YouTube, December 18, 2015. https://www.youtube.com/watch?v=VHnVsjBoHnY. Warner Bros., "The Animatrix: Trailer," YouTube, April 27, 2015. https://www.youtube.com/watch?v=94fPVqJqBGA.

27 "Venice Biennale: International Architecture Exhibition," Japan Foundation. https://www.jpf.go.jp/e/project/culture/exhibit/international/venezia-biennale/arc/ (last accessed on February 12, 2019).

28 "Little Boy: The Arts of Japan's Exploding Subculture," Japan Society. https://www.japansociety.org/little_boy_the_arts_of_japans_exploding_subculture (last accessed on February 12, 2019).

29 For his part, Morikawa is aware of his impact on the discourse (Morikawa 2008, 296–97).

30 "A New Look at Cultural Diplomacy: A Call to Japan's Cultural Practitioners (Speech by Minister of Foreign Affairs Taro Aso at Digital Hollywood University)," Ministry of Foreign Affairs of Japan, April 28, 2006. https://www.mofa.go.jp/announce/fm/aso/speech0604-2.html.

31 It seems to have worked, as Asō was hailed by some as a "cool old dude." Jean Snow, "Akihabara Nerds Rally Behind Likely Japanese PM," *Wired*, September 15, 2008. https://www.wired.com/2008/09/japan-pm-candid/.

32 Ōkura Atsuhisa, interview with the author, April 25, 2008.

33 The animated dance sequence can be viewed online. Zygreal, "SOS Brigade: Hare Hare Yukai PV (Full Dance Version)," YouTube, January 24, 2007. https://www.youtube.com/watch?v=mljdpRp41I4.

34 For well-documented predecessors, see these online videos of Haruhi dances around Akihabara from March and April 2007. Rec601Video, "Kyōi-teki ninzū de hare hare yukai wo odoru off in Akihabara (honban) 3/25 Akihabara eki mae," YouTube, March 25, 2007. https://www.youtube.com/watch?v=F1OrROuqn8M. Rec601Video, "Kyōi-teki ninzū de hare hare yukai wo odoru off in Akihabara (honban) 3/25 Yodo mae," YouTube, March 25, 2007. https://www.youtube.com/watch?v=QYvGBwzYWjA. Anachira, "'Hare hare yukai' dansu (seikō rei)," YouTube, April 8, 2007. https://www.youtube.com/watch?v=_L4krBEWS9E.

35 Filmed examples of police intervention are available online. Anachira, "'Hare hare yukai' dansu (keisatsu ni owareru tochū kaisan)," YouTube, April 8, 2007. https://www.youtube.com/watch?v=1xMaY6JYb1c. Nellis55, "Kyōi-teki na ōninzū de hare hare yukai wo odoru off sono 2: 4/8 Akihabara nite," YouTube, April 8, 2007. https://www.youtube.com/watch?v=Y_pPcdkgxts.

36 Examples of ordinances with wording that allow for this sort of intervention are available online. "Seikatsu kankyō jōrei: Yoku aru shitsumon," Chiyoda-ku Official Website. https://www.city.chiyoda.lg.jp/koho/machizukuri/sekatsu/jore/faq.html (last accessed on February 12, 2019). The appearance of signs regarding street performances in 2007 is noted online. "Akihabara," Wikipedia. https://ja.wikipedia.org/wiki/%E7%A7%8B%E8%91%89%E5%8E%9F (last accessed on February 12, 2019).

37 For comparison, see Sand 2013, 37, 41–42.

38 The video can be viewed online. Daily Onigiri, "Tommy Lee Jones Japanese Suntory Commercial: Akihabara Maid," YouTube, September 19, 2009. https://www.youtube.com/watch?v=y4BjZTz3nDU.

39 The video can be viewed online. Yoko Melon, "Shin PV: Sakuragawa Himeko Akiba ni iku non!" YouTube, November 27, 2007. https://www.youtube.com/watch?v=DBv2sAOlUUI.

40 Similarly, Morikawa describes Akihabara, where visitors come to see "otaku," as a "zoo" (*dōbutsuen*) (Morikawa 2008, 269). While he insists that this was unpleasant for "otaku," I am more interested in the corralling and disciplining of "otaku" performances.

41 For his part, Morikawa ties the concern about "weirdoes" to a general disgust toward "otaku" taste, which had taken over Akihabara from the late 1990s into the 2000s (Morikawa 2008, 289).

42 More information on the demonstration is available online. "Homepage," 6.30 Akihabara kaihō demo kōshiki saito. http://akiba630.moemoe.gr.jp/ (last accessed on February 12, 2019).

43 There is also something to be said about "the festive element of protest" and "spirit of play" (Sand 2013, 35–36), which certainly were part of the Akihabara Liberation Demonstration as a shared "otaku" performance (Galbraith and Lamarre 2010, 373). In particular, one might consider "a more public and performative politics that aims to change popular consciousness and disrupt existing sex-gender categories and to transform people's identities and identifications. Such a politics takes dominant signifiers in public realms and invests them with new (and superficially perverse) meanings" (Coombe 1998, 56).

44 This is all written on the flier that I received from Shū-chan.

45 It is noteworthy that while the male protagonist of *Train Man* is branded as an "Akihabara otaku," he is not associated with the bishōjo games and related content that transformed Akihabara into the Holy Land of Otaku. Indeed, an orientation of desire toward fictional characters does not seem to factor into this man being an "otaku," which is why it is easier to reform him through the narrative of finding his love and confidence.

46 Speaking on superhero groups in the United States, Žižek highlights the "idea of outcasts, freaks, building a society, a group of their own" (Žižek 2012). Meanwhile, writing on the new romance surrounding vampires in American popular culture, political philosophers Michael Hardt and Antonio Negri argue, "The vampires are still social outsiders, but their monstrosity helps others to recognize that we are all monsters—high school outcasts, sexual deviants, freaks, survivors of pathological families, and so forth. And more important, the monsters begin to form new, alternative networks of affection and social organization" (Hardt and Negri 2004, 193).

47 I am thinking here of regular late-night screenings of *The Rocky Horror Picture Show*, where fans turn theaters into a shared performance space. "Participation," Rocky Horror Picture Show Official Fan Site. http://www.rockyhorror.com/ (last accessed on February 12, 2019). It is also worth noting that *Urusei Yatsura*, which is often remembered as a landmark franchise in the history of moe, ended episodes in its first anime season with a very similar premise to that of *The Melancholy of Haruhi Suzumiya*. During the credits of episodes 1 through 21, the main bishōjo character, Lum, is shown dancing—quite realistically, in fact—to the song "Space Is Super Weird!" (Uchū wa taihen da, 1981). The lyrics declare that the weirder things become, the more fun, which is also the case with Lum and the cast of bizarre aliens, monsters, and others that disrupt everyday life at home and school for the male protagonist and everyone he knows. Indeed, adding weird and weird together seems to be the formula of the anime on the whole. One is invited to join this chaos by singing, if not also dancing, along with the song, which becomes a chorus, then almost a cacophony of noise toward its conclusion. At precisely this moment, Lum and other colorful characters appear in a group shot, which brings the credits to a close. While cases of fans moving along with this song in ways similar to "Sunny Sunny Happiness" are not common in the historical record, all of the elements are there, and characters within the anime do sing and dance to "Space Is Super Weird!" Like *The Rocky Horror Picture Show* and *The Melancholy of Haruhi Suzumiya*, one is

introduced to and drawn into the weirdness of aliens coming from a vast and strange universe.

48 A sign in Akihabara Park connects it to premodern Japanese history. This is not entirely unprecedented. Writing of the remapping of what was once a prostitution district but had become a site of remembering a historic "Japan," Sand explains, "This erasure of the old prostitution district from the map accorded with the broader 'de-classification' of Shitamachi [old downtown Tokyo] memory. Promoting links to the Edo [premodern] past helped culture bureaucrats in the ward government bypass a socially undesirable modern history" (Sand 2013, 85). Photos of the park and sign are available online. "Akihabara kōen, kaishū kōji shūryō de riyō saikai! Kōen to iu yorimo eki mae hiroba?" Akiba Sōken, April 25, 2014. https://akiba-souken.com/article/20008/.

49 Unless otherwise indicated, all quotes from Kobayashi are from an interview with the author on April 21, 2009.

50 The campaign poster reads, "Takaya power!" As Kobayashi sees his political function as managing Akihabara, the sign offers a very telling reversal of Morikawa's position that power is absent from the neighborhood (Morikawa 2003, 14).

51 In the interview, two- and three-dimensional forms often appeared in close proximity and blurred together. Speaking of underage girls appearing in swimsuits and posing erotically for magazines and videos, Kobayashi stated, "Japan thinks that this is something that absolutely cannot be allowed. We think it is something that can't be allowed. The city [of Akihabara] doesn't like it. The people that live in the city are very uncomfortable with it. They are uncomfortable. I am, too. The police already have a handle on these places. They know where such things are being sold." Note that, in the first instance, it is the nation that stands against this content. Akihabara residents, including Kobayashi, stand with Japan against this content and deploy police to control the streets.

52 There are parallels with the place of manga in Cool Japan. Cultural critic Azuma Hiroki opines, "The government officials I have spoken to don't seem to be aware of how strong the sexual expression is in some manga. If they were, it could well obstruct the government's support for promoting Japanese pop culture abroad" (quoted in McNicol 2004). The point is that once officials do become aware of the sexual content, which might disrupt promotional efforts, there are calls for increased policing. In her writing on a high-profile obscenity trial against manga in the 2000s, which brought up the importance of manga and "otaku" to the Cool Japan brand, legal scholar Kirsten Cather writes, "The fact that manga (and *otaku*) were symbols of national importance only fueled the state's desire to police them" (Cather 2012, 246). Note how "otaku" get brought along with the rise of manga and come under the management of the state.

53 Examples of JNTO's advertising of the "Otaku Mecca" are available online. "An Invitation to an 'Otaku' Tour: Enjoy a Shopping Spree in Akihabara," Japan: The Official Guide, Japan National Tourism Organization. https://web.archive.org/web/20180205025321/http://www.jnto.go.jp/eng/indepth/exotic/animation/d01_akiha.html (last accessed on February 5, 2018).

54 The video can be viewed online. Butthacker, "Kirsten Dunst: Akihabara Majokko Princess," Vimeo, October 8, 2012. https://vimeo.com/50971061.

55 The police were involved at times, but not to break things up so much as to direct traffic. Filmed examples are available online. Guiz, "Kirsten Dunst Akihabara Making of Turning Japanese," YouTube, March 1, 2010. https://www.youtube.com/watch?v=sehjGD1bons.

56 "Homepage," Sekai no Akiba-sai Official Website. https://web.archive.org/web/20090719044113/http://akiba-world-fes.com/ (last accessed on July 19, 2009).

57 There is a deeper history here. During the Meiji period (1868–1912), street performances were common in the area that would become Akihabara (Hyōdō and Smith 2006, 462). This came to an abrupt end in autumn 1891, when police closed street stalls and disbanded unlicensed entertainment (476). The result was the death of the plebian culture. However, afterward, the government attempted to reclaim stylish forms of popular entertainment as a "national voice" (502). In much the same way, even as "otaku" performances were policed in Akihabara, they were promoted as part of Cool Japan.

58 This speaks to a dynamic that queer theorist Jasbir K. Puar spotlights in her analysis of how the United States recuperates select forms of difference and stands against other, more confrontational difference (Puar 2007, xxiii–xxv). Even as the United States adopts the position of being sexually tolerant and liberal, the "terrorist" other is linked with the "failed and perverse" and "metonymically tied to all sorts of pathologies of the mind and body" (xxiii). This sounds very much like "weird otaku," and, in fact, some in Japan have assumed connections between "weird otaku" and terrorism (Kinsella 2000, 132; Azuma, Saitō, and Kotani 2003, 180; Cather 2012, 231).

Chapter 5. Maid Cafés

1 More specifically, design theorist Morikawa Ka'ichirō highlights the March 9, 2003, broadcast of *The Dawn of Gaia* (Gaia no yoake) as a watershed (Morikawa 2008, 265). Sponsored by Nikkei, an organization concentrated on business and economics, the episode was produced amid buzz about the future of the electric town with the Crossfield Project, and more importantly the global success of anime. One could visualize this new market in Akihabara, which worked for the television show. Instead of the bishōjo games, fanzines, and figurines that were the center of the media and material culture of the neighborhood—and were troublingly associated with two-dimensional sex—producers focused on maid cafés. According to Morikawa, there were only two or three maid cafés in Akihabara at the time, but *The Dawn of Gaia* contributed to more camera crews coming to the neighborhood to film; they, too, foregrounded maid cafés; as maids became a key visual, in *Train Man*, for example, people that saw maid cafés on television began to come to Akihabara to visit them; establishments opened to capitalize on the trend, and the number inflated to more than twenty (267). As Morikawa sees it, maid cafés originally had value as an extension of "otaku event space" (*otaku ibento kūkan*), where only people with similar tastes gather and so could relax, but tourism exposed them to the curious gaze of outsiders and transformed maid cafés into a "dangerous place" (*kiken na basho*) (268). If maid cafés had initially been a "secondary" (*fukuji-teki*) part of "otaku" culture in Akihabara, they now appeared to be even less a part of it. Describing the scene as a version of Disneyland, where one can come to interact with

"otaku" and "maids," Morikawa states his position firmly: "This scene was brought about by the Akihabara boom in the media, not by otaku" (269).

2 Anthropologist Laura Miller specifically discusses "Yōkoso! Japan: Cool Japan" (2008), a video that features "an Akihabara Maid Café," an "anime schoolgirl resin figurine," and other examples of "sexist and creepy *otaku* products" (Miller 2011, 18–19). The issue, as Miller sees it, is that the Japanese government is acting as a "pimp" selling the fantasy of sexually available young women, who become "fantasy-capital" in the global economy of desire (23). The maid as symbol of Akihabara and Cool Japan is taken advantage of by, for example, Akibaland Tours. "Akihabara Maid Cosplay Tour," Akibaland Tours. https://akibaland-tours.jimdo.com/english/akihabara/ (last accessed on February 12, 2019).

3 While acknowledging the adoption of the maid uniform in pornography and the sex industry, I found no evidence of sexual services being offered at the maid cafés in Akihabara where I conducted participant observation between 2004 and 2009.

4 This chapter does not delve as much as it might into a critique of capitalism. Like Takeyama, Hardt, and Negri, I recognize that affective labor and the affect economy can be exploitative, but also think that we should not overestimate the power of maid café owners or underestimate those involved in complex relations with, through, and as characters.

5 The name "hitomi" and all others used to refer to maids are pseudonymns, but they are also the names that these women assumed while working in cafés. I have decided not to change these names, because maids are known performers and proud of what they do. In the case of hitomi specifically, her maid name is romanized with a lowercase "h."

6 This figure was widely reported at the time, and can still be found on the website of the company behind @home café. "Profile," Infinia Co. Ltd Official Website. http://www.infinia.co.jp/company.php (last accessed on February 12, 2019). The company reports that the total number of visitors was reaching four million in 2016. In contrast to @home café, many of the other maid cafés I frequented during fieldwork have long since closed, but I leave their names unaltered in this account.

7 Furthermore, while anthropologists are increasingly working on affect theoretically and exploring methods of affective attunement in the field (Stewart 2007), there is a very real limit to how much we can understand the movement of bodies, fictional and real, in relation to one another. In the space between, things are constantly in motion, unsettled, and in play. I cannot know for certain—not for myself and not for others—those moments when the body that moves is a person in a costume or a character, or both, or something else. Affect always seems to be in excess, elusive, escaping language and frameworks. What fieldwork can do is try to convey what it is like to be there, and think through experiences of movement with others in the world.

8 *Ojō-sama*, translated here as "young miss," actually means "a daughter from a decent family" (Inoue 2006, 202). While "master" perhaps implies a higher social status, a thorough comparison of the scripts for men and women in maid cafés falls outside the scope of this chapter.

9 Rules are productive of interactions and relations between masters and maids in the café. In some ways, this brings to mind BDSM as theorized by anthropologist Margot Weiss, who sees the rules governing interaction between players as generating "circuits

and exchanges" (Weiss 2011, 62, 79, 82). Along with rules, Weiss points out that the use of "toys" contributes to the development of techniques of pleasure. Similarly, in the maid café, players use objects to set up a circuit, in which material connects bodies, as well as reality and fantasy, and energy is channeled between them. As Weiss notes, the circuit depends on commodities but is nevertheless productive of intimacy: "Mediated through commodities, such play creates intimate connections between people; the toy as prosthetic becomes a social prosthesis—a way to produce connection and intimacy" (135). Unlike BDSM, however, maid café regulars do not make a distinction between "role-playing" and "authentic energy sharing or intimate connection" (66). Rather, masters and maids share energy and forge intimate connections while role-playing, and this is no less real for the fictional aspects of it.

10 The value of such interaction in a maid café is made explicit in what Royal Milk calls "soul care" (*kokoro no kea*), in which customers pay 6,000 yen for thirty minutes of uninterrupted talk time with staff. Mikan, who works at Royal Milk, explains that most of those paying for soul care want to share their hobbies, or rather to have someone listen and show interest (see also Saitō [2000] 2011, 40–41). This can be, Mikan assures, very soothing, especially at a time of increasing isolation and alienation. Hence the name "soul care," which was originally a phrase used in the context of postdisaster therapy in Japan (Fassin and Rechtman 2009, 172).

11 The scene recalls Nakamori Akio looking at "otaku" for the third installment of his column published in *Manga Burikko* in August 1983.

12 Media scholar Thiam Huat Kam convincingly argues that "otaku" is a label for those thought to take consumption and play beyond the limits of "social common sense" (Kam 2013b, 152). In Japan, common sense demands that people fulfill socially productive roles and responsibilities. For Kam, "'Otaku' is . . . a label for those who fail . . . by engaging in play that detaches them from their roles and responsibilities" (160). This is compounded by the common sense of masculinity, which has it that men should consume and play in ways that are gender appropriate and do not interfere with relationships with women (160–61). If, as Kam suggests, "otaku" are considered to be "failed men," then this also applies to maid café regulars, whose frequent visits to maid cafés and affective relations with maids are seen as an escape from social roles and responsibilities.

13 "Dragon" and all other names used to refer to regulars are pseudonyms. In most cases, informants stuck exclusively to handles when in the maid café. For example, Dragon called himself "Doragon," a phonetic sounding out of the English word "dragon," and maids and regulars used this name when interacting with him. Although Dragon, like many other regulars, assumed a rather fantastic and "un-Japanese" name, it was his real name in the context of the maid café. He asked me to refer to him this way in the field and in my writings about him.

14 For a comparison, see Takeyama 2005, 208.

15 Queer theorist Jack Halberstam argues that the commonsense notion of success in capitalist society includes the achievement of "reproductive maturity" (Halberstam 2011, 2). Essentially heteronormative, such common sense forces intimacy into the couple and family, which are the most socially recognized and valued relational forms.

16 This is more than just "new tensions and new connections between publicly sanctioned typifications of 'Family' and popular forms of 'families'" (Kelly and White 2006, 68),

because "family" ceases to be the organizing principle of alternative intimacy. This is even more the case when we consider virtual intimacies in maid cafés.

17 I am thinking here of theorist Theodor W. Adorno, who writes, "It's a nice bit of sexual utopia not to be yourself, and to love more in the beloved than only her" (Adorno 1998, 75).

18 For his part, Morikawa proposes a different interpretation of maid cafés as an extension of "otaku event space" (Morikawa 2008, 266). To his mind, there is no real connection between maid cafés and "otaku" culture in Akihabara, but this ignores substantial ties to bishōjo games.

19 This information was confirmed on August 14, 2010, in a personal conversation with Nakamura Jin, who knows the founder of Cure Maid Café.

20 Sounding a little like renowned sexologist Alfred Kinsey, economic analyst Morinaga Takurō hypothesizes a spectrum of desire for the two- and three-dimensional (Morinaga Takurō, interview with the author, August 26, 2009). There are those attracted to primarily one or the other, and there are "two- and three-dimensional bisexuals" (*nijigen to sanjigen no baisekusharu*). Morinaga refers to manga/anime fans that have no interest at all in the three-dimensional as "fundamentalists" (*genrishugisha*). Estimating them to be the minority of manga/anime fans, perhaps only 10 percent, Morinaga asserts, "For those that can't be satisfied only with the two-dimensional world, there is a need for material. The moe market is concerned with providing this three-dimensional material to people looking for satisfaction in the two-dimensional world. Figurines of anime characters, cosplay, maid cafés, and so on are all ways of making the two-dimensional part of the three-dimensional world." While agreeing that maid cafés are experiments with bringing the two-dimensional into the three-dimensional, Honda and regulars like him represent a "fundamentalist" attitude in insisting on an orientation toward the fictional character, who is separate and distinct from the woman producing and performing it.

21 Here Honda turns to the example of Multi from *To Heart*, whose purity makes one hope for better relations and a better world (Honda Tōru 2005a, 307–11; 2005b, 147–49). Indeed, the male protagonist of *To Heart* wistfully states, "If all humans could possess a kind maid robot like Multi, wars would disappear from the world."

22 While Honda seems conservative in emphasizing marriage and the family (Honda Tōru 2005b, 177), he also imagines shifting the focus to love, equality, and nonviolence (175). On the subject of the master-maid relationship, Honda implies that not only is it distinct from man and woman, but also that the maid is often the master (140–41). He draws on the example of Mahoro from *Mahoromatic*, who is always called by her young charge "Mahoro-san," which indicates his respect for her. Wielding great power, Mahoro tells her young charge what to do—and not to do, in the case of looking at pornography. It is worth mentioning that Honda (18), Hayakawa (Hayakawa et al. 2008, 26), and others also regularly refer to maids as "maid-san."

23 For more on this "affective slop" (Berlant and Warner 1998, 560) in the context of anime conventions, see Lamerichs 2014.

24 There are reasons to keep performance and animation separate and distinct for the sake of conceptual clarity, but I agree with Silvio that "performance and animation are intertwined in specific cultural practices" (Silvio 2010, 423). I thus do not insist on calling

what happens in maid cafés "animation," but nevertheless would like to draw attention to Silvio's intervention, which is helpful for focusing in on some of the finer points of specific cultural practices in Akihabara.

25 The costuming that waitresses engage in is somewhat different from "cosplay," or the "costume play" of dressing as manga/anime characters, which is part of manga/anime fandom (Okabe 2012). Maids differ from fans in that they are making money and are not necessarily costuming as specific characters from manga, anime, and games. Rather, the maid is a general character type, with specific characters falling under it. That said, however, many maids I spoke with were manga/anime fans and enjoyed cosplay on their own time. The maid café was seen as a way to combine their personal interests in manga/anime and costuming with work.

26 In other words, role language is "fictionalized orality" (Teshigawara and Kinsui 2011, 38). In his pioneering and extensive research, linguist Kinsui Satoshi traces myriad connections between manga/anime and role language.

27 Mei, who worked at Nagomi, underscores that tsundere service is not on the menu and is something that little sisters do only for regulars that are attuned to the fantasy.

28 Schatzkiste encourages this by providing customers with manga that introduces the café's "story" and "characters," which might be considered the production materials behind the three-dimensional anime work playing out in the café.

29 I am thinking here of historian and gender and sexuality scholar John D'Emilio, who argues for "sexual expression as a form of play" (D'Emilio 2007, 256).

30 A summary of Okada's points is available online. "'Okada Toshio no yuigon bangai hen negoto 1:' Repōto teishutsu," Hashikura Rengesō, Hatena Diary, June 30, 2008. http://d.hatena.ne.jp/eg_2/20080630.

31 Others have dubbed this "life in descent" (*oriteiku ikikata*) (Mukaiyachi 2006, 3–4), which facilitates an easier existence without the pressure to ascend.

32 For example, Allison critiques how, under a neoliberal regime, "the intimacy of (a caregiving) home gets outsourced" (Allison 2013, 99). There are also questions about whether or not the maid café goes "beyond familiar and familial Japanese horizons," and if it is intimacy minus the "nuisance" of commitment and human complexity (100).

33 In her discussion of Pokémon, Allison proposes that social and economic unrest in Japan led to the "character therapy age," when people became intimate with fictional characters and derived from this a sense of well-being (Allison 2006, 91). While one might ask how "real" intimacy can be with fictional characters, Condry counters, "It makes more sense to think of media's reality (or actualization) in terms of an emotional response than in terms of a physical object" (Condry 2013, 71). So too is the maid character real based on the response to, and relationship with, her. For more on fictional-real relationships, see Pettman 2009 and Saitō (2000) 2011.

34 Maid cafés are an example of "affectional community" (D'Emilio 2007, 257) emerging in contemporary Japan. For more on these networks of support, which do not depend on bonds of blood or the state, see Allison 2013.

35 Unless otherwise indicated, all quotes from Honda Tōru in this paragraph are from an interview with the author on September 26, 2009.

Conclusion

1 Takeuchi Hiroshi, interview with the author, October 6, 2014.

2 "Homepage," MangaGamer. https://mangagamer.com/ (last accessed on February 12, 2019).

3 "Title Information: *Go! Go! Nippon!* 2016 (Download)," MangaGamer. https://web.archive.org/web/20161209033900/http://www.mangagamer.com/detail.php?goods_type=1&product_code=197&af=3a123f6214695bfacaa881bd3117c693 (last accessed on December 9, 2016).

4 Make no mistake that this is a dream, and a fraught one. In her study of reception of the Japanese cooking show *Iron Chef* in the United States, anthropologist Gabriella Lukács highlights tension in discourse about soft power, which is foundational to Cool Japan policy. On the one hand: "By providing governmental agencies with an incentive to reallocate resources in support of Japanese popular cultural exports, the soft power discourse played a vital role in fostering the globalization of Japanese popular culture" (Lukács 2010a, 414). However, on the other hand: "Dominantly, programmers and viewers did not recognize the show as a representative of 'Japan.' When they did, Japan emerged in viewers' accounts as a construct of orientalist imagination" (421). In a striking reversal of discourse about soft power, the proliferation of "Japanese" popular culture had no impact on the image of "Japan" or reinforced existing negative stereotypes. While locating "Japan" in *Iron Chef* is a dubious proposition in any case (Atkins 2007, 467), another issue is how, and if, a national image can be managed by the government as part of public diplomacy through popular culture (Daliot-Bul 2009, 257). In Japan, there is growing criticism of the use of public funds to this end (for a review, see Mihara 2014).

5 These other sites include Sekai Project, JAST USA, and J-List. "Homepage," Sekai Project. https://sekaiproject.com/ (last accessed on February 12, 2019). "Homepage," JAST USA. https://web.archive.org/web/20180417213619/https://www.jastusa.com/ (last accessed on April 21, 2018). "English Visual Novels," J-List. https://www.jbox.com/category/games-computers/visual-novels (last accessed on February 12, 2019).

6 Scholars are increasingly drawing attention to "pop as propaganda," or an approach that "promotes Cool Japan and tends to celebrate rather than critique" (McLaren and Spies 2016, 20), but it is equally problematic to critique "Japan" and "Japanese popular culture," because this too is part of the "reworking and strengthening of the national" (Iwabuchi 2010, 89). Both celebration and criticism of "Japan" can be part of nationalizing and nationalistic projects.

7 In many cases, new laws respond to the imagined threat of "Japanese" media crossing borders (Eiland 2009, 400–401; also Game Politics 2009). In the United States, orientation toward cute girl characters appears as a "virus," which has already swept Japan and is threatening to infect manga/anime fans on American shores (Schodt 1996, 54–55, 336–40). Similar language is used in the United Kingdom (Hinton 2014, 56).

8 In some ways, Hall is addressing competing schools of thought, the Frankfurt school and the Birmingham school. Many have taken issue with Frankfurt school representatives such as Theodor Adorno, who argues that mass culture pacifies and stupefies (Storey 1997, 85–94). Although himself associated with the Birmingham school (Storey

1997, 51–57), Hall does not entirely reject Adorno's intervention, and urges researchers to not lose sight of cultural domination and "cultural industries" (Hall 1998, 446–47). For an introduction to mass culture in modern Japan that reflects the teachings of the Frankfurt school, see Ivy 1993.

9 "Under such a logic," writes anthropologist Daniel White, "those arts [and more] which come under the purview of cultural administration and are labeled 'German,' 'British,' 'Chinese,' or 'Japanese,' become Japanese, Chinese, British, and German culture" (White 2015, 112). Rather than automatic, however, this is part of the ongoing processes shaping national-popular culture.

10 Writing on discourse about comics in North America, literary scholar Christopher Pizzino underscores "the scholar as legislator" (Pizzino 2016, 21). "To select materials for a comics course," Pizzino explains, "is, among other things, to negotiate the degree of one's complicity with . . . discourse" (43). I see here an invitation to consider the role of the Japan scholar as legislator, which opens into the politics of popular culture that I am discussing.

11 For more examples of invented traditions, see Vlastos 1998.

12 For comparison, see Sand 2013, 33.

13 As White points out, "The political and revisionist rhetoric linking Japan's contemporary popular arts to its traditional ones only grows stronger and more natural with the plethora of new publications trumpeting the 'pop power' of Japan's 'cool culture'" (White 2015, 112).

14 One historian writes of ukiyo-e, "The establishment of the day regarded them as trash" (Schodt 1983, 33). Another adds of pornographic ukiyo-e that the government "did not of course approve of this culture" (H. Smith 1996, 29). Regulations in Tokyo in 1722, 1790, and 1842 all seem to have affected pornographic prints, which were effectively wiped out by a police crackdown in 1907 that saw the confiscation of 143,000 prints and 5,680 printing blocks (H. Smith 1996, 32).

15 Tsutsui emphasizes how revaluation made "mass-produced *ukiyo-e* the objects of elite connoisseurship" (Tsutsui 2010, 8). Napier also indicates the potential for change over time when she writes, "Anime is a popular cultural form that clearly builds on previous high cultural traditions" and "such Japanese traditional arts as Kabuki and the woodblock print," which were "originally popular culture phenomena themselves" (Napier 2001, 4).

16 Over a century later, in 2015, there was much commotion when such ukiyo-e returned to Japan for an exhibition at the Eisei Bunko Museum.

17 This passage from an often-cited, peer-reviewed journal article is representative: "An example of the artistic pedigree of this pornographic tradition is Katsushika Hokusai's celebrated print *Octopus and Shelldiver* (*Tako to Ama*). Better known as *The Dream of the Fisherman's Wife,* this could well be the first recorded instance of 'tentacle sex,' a visual trope that, in the West, has become closely associated with animated *hentai* [pornography]" (Ortega-Brena 2009, 20).

18 On public-private alliances under the banner of Cool Japan, Iwabuchi calls attention to "the collaborative relationship between the state and media cultural industries, and culture, economy and politics" (Iwabuchi 2010, 90).

19 This is not entirely new, as demonstrated by sociologist Sharon Kinsella's analysis of the forces shaping manga into "pro-establishment pop-culture" (Kinsella 2000, 207), which

occurred amid concerns about "harmful manga" and "otaku" in Japan in the 1990s. Institutional activities and alliances around manga speak to what Kinsella calls the "regeneration of national culture" (70). As Japanese popular culture, manga began to appear in school textbooks, museums, and policy speeches. In policing some manga and promoting others, we see the process of "popular imperialism," which pushes some forms out "so that something else can take their place" (Hall 1998, 443–44). As with manga, so too with "otaku."

20 "Homepage," Eshi 100 Official Website. http://eshi100.com/ (last accessed on February 12, 2019).

21 Hattori Michisato, interview with the author, July 25, 2013.

22 Some of these same illustrators also have limited-edition prints selling for hundreds of dollars at Art Jeuness Akihabara on Chūō Street. As seen in the example of *Osamu Moet Moso* (chapter 3), Akihabara has a way of twisting things around and bringing them together in new configurations. At Art Jeuness Akihabara, some of the most famous illustrators in the history of Japanese animation—Takada Akemi, Mikimoto Haruhiko, Kei—are side by side with porn creators—Carnellian, Suzuhira Hiro, Tony. All of them, however, are bishōjo illustrators.

23 The formula of illustrations at *Eshi 100* is bishōjo against a variety of backgrounds and in a variety of settings, which are sometimes explicitly Japan, but it is more accurate to say that cute girl characters in any setting come to represent "Japan."

24 For example, *Popotan* (2002), which features character designs by Watanabe under his alias, has the most youthful-looking character engaged in the most sex acts. This is cute eroticism of a potentially disturbing sort, which is referenced in "Duck Festival."

25 Aware of this, some Japanese illustrators play up and parody the hype about Cool Japan. At Medio, a bishōjo game store in Akihabara, I came across not only fliers for *Eshi 100*, but also a book titled *Naked Apron Visual Collection 2* (Hadaka epuron visual collection 2, 2012). The book contains bishōjo drawings by illustrators much like the *Eshi 100* catalogue, but revels in the nudity and sex excluded from that more respectable publication. Rather than taking on high-minded themes such as the seasons or scenery, *Naked Apron* focuses exclusively on manga/anime-style cute girl characters that are nude except for kitchen aprons. *Naked Apron* comes with the English subtitle "Love Love Japanese Own Mode Naked Apron." Note the nationalization of the mode, whereby "otaku" fetishism becomes a "Japanese" style. An evaluation of this claim would open into questions about the politics of popular culture.

26 Unless otherwise indicated, all quotes in this paragraph come from an interview with Watanabe Akio conducted by the author on May 23, 2014.

27 For Hattori, the fact that the Ueno Royal Museum in Tokyo can host an exhibition for illustrator Aoki Ume—who worked on the bishōjo game *Sanarara* (2005), drew characters for the anime *Puella Magi Madoka Magica* (2011, scenario by Urobuchi Gen, who also works in the bishōjo game industry), and has been involved in *Eshi 100* from the beginning—is proof of growing support (Hattori 2015, 218). This is certainly not an isolated incident. Visiting the National Art Center in Tokyo for the exhibition *Japanese Manga, Anime, and Games from 1989* on June 28, 2015, I was surprised to find bishōjo games such as *Tokimeki Memorial, Love Plus, Fate/Stay Night, Higurashi no naku koro ni,* and more included in the space of national art, culture, and history. Notably, however,

references to sex and pornographic material were completely absent, which suggests some of the limits of Cool Japan.

28 Another opportunity to think about this is when Bamboo, faced with bishōjo fans around the world, asks, "Is this Japan?" While Bamboo might be suggesting that Japanese popular culture and its fans are spreading so that everywhere looks like "Japan," which smacks of Cool Japan rhetoric about soft power, one can also hear in his words a rather perverse proposition: the collective force of desire for manga/anime characters, the affective response to them, is "Japan." This in effect explodes the nation and reimagines it as "otaku" movement beyond borders.

29 Desire for, or disgust with, "Japan" makes us complicit in this, which is precisely why our relation to the imaginary other must be questioned (Allison 2012, 317–19). As anthropologist Anne Allison argues, "Power—either real or imagined—is always at work in Orientalism in that forays into foreign lands are taken with the mind of keeping one's own borders and sense of superiority intact. Even in encountering cultural difference, then, the encounter is done in a manner that confirms, rather than alters, one's own world and position in it" (298). The challenge is to journey in ways that cross and blur borders, and to be open to encounters that can alter one's world and position. Following Allison, I argue that desires are mapped and contested "in the domain of popular culture" (300), including desires for what is other. Questioning relations with others allows for desires to be contested and remapped.

BIBLIOGRAPHY

Aalgaard, Scott W. 2016. "*Summertime Blues*: Musical Critique in the Aftermaths of Japan's 'Dark Spring.'" In *Fukushima and the Arts: Negotiating Nuclear Disaster*, edited by Barbara Geilhorn and Kristina Iwata-Weickgenannt, 39–57. London: Routledge.

Abe, Shinzō. 2007. "Establishing Japan as a 'Peaceful Nation of Cultural Exchange'" Office of the Prime Minister. http://japan.kantei.go.jp/policy/bunka/050711bunka_e.html.

Adelstein, Jake, and Angela Erika Kubo. 2014. "Japan's Kiddie Porn Empire: Bye-Bye?" Daily Beast, June 3. http://www.thedailybeast.com/articles/2014/06/03/japan-s-kiddie-porn-empire-bye-bye.html.

Adorno, Theodor W. 1998. *Critical Models: Interventions and Catchwords.* Translated by Henry W. Pickford. New York: Columbia University Press.

Aera Dot. 2017. "Kitahara Minori: 'Moe kyara wa seisabetsu!'" April 14. https://dot.asahi.com/wa/2017041200020.html?page=1.

Ahmed, Sara. 2010. "Happy Objects." In *The Affect Theory Reader*, edited by Melissa Gregg and Gregory J. Seigworth, 29–51. Durham, NC: Duke University Press.

Aida, Miho. 2005. "Komikku māketto no genzai: Sabukaruchā ni kan suru kōsatsu." *Hiroshima shūdai ronshū jinbun hen* 45 (2): 149–201.

Aida, Miho. 2006. "Moeru kūkan: Meido kafe ni kan suru shakaigaku-teki kōsatsu." *Hiroshima shūdai ronshū jinbun hen* 47 (1): 193–219.

Akagi, Akira. 1993. "Bishōjo shōkōgun: Rorikon to iu yokubō." *Nyū feminizumu rebyū* 3: 230–34.

Akamatsu, Ken. 2005. "Watashi no kasetsu." July 18. http://www.ailove.net/diarybook/diary2005b.cgi.

Akatsuka, Neil K. 2010. "Uttering the Absurd, Revaluing the Abject: Femininity and the Disavowal of Homosexuality in Transnational Boys' Love Manga." In *Boys' Love Manga: Essays on the Sexual Ambiguity and Cross-Cultural Fandom of the Genre,* edited by Antonia Levi, Mark McHarry, and Dru Pagliassotti, 159–76. Jefferson, NC: McFarland.

Akiba Blog. 2008a. "'Akihabara no hokoten ga muhō jōtai' masukomi (TV kyoku) darake." April 14. http://akibablog.net/archives/2008/04/akihabara-080414.html.

Akiba Blog. 2008b. "Sawamoto Asuka-san masukomi (TV kyoku) shuzai de ketsudashi yarase?" April 21. http://akibablog.net/archives/2008/04/ketu-080421.html.

Allison, Anne. 1994. *Nightwork: Sexuality, Pleasure, and Corporate Masculinity in a Tokyo Hostess Club.* Chicago, IL: University of Chicago Press.

Allison, Anne. 2000. *Permitted and Prohibited Desires: Mothers, Comics, and Censorship in Japan.* Berkeley: University of California Press.

Allison, Anne. 2006. *Millennial Monsters: Japanese Toys and the Global Imagination.* Berkeley: University of California Press.

Allison, Anne. 2012. "American Geishas and Oriental/ist Fantasies." In *Media, Erotics, and Transnational Asia,* edited by Purnima Mankekar and Louisa Schein, 297–321. Durham, NC: Duke University Press.

Allison, Anne. 2013. *Precarious Japan.* Durham, NC: Duke University Press.

Amar, Paul. 2011. "Middle East Masculinity Studies: Discourses of 'Men in Crisis,' Industries of Gender Revolution." *Journal of Middle East Women's Studies* 7 (3): 36–70.

Anderson, Ben. 2012. "Affect and Biopower: Towards a Politics of Life." *Transactions of the Institute of British Geographers* 37 (1): 28–43.

Anderson, Benedict. [1983] 2006. *Imagined Communities.* New York: Verso.

Appadurai, Arjun. 1996. *Modernity at Large: Cultural Dimensions of Globalization.* Minneapolis: University of Minnesota Press.

Atkins, E. Taylor. 2007. "Popular Culture." In *A Companion to Japanese History,* edited by William M. Tsutsui, 460–76. Hoboken, NJ: Wiley-Blackwell.

Azuma, Hideo, and Kikichi Naruyoshi. 2012. *Posuto hi-riajū jidai no tame no Azuma Hideo.* Tokyo: Kawade shobō shinsha.

Azuma, Hideo, and Yamada Tomoko. 2011. "Azuma Hideo 2 man 5 sen ji rongu intabyū." In *Azuma Hideo: Bishōjo, SF, fujōri, soshite shissō,* edited by Nishiguchi Tōru and Anazawa Yūko, 10–44. Tokyo: Kawade shobō shinsha.

Azuma, Hideo, and Yamamoto Naoki. 2011. "Risupekuto taidan." In *Azuma Hideo: Bishōjo, SF, fujōri, soshite shissō,* edited by Nishiguchi Tōru and Anazawa Yūko, 138–54. Tokyo: Kawade shobō shinsha.

Azuma, Hiroki. 2008. "Naze Akihabara na no ka, naze keitai keijiban na no ka, naze musabetsu na no ka." Maru geki tōku on demando, June 13. https://www.youtube.com/watch?v=T1bqNYbLCOE.

Azuma, Hiroki. [2001] 2009. *Otaku: Japan's Database Animals.* Translated by Jonathan E. Abel and Shion Kono. Minneapolis: University of Minnesota Press.

Azuma, Hiroki, Saitō Tamaki, and Kotani Mari. 2003. "Otaku, yaoi, dōbutsuka." In *Mōjō genron F-kai: Posutomodan otaku sekushuariti,* edited by Azuma Hiroki, 168–96. Tokyo: Seidōsha.

Becker, Howard S. 1963. *Outsiders: Studies in the Sociology of Deviance*. New York: Free Press.

Benedict, Ruth. [1946] 2006. *The Chrysanthemum and the Sword: Patterns of Japanese Culture*. Boston, MA: Mariner Books.

Berlant, Lauren. 2007. "Nearly Utopian, Nearly Normal: Post-Fordist Affect in *La Promesse* and *Rosetta*." *Public Culture* 19 (2): 273–301.

Berlant, Lauren, and Michael Warner. 1998. "Sex in Public." *Critical Inquiry* 24 (2): 547–66.

Bessatsu Takarajima Henshūbu. 1989. "Introduction: Otaku wo shirazu shite 90 nendai wa katarenai." In *Otaku no hon*, edited by Ishi'i Shinji, 2–3. Tokyo: JICC shuppankyoku.

Boas, Benjamin, and Aoyagi Chika. 2015. *Nihon no koto wa, manga to gēmu de manabimashita*. Tokyo: Shōgakukan.

Bogue, Ronald. 1989. *Deleuze and Guattari*. London: Routledge.

Bourdain, Anthony. 2013. "Tokyo." *Parts Unknown*, November 3. http://putlockers.ch/watch-anthony-bourdain-parts-unknown-tvshow-season-2-episode-7-online-free-putlocker.html.

Brennan, Teresa. 2004. *The Transmission of Affect*. Ithaca, NY: Cornell University Press.

Briel, Holger. 2010. "The Roving Eye Meets Traveling Pictures: The Field of Vision and the Global Rise of Adult Manga." In *Comics as a Nexus of Cultures: Essays on the Interplay of Media, Disciplines and International Perspectives*, edited by Mark Berninger, Jochen Ecke, and Gideon Haberkorn, 187–210. Jefferson, NC: McFarland.

Brooker, Will. 2000. *Batman Unmasked: Analyzing a Cultural Icon*. New York: Continuum.

Brown, Steven T. 2010. *Tokyo Cyberpunk: Posthumanism in Japanese Visual Culture*. New York: Palgrave.

Buckley, Sandra. 1991. "'Penguin in Bondage': A Graphic Tale of Japanese Comic Books." In *Technoculture*, edited by Sandra Buckley and Andrew Ross, 163–96. Minneapolis: University of Minnesota Press.

Bukatman, Scott. 2012. *The Poetics of Slumberland: Animated Spirits and the Animating Spirit*. Berkeley: University of California Press.

Butler, Judith. 1988. "Performative Acts and Gender Constitution: An Essay in Phenomenology and Feminist Theory." *Theater Journal* 40 (4): 519–31.

Cather, Kirsten. 2012. *The Art of Censorship in Postwar Japan*. Honolulu: University of Hawai'i Press.

Clements, Jonathan. 2013. *Anime: A History*. New York: Palgrave.

Clements, Jonathan. 2016. "The Allure of Gravure." Schoolgirl Milky Crisis, November 28. https://schoolgirlmilkycrisis.com/2016/11/28/the-allure-of-gravure/.

Clifford, James. 1986. "Introduction: Partial Truths." In *Writing Culture: The Poetics and Politics of Ethnography*, edited by James Clifford and George E. Marcus, 1–26. Berkeley: University of California Press.

Clifford, James. 1988. *The Predicament of Culture: Twentieth-Century Ethnography, Literature, and Art*. Cambridge, MA: Harvard University Press.

Coleman, E. Gabriella. 2013. *Coding Freedom: The Ethics and Aesthetics of Hacking*. Princeton, NJ: Princeton University Press.

Comic Market Committee. 2014. "What Is Comic Market?" The Official Comic Market Site, January. http://www.comiket.co.jp/info-a/WhatIsEng201401.pdf.

Condry, Ian. 2006. *Hip-Hop Japan: Rap and the Paths of Cultural Globalization*. Durham, NC: Duke University Press.

Condry, Ian. 2013. *The Soul of Anime: Collaborative Creativity and Japan's Media Success Story*. Durham, NC: Duke University Press.

Connell, R. W. 2000. *The Boys and the Men*. Cambridge, UK: Polity Press.

Consalvo, Mia. 2016. *Atari to Zelda: Japan's Videogames in Global Contexts*. Cambridge, MA: MIT Press.

Coombe, Rosemary J. 1998. "Contingent Articulations: A Critical Cultural Studies of Law." In *Law in the Domains of Culture*, edited by Austin Sarat and Thomas R. Kearns, 21–64. Ann Arbor: University of Michigan Press.

Craig, Timothy J., ed. 2000. *Japan Pop! Inside the World of Japanese Popular Culture*. New York: M. E. Sharpe.

Craig, Timothy J., ed. 2017. *Cool Japan: Case Studies from Japan's Cultural and Creative Industries*. Ashiya, Japan: BlueSky.

Daliot-Bul, Michal. 2009. "Japan Brand Strategy: The Taming of 'Cool Japan' and the Challenges of Cultural Planning in a Postmodern Age." *Social Science Japan Journal* 12 (2): 247–66.

Dasgupta, Romit. 2005. "Salarymen Doing Straight: Heterosexual Men and the Dynamics of Gender Conformity." In *Genders, Transgenders and Sexualities in Japan*, edited by Mark McLelland and Romit Dasgupta, 168–82. London: Routledge.

Dave, Naisargi N. 2010. "Between Queer Ethics and Sexual Morality." In *Ordinary Ethics: Anthropology, Language, and Action*, edited by Michael Lambek, 368–75. New York: Fordham University Press.

De Certeau, Michel. 2005. "Walking in the City." In *Popular Culture: A Reader*, edited by Raiford Guins and Omayra Zaragoza Cruz, 449–61. London: Sage.

Deleuze, Gilles, and Félix Guattari. 1987. *A Thousand Plateaus: Capitalism and Schizophrenia*. Translated by Brian Massumi. Minneapolis: University of Minnesota Press.

D'Emilio, John. 2007. "Capitalism and Gay Identity." In *Culture, Society and Sexuality: A Reader*, edited by Richard Parker and Peter Aggleton, 250–59. London: Routledge.

Design Boom. 2008. "GEISAI 11: Tokyo's Artist Run Art Fair." August 20. http://www.designboom.com/art/geisai-11-tokyos-artist-run-art-fair/.

Diamond, Milton, and Ayako Uchiyama. 1999. "Pornography, Rape, and Sex Crimes." *International Journal of Law and Psychiatry* 22 (1): 1–22.

Dooley, Stacey. 2017. "Stacey Dooley Investigates: Young Sex for Sale in Japan." BBC Three, February 28. http://www.bbc.co.uk/iplayer/episode/po4toh2b/stacey-dooley-investigates-young-sex-for-sale-in-japan.

Dore, Ronald P. 1958. *City Life in Japan*. Berkeley: University of California Press.

Eiland, Murray Lee. 2009. "From Cartoon Art to Child Pornography." *International Journal of Comic Art* 11 (2): 396–409.

Eisenstein, Sergei. 1986. *Eisenstein on Disney*. Translated by Alan Upchurch, edited by Jay Leyda. New York: Methuen Paperback.

Eng, Lawrence. 2006. "*Otaku* Engagements: Subcultural Appropriation of Science and Technology." PhD diss., Rensselaer Polytechnic Institute.

Eng, Lawrence. 2012. "Strategies of Engagement: Discovering, Defining, and Describing Otaku Culture in the United States." In *Fandom Unbound: Otaku Culture in a Connected World*, edited by Mizuko Ito, Daisuke Okabe, and Izumi Tsuji, 85–104. New Haven, CT: Yale University Press.

Family Guy. 2012. "The Blind Side." Fox, January 15. https://www.youtube.com/watch?v=QswPVas5Qhw.

Fassin, Didier, and Richard Rechtman. 2009. *The Empire of Trauma: An Inquiry into the Condition of Victimhood*. Translated by Rachel Gomme. Princeton, NJ: Princeton University Press.

Flowers, Amy. 1998. *The Fantasy Factory: An Insider's View of the Phone Sex Industry*. Philadelphia: University of Pennsylvania Press.

FNN. 2008. "Tōkyō Akihabara musabetsu sasshō jiken Katō Tomohiro yōgisha, jiken mikka mae ni shokuba de gekido, kisei hassuru." June 11. https://web.archive.org/web/20080611072323/http://www.fnn-news.com/news/headlines/articles/CONN00134361.html.

Freedman, Alisa. 2009. "*Train Man* and the Gender Politics of Japanese '*Otaku*' Culture: The Rise of New Media, Nerd Heroes and Consumer Communities." *Intersections: Gender and Sexuality in Asia and the Pacific* (20). http://intersections.anu.edu.au/issue20/freedman.htm.

Freedman, Alisa, and Toby Slade, eds. 2017. *Introducing Japanese Popular Culture*. London: Routledge.

Freeman, Elizabeth. 2002. *The Wedding Complex: Forms of Belonging in Modern American Culture*. Durham, NC: Duke University Press.

Frühstück, Sabine, and Anne Walthall. 2011. "Introduction: Interrogating Men and Masculinities." In *Recreating Japanese Men*, edited by Sabine Frühstück and Anne Walthall, 1–24. Berkeley: University of California Press.

Fujie, Kazuhisa, and Martin Foster. 2004. *Neon Genesis Evangelion: The Unofficial Guide*. Tokyo: DH Publishing.

Fujimoto, Yukari. 1998. *Watashi no ibasho wa doko ni aru no? Shōjo manga ga utsusu kokoro no katachi*. Tokyo: Gakuyō shobō.

Fujimoto, Yukari. 2015. "The Evolution of BL as 'Playing with Gender': Viewing the Genesis and Development of BL from a Contemporary Perspective." In *Boys Love Manga and Beyond: History, Culture, and Community in Japan*, edited by Mark McLelland, Kazumi Nagaike, Katsuhiko Suganuma, and James Welker, 76–92. Jackson: University Press of Mississippi.

Fujita, Hisashi. 1989. "Kira kira omeme no hanran: Bōdāresu-ka suru shōjo manga to shōnen manga." In *Otaku no hon*, edited by Ishi'i Shinji, 127–30. Tokyo: JICC shuppankyoku.

Fujita, Kuniko, and Richard Child Hill. 2005. "Innovative Tokyo." World Bank Policy Research Working Paper no. 3507, Social Science Research Network. http://papers.ssrn.com/sol3/papers.cfm?abstract_id=660088.

Gagné, Isaac. 2008. "Urban Princesses: Performance and 'Women's Language' in Japan's Gothic/Lolita Subculture." *Journal of Linguistic Anthropology* 18 (1): 130–50.

Galbraith, Patrick W. 2009a. "*Moe*: Exploring Virtual Potential in Post-Millennial Japan." *Electronic Journal of Contemporary Japanese Studies*. http://www.japanesestudies.org.uk/articles/2009/Galbraith.html.

Galbraith, Patrick W. 2009b. *The Otaku Encyclopedia: An Insider's Guide to the Subculture of Cool Japan*. Tokyo: Kodansha International.

Galbraith, Patrick W. 2011. "Maid in Japan: An Ethnographic Account of Alternative Intimacy." *Intersections: Gender and Sexuality in Asia and the Pacific* (25). http://intersections.anu.edu.au/issue25/galbraith.htm.

Galbraith, Patrick W. 2012. *Otaku Spaces*. Seattle, WA: Chin Music Press.

Galbraith, Patrick W. 2014. *The Moe Manifesto: An Insider's Look at the Worlds of Manga, Anime, and Gaming*. North Clarendon, VT: Tuttle.

Galbraith, Patrick W. 2015a. "*Moe* Talk: Affective Communication among Female Fans of *Yaoi* in Japan." In *Boys Love Manga and Beyond: History, Culture, and Community in Japan*, edited by Mark McLelland, Kazumi Nagaike, Katsuhiko Suganuma, and James Welker, 153–68. Jackson: University Press of Mississippi.

Galbraith, Patrick W. 2015b. "'"Otaku" Research' and Anxiety about Failed Men." In *Debating Otaku in Contemporary Japan: Historical Perspectives and New Horizons*, edited by Patrick W. Galbraith, Thiam Huat Kam, and Björn-Ole Kamm, 21–34. London: Bloomsbury.

Galbraith, Patrick W. 2015c. "*Otaku* Sexuality in Japan." In *Routledge Handbook of Sexuality Studies in East Asia*, edited by Mark McLelland and Vera Mackie, 205–17. London: Routledge.

Galbraith, Patrick W. 2017. "*RapeLay* and the Return of the Sex Wars in Japan." *Porn Studies* 4 (1): 105–26.

Galbraith, Patrick W., Thiam Huat Kam, and Björn-Ole Kamm, eds. 2015. *Debating Otaku in Contemporary Japan: Historical Perspectives and New Horizons*. London: Bloomsbury.

Galbraith, Patrick W., and Thomas Lamarre. 2010. "Otakuology: A Dialogue." In *Mechademia 5: Fanthropologies*, edited by Frenchy Lunning, 360–74. Minneapolis: University of Minnesota Press.

Gallagher, Sean. 2016. "Ghost in the Plexiglass Shell: The Holographic Anime 'Robot' That Will Keep House for Lonely Salarymen." Ars Technica, December 18. https://arstechnica.com/information-technology/2016/12/the-anime-girlfriend-experience-gateboxs-ai-powered-holographic-home-robot/.

Game Politics. 2009. "In Parliament, Suggestion of 'Global Regulatory Future' for Video Games." July 21. http://webmail.vgol.com/2009/07/21/parliament-suggestion-quotglobal-regulatory-futurequot-video-games.

Gamson, Joshua. 1994. *Claims to Fame: Celebrity in Contemporary America*. Berkeley: University of California Press.

Gilbert, Ben. 2018. "Japan's $2,700 Answer to the Amazon Echo Could Make the Country's Sex Crisis Even Worse." Business Insider, June 3. http://www.businessinsider.com/gatebox-ai-the-japanese-amazon-echo-photos-2016-12.

Grassmuck, Volker. 1990. "'I'm Alone, but Not Lonely': Japanese *Otaku*-Kids Colonize the Realm of Information and Media: A Tale of Sex and Crime from a Faraway Place." http://www.cjas.org/~leng/otaku-e.htm.

Gravett, Paul. 2004. *Manga: Sixty Years of Japanese Comics*. London: Laurence King.

Greenwood, Forrest. 2014. "The Girl at the Center of the World: Gender, Genre, and Remediation in *Bishōjo* Media Works." In *Mechademia 9: Origins*, edited by Frenchy Lunning, 237–53. Minneapolis: University of Minnesota Press.

Gwern. 2012. "Interview with Hideaki Anno (English)," February 22. http://www.gwern.net/docs/eva/1997-animeland-may-hideakianno-interview-english.

Halberstam, Judith. 2011. *The Queer Art of Failure*. Durham, NC: Duke University Press.

Hall, Stuart. 1987. "Gramsci and Us." *Marxism Today*, June. http://www.hegemonics.co.uk/docs/Gramsci-and-us.pdf.

Hall, Stuart. 1998. "Notes on Deconstructing 'the Popular.'" In *Cultural Theory and Popular Culture: A Reader*, edited by John Storey, 442–53. Upper Saddle River, NJ: Prentice Hall.

Hall, Stuart, Chas Critcher, Tony Jefferson, John Clarke, and Brian Roberts. 1978. *Policing the Crisis: Mugging, the State, and Law and Order*. London: Macmillan Press.

Hardt, Michael. 1999. "Affective Labor." *boundary 2* 26 (2): 89–100.

Hardt, Michael, and Antonio Negri. 2004. *Multitude: War and Democracy in the Age of Empire*. New York: Penguin.

Hardt, Michael, and Antonio Negri. 2012. *Declaration*. New York: Perseus Books.

Harootunian, Harry, and Naoki Sakai. 1999. "Japan Studies and Cultural Studies." *positions: east asia cultures critique* 7 (2): 593–647.

Harsin, Jayson, and Mark Hayward. 2013. "Stuart Hall's 'Deconstructing the Popular': Reconsiderations 30 Years Later." *Communication, Culture and Critique* 6: 201–7.

Hattori, Michisato. 2014. "The Significance of '*Kawaii*' as the Theme of the 'Eshi 100 Vol. 4' Exhibition, and Eyeing Overseas Expansion." In *Eshi 100 nin ten*, vol. 4, edited by Ishizaka Taichi, 226–27. Tokyo: Sankei shimbunsha.

Hattori, Michisato. 2015. "Regarding the 'Eshi 100 Exhibition 05." In *Eshi 100 nin ten*, vol. 5, edited by Ishizaka Taichi, 217–19. Tokyo: Sankei shimbunsha.

Haworth, Abigail. 2013. "Why Have Young People in Japan Stopped Having Sex?" *Guardian*, October 20. http://www.theguardian.com/world/2013/oct/20/young-people-japan-stopped-having-sex.

Hayakawa, Kiyoshi, Yamazaki Ryū, Kimata Naohiro, Shimizu Ginrei, and Satō Kaede. 2008. *Meido kissa de aimashō*. Tokyo: Āruzu shuppan.

Hebdige, Dick. 2005. "Subculture." In *Popular Culture: A Reader*, edited by Raiford Guins and Omayra Zaragoza Cruz, 355–71. London: Sage.

Hills, Matt. 2002. "Transcultural Otaku: Japanese Representations of Fandom and Representations of Japan in Anime/Manga Fan Cultures." MIT. http://cmsw.mit.edu/mit2/Abstracts/MattHillspaper.pdf.

Hinton, Perry R. 2014. "The Cultural Context and the Interpretation of Japanese 'Lolita Complex' Style Anime." *Intercultural Communication Studies* 23 (2): 54–68.

Hochschild, Arlie Russell. 1983. *The Managed Heart: Commercialization of Human Feelings*. Berkeley: University of California Press.

Hofmann, Jennifer-Naomi. 2017. "Translation as Activism: An Interview with Philip Boehm." Literary Hub, March 6. http://lithub.com/translation-as-activism-an-interview-with-philip-boehm/.

Honda, Masuko. 2011. "The Genealogy of *Hirahira*: The Liminality of the Girl." Translated by Tomoko Aoyama and Barbara Hartley. In *Girl Reading Girl in Japan*, edited by Tomoko Aoyama and Barbara Hartley, 19–37. London: Routledge.

Honda, Tōru. 2005a. *Dempa otoko*. Tokyo: Sansai bukkusu.

Honda, Tōru. 2005b. *Moeru otoko*. Tokyo: Chikuma shobō.

Honda, Tōru, and Hotta Shunji. 2007. *Jisatsu suru nara, hikikomore: Mondai darake no gakkō kara mi wo mamoru hō*. Tokyo: Kōbunsha.

Honda, Tōru, and Yanashita Ki'ichirō. 2008. "Tokubetsu taidan: 'Jiken wo okoshita koto igai, hotondo boku to issho nan desu.'" In *Akiba jiken wo dō yomu ka!?*, edited by Yōsensha Mūku Henshūbu, 68–73. Tokyo: Yōsensha.

hooks, bell. 2000. "Choosing the Margin as a Space of Radical Openness." In *Gender Space Architecture: An Interdisciplinary Introduction*, edited by Jane Rendell, Barbara Penner, and Iain Borden, 203–9. London: Routledge.

Horkheimer, Max, and Theodor Adorno. 2002. "The Culture Industry: Enlightenment as Mass Deception." Translated by Edmund Jephcott. In *Dialectic of Enlightenment: Philosophical Fragments*, edited by Gunzelin Schmid Noerr, 94–136. Stanford, CA: Stanford University Press.

Hyōdō, Hiromi, and Henry DeWitt Smith. 2006. "Singing Tales of the Gishi: *Naniwabushi* and the Forty-Seven Rōnin in Late Meiji Japan." *Monumenta Nipponica* 61 (4): 459–508.

Inforest. 2005. *Meido-san taizen*. Tokyo: Inforest.

Inness, Sherrie A. 1999. *Tough Girls: Women Warriors and Wonder Women in Popular Culture*. Philadelphia: University of Pennsylvania Press.

Inoue, Miyako. 2006. *Vicarious Language: Gender and Linguistic Modernity in Japan*. Berkeley: University of California Press.

Ishikawa, Shin'ichi, Satoko Sasagawa, and Cecilia A. Essau. 2012. "The Prevalence and Nature of Child Abuse and Violence in Japan." In *Violence and Abuse in Society: Understanding a Global Crisis*, edited by Angela Browne-Miller, 307–22. Santa Barbara, CA: Praeger.

Isola, Mark John. 2010. "Yaoi and Slash Fiction: Women Writing, Reading, and Getting Off?" In *Boys' Love Manga: Essays on the Sexual Ambiguity and Cross-Cultural Fandom of the Genre*, edited by Antonia Levi, Mark McHarry, and Dru Pagliassotti, 84–98. Jefferson, NC: McFarland.

Itō, Gō. 2005. *Tezuka izu deddo: Hirakareta manga hyōgenron e*. Tokyo: NTT shuppan.

Itō, Gō. 2006. "*Manga* History Viewed through Proto-Characteristics." Translated by Shimauchi Tetsuro. In *Tezuka: The Marvel of Manga*, edited by Philip Brophy, 107–13. Melbourne, Australia: National Gallery of Victoria.

Itō, Kimio. 2005. "An Introduction to Men's Studies." In *Genders, Transgenders and Sexualities in Japan*, edited by Mark McLelland and Romit Dasgupta, 145–52. London: Routledge.

Itō, Kimio. 2010. "When a 'Male' Reads Shōjo Manga." Translated by Miyake Toshio. In *Comics Worlds and the World of Comics: Toward Scholarship on a Global Scale*, edited by Jaqueline Berndt, 169–75. Kyoto: International Manga Research Center.

Ito, Mizuko. 2008. "Mobilizing the Imagination in Everyday Play: The Case of Japanese Media Mixes." In *The International Handbook of Children, Media, and Culture*, edited by Kirsten Drotner and Sonia Livingstone, 397–412. London: Sage Publications.

Ito, Mizuko. 2012. Introduction to *Fandom Unbound: Otaku Culture in a Connected World*, edited by Mizuko Ito, Daisuke Okabe, and Izumi Tsuji, xi–xxxi. New Haven, CT: Yale University Press.

Ivy, Marilyn. 1993. "Formations of Mass Culture." In *Japan as Postwar History*, edited by Andrew Gordon, 239–58. Berkeley: University of California Press.

Iwabuchi, Koichi. 2010. "Undoing Inter-National Fandom in the Age of Brand Nationalism." In *Mechademia 5: Fanthropologies*, edited by Frenchy Lunning, 87–96. Minneapolis: University of Minnesota Press.

Jackson, John L. 2005. *Real Black: Adventures in Racial Sincerity*. Chicago, IL: University of Chicago Press.

Jenkins, Henry. 1988. "*Star Trek* Rerun, Reread, Rewritten: Fan Writing as Textual Poaching." *Critical Studies in Mass Communication* 5 (2): 85–107.

Jenkins, Henry. 1992. *Textual Poachers*. London: Routledge.

Jenkins, Henry. 2006a. *Convergence Culture: Where Old and New Media Collide*. New York: New York University Press.

Jenkins, Henry. 2006b. *Fans, Bloggers, and Gamers: Media Consumers in a Digital Age*. New York: New York University Press.

JETRO. 2005. "Japan Animation Industry Trends." *Japan Economic Monthly*, June. http://jetro.go.jp/ext_images/en/reports/market/pdf/2005_35_r.pdf.

JNTO. 2008a. *JNTO hōnichi gaikyaku jittai chōsa 2006–2007: Hōmonchi chōsa hen*. Tokyo: International Tourism Center of Japan.

JNTO. 2008b. *JNTO hōnichi gaikyaku jittai chōsa 2006–2007: Manzokudo chōsa hen*. Tokyo: International Tourism Center of Japan.

JNTO. 2010. *Official Guidebook (English): Visit Japan Year 2010 Winter Campaign*. Tokyo: International Tourism Center of Japan.

Jones, Matthew T. 2005a. "The Impact of Telepresence on Cultural Transmission through Bishoujo Games." *PsychNology Journal* 3 (3): 292–311.

Jones, Matthew T. 2005b. "Reflexivity in Comic Art." *International Journal of Comic Art* 7 (1): 270–86.

Josephy-Hernández, Daniel E. 2017. "Fansubbing Hentai Anime: Users, Distribution, Censorship and Ethics." In *Non-Professional Subtitling*, edited by David Orrego-Carmona and Yvonne Lee, 171–97. Newcastle upon Tyne, UK: Cambridge Scholars.

Kagami, Hiroyuki. 2010. *Hijitsuzai seishōnen ron: Otaku to shihonshugi*. Tokyo: Ai'ikusha.

Kam, Thiam Huat. 2013a. "The Anxieties That Make the 'Otaku': Capital and the Common Sense of Consumption in Contemporary Japan." *Japanese Studies* 33 (1): 39–61.

Kam, Thiam Huat. 2013b. "The Common Sense That Makes the 'Otaku': Rules for Consuming Popular Culture in Contemporary Japan." *Japan Forum* 25 (2): 151–73.

Kam, Thiam Huat. 2015. "'Otaku' as Label: Concerns over Productive Capacities in Contemporary Capitalist Japan." In *Debating Otaku in Contemporary Japan: Historical Perspectives and New Horizons*, edited by Patrick W. Galbraith, Thiam Huat Kam, and Björn-Ole Kamm, 179–95. London: Bloomsbury.

Kang, Nancy. 2010. "Dirty Pictures: The Metamorphosis of Erotic Art into Mass Art in Japanese Manga." In *Manga and Philosophy*, edited by Josef Steiff and Adam Barkman, 111–27. Chicago, IL: Open Court.

Katayama, Lisa. 2009a. "Love in 2-D," *New York Times Magazine*, July 21. http://www.nytimes.com/2009/07/26/magazine/26FOB-2DLove-t.html?_r=0.

Katayama, Lisa. 2009b. "Man Marries Videogame Character in Japan (First-Ever Man/Game Wedding)." Boing Boing TV, November 23. https://www.youtube.com/watch?v=hsikPswAYUM.

Kelly, William W., and Merry I. White. 2006. "Students, Slackers, Singles, Seniors, and Strangers: Transforming a Family-Nation." In *Beyond Japan: The Dynamics of East Asian Regionalism*, edited by Peter J. Katzenstein and Takashi Shiraishi, 63–84. Ithaca, NY: Cornell University Press.

Kelts, Roland. 2006. *Japanamerica: How Japanese Pop Culture Has Invaded the US*. New York: Palgrave.

Kijima, Yoshimasa. 2012. "Why Make E-*moe*-tional Attachments to Fictional Characters? The Cultural Sociology of the Post-Modern." Translated by Leonie R. Stickland. In *Pop Culture and the Everyday in Japan: Sociological Perspectives*, edited by Katsuya Minamida and Izumi Tsuji, 149–70. Melbourne, Australia: Trans Pacific Press.

Kikuchi, Satoru. 2008. "'Otaku' sutereotaipu no hensen to Akihabara burando." *Chi'iki burando kenkyū* 4: 47–78.

Kikuchi, Satoru. 2015. "The Transformation and Diffusion of 'Otaku' Stereotypes and the Establishment of 'Akihabara' as a Place-Brand." Translated by Keiko Nishimura and Björn-Ole Kamm. In *Debating Otaku in Contemporary Japan: Historical Perspectives and New Horizons*, edited by Patrick W. Galbraith, Thiam Huat Kam, and Björn-Ole Kamm, 147–61. London: Bloomsbury.

Kimi, Rito. 2015. *Hentai Manga! A Brief History of Pornographic Comics in Japan*. Translated by Patrick W. Galbraith. Los Angeles: Digital Manga.

Kinsella, Sharon. 1995. "Cuties in Japan." In *Women, Media, and Consumption in Japan*, edited by Lise Skov and Brian Moeran, 220–54. Honolulu: University of Hawai'i Press.

Kinsella, Sharon. 1998. "Japanese Subculture in the 1990s: *Otaku* and the Amateur *Manga* Movement." *Journal of Japanese Studies* 24 (2): 289–316.

Kinsella, Sharon. 2000. *Adult Manga: Culture and Power in Contemporary Japanese Society*. Honolulu: University of Hawai'i Press.

Kinsella, Sharon. 2006. "Minstrelized Girls: Male Performers of Japan's Lolita Complex." *Japan Forum* 18 (1): 65–87.

Kinsella, Sharon. 2014. *Schoolgirls, Money and Rebellion in Japan*. London: Routledge.

Kitabayashi, Ken. 2004. "The *Otaku* Group from a Business Perspective: Revaluation of Enthusiastic Consumers." Nomura Research Institute. www.nri.co.jp/english/opinion/papers/2004/pdf/np200484.pdf.

Kotani, Mari. 2003. "Otakuīn wa otakuia no yume wo mita wa." In *Mōjō genron F-kai: Posutomodan otaku sekushuariti*, edited by Azuma Hiroki, 115–27. Tokyo: Seidōsha.

KWR International. 2004. "Japan Regains Its Position as a Global Cultural and Trend Leader." February 14. http://kwrintl.com/press/2004/jet-3-27-04.html.

Lah, Kyung. 2010. "'RapeLay' Video Game Goes Viral amid Outrage." CNN, March 31. http://www.cnn.com/2010/WORLD/asiapcf/03/30/japan.video.game.rape/.

Lamarre, Thomas. 2006. "Otaku Movement." In *Japan after Japan: Social and Cultural Life from the Recessionary 1990s to the Present*, edited by Tomiko Yoda and Harry Harootunian, 358–94. Durham, NC: Duke University Press.

Lamarre, Thomas. 2009a. *The Anime Machine: A Media Theory of Animation*. Minneapolis: University of Minnesota Press.

Lamarre, Thomas. 2009b. "Platonic Sex: Perversion and Shōjo Anime (Part One)." *Animation: An Interdisciplinary Journal* 1 (1): 45–59.

Lamarre, Thomas. 2011. "Speciesism, Part III: Neoteny and the Politics of Life." In *Mechademia 6: User Enhanced*, edited by Frenchy Lunning, 110–38. Minneapolis: University of Minnesota Press.

Lamerichs, Nicolle. 2014. "Embodied Fantasy: The Affective Space of Anime Conventions." In *The Ashgate Research Companion to Fan Cultures*, edited by Linda Duits, Koos Zwaan, and Stijn Reijnders, 263–74. Surrey, UK: Ashgate.

Laycock, Joseph P. 2015. *Dangerous Games: What the Moral Panic over Role-Playing Games Says about Play, Religion, and Imagined Worlds*. Oakland: University of California Press.

Leheny, David. 2006a. "A Narrow Place to Cross Swords: 'Soft Power' and the Politics of Japanese Popular Culture in East Asia." In *Beyond Japan: The Dynamics of East Asian Regionalism*, edited by Peter J. Katzenstein and Takashi Shiraishi, 211–36. Ithaca, NY: Cornell University Press.

Leheny, David. 2006b. *Think Global, Fear Local: Sex, Violence, and Anxiety in Contemporary Japan*. Ithaca, NY: Cornell University Press.

Liberatore, Stacy. 2016. "The $2500 Holographic 'Girlfriend' That Can Double as a Virtual PA (and Even Send 'I Miss You' Messages When You're Away)," Daily Mail, December 19. http://www.dailymail.co.uk/sciencetech/article-4049486/The-2500-holographic-girlfriend-double-virtual-PA-send-miss-messages-away.html.

Lukács, Gabriella. 2010a. "*Iron Chef* around the World: Japanese Food Television, Soft Power, and Cultural Globalization." *International Journal of Cultural Studies* 13 (4): 409–26.

Lukács, Gabriella. 2010b. *Scripted Affects, Branded Selves: Television, Subjectivity, and Capitalism in 1990s Japan*. Durham, NC: Duke University Press.

Lukács, Gabriella. 2013. "Dreamwork: Cell Phone Novelists, Labor, and Politics in Contemporary Japan." *Cultural Anthropology* 28 (1): 44–64.

Lunning, Frenchy, ed. 2006. *Mechademia 1: Emerging Worlds of Anime and Manga*. Minneapolis: University of Minnesota Press.

Macias, Patrick, and Tomohiro Machiyama. 2004. *Cruising the Anime City: An Otaku Guide to Neo Tokyo*. Berkeley, CA: Stone Bridge Press.

Mackie, Vera. 2010. "Reading Lolita in Japan." In *Girl Reading Girl in Japan*, edited by Tomoko Aoyama and Barbara Hartley, 187–201. London: Routledge.

Madill, Anna. 2015. "*Boys' Love* Manga for Girls: Paedophilic, Satirical, Queer Readings and English Law." In *Children, Sexuality and Sexualization*, edited by Emma Renold, Jessica Ringrose, and R. Danielle Egan, 273–88. New York: Palgrave.

Malaquais, Laurent. 2012. *Bronies: The Extremely Unexpected Adult Fans of My Little Pony.* New York: Film Buff.

Malinowski, Bronisław. [1922] 2014. *Argonauts of the Western Pacific: An Account of Native Enterprise and Adventure in the Archipelagoes of Melanesian New Guinea.* London: Routledge.

Marshall, P. David. 2014. *Celebrity and Power: Fame in Contemporary Culture.* Minneapolis: University of Minnesota Press.

Martinez, Dolores, ed. 1998. *The Worlds of Japanese Popular Culture: Gender, Shifting Boundaries, and Global Cultures.* Cambridge, UK: Cambridge University Press.

McCarthy, Helen. 1999. *Hayao Miyazaki: Master of Japanese Animation.* Berkeley, CA: Stone Bridge Press.

McCarthy, Helen. 2009a. "And Tezuka Created Moe . . ." Helen McCarthy: A Face Made for Radio Blog, July 24. http://helenmccarthy.wordpress.com/2009/07/24/and-tezuka-created-moe/.

McCarthy, Helen. 2009b. *The Art of Osamu Tezuka: God of Manga.* New York: Abrams Comic Arts.

McCloud, Scott. 1994. *Understanding Comics: The Invisible Art.* New York: Harper Perennial.

McCloud, Scott. 2000. *Reinventing Comics: How Imagination and Technology Are Revolutionizing an Art Form.* New York: Harper Perennial.

McGlotten, Shaka. 2013. *Virtual Intimacies: Media, Affect, and Queer Sociality.* Albany: State University of New York Press.

McGray, Douglas. 2002. "Japan's Gross National Cool." *Foreign Policy* 130: 44–54.

McKnight, Anne. 2010. "Frenchness and Transformation in Japanese Subculture, 1972–2004." In *Mechademia 5: Fanthropologies,* edited by Frenchy Lunning, 118–37. Minneapolis: University of Minnesota Press.

McLaren, Sally, and Alwyn Spies. 2016. "Risk and Potential: Establishing Critical Pedagogy in Japanese Popular Culture Courses." In *Teaching Japanese Popular Culture,* edited by Deborah Shamoon and Chris McMorran, 19–43. Ann Arbor, MI: Association for Asian Studies.

McLelland, Mark. 2005. "Salarymen Doing Queer: Gay Men and the Heterosexual Public Sphere." In *Genders, Transgenders and Sexualities in Japan,* edited by Mark McLelland and Romit Dasgupta, 96–110. London: Routledge.

McLelland, Mark. 2011. "Thought Policing or the Protection of Youth? Debate in Japan over the 'Non-Existent Youth Bill.'" *International Journal of Comic Art* 13 (1): 348–67.

McLelland, Mark. 2013. "Ethical and Legal Issues in Teaching about Japanese Popular Culture to Undergraduate Students in Australia." *Electronic Journal of Contemporary Japanese Studies* 13 (2). http://www.japanesestudies.org.uk/ejcjs/vol13/iss2/mclelland.html.

McNicol, Tony. 2004. "Does Comic Relief Hurt Kids? Is the Eroticization of Children in Japanese Anime a Serious Social Problem or Just a Form of Rebellion?" *Japan Times,* April 27. http://www.japantimes.co.jp/community/2004/04/27/issues/does-comic-relief-hurt-kids/#.WKsHtBBdX-Z.

METI. 2012. "Dai 3 kai chi'iki ōpun mini shinpojiumu in Akihabara paneru disukasshon gijiroku." http://www.meti.go.jp/policy/mono_info_service/mono/creative/ref2_fy23_creative_OMS_records.pdf.

Mihara, Ryōtarō. 2010. *Haruhi in USA: Nihon anime kokusai-ka no kenkyū*. Tokyo: NTT shuppan.

Mihara, Ryōtarō. 2013. "'Character,' 'Format,' 'Cool Japan.'" In *Eshi 100 nin ten*, vol. 3, edited by Ishizaka Taichi, 224–25. Tokyo: Sankei shimbunsha.

Mihara, Ryōtarō. 2014. *Kūru Japan wa naze kirawareru no ka: "Nekkyō" to "reishō" wo koete*. Tokyo: Chūō kōron shinsha.

Miller, Laura. 2004. "You Are Doing *Burikko*! Censoring/Scrutinizing Artificers of Cute Femininity in Japanese." In *Japanese Language, Gender, and Ideology: Cultural Models and Real People*, edited by Shigeko Okamoto and Janet S. Shibamoto Smith, 148–65. Oxford, UK: Oxford University Press.

Miller, Laura. 2011. "Cute Masquerade and the Pimping of Japan." *International Journal of Japanese Sociology* 20 (1): 18–29.

Minoru, Matsutani. 2010. "Akihabara Gets Bank of Security Cameras." Japan Times, January 27. http://www.japantimes.co.jp/news/2010/01/27/national/akihabara-gets-bank-of-security-cameras/.

Mitchell, W. J. T. 2005. *What Do Pictures Want? The Lives and Loves of Images*. Chicago, IL: University of Chicago Press.

Miyamoto, Hirohito. 2011. "How Characters Stand Out." Translated by Thomas Lamarre. In *Mechademia 6: User Enhanced*, edited by Frenchy Lunning, 84–91. Minneapolis: University of Minnesota Press.

Miyamura, Noriko. 2008. "GEISAI#11 foto repōto." GEISAI. http://www.geisai.net/g20/history/g11/story.php.

Miyazaki, Hayao. 2009. *Starting Point: 1979–1996*. Translated by Beth Cary and Frederik L. Schodt. San Francisco, CA: Viz Media.

Morikawa, Ka'ichirō. 2003. *Shuto no tanjō: Moeru toshi Akihabara*. Tokyo: Gentōsha.

Morikawa, Ka'ichirō. 2004. "OTAKU: persona = space = city: The Birth of a Personapolis." In *Otaku: Jinkaku = kūkan = toshi*, edited by Morikawa Ka'ichirō, 18–37. Tokyo: Gentōsha.

Morikawa, Ka'ichirō. 2008. *Zōho shuto no tanjō: Moeru toshi Akihabara*. Tokyo: Gentōsha.

Morikawa, Ka'ichirō. 2011a. "Azuma Hideo wa ika ni shite 'otaku bunka no so' ni natta ka." In *Azuma Hideo: Bishōjo, SF, fujōri, soshite shissō*, edited by Nishiguchi Tōru and Anazawa Yūko, 179–86. Tokyo: Kawade shobō shinsha.

Morikawa, Ka'ichirō. 2011b. "Bishōjo hyōgen no hattatsu shi." Lecture held at the Yoshihiro Yonezawa Memorial Library of Manga and Subcultures, March 19.

Morikawa, Ka'ichirō. 2012. "Otaku and the City: The Rebirth of Akihabara." In *Fandom Unbound: Otaku Culture in a Connected World*, edited by Mizuko Ito, Daisuke Okabe, and Izumi Tsuji, 133–57. New Haven, CT: Yale University Press.

Morris, David Z. 2016. "The Creepy Virtual Assistant That Embodies Japan's Biggest Problems." *Fortune*, December 18. http://fortune.com/2016/12/18/gatebox-virtual-assistant-japan/.

Mukaiyachi, Ikuyoshi. 2006. *Anshin shite zetsubō dekiru jinsei*. Tokyo: NHK shuppan.

Murakami, Takashi, ed. 2000. *Superflat*. Tokyo: Madra.

Murakami, Takashi. 2005. "Earth in My Window." In *Little Boy: The Arts of Japan's Exploding Subculture*, edited by Murakami Takashi, 98–149. New Haven, CT: Yale University Press.

Nagaike, Kazumi. 2003. "Perverse Sexualities, Perversive Desires: Representations of Female Fantasies and *Yaoi Manga* as Pornography Directed at Women." *U.S.-Japan Women's Journal* 25: 76–103.

Nagaike, Kazumi. 2015. "Do Heterosexual Men Dream of Homosexual Men? BL *Fudanshi* and Discourse on Male Feminization." In *Boys Love Manga and Beyond: History, Culture, and Community in Japan*, edited by Mark McLelland, Kazumi Nagaike, Katsuhiko Suganuma, and James Welker, 189–209. Jackson: University Press of Mississippi.

Nagaoka, Yoshiyuki. 2010. *Manga wa naze kisei sareru no ka? "Yūgai" wo meguru hanseiki no kōbō.* Tokyo: Heibonsha.

Nagayama, Kaoru. 2003. "Sekushuariti no henyō." In *Mōjō genron F-kai: Posutomodan otaku sekushuariti*, edited by Azuma Hiroki, 39–58. Tokyo: Seidōsha.

Nagayama, Kaoru. 2014. *Zōho eromanga sutadīzu: "Kairaku sōchi" toshite no manga nyūmon.* Tokyo: Chikuma bunko.

Nakamori, Akio. 1989. "Boku ga 'otaku' no nazukeoya ni natta jijō." In *Otaku no hon*, edited by Ishi'i Shinji, 89–100. Tokyo: JICC shuppankyoku.

Napier, Susan J. 2001. *Anime from Akira to Princess Mononoke: Experiencing Contemporary Japanese Animation.* New York: Palgrave.

Napier, Susan J. 2007. *From Impressionism to Anime: Japan as Fantasy and Fan Cult in the Mind of the West.* New York: Palgrave.

Negri, Antonio. 1999. "Value and Affect." Translated by Michael Hardt. *boundary 2* 26 (2): 77–88.

Newitz, Annalee. 1995. "Magical Girls and Atomic Bomb Sperm: Japanese Animation in America." *Film Quarterly* 49 (1): 2–15.

Newtype. 2010. "NT Research." March.

NHK. 2007. *COOL JAPAN ~ Hakkutsu! Kakko ii Nippon.* August 30.

NHK. 2014. "Akihabara." Japanology Plus, May 8. https://www.youtube.com/watch?v=UJ7dJIwgSBY.

Nikkei Net. 2007. "Shunjū." September 1. http://web.archive.org/web/20070903120349/http://www.nikkei.co.jp/news/shasetsu/20070831AS1K3100231082007.html.

Nishimura, Yukiko. 2012. "Puns in Japanese Computer Mediated Communication: Observations from Misconversion Phenomena." *AAAI Technical Report*, 38–45.

Norma, Caroline. 2015. "Catharine MacKinnon in Japanese: Toward a Radical Feminist Theory of Translation." In *Multiple Translation Communities in Contemporary Japan*, edited by Beverley Curran, Nana Sato-Rossberg, and Kikuko Tanabe, 79–98. London: Routledge.

Novak, David. 2013. *Japanoise: Music at the Edge of Circulation.* Durham, NC: Duke University Press.

NTV. 2010. "Kyō wa nan no hi: 1998 nen 6 gatsu 28 nichi 'Harajuku no hokoten no saishūbi.'" June 28. http://www.ntv.co.jp/don/contents03/2010/06/1998628.html.

Okabe, Daisuke. 2012. "Cosplay, Learning, and Cultural Practice." In *Fandom Unbound: Otaku Culture in a Connected World*, edited by Mizuko Ito, Daisuke Okabe, and Izumi Tsuji, 225–48. New Haven, CT: Yale University Press.

Okada, Toshio. [1996] 2015a. "Introduction to Otakuology." Translated by Keiko Nishimura. In *Debating Otaku in Contemporary Japan: Historical Perspectives and New*

Horizons, edited by Patrick W. Galbraith, Thiam Huat Kam, and Björn-Ole Kamm, 89–101. London: Bloomsbury.

Okada, Toshio. [2008] 2015b. "The Transition of Otaku and *Otaku*." Translated by Björn-Ole Kamm. In *Debating Otaku in Contemporary Japan: Historical Perspectives and New Horizons*, edited by Patrick W. Galbraith, Thiam Huat Kam, and Björn-Ole Kamm, 163–78. London: Bloomsbury.

Okada, Toshio, Morikawa Ka'ichirō, and Murakami Takashi. 2005. "*Otaku* Talk." In *Little Boy: The Arts of Japan's Exploding Subculture*, edited by Murakami Takashi, 165–85. New Haven, CT: Yale University Press.

Ortabasi, Melek. 2008. "National History as Otaku Fantasy: Satoshi Kon's *Millennium Actress*." In *Japanese Visual Culture: Explorations in the World of Manga and Anime*, edited by Mark W. MacWilliams, 274–94. Armonk, NY: M. E. Sharpe.

Ortega, Mariana. 2007. "My Father, He Killed Me; My Mother, She Ate Me: Self, Desire, Engendering, and the Mother in *Neon Genesis Evangelion*." In *Mechademia 2: Networks of Desire*, edited by Frenchy Lunning, 216–32. Minneapolis: University of Minnesota Press.

Ortega-Brena, Mariana. 2009. "Peek-A-Boo, I See You: Watching Japanese Hard-Core Animation." *Sexuality and Culture* 13: 17–31.

Ostrovsky, Simon. 2015. "Schoolgirls for Sale in Japan." Vice News, July 20. https://news.vice.com/video/schoolgirls-for-sale-in-japan.

Ōtsuka, Eiji. 1991. *Tasogaredoki ni mitsuketa mono: "Ribon" no furoku to sono jidai*. Tokyo: Ōta shuppan.

Ōtsuka, Eiji. 1992. *Kasō genjitsu hihyō: Shōhi shakai wa owaranai*. Tokyo: Shinyōsha.

Ōtsuka, Eiji. 2003. *Kyarakutā shōsetsu no tsukurikata*. Tokyo: Kōdansha.

Ōtsuka, Eiji. 2004. *"Otaku" no seishin shi: 1980 nendai ron*. Tokyo: Kōdansha gendai shinsho.

Ōtsuka, Eiji. 2008. "Disarming Atom: Tezuka Osamu's Manga at War and Peace." Translated by Thomas Lamarre. In *Mechademia 3: The Limits of the Human*, edited by Frenchy Lunning, 111–25. Minneapolis: University of Minnesota Press.

Ōtsuka, Eiji. 2013. "An Unholy Alliance of Eisenstein and Disney: The Fascist Origins of Otaku Culture." Translated by Thomas Lamarre. In *Mechademia 8: Tezuka's Manga Life*, edited by Frenchy Lunning, 251–77. Minneapolis: University of Minnesota Press.

Ōtsuka, Eiji. 2015. "Otaku Culture as 'Conversion Literature.'" Translated by Patrick W. Galbraith. In *Debating Otaku in Contemporary Japan: Historical Perspectives and New Horizons*, edited by Patrick W. Galbraith, Thiam Huat Kam, and Björn-Ole Kamm, xii–xxix. London: Bloomsbury.

Patten, Fred. 2004. *Watching Anime, Reading Manga: 25 Years of Essays and Reviews*. Berkeley, CA: Stone Bridge Press.

Pettman, Dominic. 2009. "Love in the Time of Tamagotchi." *Theory, Culture and Society* 26 (2–3): 189–208.

Pizzino, Christopher. 2016. *Arresting Development: Comics at the Boundaries of Literature*. Austin: University of Texas Press.

Puar, Jasbir K. 2007. *Terrorist Assemblages: Homonationalism in Queer Times*. Durham, NC: Duke University Press.

Raku Job. 2008. "Nyūsu: Akiba otaku matsuri no goannai." May 2. http://raku-job.jp/blog/2008/05/akiba.html.

Randall, Bill. 2005. "Behold Japan's God of Manga: An Introduction to the Work of Osamu Tezuka." *Comics Journal* 5: 46–57.

Rani, Anita. 2013. "The Japanese Men Who Prefer Virtual Girlfriends to Sex." *BBC News Magazine*, October 24. http://www.bbc.com/news/magazine-24614830.

Right Stuf. 1998. "History of Anime in the U.S., Part 2." http://www.rightstuf.com/site/main/animeResources/usHistory/part2/index.html.

Ripley, Will, Hilary Whiteman, and Edmund Henry. 2014. "Sexually Explicit Japan Manga Evades New Laws on Child Pornography." CNN, June 18. http://edition.cnn.com/2014/06/18/world/asia/japan-manga-anime-pornography/.

Roberson, James E., and Nobue Suzuki. 2003. Introduction to *Men and Masculinities in Contemporary Japan: Dislocating the Salaryman Doxa*, edited by James E. Roberson and Nobue Suzuki, 1–19. London: Routledge.

Rubin, Gayle S. 2011. *Deviations: A Gayle Rubin Reader.* Durham, NC: Duke University Press.

Rushe, Dominic. 2008. "Record Sales Mask Art Fears." *Sunday Times*, May 18.

Said, Edward. 1978. *Orientalism*. New York: Pantheon Books.

Saitō, Tamaki. 2007. "*Otaku* Sexuality." Translated by Christopher Bolton. In *Robot Ghosts and Wired Dreams: Japanese Science Fiction from Origins to Anime*, edited by Christopher Bolton, Stan Csiscery-Ronay Jr., and Takayuki Tatsumi, 222–49. Minneapolis: University of Minnesota Press.

Saitō, Tamaki. [2000] 2011. *Beautiful Fighting Girl.* Translated by J. Keith Vincent and Dawn Lawson. Minneapolis: University of Minnesota Press.

Sakata, Fumihiko. 2015. "The Transition and Lineage of Beauty." In *Eshi 100 nin ten*, vol. 5, edited by Ishizaka Taichi, 222–23. Tokyo: Sankei shimbunsha.

Sakurai, Tetsuo. 2006. "Tezuka: An Artist Who Confronted His Era." Translated by Philip Brophy. In *Tezuka: The Marvel of Manga*, edited by Philip Brophy, 67–76. Melbourne, Australia: National Gallery of Victoria.

Sand, Jordan. 2013. *Tokyo Vernacular: Common Spaces, Local Histories, Found Objects.* Berkeley: University of California Press.

Sankei Shimbun. 2013. Introduction to *Eshi 100 nin ten*, vol. 3, edited by Ishizaka Taichi, 3. Tokyo: Sankei shimbunsha.

Sankei Shimbun. 2014. Introduction to *Eshi 100 nin ten*, vol. 4, edited by Ishizaka Taichi, 3. Tokyo: Sankei shimbunsha.

Sasakibara, Gō. 2003. "Kizu tsukeru sei, dankai no sedai kara otaku sedai e: Gyarugē-teki sekushariti no kigen." In *Shingenjitsu*, vol. 2, edited by Ōtsuka Eiji, 101–28. Tokyo: Kadokawa shoten.

Sasakibara, Gō. 2004. *"Bishōjo" no gendai shi: "Moe" to kyarakutā.* Tokyo: Kōdansha gendai shinsho.

Schodt, Frederik L. 1983. *Manga! Manga! The World of Japanese Comics.* Tokyo: Kodansha International.

Schodt, Frederik L. 1996. *Dreamland Japan: Writings on Modern Manga.* Berkeley, CA: Stone Bridge Press.

Schodt, Frederik L. 2007. *The Astro Boy Essays: Osamu Tezuka, Mighty Atom, and the Manga/Anime Revolution.* Berkeley, CA: Stone Bridge Press.

Schodt, Frederik L. 2009. Foreword to *The Otaku Encyclopedia: An Insider's Guide to the Subculture of Cool Japan*, by Patrick W. Galbraith, 6–7. Tokyo: Kodansha International.

Schoenberger, Karl. 1989. "Sordid Serial-Killing Case Exposes the Other Side of Innocence in Japan." *Los Angeles Times*, September 9. http://articles.latimes.com/1989-09-09/news/mn-1579_1_japan-times.

Screech, Timon. 1999. *Sex and the Floating World: Erotic Images in Japan, 1700–1820*. London: Reaktion Books.

Sedgwick, Eve Kosofsky. 1993. *Tendencies*. Durham, NC: Duke University Press.

Sedgwick, Eve Kosofsky. 2003. *Touching Feeling: Affect, Pedagogy, Performativity*. Durham, NC: Duke University Press.

Shamoon, Deborah. 2012. *Passionate Friendship: The Aesthetics of Girls' Culture in Japan*. Honolulu: University of Hawai'i Press.

Sharp, Luke. 2011. "Maid Meets Mammal: The 'Animalized' Body of the Cosplay Maid Character in Japan." *Intertexts* 15 (1): 60–78.

Shigematsu, Setsu. 1999. "Dimensions of Desire: Sex, Fantasy, and Fetish in Japanese Comics." In *Themes in Asian Cartooning: Cute, Cheap, Mad, and Sexy*, edited by John A. Lent, 127–63. Bowling Green, OH: Bowling Green State University Popular Press.

Shimotsuki, Takanaka. 2008. *Komikku māketto no sōseiki*. Tokyo: Asahi shimbun shuppan.

Shiokawa, Kanako. 1999. "Cute but Deadly: Women and Violence in Japanese Comics." In *Themes in Asian Cartooning: Cute, Cheap, Mad, and Sexy*, edited by John A. Lent, 93–125. Bowling Green, OH: Bowling Green State University Popular Press.

Siciliano, Leon. 2016. "Japan's Version of Amazon Echo Is a Female Hologram That Wants You to Be Her 'Master.'" Business Insider UK, December 20. http://uk.businessinsider.com/gatebox-female-hologram-japan-wife-ai-assistant-companion-her-master-azuma-hikari-2016-12.

Silvio, Teri. 2010. "Animation: The New Performance?" *Journal of Linguistic Anthropology* 20 (2): 422–38.

Slater, David H., and Patrick W. Galbraith. 2011. "Re-Narrating Social Class and Masculinity in Neoliberal Japan: An Examination of the Media Coverage of the 'Akihabara Incident' of 2008." *Electronic Journal of Contemporary Japanese Studies*. http://www.japanesestudies.org.uk/articles/2011/SlaterGalbraith.html.

Smith, Catharine. 2010. "'Love Plus' Resort Caters to Men with Virtual Girlfriends." Huffington Post, September 1. http://www.huffingtonpost.com/2010/09/01/love-plus-resort_n_701758.html.

Smith, Henry. 1996. "Overcoming the Modern History of Edo 'Shunga.'" In *Imaging/Reading Eros: Proceedings for the Conference Sexuality and Edo Culture, 1750–1850*, edited by Sumie Jones, 26–34. Bloomington, IN: East Asian Studies Center.

Spinoza, Benedict de. 2005. *Ethics*. Translated by Edwin Curley. London: Penguin Books.

Steinberg, Marc. 2004. "Otaku Consumption, Superflat Art and the Return to Edo." *Japan Forum* 16 (3): 449–71.

Steinberg, Marc. 2012. *Anime's Media Mix: Franchising Toys and Characters in Japan*. Minneapolis: University of Minnesota Press.

Stewart, Kathleen. 2007. *Ordinary Affects*. Durham, NC: Duke University Press.

Storey, John. 1997. *Cultural Theory and Popular Culture: An Introduction.* New York: Pearson Educational Limited.

Strategy, Johnny. 2012. "Takashi Murakami Rips Apart Cool Japan and Everyone Involved." Spoon and Tamago, January 6. http://www.spoon-tamago.com/2012/01/06/takashi-murakami-rips-apart-cool-japan-and-everyone-involved/.

Sugimoto, Arata. 2013. "Will a Government-Made 'Cool Japan' Attract More Japan Fans?" Institute for International Studies and Training, July 31. http://www.iist.or.jp/en-m/2013/0221-0896/.

Sugiura, Yumiko. 2006a. *Fujoshi-ka suru sekai: Higashi Ikebukuro no otaku onna-tachi.* Tokyo: Chūōkōron shinsha.

Sugiura, Yumiko. 2006b. *Otaku joshi kenkyū: Fujoshi shisō taikei.* Tokyo: Hara shobō.

Suzuki, CJ (Shige). 2011. "Envisioning Alternative Communities through a Popular Medium: Speculative Imagination in Hagio Moto's Girls' Comics." *International Journal of Comic Art* 13 (2): 57–74.

Szondy, David. 2016. "Gatebox Reimagines Amazon Alexa as Fawning Anime Girlfriend." New Atlas, December 18. http://newatlas.com/gatebox-ai-assistant-anime-girlfriend/47012/.

Taga, Futoshi. 2005. "Rethinking Japanese Masculinities: Recent Research Trends." In *Genders, Transgenders and Sexualities in Japan,* edited by Mark McLelland and Romit Dasgupta, 153–67. London: Routledge.

Takahashi, Mizuki. 2008. "Opening the Closed World of *Shōjo* Manga." In *Japanese Visual Culture: Explorations in the World of Manga and Anime,* edited by Mark W. MacWilliams, 114–36. Armonk, NY: M. E. Sharpe.

Takahata, Isao. 2009. "Afterword: The Fireworks of Eros." Translated by Beth Cary and Frederik L. Schodt. In *Starting Point: 1979–1996,* written by Miyazaki Hayao, 451–61. San Francisco, CA: Viz Media.

Takatsuki, Yasushi. 2010. *Rorikon: Nihon no shōjo shikōshatachi to sono sekai.* Tokyo: Basilico.

Takeda, Yasuhiro. 2005. *The Notenki Memoirs: Studio Gainax and the Men Who Created Evangelion.* Houston, TX: A. D. Vision.

Takekuma, Ken'tarō. 2003. "Otaku no dai-ichi sedai no jiko bunseki: Akumade kojin-teki na tachiba kara." In *Mōjō genron F-kai: Posutomodan otaku sekushuariti,* edited by Azuma Hiroki, 101–14. Tokyo: Seidōsha.

Takeuchi, Cory Lyn. 2015. "Regulating *Lolicon*: Toward Japanese Compliance with Its International Legal Obligations to Ban Virtual Child Pornography." *Georgia Journal of International and Comparative Law* 44: 195–236.

Takeuchi, Ichiro. 2006. "Tezuka and the Origin of Story *Manga.*" Translated by Philip Brophy. In *Tezuka: The Marvel of Manga,* edited by Philip Brophy, 87–93. Melbourne, Australia: National Gallery of Victoria.

Takeyama, Akiko. 2005. "Commodified Romance in a Tokyo Host Club." In *Genders, Transgenders and Sexualities in Japan,* edited by Mark McLelland and Romit Dasgupta, 200–215. London: Routledge.

Takeyama, Akiko. 2010. "Intimacy for Sale: Masculinity, Entrepreneurship, and Commodity Self in Japan's Neoliberal Situation." *Japanese Studies* 30 (2): 231–46.

Tamagawa, Hiroaki. 2012. "Comic Market as Space for Self-Expression in Otaku Culture." In *Fandom Unbound: Otaku Culture in a Connected World*, edited by Mizuko Ito, Daisuke Okabe, and Izumi Tsuji, 107–32. New Haven, CT: Yale University Press.

Tanimura, Kaname. 2012. "'Anime seichi' ni okeru shumi no hyōshutsu: 'Shuto' to 'anime seichi' no hikaku kara." In *Kankō shigen toshite no kontentsu wo kangaeru*, edited by Cultural Resource Management Research Team, 105–20. Hokkaidō, Japan: Center for Advanced Tourism Studies.

Tantei File News Watch. 2007. "Jimin sōsenkyō Akiba de Asō shi '2ch ni odoroita.'" September 17. http://ftp.tanteifile.com/newswatch/2007/09/17_01/index.html.

Teshigawara, Mihoko, and Kinsui Satoshi. 2011. "Modern Japanese 'Role Language' (*Yakuwarigo*): Fictionalised Orality in Japanese Literature and Popular Culture." *Sociolinguistic Studies* 5 (1): 37–58.

Tezuka, Makoto. 2011. "Nihon no sabukaruchā wo michibiita karuto no paionia." In *Azuma Hideo: Bishōjo, SF, fujōri, soshite shissō*, edited by Nishiguchi Tōru and Anazawa Yūko, 170–73. Tokyo: Kawade shobō shinsha.

Tezuka, Osamu. 1996. *Garasu no chikyū wo sukue: 21 seiki no kimi-tachi e*. Tokyo: Kōbunsha.

Tezuka, Osamu. 2010a. *Tezuka Osamu erosu 1,000 pēji (ge)*. Selected by Tezuka Rumiko. Tokyo: INFAS Publications.

Tezuka, Osamu. 2010b. *Tezuka Osamu erosu 1,000 pēji (jō)*. Selected by Tezuka Rumiko. Tokyo: INFAS Publications.

Thorn, Matthew. 2001. "Shōjo Manga—Something for Girls." *Japan Quarterly* 48 (3): 43–50.

Thorn, Matthew. 2004. "Girls and Women Getting Out of Hand: The Pleasure and Politics of Japan's Amateur Comics Community." In *Fanning the Flames: Fans and Consumer Culture in Contemporary Japan*, edited by William Kelly, 169–87. Albany: State University of New York Press.

Time. 2013. "The 100 Most Influential People Who Never Lived." September 17.

Toivonen, Tuukka, and Yuki Imoto. 2013. "Transcending Labels and Panics: The Logic of Japanese Youth Problems." *Contemporary Japan* 25 (1): 61–86.

Tokyo Otaku Mode. 2013. "'Eshi 100 Exhibit' Showcases 100 Artists' Beautiful Interpretations of Japan's Seasons." May 22. https://otakumode.com/news/519088d8197db3c155000b4c/ldquo-Eshi-100-Exhibit-rdquo-Showcases-100-Artists-rsquo-Beautiful-Interpretations-of-Japan-rsquo-s-Seasons.

Treat, John Whittier. 1993. "Yoshimoto Banana Writes Home: *Shōjo* Culture and the Nostalgic Subject." *Journal of Japanese Studies* 19 (2): 353–87.

Treat, John Whittier, ed. 1996. *Contemporary Japan and Popular Culture*. Honolulu: University of Hawai'i Press.

Tsing, Anna Lowenhaupt. 2015. *The Mushroom at the End of the World: On the Possibility of Life in Capitalist Ruins*. Princeton, NJ: Princeton University Press.

Tsuchimoto, Ariko. 1989. "Rorikon, nijikon, ningyō-ai: Kakū no bishōjo ni taku sareta kyōdō gensō." In *Otaku no hon*, edited by Ishi'i Shinji, 102–15. Tokyo: JICC shuppankyoku.

Tsutsui, William M. 2010. *Japanese Popular Culture and Globalization*. Ann Arbor, MI: Association for Asian Studies.

TV Takkuru. 2014. "Rorikon bōryoku anime kisei wa hitsuyō?" September 1. http://www.dailymotion.com/video/x25oyio_%E3%83%93%E3%83%BC%E3%83%88%E3%81%9F%E3%81%91%E3%81%97%E3%81%AE%EF%BD%94%EF%BD%96%E3%82%BF%E3%83%83%E3%82%AF%E3%83%AB-140901_news.

TV Tropes. 2017a. "Girlish Pigtails aka: Twintails." http://tvtropes.org/pmwiki/pmwiki.php/Main/GirlishPigtails?from=Main.Twintails.

TV Tropes. 2017b. "Little Sister Heroine." http://tvtropes.org/pmwiki/pmwiki.php/Main/LittleSisterHeroine.

TV Tropes. 2017c. "Meido." http://tvtropes.org/pmwiki/pmwiki.php/Main/Meido.

TV Tropes. 2017d. "Naughty Tentacles." http://tvtropes.org/pmwiki/pmwiki.php/Main/NaughtyTentacles.

TV Tropes. 2017e. "Otokonoko Genre." http://tvtropes.org/pmwiki/pmwiki.php/Main/OtokonokoGenre.

TV Tropes. 2017f. "Tsundere." http://tvtropes.org/pmwiki/pmwiki.php/Main/Tsundere.

Ueno, Chizuko. 1989. "Rorikon to yaoi-zoku ni mirai wa aru ka!? 90 nendai no sekkusu reboryūshon." In *Otaku no hon*, edited by Ishi'i Shinji, 131–36. Tokyo: JICC shuppankyoku.

Vlastos, Stephen, ed. 1998. *Mirror of Modernity: Invented Traditions of Modern Japan*. Berkeley: University of California Press.

Warner, Michael. 2000. *The Trouble with Normal: Sex, Politics, and the Ethics of Queer Life*. Cambridge, MA: Harvard University Press.

Weiss, Margot. 2011. *Techniques of Pleasure: BDSM and the Circuits of Sexuality*. Durham, NC: Duke University Press.

White, Daniel. 2015. "How the Center Holds: Administering Soft Power and Cute Culture in Japan." In *Reframing Diversity in the Anthropology of Japan*, edited by John Ertl, John Mock, John McCreery, and Gregory Poole, 99–120. Kanazawa, Japan: Kanazawa University Center for Cultural Resource Studies.

Williams, Linda. 1989. *Hard Core: Power, Pleasure, and the "Frenzy of the Visible."* Berkeley: University of California Press.

Yamanaka, Tomomi. 2009. "'Otaku' tanjō: 'Manga burikko' no gensetsurikigaku wo chūshin ni." *Kokugo kenkyū* 27: 16–34.

Yamanaka, Tomomi. 2010. "'Otaku' shi wo kaitaku suru: 1980 nendai no 'kūhaku no rokunenkan' wo megutte." *Kokugo kenkyū* 28: 10–26.

Yano, Christine R. 2013. *Pink Globalization: Hello Kitty's Trek across the Pacific*. Durham, NC: Duke University Press.

Yiu, Wai-hung, and Alex Ching-shing Chan. 2013. "'Kawaii' and 'Moe': Gazes, Geeks (*Otaku*), and Glocalization of Beautiful Girls (*Bishōjo*) in Hong Kong Youth Culture." *positions: asia critique* 21 (4): 853–84.

Yomota, Inuhiko. 2006. *Kawaii ron*. Tokyo: Chikuma shinsho.

Yonezawa, Yoshihiro. 1989. "Komiketto: Sekai saidai no manga no saiten." In *Otaku no hon*, edited by Ishi'i Shinji, 75–88. Tokyo: JICC shuppankyoku.

Yonezawa, Yoshihiro. 2004. "Dōjinshi as Otaku Expression: The State of Japanese Fanzinedoms." In *Otaku: Jinkaku = kūkan = toshi*, edited by Morikawa Ka'ichirō, 44–49. Tokyo: Gentōsha.

Yoshimoto, Taimatsu. 2009. *Otaku no kigen*. Tokyo: NTT shuppan.

Zanghellini, Aleardo. 2009. "Underage Sex and Romance in Japanese Homoerotic Manga and Anime." *Social and Legal Studies* 18 (2): 159–77.

Žižek, Slavoj. 1991. *Looking Awry: An Introduction to Jacques Lacan through Popular Culture.* Cambridge, MA: MIT Press.

Žižek, Slavoj. 2012. "Slavoj Žižek on *The Avengers.*" CBC Radio, May 29. https://www.youtube.com/watch?v=tP4pcDLI57c.

INDEX

Page locators in italics represent figures